OTHER TITLES OF INTEREST FROM ST. LUCIE PRESS

Organization Teams: Building Continuous Quality Improvement

Team Building: A Structured Learning Approach

The Motivating Team Leader

The New Leader: Bringing Creativity and Innovation to the Workplace

Organizational Transformation and Process Reengineering

Total Quality in Managing Human Resources

Total Quality in Information Systems and Technology

Total Quality in Research and Development

Total Quality in Marketing

Total Quality in Purchasing and Supplier Management

Focused Quality: Managing for Results

The Executive Guide to Implementing Quality Systems

Sustaining High Performance: The Strategic Transformation to a Customer-Focused Learning Organization

How to Reengineer Your Performance Management Process

Deming: The Way We Knew Him

For more information about these titles call, fax or write:

St. Lucie Press
100 E. Linton Blvd., Suite 403B
Delray Beach, FL 33483
TEL (407) 274-9906 • FAX (407) 274-9927

S$_{\mathrm{L}}^{t}$

Total Quality and
ORGANIZATION
DEVELOPMENT

The St. Lucie Press
Total Quality Series™

BOOKS IN THE SERIES:

Total Quality in HIGHER EDUCATION

Total Quality in PURCHASING and SUPPLIER MANAGEMENT

Total Quality in INFORMATION SYSTEMS AND TECHNOLOGY

Total Quality in RESEARCH and DEVELOPMENT

Total Quality in MANAGING HUMAN RESOURCES

Total Quality and ORGANIZATION DEVELOPMENT

Total Quality in MARKETING

MACROLOGISTICS MANAGEMENT

For more information about these books call St. Lucie Press at (407) 274-9906

Series Editor • Frank Voehl
Series Development Editor • Sandy Pearlman

Total Quality and
ORGANIZATION DEVELOPMENT

By

William M. Lindsay,
Ph.D., PE
Professor of Management
Northern Kentucky University
Highland Heights, Kentucky
Senior Associate
Performance Leadership Associates

Joseph A. Petrick,
Ph.D., M.B.A., SPHR, RODP
Associate Professor of Management
Wright State University
Dayton, Ohio
CEO, Performance Leadership Associates
CEO, Organizational Ethics Associates

S^t_L

St. Lucie Press
Delray Beach, Florida

Phone: (407) 274-9906
Fax: (407) 274-9927

S^t_L

Published by
St. Lucie Press
100 E. Linton Blvd., Suite 403B
Delray Beach, FL 33483

CONTENTS

SERIES PREFACE

The St. Lucie Press Series on Total Quality originated in 1993 when some of us realized that the rapidly expanding field of quality management was neither well defined nor well focused. This realization, coupled with America's hunger for specific, how-to examples, led to the formulation of a plan to publish a series of subject-specific books on total quality, a new direction for books in the field to follow.

The essence of this series consists of a core nucleus of eight new direction books, around which the remaining books in the series will revolve over a three-year period:

- Education Transformation: *Total Quality in Higher Education*
- Respect for People: *Total Quality in Managing Human Resources*
- Speak with Facts: *Total Quality in Information Systems and Technology*
- Customer Satisfaction: *Total Quality in Marketing and Sales*
- Continuous Improvement: *Total Quality in Research and Development*
- System Transformation: *Total Quality and Organization Development*
- Supplier Partnerships: *Total Quality in Purchasing and Supplier Management*
- Cost-Effective, Value-Added Services: *Total Quality and Measurement*

We at St. Lucie Press have been privileged to contribute to the convergence of philosophy and underlying principles of total quality, leading to a common set of assumptions. One of the most important deals with the challenges facing the transformation of the organization for the 21st century. This is a particularly exciting and turbulent time in this field, both domestically and globally, and change may be viewed as either an opportunity or a threat. As such, the principles and practices of total quality can aid in this transformation or, by flawed implementation approaches, can bring an organization to its knees.

As the authors of this text explain, the total quality orientation to organization development (OD) redefines line managerial roles and identifies new responsibilities for the traditional function to come to grips with. The

OD practitioner's role now includes strategic input and continual development of the strategic planning system to increase customer satisfaction both now and in the future. The full meaning of these changes is fully explored in light of the driving forces reshaping the environment.

As Series Editor, I am pleased with the manner in which the series is coming together. Its premise is that excellence can be achieved through a singular focus on customers and their interests as a number one priority, a focus that requires a high degree of commitment, flexibility, and resolve. The new definition of the degree of satisfaction will be the total experience of the interaction—which will be the determinant of whether the customer stays a customer. However, no book or series can tell an organization how to achieve total quality; only the customers and stakeholders can tell you when you have it and when you do not. High-quality goods and services can give an organization a competitive edge while reducing costs due to rework, returns, and scrap. Most importantly, outstanding quality generates satisfied customers, who reward the organization with continued patronage and free word-of-mouth advertising.

We trust that you will find this book both usable and beneficial and wish you maximum success on the quality journey. If it in some way makes a contribution, then we can say, as Dr. Deming often did at the end of his seminars, "I have done my best."

Frank Voehl
Series Editor

AUTHORS' PREFACE

Mark Twain is reported to have read an obituary about himself that was mistakenly published in a newspaper. He was quoted as saying: "Reports of my demise have been greatly exaggerated!" The same is true of similarly premature reports of the death of the quality management movement which have been published in recent years. On the contrary, as the global business environment becomes more and more turbulent, quality management seems more and more indispensable. In this text, we do acknowledge that there are challenges "beyond" total quality management (TQM) that managers face. For example, there are issues of organizational ethics, organization strategy development processes, organization restructuring and improvement, and developing "learning organizations" that even "world-class" organizations are struggling to comprehend and address. However, we hold the strong belief, along with countless theorists, practicing managers, and consultants, that these new challenges can most effectively be tackled within the context of a TQM philosophy. By incorporating TQM concepts and tools into the planning, design, problem-solving, and improvement processes, better decisions can be made than by the use of any other approach that has been discovered to date. Those who are trying to go beyond TQM but who have not yet seen the need to take the "quality journey" may be doomed to disappointment.

We wrote this text on *Total Quality and Organization Development* to add our efforts to those who are beginning to see the need to integrate two fields that are exhibiting signs of convergence. As far as we know, this is the first comprehensive attempt to integrate the theory and practice of these disciplines into a single text. Many of the basic concepts of TQM and organization development (OD) come from the same "roots" and may be seen as reinforcing one another.

This book is targeted toward managers, OD professionals, educators, and students who have seen the need to understand and apply the perspectives of TQM and OD, simultaneously. This is not an easy undertaking, given the vast literature that is now available in the two separate fields. We hope that our text will provide the insights and connections that will expand the vision and horizons of our readers.

KEY FEATURES

The following key features of the text make it unique:

- Provides comprehensive guidance for integrating the theory and practice of total quality and OD at all organizational levels.
- Includes useful practitioner assessment instruments for measuring individual, group, and organizational performance.
- Features up-to-date references, case studies, and literature abstracts.
- Builds upon a comprehensive total quality model of organizational structure, moving from the mission, vision, and strategy of the firm through implementation at every level, using tools and skills that OD professionals may already possess or can easily master.
- Contrasts the traditional and new perspectives of the role of OD professionals; for example, it shows how OD professionals can take on a new role of helping organizations to incorporate ethics, empowerment, and continuous improvement to achieve competitive advantages for their organization.

CHAPTER CONTENTS

The text is organized into seven chapters. In Chapter 1, we answer the question: "Why TQM and OD?" A brief history of OD is given; the convergence of OD with human resource management, organization theory, and TQM is outlined; the framework of the integrative model, the House of Total Quality, is developed; and the role of the ethical work culture is explained.

In Chapter 2, we provide a historical overview of total quality. This includes quality concepts, quality history, and the biographies and philosophies of the quality "gurus."

Chapter 3 focuses on the strategy and the importance of customer focus. The first pillar of the House of Total Quality, customer satisfaction, is presented. Within that framework, total quality business strategy, strategy planning, strategy management, and strategy implementation are addressed systematically. Implications for total quality OD strategists are then addressed using the same framework.

In Chapter 4, we explore process dimensions. The second pillar of the House of Total Quality, continuous improvement, is developed. Included in the discussion of business processes are total quality business process planning, management, and improvement. Implications for total quality OD business process improvement are also addressed.

Chapter 5 focuses on project dimensions. The third pillar of the House of Total Quality, speaking with facts, is developed. Fact-based management is then applied to team project leadership. The dimensions of total quality business projects, project planning, and project development are treated.

Total quality OD projects, project planning, and project development are tested, in turn, using the same framework.

In Chapter 6, personal performance is addressed. We introduce respect for people, the fourth and final pillar of the House of Total Quality. The relationship between respect for people and its impact on personal performance dimensions is reviewed. Following the earlier framework, total quality performance is explored on the planning and management levels, after which total quality OD performance planning and management is discussed, using the same framework.

Finally, in Chapter 7 we operationalize the entire work by addressing the specific transforming processes required for total quality OD implementation. An integrated model for managing the change and OD process is developed. Quality function deployment, barriers to implementation, an integrative case study, and international quality comparisons round out the text.

THOSE WHO DESERVE OUR THANKS

We wish to thank the series editor, Frank Voehl, for his helpful comments and support. Also, Sandy Pearlman, series development editor, and Dennis Buda, publisher, deserve special thanks. Dr. Rob Snyder, Chair of the Management and Marketing Department at Northern Kentucky University, provided support in the form of valuable information from his wealth of knowledge in the field of organization behavior and human resources, as well as tangible support in the form of departmental resources for one of the authors. The entire Management Department and the College of Business and Administration at Wright State University provided similar support for the other author. Robert S. Lindsay, son of one of the authors and a graduate student in creative writing at Kansas State University, helped in developing the abstracts and in editing parts of the manuscript. We especially appreciate the contributions of associates at Performance Leadership Associates and Organizational Ethics Associates who supported us in many ways.

Finally, we wish to thank our wives, Rebecca Lindsay and Kimberly Petrick, for their patience, understanding, love, and support. Without them, we wouldn't have been able to complete this project.

The extent to which *Total Quality and Organization Development* succeeds in presenting empowering insights, up-to-date tools, and challenging guidelines for our readers will be the final measure of our success. If we have "added value" to your professional lives, it will have made our efforts worthwhile. Please let us hear from you by giving us both your positive and negative feedback.

Bill Lindsay
e-mail: LINDSAY@NKU.EDU

Joe Petrick
e-mail: JPETRICK@DESIRE.WRIGHT.EDU

THE SERIES EDITOR

Frank Voehl has had a 20-year career in quality management, productivity improvement, and related fields. He has written more than 200 articles, papers, and books on the subject of quality and has consulted on quality and productivity issues, as well as measurement system implementation, for hundreds of companies (many Fortune 500 corporations). As general manager of FPL Qualtec, he was influential in the FPL Deming Prize process, which led to the formation of the Malcolm Baldrige Award, as well as the National Quality Award in the Bahamas. He is a member of Strategic Planning committees with the ASQC and AQP and has assisted the IRS in quality planning as a member of the Commissioner's Advisory Group.

An industrial engineering graduate from St. John's University in New York City, Mr. Voehl has been a visiting professor and lecturer at NYU and the University of Miami, where he helped establish the framework for the Quality Institute. He is currently president and CEO of Strategy Associates, Inc. and a visiting professor at Florida International University.

On the local level, Mr. Voehl served for ten years as vice chairman of the Margate/Broward County Advisory Committee for the Handicapped. In 1983, he was awarded the Partners in Productivity award for his efforts to streamline and improve the Utilities Forced Relocation Process, which saved the state of Florida some $200 million over a seven-year period.

THE AUTHORS

William M. Lindsay, Ph.D., is a professor of management at Northern Kentucky University, a registered professional industrial engineer (P.E.), and a partner in Performance Leadership Associates, a management training and organization development consulting firm based in Cincinnati, Ohio. He received a B.I.E. from Georgia Tech, a M.S. (industrial engineering) from the University of Cincinnati, and an M.B.A. and Ph.D. in business (management) from Georgia State University. Prior to entering teaching, he was an industrial engineer and operations planner at E.I. DuPont in manufacturing plants in Virginia and Tennessee; with the Department of Defense (U.S. Army) at Edgewood Arsenal, Maryland; and with Southern Airways (now a part of Northwest Airlines) in Atlanta, Georgia. Dr. Lindsay is co-author of *The Management and Control of Quality*, third edition (West Publishing, 1996). He has published articles, spoken at conferences and seminars across the United States, and performed consulting assignments on quality and productivity improvement through the use of participative approaches for over 20 years. He is past president of the Cincinnati Chapter of the Institute of Industrial Engineers and past president of the Greater Cincinnati Chapter of the Association for Quality and Participation.

Joseph A. Petrick, Ph.D., is an associate professor of management at Wright State University, a senior professional in human resources (SPHR), a registered organization development professional (RODP), and the CEO of both Performance Leadership Associates and Organization Ethics Associates, management training and organization development consulting firms based in Cincinnati, Ohio. He holds an M.B.A. in quality management/marketing from the University of Cincinnati and a Ph.D. in organizational anthropology/comparative philosophy from the Pennsylvania State University. Dr. Petrick is co-author of *Total Quality in Managing Human Resources* (St. Lucie Press, 1995) and *Management Ethics and Organization Integrity* (Sage Publishing, 1996). He has done advanced international work at the University of Bonn in Germany and the University of Tokyo in Japan. He has also had direct management experience at PepsiCo and DialAmerica. He has provided quality training and consulting for over ten years to a wide range of private, public, and nonprofit organizations and has published widely. He is vice-president of the U.S. Association for Small Business and Entrepreneurship and is president-elect of the Midwest Society for Human Resources and Industrial Relations.

CHAPTER 1

WHY TOTAL QUALITY AND ORGANIZATION DEVELOPMENT?

Why is a book about total quality and organization development (OD) an essential addition to the field? OD professionals are always looking for the latest organizational innovations. They want to know about companies that are maximizing their organizational resources. Have you ever heard of Wainwright Industries, Inc.? How about GTE Directories Corporation? You no doubt know AT&T, but do you know why AT&T Consumer Communication Services has been in the news? These three companies were the 1994 winners of the coveted Malcolm Baldrige National Quality Award. That tells you something, but you are interested in employee and organization development. To pick the best example from these three firms is not easy. They *all* excel in employee involvement and empowerment, organization designs that are focused on customer satisfaction and quality, and innovative human resource practices. Look at Wainwright, a tiny, $30-million, 275-associate, family-owned business, headquartered in St. Peters, Missouri. It makes stamped and machined parts for various products, from autos to information processing. It spends up to 7% of its payroll on training and education. Associates take quality and work-related courses during working hours, but the company also fully reimburses employees for professional and personal development courses that they take on their own time. The company reports a *99% attendance rate* for its *all-salaried workforce* and a turnover rate that is lower than industry and local averages. Business performance is also excellent. Wainwright processes 95% of all purchase orders from customers within 24 hours, on-time delivery of orders is nearly 100%, and it has reduced product cost 35% in approximately three years.

Thus, there are at least four possible reasons why you should read this book. First, total quality is an approach whose time has come. The terms total quality management (TQM), continuous quality improvement, corporate and managerial reengineering, and quality function deployment are very popular, as are OD-related concepts. The two have evolved along parallel paths, but it is time for those paths to converge. The theory of OD and the emerging theory of total quality are complementary rather than at odds with each other. Second, many OD practitioners are concerned with large-scale organizational change (sometimes called reengineering) projects, such as employee involvement processes, business process improvement, and training and development efforts (especially for quality initiatives like the ISO 9000 certification process). If you are in that group, you want to know how total quality impacts your area. Third, you may be concerned about the conditions and changes in the organizational environment surrounding the OD functions. In fact, some people may be motivated to read this book because these changes are seen as threats to OD professionals. Finally, this book may be read by those who are searching for a better way to help create a more effective and efficient work culture for the future.[1]

Whatever your reason for reading the book, a need obviously exists to transform the culture and structure of organizations so that they will be better equipped to meet the challenges of the 21st century. The American Society for Quality Control (ASQC), for example, has been co-sponsoring a research program on OD and total quality called the Transformations to Quality Organizations (TQO) Program. The preliminary results point toward a particularly exciting and turbulent time for total quality and OD, both domestically and globally.[2]

The focus of this book is on five targeted audiences: (1) practicing senior-level and line business managers involved in decision making which relates to the structure and culture of their organizations; (2) practicing OD professionals who are integrating quality concepts and practices into their repertoire of skills; (3) practicing administrators/managers involved in OD decisions in public, nonprofit, and professional contexts; (4) academicians who address OD processes in theoretical and applied courses and seminars, in strategic management, and in broad, organization-focused total quality areas; and (5) practicing and prospective business and OD professionals (students) undergoing formal or self-designed education and training to assume future work responsibilities. As we develop the concepts below, you may consider yourself to be in the role of a change agent or a facilitator of organizational change. Each group of stakeholders can benefit from this text.

This book deals with the interaction of total quality processes with OD processes. The traditional nature and scope of responsibility for most OD professionals has been that of staff support geared to organizational change and has often been driven by top management initiatives. This leads to the following requirements for OD consultants who want to develop and use a total quality approach to OD:

- To know about and promote total quality, through helping to clarify the vision, spreading the word, working alongside managers, acting as a design resource, and working as, and teaching other to become, an internal total quality OD consultant.
- To blend traditional OD techniques of diagnostic questioning, confronting, active listening, giving advice, and organization design assistance with the total quality problem-solving techniques (to be detailed later) in order to provide managers with both the factual information and the clarification of human issues that they need to make good decisions.
- To blend total quality and OD approaches to clients through a dynamic process (to be elaborated upon in Chapter 4) of: (a) establishing contact with clients and forging a working relationship, (b) agreeing on a contract and helping the client to gather and make sense of data, (c) helping to generate options and implement a plan of action, and (d) arranging for follow-up with stakeholders before disengaging.
- To understand that success is measured by the client and discover that what is really needed is, in fact, central to both the total quality and OD philosophies.

The total quality orientation to managing organizational change redefines line managerial roles and accords new responsibilities to the traditional supervisory management function. The role of the latter now includes input to strategic plans and continual development of the organization's systems and processes. The goal of these changes is to increase customer satisfaction now and in the future.

THE NATURE OF ORGANIZATION DEVELOPMENT

OD was started by an amazingly varied group of organizational psychologists, economists, and philosophers who had a hand in developing the human side of management and work. The term *organization development* has been linked to Robert Blake and Jane Mouton, Douglas McGregor, Herbert Shepherd and/or Richard Beckhard, starting in about 1957.[3]

The philosophies of the parallel movements of OD and total quality are now rapidly coming together as total quality advocates try to deal with the human factors in quality improvement and OD people attempt to deal with the technical and measurement factors that accompany the challenges of "planned" organizational change.

In this chapter, we will outline the basics of OD, provide a brief history of its development, show how it is related to human resource management within organizations today, and lay the foundation for a total quality approach to OD. Harvey and Brown[4] defined OD as: *"an attempt to achieve corporate excellence by integrating the desires of individuals for growth and development with organization goals."* Richard Beckhard,[5] one of the pioneers of the discipline, said that OD is:

- Planned
- Organization-wide
- Managed from the top
- [Designed] to increase organization effectiveness and health
- [Carried out] through planned interventions in the organization's processes using behavioral science knowledge

French and Bell added an additional insight concerning the use of change agents:

> In the behavioral science, and perhaps ideal, sense of the term, *organization development* is a long-range effort to improve an organization's problem-solving and renewal processes, particularly through a more effective and collaborative management of organization culture—with social emphasis on the culture of formal work teams—with the assistance of a change agent, or catalyst, and the use of theory and technology of applied behavioral science, including action research.[6]

This definition suggests that managers and OD planners and practitioners (internal and external consultants) are typically concerned with at least seven parts of OD.

1. **Leadership**—Leadership is a key to successful OD. It is also one of the most difficult concepts to measure, although literally hundreds of definitions and models have been proposed to explain it.
2. **Organization goals**—Organization goals are required if planned change is to take place. Vision (seeing the organization as it *could or should* be) and mission (the statement that answers the questions of *purpose*: What is our organization in business to do? Which customers must we serve?) are the starting points for organization goal setting. Individual goals must be meshed with organization goals if the vision and mission of the organization are to be accomplished.

3. **Planned improvement**—Planned improvement is the prime objective of OD. Planning requires decisions to be made in the present about an uncertain future state. The challenge of planning for OD is to outline the process that is needed to move from the current state of organizational existence to a future desired state. That challenge is often one that managers and employees hate to face.

4. **Problem-solving and renewal processes**—This facet implements planned organization-wide improvement and focuses on coordinating effective methods to collaboratively manage organizational culture, as a primary objective of the change process.

5. **Group processes and teamwork**—Group processes are how things get done in most organizations. They provide the "horsepower" for carrying out planned change within organizations. Groups must break down the overall goals and objectives of planned change into manageable "pieces" so that individuals can gather resources, agree on how the resources are to be effectively used, carry out the necessary tasks, and estimate the amount of success or failure seen in the results.

6. **Change agents/facilitators**—Change agents/facilitators bring an analytical perspective to what is otherwise an emotional process of transforming the "guts" of an organization. These OD practitioners must coax, persuade, coach, teach, and innovate if they, and the target organization, are to make planned improvements happen.

7. **Individual skills**—Individual skills are the "lowest common denominator" of planned improvement. People's skills (and accumulated knowledge and experience) represent the most valuable resource in organizations today. In a "knowledge-based society" such as we have, the human resources are the most valuable, and potentially the most perishable, ones in organizations. Individual skills, knowledge, and experience must be developed and "honed" within groups in order for planned change to take place.

To place OD in context, it is necessary to take a look at the environmental challenges that face those who work in this field. They tend to shape the context and methods that are used by OD practitioners.

ORGANIZATIONAL ISSUES RESHAPING THE ORGANIZATION DEVELOPMENT ENVIRONMENT

Six organizational issues point to the need to focus on total quality, managing organization structures, and change processes: international competition, external customer needs, internal customer needs, work force diversity and expectations, information technology and knowledge requirements, and the need for development of world-class organizational cultures.

First, *successful international competitors have challenged U.S. organization designs and human resource management* (HRM) *practices.* All businesses have three principal resources: capital, natural resources, and human resources. Many economic competitors of the United States, such as Japan, Korea, Taiwan, and Singapore, have few natural resources but use the same basic technologies as the United States. They have been forced to develop their competitive international advantage primarily through cultivation of human resources and development of organizational processes. According to Evans and Lindsay, "The human resource is the only one that competitors cannot copy, and is the only one that can synergize; that is, produce output whose value is greater than the sum of its parts."[7]

Several years ago, Japanese industrialist Konosuke Matsushita reinforced this human resource (HR) emphasis in a speech before a group of U.S. executives:[8]

> We will win and you will lose. You cannot do anything about it because your failure is an internal disease. You firmly believe that good management means executives on one side and workers on the other. On one side, men who think, and on the other side, men who can only work. For you, management is the art of smoothly transferring the executives' ideas to the workers' hands.

Japanese firms have used many different resources to achieve their stunning victories, but excellent HRM policies and practices, supportive organization structures, and an effective educational infrastructure have been contributing factors to their success and a challenge to U.S. OD professionals.[9] Japanese workers at every level are educated to use highly scientific and rational work processes, allowing them to be exceedingly data driven and rigorously scientific in researching and improving those processes—without engendering burnout. The United States continues to fall behind in technically trained high school and college graduates. Only 4% of American college graduates received degrees in engineering in 1988, versus 13% in 1960.

Second, *successful organizations place high priority on proactively and systematically understanding and responding to current and future external customer needs.* Typically, U.S. corporations place their highest priority on investor returns and focus on increasing short-term and long-term financial payoffs for stockholders. In contrast, corporations in Japan assign a relatively low priority to short-term business profits and a much higher priority to market share, attained through increased customer satisfaction and work process improvements.[10] Better financial results, such as cost reduction and higher profits, generally result from process improvements based on increased sensitivity to customer needs. Therefore, the objectives of these corporations are systematically and strategically aligned with customer satisfaction.[11]

Examples of successful international and domestic companies that place a high priority on customer satisfaction provide important signals to mainstream U.S. businesses. Companies such as Ritz-Carlton Hotels, AT&T Universal Card Services, Ford Motor Company, and others that will be profiled in this text prove that meeting and exceeding customer expectations is an area that has been neglected too long by U.S. businesses.[12] The challenge for OD professionals is to assist organizations in improving the human and technical dimensions of organizational systems by focusing on increasing customer satisfaction.[13] Those professionals who cannot or will not contribute to and support the new alignment of TQM, organizational structures, and policies designed to support strategic priorities are likely to play only marginal roles.

Third, *successful organizations seek to proactively and systematically understand and respond to current and future internal customer needs.* External customers' needs are intuitively understood by managers and workers within organizations. "They" are the people and organizations to whom "we" sell our products or services. The concept of internal customers is newer and stranger to managers. Internal customers are the next department or the next person in line to whom a product or service is delivered. Internal customers all work for the same company and will often become suppliers to their suppliers or customers to their own customers. The ultimate competitive advantage is established when an organization develops a culture that supports its internal customers. This culture harnesses the creative energies of all employees better than the competition by developing and using OD/HR processes that anticipate, meet, and exceed employee expectations. Today, employee needs are often ignored or only partially met in a frenzy of restructuring and downsizing.

Since domestic and international firms in this information age require people with high-level technical, analytical, and problem-solving skills to compete, knowledge workers (those who have those skills, or are flexible and "teachable" enough to acquire them) are at a premium.[14] Their committed contributions to organizational survival and prosperity had previously been secured through an implicit and/or explicit psychological contract (see Chapter 6 for a more complete discussion).[15] The psychological contract between employer and employee that once existed has been torn or broken by significant downsizing in every sector of the knowledge economy—often without stakeholder input. Some specific examples of this trend include:[16]

- The parking lot of G.E.'s appliance factory was built in 1953 to hold 25,000 cars; today's workforce is only 10,000.
- In 1985, 406,000 people worked for IBM, which made profits of $6.6 billion. Today, a third of the people and all of the profits are gone.
- From 1993 to 1996, Sears, Roebuck laid off over 50,000 employees.
- Cigna Reinsurance, an arm of the Philadelphia giant, has trimmed its work force 25% since 1990.

OD professionals are quickly learning that in order to attract and retain committed, sophisticated knowledge workers, they must provide a satisfying, reasonably secure, and preferably delightful work culture for them. One domestic firm, Rosenbluth Travel, experienced a 7500% growth in revenue within a 15-year span, building revenue from $20 million dollars to $1.5 billion while maintaining profitability above industry standards. CEO Hal Rosenbluth attributes the success of his company to its high HR commitment to employee satisfaction in word and deed: "For our people, the clients are priority number one. Our company has built a solid reputation in the field of customer service (in fact, our client retention rate is 96%), but we have actually done it by focusing inside on our own people."[17]

While the knowledge and skills of committed, competent employees are an asset that grows more valuable with use, many U.S. firms have come to regard human resources as expenses to be controlled or eliminated, as opposed to assets to be enhanced in order to achieve exceptional results.

Fourth, *work force diversity and mobility are creating new employee needs along with new expectations about the present and future work culture.* Another key trend is the composition of the work force in the United States. The work force is becoming more diverse, with a different ethnic and racial mix. More women continue to enter the work force, the educational profile of the new work force members is changing (with an education gap widening among workers), and workers with disabilities are emerging as an untapped resource.[18] These work force changes have led to heightened expectations that traditional OD and HR managers have not previously encountered. Employees and managers need to be taught to view diversity as a strategic advantage; workers need the flexibility to rapidly accommodate changes and diversity in work settings. Corporate HR policies must be modified to permit more flexible schedules, a wider range of employee services, and ongoing personal and professional development of all employees, not just managers. In addition, nations with slowly growing work forces but rapid growth in service jobs (Japan, U.S., Germany) have become magnets for immigrants. U.S. workers are relocating with even greater frequency.[19]

Fifth, *the information technology revolution is reshaping the core competencies needed in a knowledge economy.* In 1991, for the first time, business investment in computers and telecommunication equipment tools of the new economy—tools that create, sort, store, and ship knowledge—exceeded capital spending for industrial, construction, and other "old economy" equipment.[20] These impressive figures still understate investment in knowledge machines because they do not show the growing capability of sophisticated industrial gear, using microprocessor controls, to perform complex operations automatically. For example, more than half of machine tool spending in the United States is for equipment with built-in computerized numerical controls.[21]

The revolution in information technology impacts most OD professionals in four major ways. (1) It intensifies the need for everyone in the organization (including OD professionals) to continually develop and update computer literacy skills. This is a challenging training and development problem for OD/HRM professionals. (2) The distribution of technical, problem-solving, and decision-making abilities throughout the organization through computer networks creates a redistribution of power. This redistribution of power based on competency expands the change-related responsibilities of OD professionals. (3) The speed, directness, and immediacy of information exchange, both within the work organization at all levels and between organizations and key external stakeholders (suppliers and customers), is redefining business relationships and responsibilities, from the ordering of products and services to the sharing of feedback on effective performance, organizational change, and satisfaction. (4) Employee expectations for sophisticated information systems to give them access to decision support information, team members, and managers; support for developing and "marketing" their skills, company-wide (or beyond); and computer-assisted career tracking and feedback will only increase. OD professionals will have to take an active role in helping individuals and teams transform their modes of working and interacting to cope with rapid technological advances such as these.

Sixth, *OD and HR leaders are challenged to become effective strategic partners in the creation of world-class learning cultures.* Within both the OD and the related HR profession, there has been a growing movement away from the staff support functional role to the strategic partner role.[22] OD professionals are encouraged to strengthen the linkage between business strategies and OD change practices such as team and intergroup process development.[23] In addition, senior managers need the advice of OD professionals in developing learning organizations that will use empowered, dedicated employees to structure high-performing units for strategic success.[24] In well-developed ethical work cultures, where trust, loyalty, and creativity are respected, investments in R&D, training, and associate employability generally yield high returns. OD practitioners can be catalysts for creating this environment. Some of the payoffs include consistently high levels of innovation, low employee turnover, and an increased tendency of employees to embrace and skillfully use new technology. Organizational redesign approaches such as virtual organizations,[25] organizational federalism,[26] reengineering,[27] and organizational architecture theory[28] present competing and confusing options for aligning business strategy and corporate structure. For example, process reengineering now requires extensive cross-functional cooperation and information sharing. This, in turn, demands more OD and HR involvement for group facilitation, privacy protection, and project support. To effectively address these six driving forces, integration of strategy, quality, organization, and HR concerns will require forging new, strong partnerships between senior managers and OD/HR professionals.

HISTORY AND APPROACHES TO ORGANIZATION DEVELOPMENT IN THE UNITED STATES[29]

A brief history of U.S. OD from both an "organic" and a "spectrum" approach suggests the role that OD may play in meeting the challenges posed by the current driving forces for change. The organic approach uses the metaphor of a tree to examine the growth of OD from its beginning "roots" and "stems." The spectrum approach uses a logical, analytical model to capture the broad range of views and theories developed by the major OD theorists. Unlike scientific management, which had one identifiable founder, Frederick W. Taylor, OD grew out of a collaborative effort to improve the management of organizations by application of multiple behavioral science theories and associated techniques. If there can be said to be a "founding father" of OD, it would probably have to be Kurt Lewin.

Organic Approach: The "Roots" of Organization Development

Kurt Lewin was an applied social scientist at the Massachusetts Institute of Technology during and after World War II. He had been recruited by Douglas McGregor, who was then at the Sloan School of Management. He developed two tools which later became the focal techniques used by his peers and followers in OD work. These were called laboratory-training methods (sometimes labeled T-group methods) and survey research and feedback (sometimes called the action research model). Lewin created the National Training Laboratory (NTL), where professors and social scientists later came, beginning in 1947, to learn new methods for conceptualizing and applying theories of group dynamics, change processes, and action research. French and Bell defined three "stems" coming from the "roots" of OD as: (1) the laboratory training stem, (2) the survey research and feedback stem, and (3) the action research stem.

Organic Approach: The Laboratory Training Stem

Lewin founded his Research Center for Group Dynamics (RCGD) in 1945 with the help of staff members Marian Radke, Leon Festinger, Ronald Lippitt, and Dorwin Cartwright. Kenneth Benne, Leland Bradford, and Gordon Lippitt formed the NTL after Lewin died unexpectedly in 1947.

The laboratory training stem expanded following a conference at the Gould Academy in Bethel, Maine, in the summer of 1947. Representatives of the RCGD met there with others from the National Education Association, Teachers College of Columbia University, University of California at Los Angeles, Springfield College, and Cornell University. The participants met with a trainer and an observer in Basic Skill Training Groups (later called T-groups) for the major part of each day over a three-week period. Later, laboratory training centers were set up, generally at universities, and group dynamics and change methods were taught around the country. French and Bell[30] pointed out that:

> ...The training of "teams" from the same organization that had emerged early at Bethel undoubtedly was a link to the total organizational focus of Douglas McGregor, Herbert Shepard, and Robert Blake, and subsequently the focus of Richard Beckhard, Chris Argyris, Jack Gibb, Warren Bennis, and others.

In 1952 and 1953, Robert Tannebaum, a Ph.D. in industrial relations from the School of Business at the University of Chicago, developed an original OD concept of team building through what he called *vertically structured groups*, at the U.S. Naval Ordnance Test Station at China Lake, California. Douglas McGregor began to transfer T-group skills to complex organizations at Union Carbide in 1957. He helped to form what was later called "an organization development" group under the direction of John Paul Jones, an industrial relations manager at Union Carbide. Also in 1957, Herbert Shepard, who had completed a doctorate at MIT and taught there in the industrial relations section, joined the employee relations department at Esso Standard Oil (now Exxon). In 1958 and 1959, Shepard, along with Robert Blake, a clinical psychologist, conducted a series of experiments in OD aimed at improving managerial understanding of top management and performance of middle managers. The two OD consultants used interview surveys and feedback, T-groups, and other methods at three Esso refineries. Shepard later developed the first Ph.D. program in OD at Case Institute of Technology (later Case Western Reserve University). Blake was the co-developer (with Jane Mouton) of the managerial grid® approach to OD.

Richard Beckhard came out of the unlikely background of a career in the theater. He was associated with the NTL's summer programs as a staff member for a few years until Douglas McGregor, who had already moved from MIT to the presidency of Antioch College, recruited Beckhard for work at MIT. Between 1958 and 1963, Beckhard worked with McGregor on several projects at Union Carbide, Pennsylvania Bell, and General Mills. Beckhard was also instrumental in setting up the first major nondegree programs in OD at the NTL. These included conferences and seminars for specialists, middle managers, senior executives, and presidents.

Organic Approach: The Survey Research and Feedback Stem

Survey research and feedback is a specialized type of action research. It was developed by Rensis Likert, founder and director of the Institute for Social Research and the Survey Research Center at the University of Michigan.

Likert received his Ph.D. in psychology from Columbia and as part of his dissertation research developed the Likert scale for measuring attitudes. After several years of university teaching, working for government agencies during World War II, and doing research on leadership, motivation, morale, and productivity for the Life Insurance Agency Management Association, he moved to Michigan. After Lewin's death, the RCGD was moved from MIT and placed under Likert as part of the Institute for Social Research.

Beginning in 1947, survey research studies directed by Floyd Mann were done at Detroit Edison Company. Surveys of employee attitudes and organizational issues were used as a focal point for organization changes. It was found that if a manager was given the results of an employee survey but did not discuss them with subordinates, no changes took place. However, if discussion of the survey results between managers and subordinates took place, substantial favorable changes occurred.

Likert also met with Lewin and McGregor and encouraged the formation of the group dynamics center at MIT, helped to launch the first NTL lab for managers in 1956, and influenced the extension of OD research after the RCGD was moved from MIT to Michigan. Staff members at MIT, including Festinger, Cartwright, Lippitt, and John R.P. French, Jr., moved to Michigan and worked with Likert when the RCGD was moved.

Organic Approach: The Action Research Stem

French and Bell[31] define action research as:

> ...a collaborative, client–consultant inquiry consisting of prelimi-
> nary diagnosis, data gathering from the client group, data feed-
> back to the client group, data exploration and action planning by
> the client group, and action.

William F. Whyte and Edith Hamilton used action research in their work at the Tremont Hotel in Chicago in 1945 and 1946, and Kurt Lewin did a number of studies with his students using action research. French and Bell noted that survey research, as developed by Likert and his colleagues, is a specialized form of action research.

The Tavistock Clinic in England became a center from which the action research approach developed. It was founded in the 1920s to provide psychotherapy, based on psychoanalytic theory that had been developed from the treatment of battle neurosis in World War I. Using this "clinical" approach, social psychologists such as W.R. Bion, John Rickman, and especially Eric Trist developed their concepts of group dynamics and behavior.

Trist, using studies of work and the need for group restructuring in coal mining operations, founded the *sociotechnical systems* approach to work design. He did a number of experiments in work redesign and use of semi-autonomous work groups. He was influenced in his work by the systems concepts of Von Bertalanffy and Andras Angyal and in group dynamics by Lewin, Likert, and others in the United States. Robert Blake and Warren Bennis, among other OD pioneers, studied at Tavistock.

Spectrum Approach: Individual, Group, and Systems Influences on Organization Development

Warner Burke, another pioneer in OD, categorized the OD theories into perspectives, emphases, and applications according to Table 1.1.

It should be noted that there is considerable overlap between the theorists listed in Burke's table and the "roots and stems" suggested by French and Bell. Perhaps the most striking difference is that Burke included the *individual behavior* theorists Maslow, Herzberg, Vroom, Lawler, Hackman,

Table 1.1 Summary of Primary Organization Development Theorists According to Their Perspectives, Emphases, and Applications

Perspective	Theorist	Emphasis	Application
Individual	Maslow and Herzberg	Individual needs	Career development, job enrichment
	Vroom and Lawler	Individual expectancies and values	Reward system design, performance appraisal
	Hackman and Oldham	Job satisfaction	Job and work design, job enrichment
	Skinner	Individual performance	Incentive systems, reward system design
Group	Lewin	Norms and values	Changing conformity patterns
	Argyris	Interpersonal competence and values	Training and education
	Bion	Group unconscious, psychoanalytic basis	Group behavior diagnosis
System	Likert	Management style and approach	Change to participative management
	Lawrence and Lorsch	Organizational structure	Change contingent on organizational environment
	Levinson	Organization as a family, psychoanalytic basis	Diagnosis of organization according to familial patterns

Source: Burke, W. Warner (1982). *Organization Development: Principles and Practices*. Glenview, IL: Scott-Foresman, p. 42. Reprinted by permission of HarperCollins College Publishers.

Oldham, and Skinner among the OD "greats." The following is a brief summary of the contributions of these motivational theorists, whose work was in many ways entwined with the "roots" of OD. The contributions of B.F. Skinner and Hackman and Oldham's job design model will be discussed in detail in the section on OD and HRM later in this chapter.

The six theorists who provided the content and process motivational models to undergird the human relations approach included Abraham Maslow, Frederick Herzberg, Douglas McGregor, Victor Vroom, Lyman Porter, and Edward Lawler.[32] Content theories specify what sort of events, needs, or outcomes motivate behavior, while process theories specify how different kinds of events, conditions, or outcomes motivate behavior. The first three theorists above were pioneers in the development of content theories of motivation. The last three developed process theories.

Maslow, in his "hierarchy of needs," argued for the existence of five innate, genetically determined needs: physiological, safety, belonging, esteem, and self-actualization. Behavior is driven by the urge to fulfill these five prepotent needs in ascending order, i.e., higher order needs (esteem and self-actualization) could only influence motivation if lower order needs (physiological, safety, and belonging) were largely satisfied. For OD and HR professionals, this meant that additional job recognition would not motivate a hungry employee since physiological needs are prepotent needs which require a different level of fulfillment than the higher order needs.

Herzberg developed a motivation–maintenance model that separated motivational factors (the work itself, achievement, possibility for growth, responsibility, advancement, and recognition) from maintenance or hygiene factors (status, job security, interpersonal relations, salary, working conditions). Only the former, according to Herzberg, positively motivated behavior, while the latter, if absent, could be demotivators that would never act as motivators. Herzberg applied his model to work contexts and argued that job enrichment, defined as increasing the areas of responsibility of workers, should be used to increase motivation rather than relying on salary increases. Job enrichment has been utilized by OD and HR professionals to support employee involvement programs and self-managed work teams, as well as motivational work, through work redesign programs. Thus, professionals who want to be effective enablers of organization change must be sensitive to true motivators and must cultivate internal flexibility.

McGregor, who has already been mentioned as a pioneer in OD, also provided a well-known model of managerial leadership assumptions: Theory X and Theory Y. Theory X assumes that employees dislike work, need to be coerced to perform, and will avoid responsibility whenever possible. Theory Y assumes that employees do *not* dislike work, that they can become committed to meet organizational objectives without coercive pressures, and that they will learn not only to accept but also to seek responsibility. Under Theory X, scientific management advocates focused on incentives and penalties, along with close supervision and inspection, to guarantee productivity. Under Theory Y, organization change agents focused on system improvements that required participation, delegation of responsibility, and appropriate resources for competent, trustworthy people to be productive. McGregor was one of the first to codify the win–win vs. lose–lose concept of behavior.

Porter and Lawler proposed a dynamic process model of motivation to supplement the prior static content models. The Porter and Lawler Expectancy Model (based on earlier work by Victor H. Vroom) utilizes Vroom's three major concepts: valence (perceived value of reward), instrumentality (subjective belief about effort–reward probability), and expectancy (perceived link between effort–performance and performance–outcome). The first letters of these concepts form the acronym VIE, which is sometimes used to identify the model. According to their theory, the combination of initial employee valence (incorporating Maslow and Herzberg's theories) and employee belief about effort–reward probability determines the initial work effort exerted. Effort, in turn, leads to performance which is affected by abilities and traits, as well as accurate role perceptions. In the dynamic flow of motivation, performance influences actual intrinsic and extrinsic rewards and the perceived equity of rewards determines future employee work effort expended. If rewards are perceived as equitable, then satisfaction occurs and accelerates a cycle of renewed motivation to produce. The goal of organization change professionals, as implied by Porter and Lawler's model, is to optimize motivated performance by focusing on people and work processes and increasing employee valence, instrumentality, and expectancy.

Including the individual motivational pioneers might generate arguments from some OD theorists who would hold that organization change processes have little to do with individual motivation, since that is the territory of the organization behaviorists. However, Sashkin and Burke,[33] in a review of the development of the OD discipline during the 1980s, point out that:

> ...there has been an effective integration, resolving the long-standing conflict between structural OD concerns and behavioral process issues as the focus of OD activities...In the 1980's *team building* rarely (if ever) consists of open-ended examination of interpersonal relations. Team building interventions today typically have a clear task focus; process is a way of improving how the team accomplishes its tasks, not an end in itself.

Thus, it appears that OD theorists are now content to draw on the work of organizational psychologists, while drawing the dividing line at the point of *tasks* within work groups. Rather than addressing issues relating to individual behavior, they simply focus on the tasks and the processes that are related to how the individual will contribute to the group and its effectiveness.

As the OD discipline has evolved in the United States, different approaches have demanded different competencies of OD professionals (e.g., the skills required to devise policies needed to "reengineer" organizations are different than those needed to build self-managing teams). Today, the demands for both external flexibility and internal control are also stretching OD professionals to address quality concerns. Practitioners in the HRM field have applied some of the same organization theory assumptions adopted by OD practitioners. This "blended" theory has positively influenced their openness to total quality philosophies and practices.

HUMAN RESOURCE MANAGEMENT, ORGANIZATION THEORY, AND TOTAL QUALITY

Recognition of the increasing importance of HR activities, in fact, contributed to the emergence in the 1970s of the term "human resource management." Early references to this discipline used terms such as personnel management, personnel administration, or industrial relations. While most U.S. corporations have not granted full strategic partnership to HR professionals, senior managers are now acknowledging the impact of HR professionals on organizational effectiveness.

It is precisely during rapidly changing times that HR professionals have the opportunity for high impact. The traditional definition of the discipline of *human resource management* as a specialty field that attempts to develop programs, policies, and activities to promote the satisfaction of both individual and organizational needs, goals, and objectives is taking on new dimensions.[34] The prospect of substantially contributing to organizational, national, and global economic leadership is both daunting and appealing.

During the early periods of U.S. history, there was no systematic, uniform HR policy in the private or public sectors. The predominantly Christian European background of U.S. immigrant workers supported the belief in hard work and pride in sound craftsmanship.[35] Early U.S. associations of artisans and craftspeople paralleled European medieval guilds. Early craftspeople (e.g., New England shipbuilders, colonial Williamsburg artisans, New York garment makers) brought with them detailed knowledge of materials, skills in developing processes and using tools to work on the materials, and attitudes toward work and its prime beneficiary—customers—that provided the bedrock upon which the major changes of the Industrial Revolution were built in the late 19th century in America.

Human resource professionals today are struggling with retrieving the U.S. worker commitment to quality craftsmanship in a world that does not offer employees feudal protections. They have relied on balancing the competing theories and practices of a wide range of experts to cope with massive HR changes in the last century. The shifting priorities of HR professionals at various times in history have caused some senior managers to regard the field as "mostly good intentions and whistling in the dark or averting unionization."[36] The absence of consideration for employees' personal well-being and economic anxiety in many U.S. organizations has further blocked the deepening of worker commitment to OD. Yet, one of the most basic OD dynamics at work is "how you treat your employees is how they will treat customers."

In addition to HRM approaches, the organization theory (OT) assumptions adopted by OD professionals also influence their openness to total quality initiatives. They have endorsed OT assumptions that emphasize external flexibility as key to organizational success. Therefore, it is only a "short step" to embracing TQM perspectives.

A framework of competing approaches to OT is shown in Figure 1.1. These OT options explicitly deal with the identity and purpose of an organization. They implicitly limit or expand the roles that OD practitioners take on, depending on which perspective is the prevailing one in their area of influence. In other words, it is important for OD professionals to be aware of how the following OT assumptions influence their attitudes toward the total quality approach.

Organizational outcome theories hold that an organization is determined (or driven) by the mechanistic and/or systematic attainment of goals.[37] The

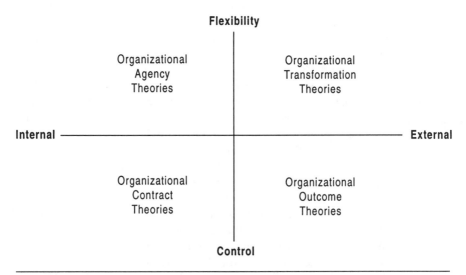

Figure 1.1 Framework of Competing Organization Theory Approaches

organization *is* its attained goals. OD professionals who support these theories emphasize the *external control* of the business environment by focusing on productivity and profitability outcomes. If achievement of organizational outcomes violates established procedures, contractual rights, or work community values or deprives the work system of resources for innovation and renewal, these OD professionals may simply state that sacrifices must be made to secure the desired organizational goals. In this context, a mechanistic approach to goal attainment would be taken by an organization such as UPS, where its traditional purpose has been to move more than one million packages per day from the sender to the recipient and to get every one of them there on time! It should be noted that UPS is in the midst of a cultural change in which it is attempting to become less mechanistic in its approach, in order to encourage more innovative and participative contributions.

Organizational contract theories hold that an organization is determined by a set of agreements or contracting relationships among members.[38] The organization *is* its network of contracting relationships. OD professionals who support these theories focus on abiding by the terms of the contract, whether or not the organization is unionized. Struggles over *internal control* of policies, processes, and procedures divide managers and workers, or contractor and contractee. Managers, line employees, and OD professionals may rigorously adhere to such contracts, which can lead to such actions as refusing to alter historic work patterns, even under adverse economic conditions; insisting on not contracting with a nonunion supplier, even when it damages the company or its objectives; or suppression of innovation or performance, even if the contract does not prohibit such actions. The automotive industry, and especially several American firms, has been hampered by extreme "contractitis," or overemphasis of the contract, over the years.

Organizational agency theories hold that the organization is determined by the quality of human relationships, freely formed and sustained by committed involvement.[39] The organization *is* a human relations community with character. OD professionals and managers who regard organizations according to agency theories focus on enhancing the quality of human relations. When the development of organizational character and work community relations delay meeting productivity/profit goals, bypass procedures or contractual processes, or threaten resources that might have gone to system improvement or innovation, these OD professionals simply assume that sacrifices must be made to enhance organizational character and work community relations. An extreme example of this was a family-owned meatpacking plant that was established by the patriarch of a family after World War II. His sons were tapped to run the business when the founder went into semi-retirement. However, the founder retained control over all of the major decisions. When it came time to make the critical decision on whether to automate the process or risk the company folding because of its inability to compete, he would not permit the sons to automate because his "agency" philosophy was that the welfare of his long-time employees was more important than profits, or even the eventual survival of the firm.

Organizational transformation theories hold that an organization is determined by its capacity to continuously learn, create, and sustain an adaptable, just system that continuously interacts with the human and natural environment.[40] The organization is a collective learning system that is able to transform and improve itself over time. OD practitioners who regard organizations primarily as innovative, transformational systems focus on shared creativity and organizational justice. When system transformation activities delay achievement of short-term economic goals, override policies and procedures, or reduce the opportunities for solidifying work community relations, these OD professionals assume that sacrifices must be made to promote system innovation and organizational justice.

Organizational transformation theories seem to fit the requirements for OD work in a total quality setting better than the other approaches. Requirements for external flexibility are held in common by both HRM and OT approaches. By visualizing the organization as a transformational system, OD practitioners may adapt the total quality concepts for their use in continually improving processes, developing innovative projects, and working to empower people to achieve their goals through creative individual performance. Efforts to establish an ethical work culture and achieve organizational justice (see discussion in this and later chapters) help ensure that transformations result in moral improvements in organizations, instead of just change for the sake of change or as a demonstration of political clout. With a commitment to improving the system, OD professionals can be free to recommend minor incremental improvements or radical innovative organizational redesign, as the need for transformation requires. An organizational transformation approach seems to have been taken by David Kearns,[41] the CEO at Xerox who was most responsible for leading the turnaround of the troubled copier company in the 1980s. Through his vision for Xerox to become "the document company," his refusal to let an initial failure of the quality effort stop its forward movement, and his eventual establishment of the Leadership Through Quality approach which was adopted by managers across the company, he was able to lead the core division of Xerox to win a Baldrige Award in 1989.

THE HOUSE OF TOTAL QUALITY: AN ORGANIZATION DEVELOPMENT OPPORTUNITY

If our analysis of the environmental changes and OD history is accurate, then we can conclude that OD professionals are facing unprecedented challenges. The question to be asked is whether these challenges will be viewed as threats or opportunities. OD professionals who define their world in terms of threats may engage in defensive actions, focus on preservation of the past, or retreat into narrow technical specialties. In contrast, OD professionals who define their world in terms of opportunities will focus on the future and carry forward the best of the past. As they become familiar with and understand the promise of total quality, the urgency of seizing the opportunity will become evident.

To begin that process of understanding, one definition of total quality recently endorsed by the *Total Quality Forum* is:

> …a people-focused management system that aims at continual increase in customer satisfaction at continually lower cost. TQ is a total system approach (not a separate area or program), and an integral part of high-level strategy. It works horizontally across functions and departments, involving all employees, top to bottom, and extends backwards and forwards to include the supply chain and the customer chain.[42]

This definition will be expanded in Chapter 2, but it is clear that OD professionals who adopt total quality will become strategic partners in system analysis and improvement. They will assist their clients in empowering employees to control their own work across traditional organizational barriers in order to achieve world-class performance. In fact, the principles and practices associated with total quality impact all the traditional OD approaches. They will require role changes and increased flexibility for line managers, OD specialists, and related HR professionals.

Figure 1.2 presents an overview of the total quality philosophy by introducing the model and related concepts around which this book is organized.[43] The House of Total Quality provides a comprehensive frame of reference, integrating key aspects of organization design and operation, as opposed to the more limited scope and meaning of the House of Quality as a means of quality function deployment in *hoshin* planning.[44] The House of Quality and *hoshin* planning concepts will be explored more fully in Chapters 3 and 7.

The House of Total Quality consists of six components, as depicted in Figure 1.2: (1) the roof or superstructure consists of *four organizational subsystems* within which the actual work of any organization takes place: *the management, social, technical, and educational* subsystems; (2) the *four pillars of quality: customer satisfaction, continuous improvement, speaking with facts, and respect for people*; (3) the *four foundations: strategy management, process management, project management, and individual task management*; (4) the *four cornerstones: strategic planning, process planning, project planning, and task planning*; (5) the *mortar of deployment* between the joints of the roof, the pillars, the foundations, and the cornerstones; and (6) the *ethical work culture*. Each of the pillars with its related foundations and cornerstones is treated in a separate chapter. The ethical work culture is treated later in this chapter.

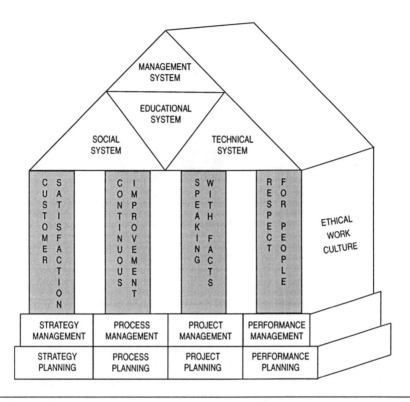

Figure 1.2 The House of Total Quality (Source: Voehl, Frank (1992). *The House of Total Quality*. Coral Springs, FL: Strategy Associates, p. 17. Modified by the authors.)

The Roof Subsystem

The roof or superstructure subsystem of the House of Total Quality is a self-contained system composed of four subsystems. The four subsystems are social, technical, educational, and managerial. Their interdependencies are shown in the three interlocking circles of the ballantine (Figure 1.3). Successful implementation of total quality and continuous improvement requires refocusing OD to recognize the importance of systems. Deming states: "The people work in a system. The job of the manager is to work on the system, to improve it continuously, with their help." Within the roof subsystem of the House of Total Quality, the OD manager must work on these four subsystems.

The social system advocated by Deming (see Chapter 2 for details) includes factors associated with the formal and informal characteristics of the "personality" of the organization: (1) organizational norms, role responsibilities, and sociopsychological relationship expectations; (2) status and power

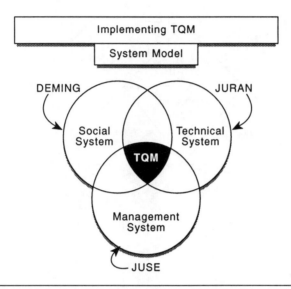

Figure 1.3 The Roof Subsystem of the House of Total Quality

relationships between individual members and among groups; and (3) the extent to which profound knowledge is part of the work community. It is the social system that has the greatest impact on such factors as competition, cooperation, motivation, creativity, innovative behavior, and teamwork. OD practitioners and HR managers share a major responsibility for "shaping" the "personality" of the organization. To achieve total quality, a social system must be developed in which internal and external customer satisfaction, continuous improvement, speaking with facts, and genuine respect for people are accepted social practices in the organization.

The technical system advocated by Juran (see Chapter 2) is concerned with the flow of work through the organization. It includes all the tools and machinery, the practice of quality, and the quantitative aspects of quality.[45] If you can measure it, you can probably describe and perhaps improve it, using the technical system approach. In most organizations, the technical system contains the following core elements:

- Accumulation of technology
- Pursuit of standardization
- Work flow, materials, and specifications
- Job definitions and responsibility
- Machine/person interface
- Number and type of work steps
- Availability and use of information
- Decision-making processes

- Problem-solving tools and processes
- Physical arrangements of equipment, tools, and people

The expected benefits of analyzing and improving the technical system(s) are to:

- Reduce (eliminate) waste and rework
- Reduce (eliminate) negative variation
- Reduce (eliminate) interruptions and idle time
- Save time and money
- Increase employee control over the work process
- Reduce bottlenecks and frustration
- Improve safety and quality of work life
- Increase speed and responsiveness
- Improve customer satisfaction

The educational system is focused on creating and developing a global learning organization dedicated to continuously expanding the knowledge horizons of its stakeholders to gain competitive advantage. Honda, Xerox, Motorola, and GE are examples of organizations that place a premium on developing their quality educational systems. The educational system not only requires OD professionals and their HR counterparts to enhance their internal training and development efforts, but also demands that learning partnerships with other public and private institutions be forged to continuously network and upgrade the knowledge of all employees.

Yahagi[46] wrote an article on what the Japanese are doing about going "beyond" TQM. He indicated that there are at least 12 factors that relate to excellent quality management: corporate history, corporate climate, strategic alliances, channels, management cycle, environment, management targets, business structure, management resources, management design, management functions, and management performance. His research indicates that six of these are *critical* to the success of an organization, including:

- **Corporate climate**—Core climate and culture
- **Management cycle**—Vision, strategy, planning, organizing, implementing, and controlling
- **Business structure**—Business fields, business mix, and market standing
- **Management resources**—Money, materials, information, and people
- **Management design**—System, organization, authority, and responsibility
- **Management performance**—Growth, scale, stability, profit, and market share

He indicates that what follows product quality must be *management quality*. These critical factors will be incorporated in the discussion of policy deployment in the House of Total Quality.

Thus, management provides the leadership and framework for the policies, procedures, and practices of the organization. The management system is deployed at four levels: strategy, process, project, and personal performance management. These comprise the foundations and cornerstones of the House of Total Quality and will be introduced now.

Pillar, Cornerstone, Foundation Subsystem

The roof and four pillars of the House of Total Quality rest upon the four cornerstones of planning and the four foundations of management which relate to strategies, processes, projects, and performance. While the roof (subsystem) is the most theoretical part of the House of Total Quality, with the pillars providing direction for desired system outcomes, it still does not ground the structure in reality. Planning and managerial operations must be put into action in order to implement the quality improvement process.

The cornerstone of the first pillar (customer satisfaction) is *strategy planning*. Strategy planning is done through the process of environmental analysis and strategy formulation to determine an organization's future direction. It is most effectively conducted as an iterative, participative design process. It enhances the adequacy, increases the accuracy, and generates the commitment of organizational stakeholders to adapt to or transform the environment, as needed or possible.

The foundation of the first pillar is *strategy management*. Strategy management is the process of strategic plan implementation, evaluation, and control to develop competitive advantage and to ensure a favorable organizational future. It is most effectively conducted as an active, iterative, feedback process to determine the long-run performance of an organization. The strategy dimension is discussed in Chapter 3.

The cornerstone of the second pillar (continuous improvement) is *process planning*. Process planning assures that all key processes work in harmony with the mission and meet the needs and expectations of the constituents or customers by maximizing operational effectiveness. The focus of process planning is to design operations to identify, hear, and respond rapidly to the changing voices of the customer.

The foundation of the second pillar is *process management*. Process management is required to implement and coordinate measured, streamlined, and controlled processes to continually improve operations. This managerial stage often requires cross-functional efforts, since many functions cross departmental boundaries. The outcomes are a common language for documenting activities and shared decision making to eliminate waste, redundancy, and bottlenecks. Process management tools, which enhance OD professional performance, include affinity diagram/KJ method, interrelationship digraphs, tree diagrams, matrix diagrams, arrow diagrams, process decision program charts, matrix data analysis, competitive benchmarking, flowcharting, nominal group techniques, structured surveys, trend charts, and computerized systems analysis. These are discussed in greater detail in Chapter 4.

The cornerstone of the third pillar (speaking with facts) is *project planning*. Project planning establishes a system to effectively plan, organize, implement, and control all the resources and activities needed for successful completion of projects. At this stage, teams are formed to solve and carry out both process- and policy-related tasks. Team activities are linked to operational objectives and improvement targets and are designed to develop the critical success factors: control systems, schedules, tracking mechanisms, performance indicators, and skill analysis.

The foundation of the third pillar is *project management*. Project management focuses on the implementation and control of a single, nonrecurring event that activates organizational change through structured phases and specified outcomes and requires teamwork for successful completion. Sound project management links organizational objectives and processes, implements a work plan with designated milestones, establishes a communication process for documenting key decisions and improvements, resolves project problems, and results in a project completed on time and within budget. Project management tools that enhance performance of the OD professional are: cause-and-effect diagrams, check sheets, display graphs, histograms, Pareto charts, scatter diagrams, control charts, force-field analysis, prioritization matrices, run charts, block diagrams, customer/supplier relations checklists, and quality mapping. These tools are treated in Chapter 5.

The cornerstone of the fourth pillar (respect for people) is *performance planning*. Personal performance planning provides all employees with the means to implement continuous improvement of the above processes and systems through completion of individual tasks and activities. By developing an individual performance plan, one can become aware of how his or her work performance contributes to the success and sense of community of the rest of the organization.

The foundation of the fourth pillar is *performance management*. Performance management may be defined as the implementation and control of, and respectful regard for, oneself and others in line with total quality strategies, processes, and projects. Key objectives, with quality indicators and personal controls, must be developed. The outcome of personal performance management is a committed organizational vision, people empowered to make decisions and solve problems, a greater sense of job satisfaction and work community, improved communication, respect and trust, and better integrated work systems. Performance dimensions are discussed in Chapter 6.

The mortar of deployment bonds the roof, pillars, foundations, and cornerstones of the House of Total Quality. Deployment is the interactive process of participation and feedback that builds a sense of ownership and commitment to the expansion of the House of Total Quality, domestically and internationally. Deployment is most successful when a supportive ethical work culture has been established within an organization. Characteristics of this type of culture are explained in the next section.

ETHICAL WORK CULTURE AND EXPANDED ORGANIZATION DEVELOPMENT ROLES

While the House of Total Quality provides the height and breadth of total quality, the organizational ethical work culture provides its depth and determines what it "feels like" to internal and external stakeholders who dwell there.[47] The ethical work culture of an organization determines whether the house becomes a home—a place where respect, cooperation, trust, caring, justice, and high performance standards prevail. Organizations with highly developed ethical work cultures demonstrate *organizational integrity*, which can be defined as the collective alignment of moral awareness, judgment, intention, and conduct around principled standards.[48] Habitual patterns of practice from highly developed ethical cultures lead to formation of *organizational character*. Organizational character is different than organizational personality; the former gives principled caring relationships and reputation a higher priority than rapid socioeconomic adaptability. The latter is neutral on the questions of morality or organizational values. Total quality organizations are organizations that stand for certain principles and caring relationships which OD practitioners are expected to nurture and sustain through sound system development.

Culture has been defined as a pattern of basic assumptions—invented, discovered, or developed by a given group as it learns to cope with its problems of external adaptation and internal integration—that has worked well enough to be considered valid and, therefore, to be taught to new members as the correct way to perceive, think, and feel in relation to those problems.[49] The word "culture" can be applied to any size of social unit, from entire civilizations, countries, or ethnic groups down to organizations or groups. Culture can be viewed from three levels: artifacts and creations (technology, art, visible and audible behavior patterns), values (normative claims by group members that may be tested in the physical environment or by social consensus), and assumptions (fundamental beliefs about the nature of reality, human beings, human activity, and human relationship to the environment).

Ethical work cultures can also be changed by interventions that focus on key leverage points.[50] If the current organizational ethical values are not strongly held, organizations have the opportunity to move to alternative (preferably *higher*) ethical culture stages of development. Thus, the less members are committed to the status quo, the easier it will be to effect organizational ethical work culture and subculture change.[51]

Organizational work cultures and subcultures differ, but they can be morally developed by appropriately introducing the next maturity stage of ethical work culture. It is important for OD professionals to be able to identify and support those ethical work cultures that provide the depth of principled commitment to the House of Total Quality. Ethical work cultures provide continuity of commitment to principles and practices that survive leadership transitions. Leaders and all employees must hold themselves and others accountable to standards of integrity if a strong ethical work culture is to survive. Organizations without well-developed ethical work cultures do not have the staying power to implement total quality. They are rightly regarded as lacking character or being shallow. The work of Kohlberg[52] and Gilligan[53] on individual moral development can be extended to organizational moral development to provide a six-stage road map of ethical work cultures and the work environments they sustain (Table 1.2).

Stages 1 and 2: The House of Manipulation. The House of Manipulation is the work environment that is created and sustained by stages one and two of organization ethical work culture: Social Darwinism and Machiavellianism. Social Darwinism may be considered an amoral stage of organizational existence—the lowest or first stage of organizational ethical work culture formation—and can be described as a form of survival of the fittest. At this stage, the most powerful individual, coalition, or network determines what is right or wrong and punishes those who deviate from accepted behavior. The lion or lion prides are appropriate metaphors for forceful ruling individuals and cliques that devise and monitor organizational policies and procedures.

At the next level of development is Machiavellianism, which assumes that members will routinely accept dishonest behavior for organizational advantage. Unlike the forceful lion, the Machiavellian fox is more likely to resort to back-stabbing, cunning, and treachery to maximize organizational gain. Organizations operating at the second stage are above the stage 1 bloodbaths, but an atmosphere of distrust is created, where every employee seeks to get ahead by stepping on others, which precludes collaborative activity. Organizations that operate at the first two stages are mired in a moral jungle, and their predatory rewards are meager compared to the benefits that await them at higher levels.

Stages 3 and 4: The House of Compliance. At the third and fourth stages, Popular Conformity and Allegiance to Authority are the two leading strategies. At the third stage, an organization adopts conventional procedures to which members must adhere if they are to remain employed. Lions and foxes are not tolerated at this stage. Organizations such as public bureaucracies and family businesses often become fixed on complying with rules and familiar operating procedures, forgetting that the rules were set up to better

Table 1.2 Model of Organizational Ethical Work Culture Stages and the Work Environments They Sustain

Organizational Ethical Work Culture Stage	Work Environment
Stage 1: *Social Darwinism* Dread of extinction and the urgency of financial survival dictate moral conduct. The direct use of force is the accepted norm. An atmosphere of fear pervades. Stage 2: *Machiavellianism* Organization's gain guides actions. Successfully attaining goals justifies the use of any effective means, including dishonesty. An atmosphere of distrust pervades.	**House of Manipulation**
Stage 3: *Popular Conformity* There is a tradition of standard operating procedures. Peer pressure to adhere to social norms dictates what is right or wrong behavior. Stage 4: *Allegiance to Authority* Directions from legitimate authority, inside and outside the firm, determine organizational moral standards. Right and wrong are based on the decisions of those with legal and hierarchical power to legitimately optimize investor wealth.	**House of Compliance**
Stage 5: *Democratic Participation* Egalitarian participation in decision making and reliance on majority rule become organizational moral standards and shape investor financial expectations. Stage 6: *Principled Integrity* Justice, utility, caring, dignity, freedom, service, and accountability become guiding principles and serve as the basis for creating multiple stakeholder relationships. Sustained enhancement of these relationships forms organization character. Conscious, daily integration of the guiding principles in all systems and processes overrides other value culture stages and creates an atmosphere of trust and commitment.	**House of Integrity**

serve customers or clients. Their resistance to change, based on traditional or popular conformity, can lead to institutionalized mediocrity.

At the fourth stage, compliance is based not on a need for peer approval but on obedience to legitimate internal and/or external organizational authority. The work climate is one in which employees do not think and act for themselves, but always check out the position of legal officers and/or senior managers before uttering an opinion. Employees are conditioned to comply with authority by a process of hierarchical socialization. Sometimes this involves indoctrination processes, detailed by William Whyte in *The Organization Man* in the 1950s, or powerful socialization pressures, identified by Terrence Deal and Allan Kennedy in *Corporate Cultures* in the 1990s. The absence of individual moral autonomy severely limits the ability of organizations to move to stage 5 of moral development. The group-centered mentality of stages 3 and 4 can blind the organization to environmental challenges, resulting in a habitually reactive posture to external change. These conditions can stunt an organization's growth or threaten its survival in a globally competitive environment. Recent moral development research on American business professionals and business school graduate students indicates that a majority of business practitioners seem to be reasoning at a level that will sustain the House of Compliance.[54] *Thus, OD professionals need to stretch themselves and challenge their clients in order to move up from the House of Compliance to the House of Integrity.*

Stages 5 and 6: The House of Integrity. At the fifth and sixth stages of organizational ethical work culture development, Democratic Participation and decision making and Principled Integrity are the dominant stages. Employees who work in organizations operating at the fifth stage are not guided by seeking social approval or the authoritative command typical of the House of Compliance. Instead, majority vote of individual members, or their representatives, ultimately determines policy and procedure.

Surveying majority trends is an important basis for organizational decision making at this stage. An obvious defect in this stage is that, just as a lion, fox, peer groups, or heavy-handed authority figures can abuse power to the detriment of the organization, so can the tyranny of the majority. The majority can override the creative few and prematurely silence excellent minority contributors. This deprives the organization of vital inputs and potential innovations. However, the roots of participative management are found in democratic ideals. A stage 5 organizational ethical work culture, therefore, is more conducive to the growth of participative quality processes than any of the earlier stages. It is important for OD professionals to be aware of an organization's ethical work culture to prevent premature introduction of the technical subsystems of quality into a culture that resists democratic participation.

The sixth stage of organizational ethical work culture development requires respect for justice and the minority rights of productive and creative individuals. A key characteristic of this stage is use of problem-solving and decision-making processes that involve searching for consensus and community building, rather than relying on a majority vote. Effective, efficient, caring, and just systems that protect organizational contributors from scapegoating are abiding features at level six. The organization thrives by nurturing consensus, thus gaining valuable insights from creative individuals and groups who dare to go beyond the majority view.

Employees who work in organizations at the sixth stage of ethical work culture development do not rest on their laurels. They are continually strengthening organizational character, or readiness to act, by developing their intellectual virtues (knowledge, understanding, and wisdom), their moral virtues (justice, honesty, courage, moderation, and prudence), and their social-emotional virtues (caring, assertiveness, humility, openness, and cooperativeness). Various habits and stable processes constitute the work culture that supports the House of Integrity. In turn, the House of Integrity is the best climate in which to create and implement new technologies that sustain the competitive advantage of learning organizations.

Since competent, committed employees will expect to be a part of a learning organization with the ethical work culture of the House of Integrity, OD professionals need the concepts, practices, and tools to bring it about.[55] Development of the best operating, technical, and managerial talent now demands expanded OD competency. OD professionals are expected to know how to assess and develop the ethical work culture of a work organization so that the House of Integrity can become an inviting "work home" for the best available talent. Otherwise, the best talent will migrate to competitors that can create the House of Integrity ethical climate that is a necessary requirement for the optimal functioning of the House of Total Quality.

Thus, developing the organization's ethical work culture and key cultural assumptions is critical if total quality implementation is to succeed. The roof, pillars, foundations, and cornerstones provide the height and breadth of the House of Total Quality, but the ethical work culture determines its depth. An organization with a weak ethical work culture will not have the character for sustained implementation of total quality.

It is important for general managers and OD professionals to realize that the ethical work culture is part of the system of total quality that requires regular assessment, monitoring, and development. Expecting sustained world-class quality performance from an organization that has not institutionalized the ethical level of the House of Integrity through an ethics development system is unrealistic.

Ten components of an ethics development system in a total quality ethical work culture are:[56] (1) organizational leaders who are personally committed, credible, visible, and willing to take action on the ethical values of the work culture; (2) a statement of prioritized core values, guiding principles, and a code of ethics to provide broad and specific guidance for employees; (3) an ethics council or coordinating group to establish and update policies, ultimately resolve ethical disputes, and provide a top-level conduit for the internal and external ethical voice of customers; (4) routine ethical work culture assessments, with results shared and problems addressed; (5) organizational ethical impacts considered in HR selection, performance appraisal, promotion, and development decisions, as well as OD design and processes; (6) ongoing ethics training at all levels to ensure both compliance to standards and autonomous decision-making skills that enable responsible conduct on a daily basis; (7) a formal mechanism for reporting unethical and/or illegal practices to an individual and/or office with the authority to take action (e.g., a policy of whistleblower protection for person(s) reporting unethical practices to an organizational ethics officer); (8) a mechanism and/or process for the resolution and enforcement of ethical standards with timely, fair, and just decisions rendered to the person(s) and/or systems involved; (9) formal and informal communication channels that reinforce the importance of continually improving the ethical work culture; and (10) regular recognition and/or commendation rituals for individuals and/or groups that show exemplary ethical contributions.

The House of Total Quality graphically shows the triple impact of total quality on the responsibilities of OD managers who must assist in planning and deployment: (1) *developing the full vertical dimension* of each pillar supporting the roof of the House of Quality; (2) *developing the full horizontal alignment* of the foundation stones and columns of the house, with each depending on the other; and (3) *developing the full depth* of the house through assessing and implementing the ethical work culture of the House of Integrity.

Each component of the House of Total Quality can benefit from input from competent OD professionals. This integrated view of an organization requires more than mastering the traditional OD and HR subspecialties. It also requires increased strategic thinking and work/organization redesign competencies.

TOTAL QUALITY MANAGEMENT STANDARDS AND THE HOUSE OF TOTAL QUALITY

Two of the most widely recognized lists of quality characteristics are W. Edwards Deming's 14 Points and the Malcolm Baldrige National Quality Award criteria. Deming's points reflect his approach to the attitudes, behaviors, policies, and culture change which must take place in order to have a successful quality system. The Baldrige criteria provide a tool for assessing how organizations have implemented total quality and what the impact has been. We will briefly consider each of these.

Deming's 14 Points

The origins and background of Deming are presented in Chapter 2. However his philosophy, which is captured in his famous 14 Points, is most appropriate for use here. Deming developed his philosophy over a number of years and continuously improved his 14 Points, given in Exhibit 1.1. Deming did not provide a clear rationale for the 14 Points, many of which go against generally accepted practices of "conventional" management. Recently, however, he synthesized the underlying foundation behind the 14 Points in what he called "A System of Profound Knowledge," which is also presented in Chapter 2.

After a series of conferences on productivity, mandated by President Reagan in 1983, a proposal for a national quality award, similar to the Deming Prize in Japan, was developed and sent to Congress. The Malcolm Baldrige National Quality Award was named after the secretary of commerce who was killed in an accident shortly before the bill was passed. President Reagan signed the bill into law on August 20, 1987.

The Baldrige criteria were developed, and are constantly being improved, by a volunteer group of quality experts from business, consulting, and academic organizations, now called the Board of Overseers. The award is administered by the National Institute of Standards and Technology, a division of the Department of Commerce. However, all evaluations and determination of awards are done by volunteer examiners. The core values are contained in the seven categories for the assessment. Priorities are designated by the points assigned to each category. These point values have shifted somewhat since the award was first established to reflect the maturing understanding of the components of quality, as well as "continuous improvement." The 1995 criteria and their point scores are presented in Exhibit 1.2.

Table 1.3 compares the components of the House of Total Quality with the Baldrige categories and Deming principles. The second column in the table presents the seven categories and core values and concepts of the Malcolm Baldrige National Quality Award. The third column presents an abridged listing of the principles and concepts developed by W. Edwards Deming; a complete listing is presented in Chapter 3. Deming's beliefs are included for two reasons. First, Deming was an early practitioner of total quality, and much of the work in the field is directly or indirectly influenced by his ideas. Second, they are provocative; his 14 Points stimulate exploration of their implications for individual institutions.

The House of Total Quality model incorporates the quality principles of Deming and the Baldrige criteria. Its comprehensiveness provides an excellent structure for exploration of the relations between total quality and OD.

ORGANIZATION DEVELOPMENT, HUMAN RESOURCE MANAGEMENT, AND THE TOTAL QUALITY DIFFERENCE

The total quality approach is changing the role of OD and HR professionals by changing the expectations of stakeholders, within and outside the profession. The responsibilities of the organizational change agent are also chang-

1. Create and publish to all employees a statement of the aims and purposes of the company or other organization. The management must demonstrate constantly their commitment to this statement.
2. Learn the new philosophy, top management and everybody.
3. Understand the purpose of inspection, for improvement of processes and reduction of cost.
4. End the practice of awarding business on the basis of price tag alone.
5. Improve constantly and forever the system of production and service.
6. Institute training.
7. Teach and institute leadership.
8. Drive out fear. Create trust. Create a climate for innovation.
9. Optimize toward the aims and purposes of the company the efforts of teams, groups, staff areas.
10. Eliminate exhortations for the work force.
11. a. Eliminate numerical quotes for production. Instead, learn and institute methods for improvement.
    b. Eliminate M.B.O. Instead, learn the capabilities of processes, and how to improve them.
12. Remove barriers that rob people of pride of workmanship.
13. Encourage education and self-improvement for everyone.
14. Take action to accomplish the transformation.

W. EDWARDS DEMING, PH.D.
Consultant in Statistical Studies
10 January 1990

Exhibit 1.1   Deming's 14 Points

• Leadership	90 Points
• Information and Analysis	75 Points
• Strategic Planning	55 Points
• Human Resource Development and Management	140 Points
• Process Management	140 Points
• Business Results	250 Points
• Customer Focus and Satisfaction	250 Points

Exhibit 1.2   Baldrige Award Criteria (Source: 1995 Malcolm Baldrige National Quality Award Criteria, NIST.)

Table 1.3 A Comparison of the House of Total Quality with the Baldrige Categories and Deming Principles

HOUSE OF TOTAL QUALITY[a]	BALDRIGE CATEGORIES[b]	DEMING PRINCIPLES[c]
THE ROOF		
Management System		
1. Systems, process	**SYSTEM**	1. Publish the aims and purpose of the organization
2. Leadership	1.0 Leadership	2. Learn the new philosophy
3. Strategy	3.0 Strategic quality planning	7. Teach and institute leadership
4. Mission, vision, values	• Long-range planning	
Social System		
1. Structure	4.0 Human resource development and management	14. Take action to accomplish the transformation
2. Social norms	• Employee development	• Hierarchic style of management must change
	• Partnership development	• Transformation can only be accomplished by people, not hardware
3. Teams	• Cross-functional teams	
4. Organizational personality		
Technical System		
1. Work processes	5.0 Process management	9. Optimize efforts of teams, groups, staff toward aims and purposes
2. Job descriptions	• Reduced cycle time	• Statistical measurement
3. Problem-solving tools	• Design quality and QFD	
4. Decision making		
6. Measurement tools		
Educational System		
1. Lifelong learning	4.0 Human resource development and management	• Continual learning
2. Retraining	• Employee participation and development	6. Institute training

THE PILLARS

Customer satisfaction	7.0 Customer focus and satisfaction	4. End the practice of awarding business on price tag alone • Aim quality at the needs of the customer, present and future
Continuous improvement	2.0 Information and analysis 5.0 Process management 6.0 Business results	3. Understand the purpose of inspection—improve processes, reduce costs 11a-b. Eliminate quotas & MBO. Concentrate on improvement
Speak with facts	2.0 Information and analysis • Management by fact	3. Understand the purpose of inspection—improve processes, reduce costs • In God we trust; all others bring facts • Statistical measurement
Respect for people	4.0 Human resource development and management • Job design • Compensation and recognition • Employee well-being and satisfaction	14. Take action to accomplish the transformation 11a. Eliminate numerical quotas 11. Eliminate MBO 12. Remove barriers that rob people of pride in workmanship

ETHICAL WORK CULTURE

Ethical work culture	1.0 Leadership 4.0 Human resource development and management • Manage for organizational integrity	8. Drive out fear 7. Teach and institute leadership • Create and maintain system integrity

[a] Voehl, Frank (1992). *The House of Total Quality*. Coral Springs, FL: Strategy Associates.
[b] 1995 Award Criteria, Malcolm Baldrige National Quality Award, Milwaukee: American Society for Quality Control.
[c] Deming, W. Edwards (1986). *Out of the Crisis*. Cambridge, MA: MIT Center for Advanced Engineering Studies, as modified by W. Edwards Deming, 1990.

ing, as shown in Exhibit 1.3. Thus, while OD and HRM professionals reflect the organizational culture within which they are working, they also are expected to influence and shape it.

OD practitioners must walk a fine line in order to embrace the TQM philosophy and not lose the advantages of the vision and philosophy that are badly needed in today's climate of constant organizational change. Schein[57] claimed that the OD field has recently become more "technology driven" as professionals have focused on application of tools, techniques, and programs. This has led to neglect of the field's early vision and philosophy of working with organizational systems. Schein stated that the early OD vision and philosophy were based on: (1) helping systems help themselves, (2) focusing on process rather than content, and (3) not trusting any specific technology or approach to provide a "ready-made" solution to a given organizational problem. Thus, OD practitioners can feel safe in retaining their historic identity while applying the total quality philosophy, approaches, and techniques in a "contingency" fashion, where they are appropriate. OD

SOUNDING BOARD
- Facilitates exploration, clarification, and deeper understanding of client attitudes, values, and motivation for adopting a total quality strategy
- Assists clients in assessing the fit between their personal management beliefs and those of TQM
- Helps clients attend to and explore the complex implications of implementing TQM

ORGANIZATION CHANGE CONSULTANT
- Helps clients plan and manage the organization change process during adoption of TQM by facilitating the process of crafting a vision for change and designing specific strategies for achieving the vision
- Helps the client system cope with the stress produced by change

TRAINING CONSULTANT
- Helps plan and design effective learning/educational activities to support the TQM implementation effort
- Coaches instructor–managers in skills required for group training

SHADOW CONSULTANT TO QUALITY IMPROVEMENT TEAMS
- Consults with quality improvement team leaders and facilitators regarding management of group processes
- Assists teams in developing strategies to prepare the rest of the organization to accept and support the improvement they will be implementing

---

Exhibit 1.3 Value-Added Roles for Organization Development Professionals Working in Total Quality Organizations (Source: Adapted from F.W. Voehl, Coral Springs, FL: Strategy Associates.)

practitioners may be able to add the greatest value to their clients' systems by intervening in such a way as to help clients manage complex processes. Some of these processes involve how organizations and people learn, how decisions are made, how strategy is developed and implemented, and how organization change is produced and managed. To do so is to be consistent with the OD field's traditions, roots, and core values.

A list of these changing expectations and the difference total quality makes is indicated in Table 1.4, which provides a comparison of traditional and total quality HRM approaches.

In the traditional business organizational approach, the key objectives are productivity, profits, and smoothly managing change processes, while the quality objective is often restricted to meeting minimum required standards or federal regulations or keeping the stockholders satisfied. Information is shared only if it is needed, since the primary constituencies in the organization are managers and stockholders; customers and employees are accorded a much lower priority by the organization. Employee involvement programs, if they exist at all, are primarily suggestion plan approaches. Education and training are strictly job related rather than broadening the overall capacities of employees. Finally, rewards are management designed and driven by productivity requirements. Regular layoffs and plant shutdowns occur without retraining, thereby undermining job security for the average employee.

In contrast, the business objectives of the total quality OD/HRM approach are to increase customer satisfaction and market share through improved quality and to develop a more cooperative, flexible, loyal, and innovative work environment. They are based on according preeminence to human resources in meeting customer needs, with a focus on sharing information, responsibility, and rewards. Changing the organization to enhance employee involvement within and between levels and functions becomes a way of life, with ongoing education and multiple skill training. Training and development resources are available to all employees. The reward structure is designed and adjusted through management and employee input, and involvement in the formation of HR policies and practices is built into the infrastructure of the organization. Job security and job transitioning become partially an organizational responsibility that OD and HRM leaders routinely address.

A more detailed treatment of the difference total quality makes for OD and HRM practices is provided in Chapters 3 to 6. It is important to recognize, however, that "changes in corporate culture come slowly, and even managers who have adopted the TQM philosophy do not necessarily have the power to move their organization and its systems overnight."[58] OD and HRM professionals, therefore, need to be aware of the barriers to total quality OD implementation.

Table 1.4 Comparison of Traditional and Total Quality and Organization Development/Human Resource Management Approaches

	Traditional OD/HRM approach	Total quality OD/HRM approach
Philosophy	Fair day's work for a fair day's pay	Shared responsibility, commitment, rewards
Business objectives	Increased productivity, profitability; quality is secondary; focus on labor	Increased quality, productivity, customer satisfaction, employee satisfaction and loyalty
Quality objectives	Adequate quality to remain in business; staff-driven approaches to quality improvement	TQM and continuous improvement at and across every level
Business information sharing	Limited to information on an as-needed basis for job performance	Open books—share broad information on profits, productivity, quality, costs, capital spending plans
Major constituencies	Managers, stockholders, customers, employees	Customers, all employees, stockholders
Employee involvement	Programs—suggestions, plans, individual employee awards; usually no formal system	Extensive, within and between levels and functions; "way of life"
Education and training	On-the-job training; feedback on job performance	Quality and economic education; multiple skill training; problem solving and group process
Reward structure	Management designed and administered	Designed and adjusted by management–employee committee; formal, early union involvement
Job security	Labor as a variable cost; layoffs common during business downturns	Formal commitment; a key consideration in all decisions

Source: Adapted from O'Dell, Carla, "Sharing the Productivity Payoff," reprinted from Production Brief 24 with permission of the American Productivity and Quality Center, Houston. Reprinted by permission from page 336 of *Productivity Through People* by Werther, William B. et al. Copyright ©1980 by West Publishing Co. All rights reserved.

BARRIERS AND RESPONSES TO TOTAL QUALITY ORGANIZATION DEVELOPMENT IMPLEMENTATION

It is important for OD professionals to realize that pitfalls to total quality practices exist but can be overcome. Successful total quality efforts recognize cultural change as a continuous, long-term process, with initial concentrations of support investments required for at least three to five years. Some factors may make it difficult to successfully carry out these efforts in organizations, but the total quality subsystems (management, social, technical, and educational) can address each barrier.

1. Strategic Barrier #1 and the Management System Response. Differences over strategic priorities is often a major corporate barrier. If managers risk losing power and perks or investors risk losing financial returns in the short run, expect direct opposition to quality strategic priorities for customer satisfaction and increased market share. The intense North American emphasis on short-term financial returns at all organizational levels is probably the most potent deterrent to long-term total quality progress. The management system addresses this issue by strategic planning that integrates multilevel requirements, discussed in Chapter 3.

2. Strategic Barrier #2 and the Educational System Response. Resistance to the OD/senior management strategic partnership from either side can become a barrier to effective implementation of total quality. Active involvement of senior leadership and the strategic co-partnership of OD professionals will be necessary to change the House of Compliance into the House of Integrity. To this end, OD professionals must strengthen and expand their understanding of their organizations' core businesses. OD professionals should try to build some practical line experience with "bottom-line" accountability into their career paths. This will help close the credibility gap that they often suffer in the eyes of business executives. The educational system addresses this issue by adequate strategic and operations planning for senior- and functional-level managers. This is expanded upon in Chapters 3 and 4.

3. Cultural Barrier #1 and the Social System Response. Employees who work in an underdeveloped organizational ethical work culture that supports either the House of Manipulation or the House of Compliance will criticize the House of Integrity as being too idealistic, overly optimistic, or naive and question the need for initiating the change to move to higher levels. The path toward ethical work culture maturity is a long one but worth the effort of OD professionals. The social system addresses this issue by adequate ethical work culture assessment and development, as will be seen in Chapters 3 to 6.

4. Cultural Barrier #2 and the Social System Response. Unrealistic social expectations can be created by introducing too much improvement at once. Employees often feel frustrated when these unrealistic expectations are unmet. The social system addresses this issue by adequate incremental project planning, as discussed in Chapter 5.

5. Specialization Barrier #1 and the Educational System Response. OD specialists who focus on team building, organization change processes, training and development, or other specialties may resist the expansion of role responsibilities beyond these narrow technical areas. Specialization accords professional status to many individuals in the OD field. Relinquishing some of these duties to line managers and learning new skills is psychologically uncomfortable. In some firms, however, OD professionals need to change or they will be marginalized. The way that the educational system addresses this issue by providing training and development for OD professionals to prepare them for confidently assuming new responsibilities is discussed in Chapter 6.

6. Specialization Barrier #2 and the Social System Response. Some OD specialists will claim that continuous improvement and participation already exist, so there is no need to change. After all, the very nature of OD is about organizational change and development. Granted, there are ongoing professional development, collegial relations, and professional codes to sustain specialization improvement, but organization-wide, cross-functional system improvement rarely exists. Functional myopia can be cured with TQM of change processes. The social system addresses this issue thorough broadened role expectations and reward systems and is treated in Chapter 4.

7. Structural Barrier #1 and the Management System Response. Intensive divisionalization encourages identification with groups, departments, or subdivisions rather than the total institution. Total quality emphasizes interdepartmental, interdisciplinary, and system-wide collaboration on problem solving and project completion. OD professionals face resistance to matrix and other process-oriented organization structures that may promote quality but not be "conventional." This is closely related to the next barrier. The management system addresses this issue of cross-functional integration in the operations planning section of Chapter 4.

8. Structural Barrier #2 and the Management System Response. Hierarchy inertia is likely to exercise benign or not-so-benign neglect to total quality. Total quality supporters advocate a pancake-style rather than a pyramid-style structure. Persons who have hierarchical power are likely to resist total quality initiatives because they will entail some loss of power and authority. OD professionals who support quality, however, cannot prevent the inevitable drift toward flatter organizations that are technically linked. The management system addresses this issue of facilitating horizontal structures and process in the operations planning section of Chapter 4.

9. Structural Barrier #3 and the Management System Response. The compensation system in most organizations is geared toward individual performance, and the lack of widespread gainsharing, profit sharing, and group rewards provides a convenient excuse for OD professionals not to adopt an advocacy role in changing the system to build a quality work culture. After all, they may reason, that is the focus and agenda of the compensation specialists. The management system addresses this issue by restructuring the reward system to include a wide range of group reward policies, as treated in Chapter 4.

10. Linguistic Barrier #1 and the Educational System Response. By encouraging standardization and minimizing variation, the language of statistical process control generates negative reactions from individuals geared toward innovation and creativity. It seems to require limits on individual freedom. In total quality improvement, however, positive variations within desired outcomes are encouraged, so that creativity is not squelched but unacceptable variation is controlled. The educational system addresses this issue on creativity, self-discipline, and system stability in Chapter 6.

11. Linguistic Barrier #2 and the Educational System Response. Managing quality control often generates linguistic opposition because it seems to imply unnecessary limits on personal work style. In total quality improvement, however, the emphasis is on identifying and doing whatever is necessary to achieve what the members see as benefits to the organization, rather than an excessive focus on what top management orders them to do. In Chapter 6, readers will see how the educational system addresses this issue by increasing awareness of the expanded freedom that proper quality processes provide.

12. Operational Barriers and the Technical System Response. Busy OD professionals can claim that there is insufficient time to do their jobs and work on job improvement, but that is the total quality operational challenge—to simultaneously do the job and improve the way the job is done. However, once OD managers learn the technical skills required to think statistically, they will save time because they stop treating all variation as if it were due to special causes, and therefore stop overreacting. By focusing on the vital few improvements possible in an organization, the technical system can address this issue, as discussed in Chapter 5.

13. Attitudinal Barriers and the Educational System Response. Employees may regard total quality as a passing fad which won't work and which focuses attention on internal processes rather than external results.[59] The educational system addresses this issue by pointing to specific global benefits of total quality implementation (as developed in Chapter 7): employee relations are enhanced, operating procedures are improved, customer satisfaction is increased, and financial performance is strengthened.

In short, the potential for change exists and the degree of change required is dependent upon the balance of driving and resistant forces to the principles of total quality improvement. The resistant forces may be so severe that a radical transformation may be required. The intent of this book is to help sensitize all managers of organizational change, and specifically OD professionals, to these issues in order to realistically and constructively develop world-class competitive work cultures.

REVIEW QUESTIONS

1.1 What are the six driving forces reshaping the OD environment of the future?

1.2 What are the "organic" and "spectrum" approaches to OD that have emerged in the United States since the late 1930s?

1.3 What are the "perspectives" that Warner Burke provided on the individual, group, and systems influences in the development of OD?

1.4 Compare and contrast the competing organizational theories and relate them to the total quality approach.

1.5 What is the House of Total Quality, and how might it be a useful model for OD practitioners?

1.6 What are the six essential components of the House of Total Quality, and why is each one important to the strength and solidity of the overall structure?

1.7 How would you characterize each of the six stages of ethical work culture development and their relationship to the realization of a total quality environment?

1.8 What are the ten components of a total quality ethical work culture?

1.9 What are the differences between the traditional and total quality approaches to OD/HRM?

1.10 What are two strategic barriers to successful implementation of total quality, and how can the total quality subsystems effectively address each one? (This question can be repeated using other categories of barriers, i.e., cultural, specialization, structural, linguistic, operational, and attitudinal).

DISCUSSION QUESTIONS

1.1 What challenges or opportunities has the changing nature and diversity of the work force presented to you personally? How have you addressed those challenges or opportunities, and what insights have you gained from your experience?

1.2 Compare and contrast the four OT approaches and their influence on OD professionals' attitude toward total quality.

1.3 Discuss the difference in approach that seems to be presented by the Baldrige criteria and by Deming's 14 Points. Do they seem to complement or contradict each other?

1.4 Elaborate on your experiences if you have worked in an ethical work culture that supports the House of Manipulation, the House of Compliance, and/or the House of Integrity.

1.5 Why do you agree or disagree with the claim that the total quality approach to OD is another form of worker exploitation?

ENDNOTES

1. Adapted from Lewis, Ralph G. and Smith, Douglas H. (1994). *Total Quality in Higher Education*. Delray Beach, FL: St. Lucie Press.

2. Kochan, Thomas and Useem, Michael, Eds. (1994). *Transforming Organizations*. New York: Oxford University Press; Ackoff, Russell L. (1994). *The Democratic Corporation*. New York: Oxford; Gouillart, F.J. and Kelly, J.N. (1995). *Transforming the Organization*. New York: McGraw-Hill.

3. Harvey, Donald F. and Brown, Donald R. (1988). *An Experiential Approach to Organization Development*, 3rd edition. Englewood Cliffs, NJ: Prentice-Hall, p. 9. Also see French, Wendell L. and Bell, Cecil H. Jr. (1994). "A History of Organization Development." Cited in Wendell L. French, Cecil H. Bell, Jr., and Robert A. Zawacki, Eds. (1994). *Organization Development and Transformation: Managing Effective Change*, 4th edition. Burr Ridge, IL: Irwin, p. 30.

4. Harvey and Brown (endnote 3), p. 3.

5. Beckhard, Richard (1969). *Organization Development Strategies and Models*. Reading, MA: Addison-Wesley, p. 9.

6. French, Wendell L. and Bell, Cecil H. Jr. (1978). *Organization Development*, 2nd edition. Englewood Cliffs, NJ: Prentice-Hall, p. 14, cited in French, Bell, and Zawacki (endnote 3), p. 7.

7. Evans, James R. and Lindsay, William M. (1993). *The Management and Control of Quality*, 2nd edition. Minneapolis: West Publishing, p. 281.

8. Cited in Shores, A. Richard (1990). *A TQM Approach to Achieving Manufacturing Excellence*. Milwaukee: ASQC Quality Press, p. 270.

9. Bartlett, Christopher and Ghoshal, Sumantra (1987). *Managing Across Borders*. Cambridge, MA: Harvard Business School Press; Fingleton, E. (1995). *Blindside: Why Japan Is Still on Track to Overtake the U.S. by the Year 2000*. Boston: Houghton Mifflin, pp. 6–47.

10. Yoshida, Kosaku (1992). "New Economic Principles in America—Competition and Cooperation: A Comparative Study of the U.S. and Japan." *Columbia Journal of World Business*. Vol. 26, No. 4, pp. 2–15; Ishihara, S. (1991). *The Japan that Can*

Say No: Why Japan Will Be First Among Equals. New York: Simon & Schuster, pp. 95–105.

11. Ishikawa, K. and Lu, D. (1985). *What Is Total Quality Control?* Englewood Cliffs, NJ: Prentice-Hall, pp. 45–46.

12. Spechler, J.W. (1988). *When America Does It Right: Case Studies in Service Quality.* Norcross, GA: Industrial Engineering and Management Press.

13. Bounds, G.M. and Pace, L.A. (1991). "Human Resource Management for Competitive Capability." In M.J. Stahl and G.M. Bounds, Eds. *Competing Globally through Customer Value: The Management of Strategic Suprasystems.* New York: Quorum Books, pp. 95–112.

14. Reich, Robert B. (1991). *The Work of Nations: Preparing Ourselves for 21st Century Capitalism.* New York: Vintage Books, pp. 171–242.

15. Robinson, S. and Rousseau, D. (1994). "Violating the Psychological Contract: Not the Exception But the Norm." *Journal of Organizational Behavior.* Vol. 15, No. 6, pp. 245–259.

16. Boroughs, D.L. (1996). "Winter of Discontent." *U.S. News & World Report.* January 22, pp. 47–54.

17. Rosenbluth, Hal F. and Peters, D.M. (1992). *The Customer Comes Second: And Other Secrets of Exceptional Service.* New York: William Morrow, pp. 14–15.

18. Fernandez, J. and Bass, M. (1993). *The Diversity Advantage.* Lexington, MA: Heath and Company.

19. Marquardt, Michael and Reynolds, Angus (1994). *The Global Learning Organization.* Burr Ridge, IL: Irwin, pp. 16–18.

20. Wriston, Walter (1992). *The Twilight of Sovereignty: How the Information Revolution Is Transforming the World.* New York: Charles Scribner & Sons, pp. 50–70.

21. Ibid., p. 75.

22. Lengnick-Hall, Cynthia A. and Lengnick-Hall, Mark L. (1988). "Strategic Human Resources Management: A Review of the Literature and a Proposed Typology." *Academy of Management Review.* Vol. 13, No. 3, pp. 454–470.

23. Schuler, Randall S. and Harris, Drew L. (1992). *Managing Quality.* Reading, MA: Macmillan, pp. 25–53; Schuler, R.S. (1990). "Repositioning the Human Resource Function: Transformation or Demise?" *Academy of Management Executive.* Vol. 14, No. 3, pp. 49–60.

24. Jones, Alan and Hendry, Chris (1992). *The Learning Organization.* Coventry, UK: HRD Partnership, pp. 10–60; Dixon, Nancy (1992). "Organizational Learning: A Review of the Literature with Implications for HRD Professionals." *Human Resource Development Quarterly.* Vol. 3, No. 1, pp. 29–49; Senge, Peter (1990). "The Leader's New Work: Building Learning Organizations." *Sloan Management Review.* Vol. 32, No. 1, pp. 7–23.

25. Harrington, John (1991). *The Virtual Organization and Information Technology.* Englewood Cliffs, NJ: Prentice-Hall, pp. 12–65; Davidow, William H. and Malone, Michael S. (1992). *The Virtual Corporation.* New York: Harper Business, pp. 1–72.

26. Handy, Charles (1989). *The Age of Unreason.* London: Basic Books, pp. 40–70.

27. Hammer, Michael and Champy, James (1993). *Reengineering the Corporation.* New York: Harper, pp. 10–39.

28. Sturner, William F. (1993). *Impact: Transforming Your Organization.* Buffalo, NY: Creative Education Foundation; Fletcher, Beverly R. (1990). *Organization Trans-*

formation: Theorists and Practitioners. Westport, CT: Greenwood Publishing Group; Jaccaci, August (1989). "The Social Architecture of a Learning Organization." *Training and Development Journal.* Vol. 43, No. 11, pp. 49–51.

29. The historical facts and references in this section are adapted from French and Bell (endnote 3), pp. 25–40.

30. Ibid., p. 26.

31. Ibid., p. 32.

32. Maslow, Abraham (1954). *Motivational Personality.* New York: Harper and Row; Herzberg, F., Mausner, B., and Snyderman, B. (1959). *The Motivation to Work,* 2nd edition. New York: John Wiley and Sons; McGregor, Douglas (1960). *The Human Side of Enterprise.* New York: McGraw-Hill; Porter, Lyman W. and Lawler, Edward E. (1968). *Managerial Attitudes and Performance.* Homewood, IL: Irwin.

33. Sashkin, Marshall and Burke, W. Warner (1994). "Organization Development in the 1980's." in French, Bell, and Zawacki (endnote 3), p. 55.

34. Singer, Marc G. (1990). *Human Resource Management.* Boston: PWS-Kent, pp. 5–7.

35. *The Craftsman in America.* Washington, DC: The National Geographic Society, 1975, pp. 164–166.

36. Kinner, Wickham (1981). "Big Hat—No Cattle: Managing Human Resources." *Harvard Business Review.* September–October, p. 109.

37. Jackson, Norman and Carter, Pippa (1991). "In Defense of the Paradigm of Incommensurability." *Organization Studies.* Vol. 12, pp. 109–127; Scott, W. Richard (1981). *Organizations: Rational, Natural and Open Systems.* Englewood Cliffs, NJ: Prentice-Hall, pp. 54–76; Parsons, Talcott (1951). *The Social System.* New York: Free Press.

38. Keeley, Michael (1988). *A Social Contract Theory of Organizations.* Notre Dame, IN: University of Notre Dame; Williamson, O.E. (1987). *The Economic Institution of Capitalism: Firms, Markets and Relational Contracting.* New York: Free Press; Hall, Richard H. (1996). *Organizations: Structures, Processes and Outcomes.* Englewood Cliffs, NJ: Prentice-Hall, pp. 70–74.

39. Argyris, Chris (1962). *Personality and Organization.* Homewood, IL: Irwin; Likert, Rensis (1967). *The Human Organization.* New York: McGraw-Hill; Mayer, Roger C., Davis, James H., and Schoorman, F. David (1995). "An Integrative Model of Organizational Trust." *Academy of Management Review.* Vol. 20, No. 3, pp. 709–734; Wilkins, Alan (1989). *Developing Corporate Character.* San Francisco: Jossey-Bass.

40. Kochan, Thomas A. and Useem, Michael, Eds. (1992). *Transforming Organizations.* New York: Oxford University Press; Van de Ven, Andrew H. and Poole, M. Scott (1995). "Explaining Development and Change in Organizations." *Academy of Management Review.* Vol. 20, No. 3, pp. 510–540; Jones, Alan and Hendry, Chris (1992). *The Learning Organization.* Coventry, UK: HRD Partnership; Nonaka, Ikujiro and Takeuchi, Hirotaka (1995). *The Knowledge-Creating Company.* New York: Oxford University Press.

41. Kearns, David and Nadler, David (1993). *Prophets in the Dark.* New York: HarperBusiness.

42. Rampey, J. and Roberts, H. (1992). "Perspectives in Total Quality." *Proceedings of Total Quality Forum IV.* Cincinnati, OH: Procter & Gamble, November.

43. With slight modifications, taken from Voehl, Frank (1992). *Total Quality: Principles and Practices within Organizations*. Coral Gables, FL: Strategy Associates.
44. Akao, Yoji (1990). *Quality Function Deployment*. Cambridge, MA: Productivity Press; Taguchi, Genichi (1986). *Introduction to Quality Engineering*. Tokyo: Asian Productivity Organization.
45. Evans and Lindsay (endnote 7), p. 287.
46. Yahagi, Seiichiro (1992). "After Product Quality in Japan: Management Quality." *National Productivity Review*. Autumn, pp. 46–59.
47. Petrick, Joseph A. and Furr, Diana S. (1995). *Total Quality in Managing Human Resources*. Delray Beach, FL: St. Lucie Press, pp. 26–32.
48. Petrick, Joseph A. and Quinn, John F. (1996). *Management Ethics and Organization Integrity*. Newbury Park, CA: Sage Publications, pp. 50–60; Paine, Lynne S. (1994). "Managing for Organizational Integrity." *Harvard Business Review*. March–April, pp. 110–115.
49. Schein, Edgar H. (1988). *Organizational Culture and Leadership*. San Francisco: Jossey-Bass, pp. 1–120.
50. Trice, Harrison M. and Beyer, Janice M. (1993). *The Cultures of Work Organizations*. Englewood Cliffs, NJ: Prentice-Hall, p. 18.
51. Wilkins, Alan and Dyer, W. Gibb Jr. (1988). "Toward Culturally Sensitive Theories of Culture Change." *Academy of Management Review*. Vol. 13, No. 4, pp. 522–533; Wilkins, Alan (1989). *Developing Corporate Character: How to Successfully Change an Organization without Destroying It*. San Francisco: Jossey-Bass; Trice, Harrison M. and Morand, David (1991). "Cultural Diversity: Organizational Subcultures and Countercultures." In Gale Miller. *Studies in Organizational Sociology*, Vol. 10. Greenwich, CT: JAI Press, pp. 69–105.
52. Kohlberg, Lawrence (1981). *The Philosophy of Moral Development*. San Francisco: Harper and Row. This model can incorporate the five-stage model proposed by Starke, Linda (1993). "The Five Stages of Corporate Moral Development." In Michael Ray and Alan Ringler, Eds. *The New Paradigm in Business*. New York: Putnam, pp. 203–204.
53. Gilligan, Carol (1982). *In a Different Voice*. Cambridge, MA: Harvard University Press.
54. Petrick, Joseph A. and Manning, George E. (1990). "Developing an Ethical Climate for Excellence." *The Journal for Quality and Participation*. Vol. 14, No. 2, pp. 85–87.
55. Petrick, Joseph A. and Pullins, Ellen B. (1992). "Organizational Ethics Development and the Expanding Role of the HR Professional." *The Healthcare Supervisor*. Vol. II, No. 2, pp. 52–61.
56. Petrick and Quinn (endnote 48), pp. 75–80.
57. Schein (endnote 49), pp. 75–80.
58. Evans and Lindsay (endnote 7), p. 287.
59. Harari, Oreu (1993). "Ten Reasons Why TQM Doesn't Work." *Management Review*. Vol. 28, No. 1, pp. 33–38; also see articles by Becker, Selwyn W. and Harari, Oreu (1993). *Management Review*. May, pp. 30–36.

ABSTRACTS

ABSTRACT 1.1
DRIVING FORCES FOR QUALITY IMPROVEMENT IN THE 1990S

Stupak, Ronald J.
The Public Manager, The New Bureaucrat, Spring 1993, pp. 32–35

This article focuses on the use (or lack) of TQM in the public sector. The author first examines the reasons why TQM has been labeled an incompatible program for management of federal government organizations by OD thinkers. Reasons include the government's penchant for dealing in services rather than manufacturing, the lack of high priority on TQM by top managers, low national priority on quality in government, lack of competition to lose customers to, the perception of loss of power by middle managers within the organization, and the reluctance to use a program that was "not invented here" (i.e., in government).

The author next examines the driving forces currently leading government managers to adopt TQM strategies, such as the demands for improved productivity, for increased customer and employee involvement in company management, and for increased performance measurement and long-term strategic planning. The article cites the Defense Systems Management College at Fort Belvoir, Virginia as a case study of increased employee involvement. Productivity, employee morale, and customer satisfaction all increased after TQM administrative and support services were provided to teachers, students, and other school staff. The college implemented an integrated organizational change model, one consistent with its organizational culture and external environment, through the use of OD techniques and TQM tools.

ABSTRACT 1.2
WORKPLACE MANAGEMENT 2000

Coates, Joseph F., Jarratt, Jennifer, and Mahaffie, John
Personnel Administrator, December 1989, pp. 51–55

This article starts by examining the half-dozen overarching drivers of change currently affecting the work force. These include the aging of the work force and the emergence of baby boomers as the dominant generation in work and politics, the alteration of workplaces and neighborhoods resulting from increased immigration of ethnic groups, and changes in family life, including increases in the populations of working women and dual income households. These, in turn, bring social change in the form of new values and attitudes about work, family life, and society. Transportation and communications technologies have also made people, money, information, and goods more mobile. The new worldwide economic market will allow capital, labor, and goods to flow across oceans and borders. International competition pushes corporations to restructure and change managerial practices and relationships with workers, thus increasing the need for innovative, risk-taking leaders.

The article next examines seven themes which characterize emerging trends in the North American work force. The first of these is diversity in the work force and flexibility in management. Fewer numbers of young people are entering the job market. This increases opportunities for traditionally underemployed work groups such as the handicapped and retirees. The society is aging, and corporations must maintain their productivity, adapt to differences, and develop flexibility in managing change. The second theme is the integration of home and work life. Corporations must account for the pressure for flexible work hours, unconventional work sites and arrangements, child care, and time off for family matters.

The third theme is globalization, the integration of the world's economies. As nations upgrade their science and technology to compete with the United States, corporations have opportunities to participate in international joint ventures. International events such as the consolidation of markets in the EEC and the upcoming Chinese takeover of Hong Kong will drastically alter world markets, creating shifts in capital and the work force. The fourth theme is the integration of HR planning with business unit planning. The new emphasis on managing people as assets will encourage the integration of HR planning with the organization's strategic thinking, goals, visions, and OD.

The fifth theme is the changing nature of work, the shift from craft skills to knowledge-based work, such as information services, and the subsequent necessity of re-educating and training the work force. Computer literacy, and the ability to interpret and absorb information, will be in high demand. Developing educational and recruitment programs capable of anticipating, and building for, crucial skills and higher technologies will come under greater scrutiny. The sixth theme is striking a balance between cost and demand for benefits. Corporations must find cost-effective yet efficient ways to provide their employees with health and other benefits as the baby-boomer work force ages.

The seventh theme is the new ways the corporation interacts with the social agenda. Since people no longer expect the federal government to solve everything, corporations are now being pushed to help in resolving such problems as the trade deficit, the declining quality of public education, environmental pollution, and drug abuse. At the same time, corporate activities such as restructuring, downsizing, and mergers and acquisitions are triggering interest in regulation and worker protection. Meeting the corporation's goals can probably only be done by meeting some of the public's.

The article next takes a look at countervailing forces, those factors and possibilities that could act against the prevailing direction of change. These include:

1. Recession, depression, or inflation, with which we are already having problems.

2. Globalization, which would change the business environment since imbalance in one country affects all others, and protectionism, which may be invoked to control supply and demand.
3. Restructuring, cost cutting, and downsizing—Restructuring and downsizing may demoralize the work force, reduce internal experimentation, and restrict flexibility in reward structures and innovation. Cost cutting, if done improperly, may reduce capital investments and create a fragile internal financial balance.
4. Automation, new technology, reforms, and alternatives can reduce the work force but, on the other hand, give greater selectivity of available skills from the work force pool.
5. Actions of the national government—regulation, legislation, and tax and budget reform. No further comment needed here.
6. Resistance to change by unions or old-guard management.
7. Attitudes—A widespread change in the attitude of a group or institution would change the direction of the trend their attitude was driving. An example given is a hostile rather than positive response to foreign competition.

Although the article does not specifically address the role of total quality in dealing with socioeconomic and political problems, the implication is that managerial experience and a total quality philosophy may be key in efficiently and effectively dealing with the larger issues of society, particularly by firms that strive to reach the peak of the ethical work culture paradigm.

CASE STUDY

GTE DIRECTORIES COMPANY*

In the hotly contested advertising business, "delight your customer" is more than just a quality management motto. It is often the difference between success and failure. With that fact of business life in clear view, operations at GTE Directories Corporation are driven by a comprehensive, continuous focus on customer satisfaction that combines market research with clear-cut quality improvement processes and techniques.

It hasn't always been that way. The company has been a leading Yellow Pages publisher for more than 50 years. In the 1980s, GTE Directories began to face competition from other publishers and other media that began to move into the advertising niche previously reserved for Yellow Pages publishers. With the economy slowing, businesses increasingly replaced faith in advertising with a demand for proof that advertising worked.

It was a wake-up call for GTE Directories. The company responded by transforming itself from an organization that relied on experience, enthusiasm, and the gut instinct of an aggressive sales force to a company focused on anticipating and satisfying customer needs based on concrete, systematic customer input.

Today, as one of the largest players in its business, with $1.4 billion in annual revenue, the company's primary focus is on publishing and selling advertising for telephone directories. It produces more than 1,200 directory titles in 45 states and 17 countries, including more than 75 different directories in international markets. The company's 5,150 employees work at its headquarters in Dallas/Ft. Worth, Texas, and at dozens of other sites in North America, Canada, and overseas.

QUALITY COMMITMENT STARTS AT THE TOP

GTE Directories has three distinct customer groups: the businesses that advertise in its directories; consumers using the directories and related services; and companies that contract for Yellow Pages publishing, printing, distribution, and sales services, either directly or through joint venture partnerships.

Knowing its customers and satisfying their needs drives business decisions at the company. The company first introduced formal quality improvement techniques into its management mainstream in 1986, with strong leadership by the

---

* This case was taken from the Malcolm Baldrige National Quality Award: Profile of Winners, 1994, published by NIST, Department of Commerce.

company's executive management. Convinced that commitment to quality starts at the top, the company's senior management attended parent GTE's quality improvement course and then taught a similar course to more than 400 senior and middle managers. Covering basic tools, techniques, and philosophies for quality improvement, the training stressed the use of quality improvement teams to address quality issues. Action plans developed by the first teams emerged to become the company's initial quality improvement plan.

Since 1991, GTE Directories has used the Baldrige Award criteria to drive its internal examination and improvement process. The company employs a comprehensive, disciplined approach to anticipate, meet, and exceed customers' needs. This Customer Satisfaction Measurement Program (CSMP) also provides quantitative data on customers' perceptions of the company's performance in delivering products and services that meet their needs.

"100 PERCENT CUSTOMER SATISFACTION"

GTE Directories' vision is "100 Percent Customer Satisfaction through Quality." The CSMP is a framework for understanding customer needs, benchmarking company performance, establishing priorities, and monitoring the company's progress toward meeting customer satisfaction goals.

GTE Directories also puts a premium on constantly measuring, reviewing, and refining its processes for collecting key operational data. But to ensure that its data are relevant, customer satisfaction priorities are used to set corporate goals and to determine which activities will be measured. To ensure that the scope, management, and quality of key operational measurement data are always up to date, functional and cross-functional process management teams are formed throughout the company.

The team approach, in fact, is pervasive and popular at GTE Directories, where employees use quality improvement teams to identify problems and change work processes. It is not unusual for individuals to have served on 10 or more quality improvement teams and virtually every employee serves on at least one per year. The company also has 13 permanent process management teams that continually monitor and refine core business and support service processes. The team approach to management is rounded out by 14 active self-managed work teams.

To ensure that GTE Directories is comparing itself with the best-in-class business, heavy use is made of competitive comparisons and benchmarks. Six broad data categories relating to customers, products, operations, employees, business and support services, and supplier performance are benchmarked.

Convinced that satisfaction and loyalty are the bedrock of effective and long-lasting customer–supplier relationships, GTE Directories uses its CSMP process and multiple customer and market research techniques to identify customer service requirements, such as professionalism, timeliness, accessibility, and credibility of specific customer service standards and performance measures, and weighs the relative importance of product and service delivery features to each of the company's three customer groups. Those service standards and operating goals are used as the basis for individual and team performance goals, improvements, and rewards.

QUALITY PLANNING YIELDS RESULTS

Results. Ultimately, that is how any organization's quality management system is judged. GTE Directories keeps close tabs on results in traditional quality categories. It is proud to claim a published error ratio in 1993 of just over 350 per 1 million listings. In addition, it rates best-in-class in errors per 1,000 paid items according to industry benchmark studies. The number of advertisers handled by individual sales representatives has increased each of the last three years. At the same time, the number of sales hours spent by each representative with advertisers has jumped—an indicator that what GTE Directories' research has shown as especially important to its customers has been put into practice.

Quality results show up in other measures too. The company points proudly to independent studies that show that its directories are preferred in 271 of its 274 primary markets. And, in a very competitive market, GTE Directories has sustained increasing revenue growth.

The company knows that error ratios, customer preference studies, and revenue reports are useful—but insufficient—indicators of results. What counts in the long run is customer satisfaction. GTE Directories knows that its best hope for continued market and financial success rests with its ability to achieve its vision of 100 percent customer satisfaction.

QUESTIONS

1 What indications are there that GTE follows Deming's 14 Point philosophy?
2 What seems to be the driving force (or combination of forces) that has led to GTE's quality success?

CHAPTER 2

OVERVIEW OF TOTAL QUALITY

Frank Voehl and William M. Lindsay

During the past five years, there has been an explosion of books in the field of total quality. Yet in all of thousands of books and millions of words written on the subject, there is an absence of three essential ingredients: a good working definition, a comprehensive yet concise history, and a clear and simple systems model of total quality. The comprehensive systems model for total quality was introduced in Chapter 1 and will be extended throughout the text.

The focus of Chapter 2 is on three areas: the concept of total quality, the difference between total quality control and traditional control, and a history of total quality. The history of total quality is divided into four parts: the early technical systems development, the early management systems development, the early sociotechnical systems development, and the era of the gurus.

THE CONCEPT OF TOTAL QUALITY

The conceptual analysis of total quality involves clarifying the meaning of "quality," "total," and finally treating the combined dimensions of "total quality." The American National Standards Institute (ANSI) and the American Society for Quality Control (ASQC) define quality as:[1] *"the totality of features and characteristics of a product or service that bears on its ability to satisfy given needs."* In highly competitive markets, however, merely satisfying customer needs will not achieve success. To beat the competition, organizations often must exceed customer expectations by providing products and/or services that delight and excite customers. Therefore, most progressive organizations now define quality as *meeting or exceeding customer expectations.*[2] The phrase "total customer satisfaction" is used to incorporate both meeting and exceeding customer expectations over time.

In Chapter 1, we defined total quality management as:

> ...a people-focused management system that aims at continual increase in customer satisfaction at continually lower cost. TQ is a total system approach (not a separate area or program), and an integral part of high-level strategy. It works horizontally across functions and departments, involving all employees, top to bottom, and extends backwards and forwards to include the supply chain and the customer chain.[3]

Note the similarities and differences between this definition and ANSI's. Quality, when defined as providing total customer satisfaction, provides a unifying perspective for treating quality in manufacturing and quality in services. Thus, our earlier definition focuses on customer satisfaction, which is outlined in this chapter and highlighted in Chapter 3. Notice also that our definition emphasizes things that may be implied but are not made specific in the ANSI definition. Specifically, you can see *increasing* customer satisfaction, *decreasing* costs, a total *system* approach, high-level *strategy*, a *cross-functional* approach (which implies a process focus), and extension across the *customer–supplier* chain. We can extend these definitions even further by looking at the characteristics of quality in products and services.

Quality in manufacturing products includes the following dimensions:[4]

1. **Performance**—A product's primary operating characteristics
2. **Features**—The "bells and whistles" of a product
3. **Reliability**—The probability of a product's surviving over a specified period of time under stated conditions of use
4. **Conformance**—The degree to which physical and performance characteristics of a product match pre-established standards
5. **Durability**—The amount of use one gets from a product before it physically deteriorates or until replacement is preferable
6. **Serviceability**—The ability to repair a product quickly and easily
7. **Aesthetics**—How a product looks, feels, sounds, tastes, or smells
8. **Perceived quality**—Subjective assessment resulting from image, advertising, or brand names

Quality in providing services includes the following dimensions:[5]

1. **Time**—How much time must a customer wait?
2. **Timeliness**—Will a service be performed when promised?
3. **Completeness**—Are all items in the order included?
4. **Courtesy**—Do front-line employees greet each customer cheerfully and politely?
5. **Consistency**—Are services delivered in the same fashion for every customer, and every time for the same customer?
6. **Accessibility and convenience**—Is the service easy to obtain?
7. **Accuracy**—Is the service performed right the first time?
8. **Responsiveness**—Can service personnel react quickly and resolve unexpected problems?

The "total" in total quality is total in three senses: it covers every process, every job, and every person. First, it covers *every process*, rather than just manufacturing or production. Design, construction, R&D, accounting, marketing, repair, and every other function must also be involved in quality improvement. Second, total quality is total in that it covers *every job*, not just those involved in making the product. Secretaries are expected not to make typing errors, accountants not to make posting errors, and presidents not to make strategic errors. Third, total quality recognizes that *each person* is responsible for the quality of his or her work and for the work of the group.

The phrase "quality as total customer satisfaction" provides directional stability and integration throughout the entire operation of an organization. Only the outer edges of the company actually have contact with customers in the traditional sense, but each department can treat the other departments as its customer. The main judge of the quality of work is the customer, for if the customer is not satisfied, the work does not have quality. This, coupled with the achievement of corporate objectives, is the bottom line of total quality.

In that regard, it is important, as the Japanese say, to "talk with facts and data." Total quality emphasizes the use of fact-oriented discussions and statistical quality control techniques by everyone in the company. Everyone in the company is exposed to basic quality control ideas and techniques and is expected to use them. Thus, total quality becomes a common language and improves "objective" communications.

Total quality also radically alters the nature and basic operating philosophy of organizations. The specialized, separated system developed early in the 20th century is replaced by a system of *mutual feedback and close interaction between departments*. Engineers, for example, work closely with construction crews and storekeepers to ensure that their knowledge is passed on to workers. Workers, in turn, feed their practical experience directly back to the engineers. The information interchange and shared commitment to product quality are what make total quality work. Teaching all employees how to apply process control and improvement techniques makes them party to their own destiny and enables them to achieve their fullest potential.

However, total quality is more than an attempt to make better products; it is also a search for better ways to make them. Adopting the total quality philosophy commits the company to the belief that there is always a better way of doing things, a way to make better use of the company's total quality resources, a way to be more productive. In this sense, total quality relies heavily upon value analysis as a method of developing better products and operations in order to maximize value to the stakeholder, whether customers, employees, or shareholders.

Total quality also implies a different sort of worker and a different attitude toward the worker from management. Under total quality, workers are generalists rather than specialists. *Both workers and managers are expected to move from job to job, gaining experience in many areas of the company.*

Finally, the integrated concept "total quality" combines the essential features of both prior concepts. Thus, the working definition of total quality for this text is as follows: *total quality is a set of philosophies and concepts by which management systems can be directed to the efficient achievement of the organization's objectives to assure ongoing, comprehensive customer satisfaction and maximum stakeholder value.* This is accomplished through the continuous improvement of the quality system, which consists of the social system, the technical system, the management system, and the educational system. Thus, it becomes a way of life for doing business for the entire organization.

One of the essential total quality concepts says that a company should *design quality into its products,* not inspect for it afterwards. Only by having a devotion to quality throughout the organization will the best possible products be made. Or, as stated by Union of Japanese Scientists and Engineers counselor and Japanese quality control scholar Dr. Noriaki Kano,[6] "Quality is too important to be left to inspectors."

Total quality is also too important to take second place to any other goals. Specifically, it should not be subsidiary to profit or productivity. Concentrating on quality will ultimately build and improve both profitability and productivity. Failure to concentrate on quality will quickly erode profits, as customers resent paying for products that they perceive as low quality.

The main focus of total quality is on *why.* It goes beyond the *how to* to include the *why to.* It is an attempt to identify the causes of defects in order to eliminate them. It is a continuous cycle of detecting defects, identifying their causes, and improving the process so as to totally eliminate the causes of defects.

Accepting the idea that the customer of a process can be defined as the next process is essential to the real practice of total quality. According to total quality, control charts should be developed for each process, and any errors identified within the process should be disclosed to the next process in order to raise quality. However, it often seems to be contrary to human nature to seek out one's own mistakes. People tend to find the errors caused by others and to neglect their own. Unfortunately, exactly that kind of self-disclosure is what is really needed.[7]

Instead, management too often tends to blame and then take punitive action. This attitude prevails from front-line supervisors all the way up to top management. In effect, we are encouraged to hide the real problems we cause, and instead of looking for the real causes of problems, as required by total quality, we look the other way.

The Concept of Control

The Japanese notion of *control* differs radically from the American; that difference of meaning does much to explain the failure of U.S. management to adopt total quality. In the United States, control connotes someone or something that limits an operation, process, or person. It has the overtones of a "police force" in the industrial engineering setting and is often resented.

In Japan, Dr. Kano[8] has stated that *control* means "all necessary activities for achieving objectives in the long-term, efficiently and economically." Control, therefore, is doing whatever is needed to accomplish what we want to do as an organization.

To further address this distinction, William Ouchi[9] offered three different approaches to managerial and social control: *bureaucratic, market, and clan control.* Bureaucratic control has been the most prevalent in American businesses until recently. It is based on rules, regulations, and "thou shalts" or "thou shalt nots." This type of control is fine for organizations in static environments where there is no need for change or innovation. It worked well for years in the federal government and AT&T. It no longer works well in either place, because the environment is changing too rapidly.

Market control is where market forces determine the standards and people's performance is evaluated based on meeting sales or profit goals. This type of control works reasonably well where there is a profit objective for the organization that is understood by everyone and where profit sharing is a well-developed reward strategy. Unfortunately, many organizations in government and the nonprofit sector cannot relate their goals to the profit motive. Even those organizations that do have a profit focus sometimes have difficulty translating that to the various parts of the organization. For example, how does a training and organization development (OD) department contribute to the profit goals of the parent organization?

Clan control is a Japanese management concept that can be translated to American firms as "commitment." In Japan, the family or the organization is the lowest unit of society. In the United States, the individual is the focus, even when people work in groups or organizations.

With increased competition, managers have begun to realize that they cannot control people or processes in the same old bureaucratic way. Instead of thinking that: (1) people are part of the process, (2) the process needs to be controlled, and (3) managers have to carefully control the activities of people as part of the process, the conventional wisdom is changing. The current approach that seems to be evolving is: (1) people must design and redesign processes, (2) the process must be controlled by people to be productive, and (3) managers must obtain commitment from people to design, redesign, and control processes so that they will remain productive.

A recent study revealed that the benefits of going from a control to a commitment model include:[10] higher in-plant quality, lower warranty costs, less waste, higher machine utilization, increased capacity with the same plant and equipment, reduced operating and support personnel, reduced absenteeism and turnover, faster implementation of change, and development of human skills and individual self-esteem. The burden of "cost" of these changes which were typically borne by managers included investment in extra effort to make the changes work; development of new skills and relationships; coping with higher levels of ambiguity and uncertainty; the pain and discomfort associated with changing habits, attitudes, and skills; and the uncertainty associated with increased responsibility.

Recognizing the need for changes in the way that people and systems are empowered, led, and controlled is the starting point for blending the two disciplines of quality planning and control with OD. In the next chapter, we will take a brief look at the field of OD and see how it is being blended with total quality concepts to bring about changes in people, systems, and organizations.

Differences Between "Classical" and "Total Quality" Control

The differences can be seen very graphically in the PDCA (Plan-Do-Check-Act) continuous improvement chart which is widely used in Japan to describe the cycle of control (Figure 2.1) Proper control starts with planning, does what is planned, checks (studies) the results, and then applies any necessary corrective action. The cycle represents these four stages—Plan-Do-Study (Dr. Deming recently replaced "Check" with "Study")-Act—arranged in circular fashion to show a continuing cycle. Since we will sometimes adapt or use models from other sources in later chapters, you should equate PDSA = PDCA. Keep in mind that Dr. Deming actively practiced "continuous improvement" in his own work and writings until the day he died.

In the United States, where specialization and division of labor are emphasized, the cycle is more likely to look like Fight-Plan-Do-Study. In-

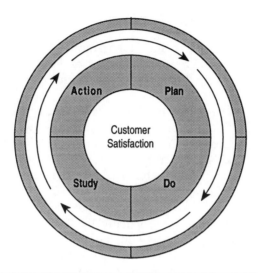

Figure 2.1 The Deming–Shewhart PDSA Model (Adapted with permission from Evans, James R. and Lindsay, William M. (1996). *The Management and Control of Quality*, 3rd edition. St. Paul, MN: West Publishing, p. 345.)

stead of working together to solve any deviations from the plan, time is spent arguing over who is responsible for the deviations. This *sectionalism*, as the Japanese refer to it, hinders collective efforts to improve the way things are done and lowers national productivity and the standard of living. *There need be nothing threatening about control if it is perceived as exercised in order to gather the facts necessary to make plans and take action toward making improvements.*

Total quality includes the control principle as part of the set of philosophies directed toward the efficient achievement of the objectives of the organization. Many of the individual components of total quality are practiced by American companies, but few practice total quality as a whole.

HISTORY OF TOTAL QUALITY

About the year one million B.C., give or take a few centuries, man first began to fashion and use stone tools for hunting and survival.[11] Up until 8000 B.C., however, very little progress was made in the quality control of these tools. It was at this time that man began assembling instruments with fitting holes, which suggests the first use of interchangeable parts on a limited basis. Throughout this long period, each person made his or her own tools. The evidence of quality control was measured to some extent by how long a person stayed alive. If the tools were well made, the chances of survival increased. A broken axe handle usually spelled doom.

The Craft Era and American Quality

The Craft Era extended from the Stone Age up to and overlapping the Industrial Revolution. Americans still hunger for the simplicity, the attention to detail, and the quality "image" that crafts and craftsmanship bring to mind.

It is impossible to visit any of America's historic centers—such as Colonial Williamsburg; Old Sturbridge Village; Shakertown in Pleasant Hill, Kentucky; or Mystic Seaport, Connecticut—without feeling a touch of nostalgia for the fine old skills of the craftsman, now largely lost in our fast-paced, mass-produced, throw-away society. What was it that made the craftspeople of bygone days, and the few who remain today, so conscious of the quality of their work? Perhaps it was the pursuit of the mysterious concept of "profound knowledge" that was articulated by the late W. Edwards Deming. We will discuss Deming's concept in more detail below. The profound knowledge of craftspeople may be encompassed in three categories: knowledge of materials and their strengths and limitations, skill in developing processes and using the best tools and techniques to work on the materials, and attitudes toward work and its beneficiary, the customer who purchased the final object of the craftsman's manufacture. A few quotations from an unidentified author in a National Geographic book on craftsmen illustrate these concepts.[12]

Concerning knowledge of the materials, their interaction with skills, and the quality imperative, the author focused on the shipbuilding craft, when "wooden ships and iron men" ruled the oceans. He wrote:

> Shipwrights felt a heavier responsibility, for their work—from grand paddle-wheeler to dory, frigate to clipper ship—had to stand up to the united wrath of sea and weather.

Later, this author interviewed Henry B. Jarvis, a modern shipwright with ancient craftsman's skills, at Mystic Seaport, Connecticut. Part of Jarvis' responsibility was to maintain the whaling vessel the *Charles W. Morgan*, which was launched in 1841 and sailed for 80 years before eventually being retired to Mystic Seaport. As noted by Jarvis:

> "To build a ship, you've got to know what woods go where," Henry began, listing examples of nautical know-how. Pine provides ceiling amidships but green oak serves fore and aft, where curves demand a wood that can bend. Instead of nails, trunnels—inch-thick, foot-long pegs of black locust—bond the ship's sheathing to its ribs.
>
> "Black locust, see, is tough and close-grained. It won't break or rot, and it doesn't shrink much. Some places, you might best use copper spikes. But wood on wood is best."

Another author in the same text[13] described the philosophy of work of Lenore Tawney, a craftswoman who created fiber sculptures in a converted shoe factory in Manhattan in the 1970s. She said:

> When you work, you must involve yourself totally. You can't be bored with your work. Because, if you are bored, you put that boredom into the fiber. It stays there, it becomes part of that work. And that work then becomes everything you were at the moment you created it. If you were aware, involved in its creation, the work will become aware and involved. If you were bored, it will be forever boring.
>
> ...For my work is very simple, nothing about it is really so complicated. Anybody can look and "see" the techniques, use the same linen, the same colors.
>
> ...It's what you do with those materials that's important. You have to be in touch with yourself. When people ask me about my work, how I created it, I tell them, "Don't look at other people's work for your creation, don't look outside, look in. If you look at other people's work, and not within yourself, you are only imitating. The challenge is, with each new work, to create a new part of yourself, a new being."

The Industrial Revolution obviously did not "kill" the concept of craftsmanship, but it was the beginning of a focus on output and mass production as opposed to one-of-a-kind, unique production of single items.

Interchangeable Parts and Division of Labor

A little over 200 years ago, in 1787, the concepts of interchangeable parts and division of labor were first introduced in the United States. Eli Whitney, inventor of the cotton gin, applied these concepts to the production of 10,000 flintlock military rifles for the U.S. arsenal. However, Whitney had considerable difficulty in making all the parts exactly the same. It took him ten years to complete the 10,000 muskets that he promised to deliver in two years.

Three factors prevented Whitney from delivering the 10,000 muskets in two years as promised. First, there was a dramatic shortage of qualified craftsmen needed to build the muskets. Consequently, Whitney correctly saw the solution to the problem—machines must do what men previously did. If individual machines were assembled to create each individual part needed, then men could be taught to operate these machines. Thus, Whitney's application of division of labor to a highly technical process was born. Whitney called this a *manufactory*.

Next, it took almost one full year to build the manufactory, rather than two months as Whitney originally thought. Not only did the weather inflict havoc on the schedule, but epidemics of yellow fever slowed progress considerably.

Third, obtaining the raw materials in a timely, usable manner was a hit-or-miss proposition. The metal ore was often defective, and the castings made from it were flawed and pitted. In addition, training the workers to perform the actual assembly took much longer than Whitney imagined and required a considerable amount of his personal attention, often 15 to 20 hours a day. Also, once the men were trained, some left to work for competing armories.[14]

To compound these factors, his ongoing cotton gin patent lawsuits took a considerable amount of his highly leveraged attention and time. Fortunately for Whitney, his credibility in Washington granted him considerable leeway in letting target dates slip. War with France was no longer imminent. Thus, a quality product and development of the associated manufacturing expertise were deemed more important than schedule. What was promised in 28 months took almost 120 to deliver.

Luckily for Whitney, the requirement of "on time and within budget" was not yet in vogue. What happened to Whitney was a classic study in the problems of trying to achieve a real breakthrough in operations. Out of this experience, Whitney and others realized that creating parts exactly the same was not possible and, if tried, would prove to be very expensive. This concept of interchangeable parts would eventually lead to statistical methods of control, while division of labor would lead to the factory assembly line.

THREE STREAMS OF QUALITY HISTORY

Eli Whitney's work on the development of interchangeable parts for muskets can be seen as the starting point for the movement away from the craft system to the factory system. It can also be seen as the beginning of modern problems and concepts of statistical quality control. In some ways, it can be seen as the starting point of the "dehumanization" of workers, as they became just another "cog in the wheel" in the developing Industrial Revolution. Although the social system was neglected through the early decades of the 20th century, there is a thread of history that pulls them together. Thus, we can use our previous classifications of technical systems, management systems, and social systems to develop a three-pronged history of total quality. What we now call total quality has evolved from these major streams.

Early Technical Systems Development

The movement away from craft to manufactory systems generated an interest in developing technical systems first. Only a few forward-looking visionary owner/managers, such as Robert Owen in England,[15] were concerned with administrative or social systems. To most, it seemed to be important to explore the technical aspects of manufacturing. It was assumed that people could be made to conform to the technical system.

The First Control Limits

The experiences of Whitney and others who followed led to a relaxation of the requirements for exactness and a movement toward the use of tolerances. This allowed for a less than perfect fit between two (or more) parts. The concept of "go–no-go" tolerance was introduced between 1840 and 1870.[16]

This idea was a huge step forward in that it created the concept of upper and lower tolerance limits for each part, thus allowing the production worker more freedom to do his or her job at a lower cost. All the worker had to do was stay within the tolerance limits, instead of trying to achieve unnecessary or unattainable perfection.

Defective Parts Inspection

The next advancement centered around expanding the concept of tolerance and using specifications, where variation is classified as either meeting or not meeting requirements. For those pieces of product that every now and then fell outside the specified tolerance range (or limits), the question arose as to what to do with them. To discard or modify these pieces added significantly to the cost of production. However, to search for the unknown causes of defects and then remove them also cost money. The heart of the problem was how to reduce the percentage of defects to a point where (1) the rate of increase in the *cost of control* equals the rate of *increase* in *savings* which is (2) brought about by *decreasing the number of rejected parts*.

In other words, inspection/prevention had to be cost effective. The problem of minimizing the percentage of defects in a cost-effective manner was not the only one to be solved. Some tests for quality characteristics require destructive testing. Examples include tests for strength, chemical composition, fuse blowing time, etc. Since not every piece can be tested, the statistical sample was first used around the turn of the century.

Statistical Theory

During the early part of the 20th century, a tremendous increase in quality consciousness occurred. What were the forces at work that caused this sudden acceleration of interest in the application of statistical quality control (SQC)? There were at least three key factors.

The first was a rapid growth in standardization, beginning in 1900. Until 1915, Great Britain was the only country in the world with some type of national standardization movement. The number of industrial standardization organizations throughout the world, especially between 1916 and 1932, rose dramatically.[17] During that 15-year period, the movement grew from one country (Great Britain) to 25, with the United States coming on line about 1917, just at the time of World War I.

The second major factor ushering in a new era was a radical shift in ideology which occurred in about 1900. This ideological shift was away from the notion of exactness of science (which existed in 1787 when interchangeability of parts was introduced) to probability and statistical concepts, which developed in almost every field of science around 1900.

The third factor was the evolution of division of labor into the factory system and early assembly-line systems of the early 20th century. These systems proved to be ideal for employing an immigrant work force quickly.

In the next section, we will consider the first two major factors, since they were part of the development of technical systems. Later, we will explore the development of the management and social systems, which grew out of the third factor. One of the early champions in the U.S. quality movement was Walter Shewhart, of Atlantic Telephone and Telegraph's Bell Laboratories. Shewhart is rightly called the "founding father of SQC."

Walter Shewhart—The Founding Father of Statistical Quality Control

Walter Shewhart was an engineer, scientist, and philosopher. He was a very deep thinker, and his ideas, although profound and technically perfect, were difficult to fathom. His style of writing followed his style of thinking—very obtuse. But he was brilliant and his works on variation and sampling, coupled with his teachings on the need for documentation, influenced forever the course of industrial history. Shewhart was familiar with Whitney's innovations—division of labor and the use of interchangeable parts. However, he was most concerned with the latter, for interchangeable parts meant variation, rejects, and waste.

To deal with the issue of variation, Shewhart developed the control chart in 1924. He realized that the traditional use of tolerance limits was shortsighted, because they only provided a method for judging the quality of a product that has already been made.[18]

The control limits on Shewhart's control charts, however, provided a ready guide for taking action on the process to remove what he called *assignable causes*[19] of variation, thus preventing nonconforming products from being produced in the future. This allowed management to focus on the future, through the use of statistical probability—a prediction of future production based upon historical data. Thus, the emphasis shifted from costly correction of problems to prevention of problems and improvement of processes.[20]

Shewhart's focus shifted from individual parts to a systems approach. The notion of zero defects of individual parts was replaced with zero variability of system operations.

Shewhart's Control System

Shewhart identified the traditional act of control as consisting of three elements: the act of specifying what is required, the act of producing what is specified, and the act of judging whether the requirements have been met. This simple picture of the control of quality would work well if production could be viewed in the context of an exact science, where all products are made exactly the same. Shewhart knew, however, that because variation is pervasive, the control of quality characteristics must be a matter of probability. He envisioned a statistician helping an engineer to understand variation and arrive at the economic control of quality.[21]

Shewhart's Concept of Variation

Determining the *state of statistical control* in terms of the degree of variation is the first step in the Shewhart control system. Rather than specifying what is required in terms of tolerance, Shewhart viewed variation as being present in everything and identified two types of variation: *controlled* and *uncontrolled*. This is fundamentally different from the traditional way of classifying variation as either acceptable or not acceptable (go–no-go tolerance). Viewing variation in terms of being controlled or uncontrolled enables one to focus on the causes of variation in order to improve a process (before the fact) as opposed to focusing on the output of a process to judge whether the product or the process is acceptable (after the fact).

Shewhart taught that controlled variation is a consistent pattern of variation over time that is due to *random* or *chance causes*. He saw that there are many chance causes of variation, but the effect of any one of these is relatively small; therefore, which cause or causes are responsible for observed variation is a matter of chance. Shewhart stated that a process that is being affected only by *chance* causes of variation is said to be in a *state of statistical control*.

All processes contain chance causes of variation, and Shewhart taught that it is possible to reduce the chance causes of variation, but it is not realistic or cost effective to try to remove them all. The control limits on Shewhart's control charts represent the boundaries of the occurrence of chance causes of variation operating within the system.

The second type of variation—uncontrolled variation—is an inconsistent or changing pattern of variation over time that is due to what Shewhart classified *assignable* causes. Because the effects of assignable causes of variation are relatively large compared to chance causes, they can and must be identified and removed.[22] Shewhart said a process is *out of statistical control* when it is being affected by assignable causes.

One of Shewhart's main problems was how to communicate this newfound theory without overwhelming the average businessman or engineer. The answer came in the form of staged experiments using models which demonstrated variation. His *ideal bowl experiment*[23] with poker chips was modeled by his protégé, W. Edwards Deming, some 20 years later with his famous *red bead experiment*.

Another major contribution of Shewhart's first principle of control was his recognition of the need for operational definitions that are communicated to operators, inspectors, and scientists alike. He was fond of asking, "How can an operator carry out his job tasks if he does not understand what the job is? And how can he know what the job is if what was produced yesterday was O.K., but today the same product is wrong?" He believed that inspection, whether the operator inspects his own work or relies on someone else to do it for him, must have operational definitions. Extending specifications beyond product and into the realm of operator performance was the first attempt to define the "extended system of operations" which would greatly facilitate the production process.

Next, we will explore the management and social systems concepts, which grew out of Whitney's division of labor. Frederick W. Taylor was the "founding father" of both management and industrial engineering and the first to recognize the need for a systematic approach to management.

Early Management Systems Development— The Taylor System versus Quality

Frederick Winslow Taylor was born in 1856 and entered industry as an apprentice in the Enterprise Hydraulics Shop in 1874. According to popular legend, the old-timers in the shop told him: "Now young man, here's about how much work you should do each morning and each afternoon. Don't do any more than that—that's the limit."[24]

It was obvious to Taylor that the men were producing below their capacity, and he soon found out why. The short-sighted management of that day would set standards, often paying per-piece rates for the work. Then, when a worker discovered how to produce more, management cut the rate. In turn, management realized that the workers were deliberately restricting output, but could not do anything about it.

It was Taylor's viewpoint that the whole system was wrong. Having studied the writings and innovations of Whitney, he came to realize that the concept of division of labor had to be revamped if greater productivity and efficiency were to be realized. His vision included a super-efficient assembly line as part of a management system of operations. He, more than anyone at the time, understood the inability of management to increase individual productivity, and he understood the reluctance of the workers to produce at a high rate. Because he had been a working man, it was apparent to him that there was a tremendous difference between *actual* output and *potential* output. Taylor thought that if such practices applied throughout the world and throughout all industry, the potential production capacity was at least three or four times what was actually being produced. When he became a foreman, Taylor set out to find ways to eliminate this waste and increase production.

At the turn of the century, Taylor wrote a collection of reports and papers that were published by the American Society of Mechanical Engineers. One of the most famous was *On the Art of Cutting Metals*, which had worldwide impact. With Maunsel White, Taylor developed the first high-speed steel. Taylor was also instrumental in the development of one of the first industrial cost-accounting systems, even though, according to legend, he previously knew nothing about accounting.

For more than 25 years, Taylor and his associates were busy exploring ways to increase productivity and build the model factory of the future. The techniques they developed were finally formalized in writing and communicated to other people. During the early years of this experimentation, most who knew about it were associated with Taylor at the Midvale Steel Company and Bethlehem Steel.

Other pioneers began to come into the picture and make contributions to the body of science of the new management thinking. Among them was Carl G.L. Barth, a mathematician and statistician who assisted Taylor in analytical work, and Henry L. Gantt (famous for the Gantt chart), who invented the slide rule. Another associate of Taylor's, Sanford E. Thompson, developed the first decimal stopwatch.[25] Finally, there was young Walter Shewhart, who was to transform industry with his statistical concepts and thinking and his ability to bridge technical tools with a management system.

Frank G. and Lillian Gilbreth, who were aware of Taylor's work in measurement and analysis, turned their attention to mechanizing and commercializing Taylorism. For their experimental model, they chose the ancient craft of bricklaying, because Frank had been a master bricklayer before starting his consulting career. It might have been assumed that production in bricklaying certainly should have reached its zenith thousands of years ago, with nothing more to be done to increase production. Yet Frank Gilbreth was able to show that by following his techniques and with proper management planning, production could be raised from an average of 120 bricks per hour to 350 bricks per hour, and the worker would be less tired than he had been under the old system.

By 1912, the "efficiency movement" was gaining momentum. Taylor was called before a special committee of the House of Representatives which was investigating scientific management and its impact on the railroad industry. He tried to explain scientific management to the somewhat hostile railroad hearings committee which regarded it as a method for "speeding up" work.

Referring to his early experiences in seeking greater output, Taylor described the strained feelings between himself and his workmen as "miserable." Yet he was determined to improve production. He continued his experiments until three years before his death, when he found that human motivation, not just engineered improvements, could alone increase output.

Unfortunately, the human factor was ignored by many. Shortly after the railroad hearings, self-proclaimed "efficiency experts" did untold damage to scientific management. Time studies and the new efficiency techniques were used by incompetent "consultants" who sold managers on the idea of increasing profit by "speeding up" employees. Consequently, many labor unions, just beginning to feel their strength, worked against the new science and all efficiency approaches. With the passing of Taylor in 1915, the scientific management movement lost, for the moment, any chance of reaching its true potential as the catalyst for the future total quality management system. Still, the foundation was laid for the management system that was soon to become a key ingredient of organizations of the future.

The Shewhart Cycle: When Control Meets Scientific Management

From the "exact science" days of the 1800s until the 1920s, *specification, production,* and *inspection* were considered to be independent of each other when viewed in a straight line manner. They take on an entirely different picture when viewed from the perspective of an inexact science. When the production process is viewed from the standpoint of the control of quality as a matter of probability, then specification, production, and inspection are linked together as represented in a circular diagram or wheel. *Specification* and *production* are linked because it is important to know how well the tolerance limits are being satisfied by the existing process and what improvements are necessary. Shewhart likened this process (which he called the Scientific Method) to a dynamic process of acquiring knowledge, which is similar to an experiment. Step 1 was formulating the hypothesis. Step 2 was conducting the experiment. Step 3 was testing the hypothesis.[26] In the Shewhart Wheel, the successful completion of each interlocking component led to a cycle of continuous improvement. (Years later, Deming was to popularize this cycle of improvement in his famous Deming Wheel.)

Early Sociotechnical Systems Development

Although the term "sociotechnical systems" would not be coined until the 1950s or 1960s, much of what W. Edwards Deming did during the pre- and post-World War II years, as he developed his 14 Points and management philosophy, was to anticipate the work of OD and sociotechnical systems theorists, who were probably unaware of Deming's work. Much of this background was presented in Chapter 1. However, the "Deming thread" and the post-war "gurus" are introduced here.

Shewhart Meets Deming

It was at the Bell Laboratories in New Jersey that Shewhart, who was leading the telephone reliability improvement efforts during the 1930s, first met Deming. Shewhart, as discussed earlier, was developing his system of improving worker performance and productivity by measuring variation using his control charts and statistical methods. Deming was impressed and liked what he saw, especially Shewhart's intellect and the *wheel*—the Shewhart cycle of control. He realized that with training, workers could retain control over their work processes by monitoring the quality of the items they produced. Deming also believed that once workers were trained, educated, and empowered to manage their own work processes, quality would increase and costly inspections could once and for all be eliminated. He presented the idea that higher quality would cost less, not more. Deming studied Shewhart's teachings and techniques and learned well, even if at times he was lost. He said that his genius was in knowing when to act and when to leave a process alone. At times, he was frustrated by Shewhart's obtuse style of thinking and writing.[27]

In 1938, Shewhart delivered four lectures to the U.S. Department of Agriculture (USDA) Graduate School at the invitation of Deming. In addition to being in charge of the mathematics and statistics courses at the USDA Graduate School, Deming was responsible for inviting guest lecturers. He invited Shewhart to give a series of lectures on how statistical methods of control were being used in industry to economically control the quality of manufactured product. Shewhart spent an entire year developing the lectures, titled them *Statistical Method from the Viewpoint of Quality Control*, and delivered them in March of 1938. They were subsequently edited into book format by Deming and published in 1939.

In a couple of years, both he and Shewhart were called upon by the U.S. government to aid the war effort. As David Halberstam recounted, the War Department, impressed by Shewhart's theories and work, brought together a small group of experts on SQC to establish better quality guidelines for defense contractors.[28] Deming was a member of that group and he came to love the work.

THE ERA OF THE QUALITY GURUS

The development of the quality gurus is really an international story. It started in Japan in the 1940s, when the need for American quality expertise was recognized. It spread to the United States 40 years later only because of the growing perception of the international quality gap. It is interesting to note, however, that there may be a parallel between the Japanese and American experiences of the need for "gurus"—both countries were in a crisis when the need was recognized.

Origins of Deming

Who was W. Edwards Deming, the man who was to take Shewhart's teachings, popularize them, and even go beyond? He was born at the turn of the century, October 14, 1900, and received his Ph.D. in physics at Yale University in the summer of 1927, which is where he learned to use statistical theory. As a graduate student in the late 1920s, he did part-time summer work at the famous Western Electric Hawthorne Plant in Chicago.

It was at this plant in 1927 that Elton Mayo, of Harvard's Department of Industrial Research, began his 20-year study of attitudes and reactions of groups under differing work conditions. He and his group performed industrial experiments which later became known as the Hawthorne Experiments.[29]

While working at Hawthorne, Deming could not help noticing the poor working conditions in this sweatshop environment, which employed predominantly female laborers to produce telephones. Deming was both fascinated and appalled by what he saw and learned. It was at Hawthorne that he saw the full effects of the abuses of the Taylor system of scientific management. He also saw the full effect of Whitney's second great innovation—division of labor—when carried to extremes by ivory tower management that did not care to consider the state of the social system of the organization. So what if the worker environment resembled a sweatshop—the workers were paid well enough. "The women should be happy just to have a job" seemed to be the unspoken attitude.

A couple of years before meeting Shewhart, when Deming encountered Taylorism at Hawthorne, he found a scientific management system with the following objectives:

- Develop a science for each element of work.
- Scientifically select a workman and train and develop him.
- Secure whole-hearted cooperation between management and labor to ensure that all work is done in accordance with the principles developed.
- Divide the work between management and labor. The manager takes over all work for which he is better suited than the workman.

It was the fourth point, which evolved out of the division of labor concept, that Deming found to be the real villain. In practice, this meant removing from the worker basic responsibility for the quality of the work. What Deming disliked was that workers should not be hired to think about the work they did. That was management's job. Errors will occur, but the worker need not worry—the inspector will catch any mistake *before* it leaves the plant. In addition, management could always lower the per-piece pay to reflect scrap and rework. Any worker who produced too many inferior quality pieces would be fired.

The problem with Taylorism is that it views the production process mechanically instead of as a holistic system, which includes the human elements of motivation and respect. Taylorism taught American industry to view the worker as "a cog in the giant industrial machine, whose job could be defined and directed by educated managers administering a set of rules."[30] Work on the assembly lines of America and at Hawthorne was simple, repetitive, and boring. Management was top-down. Pay per piece meant that higher output equals higher take-home pay. Quality of work for the most part was not a factor for the average, everyday worker.

This system found a friend in the assembly-line process developed by Henry Ford and was widely incorporated into America's private and public sectors. Taylor's management system made it possible for waves of immigrants, many of whom could not read, write, or speak English (or sometimes not even communicate with one another), to find employment in America's factories. Taylor's ideas were even introduced into the nation's schools.[31]

Edwards Deming had various colleagues at the time, one of whom was Joseph Juran, another pioneer who was later to be recognized as a quality "guru." They rebelled against the scientific management movement. They probably felt, as did Elton Mayo,[32] that the authoritarian Taylorism method of management was degrading to the human spirit and counterproductive to the interests of employees, management, the company, and society as a whole.

Mayo and his Hawthorne research team confirmed these feelings with their findings: good leadership leads to high morale, motivation, and to higher production. Good leadership was defined as democratic, rather than autocratic, and people centered, as opposed to production centered. Thus began the human relations era.

Post-World War II

When the war ended, American industry converted to peacetime production of goods and services. People were hungry for possessions and an appetite developed worldwide for products "made in the U.S.A." The focus in the

United States returned to quantity over quality, and a gradual deterioration of market share occurred, with billions of dollars in international business lost to Japanese and European competitors. These were the modern-day phoenixes rising from the ashes of war. America became preoccupied with the mechanics of mass production and its role as world provider to a hungry people. What followed was an imbalance between satisfying the needs of the worker and lack of appreciation for and recognition of the external customer. America moved away from the things that had made it great!

The Japanese Resurrection

Japan first began to apply statistical control concepts in the early 1920s but moved away from them when the war began.[33] In 1946, under General Douglas MacArthur's leadership, the Supreme Command for the Allied Powers (SCAP) established quality control tools and techniques as the approach to effect the turnaround of Japanese industry. Japan had sacrificed its industry and eventually its food supply to support its war effort. Subsequently, there was little left in post-war Japan to occupy. The country was in shambles. Only one major city, Kyoto, had escaped wide-scale destruction; food was scarce and industry was negligible.

Against a backdrop of devastation and military defeat, a group of Japanese scientists and engineers—organized appropriately as the Union of Japanese Scientists and Engineers (JUSE)—dedicated themselves to working with American and Allied experts to help rebuild the country. Reconstruction was a daunting and monumental task. With few natural resources or immediate means of producing them, export of manufactured goods was essential. However, Japanese industry—or what was left of it—was producing inferior goods, a fact that was recognized worldwide. JUSE was faced with the task of drastically improving the quality of Japan's industrial output as an essential exchange commodity for survival.

W.S. Magill and Homer Sarasohn, among others, assisted with the dramatic transformation of the electronics industry and telecommunications. Magill is regarded by some as the "father of SQC" in Japan. He was the first to advocate its use in a 1945 lecture series and successfully applied statistical process control techniques to vacuum tube production in 1946 at NEC. Hopper[34] reviewed the history of how Magill, Sarasohn, and other U.S. engineers assisted the Japanese in their post-World War II recovery efforts.

Sarasohn worked with supervisors and managers to improve reliability and yields in the electronics field from 40% in 1946 to 80 to 90% in 1949; he documented his findings for SCAP, and MacArthur took notice. He ordered Sarasohn to tell Japanese businessmen how to get things done. The Japanese listened, but the Americans forgot. In 1948, Deming replaced Sarasohn, and the rest is history.

In July 1950, Deming began a series of day-long lectures to Japanese management in which he taught the basic "Elementary Principles of Statistical Control of Quality." The Japanese embraced the man and his principles and named their most prestigious award for quality the Deming Prize. During the late 1970s, Deming turned his attention back to the United States and worked tirelessly on a "mission" to help U.S. industry revive its quality, until his death in 1994. His 14 Points go far beyond statistical methods and address the management system as well as the social system, or culture, of the organization. In many ways, he began to sound more and more like Frederick Taylor, whose major emphasis in later years was on the need for a *mental revolution*—a transformation! Deming's "Theory of Profound Knowledge"[35] brings together all three systems of total quality. It is discussed briefly below.

The Other "Gurus" Arrive

What started in Japan in the 1940s and 1950s became a worldwide quality movement, albeit a limited one, within 30 years. It was during this period that the era of the "gurus" (Deming, Juran, Ishikawa, Feigenbaum, and Crosby) evolved. Starting with Deming in 1948 and Juran in 1954, the movement was eventually carried back to the United States by Feigenbaum in the 1960s and Crosby in the 1970s. Meanwhile, Ishikawa and his associates at JUSE kept the movement alive in Japan. By 1980, the bell began to toll loud and clear in the West with the NBC White Paper entitled "If Japan Can, Why Can't We?" The following are thumbnail sketches of the teachings of the other gurus.

Joseph Juran

Joseph Juran, the son of an immigrant shoemaker from Romania, began his industrial career at Western Electric's Hawthorne Plant before World War II. He later worked at Bell Laboratories in the area of quality assurance. He worked as a government administrator, university professor, labor arbitrator, and corporate director before establishing his own consulting firm, the Juran Institute, in Wilton, Connecticut. In the 1950s, he was invited to Japan by JUSE to help rebuilding Japanese corporations develop management concepts. Juran based some of his principles on the work of Walter Shewhart and, like Deming and the other quality gurus, believed that management and the system are responsible for quality. Juran is the creator of many of the basic concepts of statistical quality control and authored a book entitled *The Quality Control Handbook*,[36] which has become an international standard reference for the quality movement.

Juran's definition of quality is described as "fitness for use as perceived by the customer." If a product is produced and the customer perceives it as fit for use, then the quality mission has been accomplished. Juran also believed that every person in the organization must be involved in the effort of making products or services that are fit for use.

Juran described a perpetual spiral[37] of progress or a continuous striving toward quality. Steps on this spiral are, in ascending order, customers, product development, operations, marketing, and then back to customers and product development again. The idea behind the spiral is that each time the steps in the spiral are completed, products or services would increase in quality. Juran explained that chronic problems should be solved by following this spiral; he formulated a breakthrough sequence to increase the standard of performance so that problems are eliminated. To alleviate sporadic problems, which he found are often solved with temporary solutions, he suggested carefully examining the system causing the problem and adjusting it to solve the difficulty. Once operating at this improved standard of performance, with the sporadic problem solved, the process of analyzing chronic and sporadic problems should start over again.

Juran pointed out that companies often overlook the cost of producing low-quality products. He suggested that by implementing his theories of quality improvement, not only will higher quality products be produced, but the actual costs would be lower. His Cost of Quality principle was known as "Gold in the Mine."

Juran is known for his work with statistics, and he relied on the quantification of standards and statistical quality control techniques. He is credited with implementing the use of the Pareto diagram and developing the concepts of quality cost to improve business systems as well.

Juran's concept of quality included the managerial dimensions of quality planning, quality control, and quality improvement (known as the Juran Trilogy®) and focused on the responsibility of management to achieve quality and the need for setting goals. His ten steps to quality are as follows:

1. Build awareness of opportunities to improve.
2. Set goals for improvement.
3. Organize to reach goals.
4. Provide training.
5. Carry out projects to solve problems.
6. Report progress.
7. Give recognition.
8. Communicate results.
9. Keep score.
10. Maintain momentum by making annual improvement part of the regular systems and processes of the company.

Ishikawa and the Japanese Experts

Kaoru Ishikawa studied under both Homer Sarasohn and Edwards Deming during the late 1940s and early 1950s. As president of JUSE, he was instrumental in developing a unique Japanese strategy to total quality: the broad involvement of the entire organization in its *total* sense—every worker, every process, and every job. This also included the complete life cycle of the product from start to finish.

Some of his accomplishments include the successful development of the quality control circle movement in Japan, in part due to innovative tools such as the cause-and-effect diagram (often called the Ishikawa fishbone diagram because it resembles a fish skeleton). His approach was to provide easy-to-use analytical tools that could be used by all workers, including those on the line, to analyze and solve problems.

Ishikawa identified seven critical success factors that were essential for the success of total quality control in Japan:

1. Company-wide quality control and participation by *all* members of the organization
2. Education and training in all aspects of total quality, which often amounts to 30 days per year per employee
3. Use of quality control circles to update standards and regulations, which are in constant need of improvement
4. Quality audits by the president and quality council members (senior executives) twice a year
5. Widespread use of statistical methods and a focus on problem prevention
6. Nationwide quality control promotion activities, with the national imperative of keeping Japanese quality number one in the world
7. Revolutionary *mental* attitude on part of both management and workers toward one another and toward the customer, including welcoming complaints, encouraging risk, and a wider span of control

Ishikawa believed that Japanese management practices should be democratic, with management providing the guidelines. Mission statements were used extensively, with operating policies derived from them. Top management must assume a leadership position to implement the policies so that they are followed by all.

The impact on Japanese industry was startling. In seven to ten years, the electronics and telecommunications industries were transformed, with the entire nation was revitalized by the end of the 1960s.

Armand Feigenbaum

Unlike Deming and Juran, Feigenbaum did not work extensively with the Japanese. He was vice president of worldwide quality for General Electric until the late 1960s, when he set up his own consulting firm, General Systems, Inc. He is best know for coining the term *total quality control* and for his pioneering 850-page book on the subject.[38] His teachings center around the integration of people–machine–information structures in order to economically and effectively control quality and achieve full customer satisfaction.

Feigenbaum taught that there are two requirements to establishing quality as a business strategy: establishing customer satisfaction must be central and quality/cost objectives must drive the total quality system. His systems theory of total quality control includes four fundamental principles:

- Total quality is a continuous work process, starting with customer requirements and ending with customer satisfaction.
- Documentation allows visualization and communication of work assignments.
- The quality system provides for greater flexibility because of greater use of alternatives provided.
- Systematic reengineering of major quality activities leads to greater levels of continuous improvement.

Like Juran and Deming, Feigenbaum used a visual concept to capture the idea of waste and rework—the so-called Hidden Plant. Based upon studies, he taught that this "Hidden Plant" can account for between 15 and 40% of the production capacity of a company. In his book, he uses the concept of the "9 M's" to describe the factors which affect quality: (1) markets, (2) money, (3) management, (4) men, (5) motivation, (6) materials, (7) machines and mechanization, (8) modern information methods, and (9) mounting product requirements.

According to Andrea Gabor in the Deming-focused television biography "The Man Who Discovered Quality," Feigenbaum has taken a nut-and-bolts approach to quality, while Deming is often viewed as a visionary. Nuts and bolts led him to focus on the benefits and outcomes of total quality, rather than only the process to follow. His methods led to increased quantification of total quality program improvements during the 1970s and 1980s.

Philip Crosby

Unlike the other quality gurus who were scientists, engineers, and statisticians, Philip Crosby is known for his motivational talks and style of presentation. His emergence began in 1961, when he first developed the concept of zero defects while working as a quality manager at Martin Marietta Corporation in Orlando, Florida. He believed that "zero defects" motivated line workers to turn out perfect products. He soon joined ITT, where he quickly moved up the ranks to vice president of quality control operations, covering 192 manufacturing facilities in 46 countries. He held the position until 1979, when he opened up his own consulting company, which became one of the largest of its kind, employing over 250 people worldwide.

He established the Quality College in 1980 and used that concept to promote his teachings and writings in 18 languages. It has been estimated that over five million people have attended its courses, and the growing library of books[39] that he has written are popular and are easy to read. It is in these works that he introduces the four absolutes of his quality management philosophy:

1. The definition of quality is conformance to requirements.
2. The system of quality is prevention of problems.
3. The performance standard of quality is zero defects.
4. The measurement of quality is the price of nonconformance, or the cost of quality.

The fourth principle, the Cost of Quality, is similar to Feigenbaum's Hidden Plant and Juran's Gold in the Mine. Like Deming, Crosby has 14 steps to quality improvement. Also like Deming, he has been very critical of the Malcolm Baldrige National Quality Award, although his influence (like Deming's) can be seen in virtually every one of the seven categories.

He departs from the other gurus in his emphasis on performance standards instead of statistical data to achieve zero defects. He believes that identifying goals to be achieved, setting the standards for the final product, removing all error-causing situations, and complete organizational commitment comprise the foundation for excellence.

A Brief Summary of the Deming Quality Philosophy[40]

To the very end, Deming was a "maverick." A few months before his death, his final book was published.[41] In it, he explained his "Theory of Profound Knowledge," which he had talked of but had never explained.

Unlike other gurus and consultants, Deming never defined quality precisely. In his last book, he stated, "A product or a service possesses quality if it helps somebody and enjoys a good and sustainable market."[42] Deming focused on the improvement of product and service quality by reducing uncertainty and variability in the design and manufacturing process. In Deming's view, variation is the chief culprit of poor quality. In service operations, for example, variations from service standards, such as on-time arrival of airline flights, lead to inconsistent performance, waste of passengers' time, and possible failure of the firm. Deming proposed using a continuous cycle of product design, manufacture, test, and sales, followed by market surveys and then redesign to reduce variation, In his Deming "chain reaction," higher quality leads to higher productivity, which in turn leads to long-term competitive strength. He recommended the following steps. (1)

Make improvements in quality, which leads to (2) lower costs because of less rework, fewer mistakes, fewer delays and snags, and better use of time and materials. (3) Lower costs then lead to (4) productivity improvements. With better quality and lower prices, the firm can (5) achieve a higher market share and thus stay in business, (6) providing more and more jobs. Deming places the ultimate responsibility for quality improvement in the hands of top management.

Deming developed a statement called "A System of Profound Knowledge" in his recent book. Profound Knowledge provides the underlying foundations behind the 14 Points. A brief discussion of the elements of Profound Knowledge (given below) will help you understand and appreciate the 14 Points.

Profound Knowledge consists of four parts, all related to each other:

1. Appreciation for systems
2. Understanding variation
3. Theory of knowledge
4. Psychology

Systems—A system is a set of functions or activities within an organization that work together for the aim of the organization. Any system is composed of many smaller, interacting subsystems (as mentioned in the discussion of the House of Total Quality in Chapter 1). For example, a McDonald's restaurant is a system, which includes the order-taking/cashier system, grill and food preparation system, drive-through system, purchasing system, and training system. These systems are linked together as internal customers and suppliers.

The components of any system must work together in order for the system to be effective. When there are interactions among the parts of a system, managers cannot manage the system by simply managing the parts. This is one of the problems with functionally oriented organizations. Many companies manage by using a *vertical* organization chart rather than using *horizontal* cross-functional relationships.

Management's job is to *optimize* the system. Suboptimization results in loss for everybody in the system. According to Deming, it would be poor management, for example, to purchase materials or services at the lowest price or to minimize the cost of manufacturing at the expense of the rest of the system.

Management must have an *aim*, a purpose toward which the system continually strives. Deming believed that the aim of any system is for everyone—stockholders, employees, customers, community, the environment—to gain over the long term. Stockholders can realize financial benefits, employees can receive opportunities for training and education, customers can receive products and services that meet their needs and create satisfaction, the community can benefit from business leadership, and the environment can benefit from socially responsible management.

This theory applies to managing people also. All the people who work within a system can contribute to improvement and thus enhance their joy in work. For example, many factors within the system affect the individual performance of an employee:

- Training received
- Information and resources provided
- Leadership of supervisors and managers
- Disruptions on the job
- Management policies and practices

Performance appraisals usually do not recognize these factors. According to Deming, pitting individuals or departments against each other for resources is self-destructive. The individuals or departments will perform to maximize their own expected gain, and not that of the entire firm. Optimizing the system requires internal cooperation. Similarly, using sales quotas or arbitrary cost reduction goals will not motivate people to improve the system and customer satisfaction; people will only perform to meet the quotas and goals.

Variation—The second part of Profound Knowledge is a basic understanding of statistical theory and variation. Variation is everywhere, from hitting golf balls to service in a restaurant. Variation has already been discussed in the context of control in this chapter. This area will be revisited several times throughout the book.

Theory of Knowledge—The third part of Profound Knowledge is the Theory of Knowledge. Theory of Knowledge is a branch of philosophy that is concerned with the nature and scope of knowledge, its presuppositions and basis, and the general reliability of claims to knowledge. Deming was strongly influenced by Clarence Irving Lewis, author of *Mind and the World*.[43] Lewis stated: "There is no knowledge without interpretation. If interpretation, which represents an activity of the mind, is always subject to the check of further experience, how is knowledge possible at all?...An argument from past to future at best is probable only, and even this probability must rest upon principles which are themselves more than probable."

Deming emphasized that there is no knowledge without theory, and experience alone does not establish a theory. Any rational plan, however simple, requires prediction concerning conditions, behavior, and comparison of performance. A statement devoid of prediction or explanation of past events conveys no knowledge. Experience alone is no help in management. To copy an example of success without understanding it with theory may lead to disaster. Experience only *describes*; it cannot be tested or validated.

Theory shows a cause-and-effect relationship that can be used for prediction. Many companies have jumped on the latest fads advocated by popular business consultants, and many of these approaches have failed. Methods that have sustained success are grounded in theory. This notion implies that management decisions must be based on fact, not instinct. Objective data and a systematic problem-solving process provide a rational basis for making decisions. Thus, the purpose of theory is to develop a science. The purpose of science is to describe, predict, and control practice. This will be discussed further in a later chapter, particularly in the context of "learning organizations."

Psychology—Psychology helps us to understand people, interactions between people and circumstances, interactions between leaders and employees, and any system of management. Much of Deming's philosophy is based on understanding human behavior and treating people fairly. People differ from one another. A leader must be aware of these differences and use them to optimize everyone's abilities and preferences. Most managers operate under the supposition that all people are alike. However, people learn in different ways and at different speeds. A true leader understands this and manages the system accordingly.

People are motivated intrinsically and extrinsically. Fear is not a motivator, but instead prevents the system from reaching its full potential. People are born with a need for relationships with other people and with the need to be loved and esteemed by others. Circumstances provide some people with dignity and self-esteem and deny other people these advantages. The latter will smother intrinsic motivation. If people cannot enjoy work, they will not be productive and focused on quality principles. Psychology helps us to nurture and preserve these positive innate attributes of people.

One of Deming's more controversial beliefs is that pay is not a motivator, although industrial psychologists have said this for decades. The chairman of General Motors once stated that if he doubled the salary of every employee, nothing would change. Monetary rewards are a way out for managers who do not understand how to manage intrinsic motivation. Joy in work becomes secondary to getting good ratings. Employees are ruled by external forces and try to protect what they have and avoid punishment.

Very little in Deming's system of Profound Knowledge is original. Walter Shewhart developed the distinction between common and special causes of variation in the 1920s, business schools taught many behavioral theories to which Deming subscribes in the 1960s, management scientists refined systems theory in the 1950s through 1970s, and scientists in all fields have long understood the relationships among prediction, observation, and theory. Deming made a major contribution in tying these concepts together. He recognized their synergy and developed them into a unified theory of management that is universal. However, Deming cautioned that Profound Knowledge cannot be forced on people. He emphasized that it must come from the outside and by invitation. Managers must want to learn and apply it. Otherwise, it's business as usual.

ISO 9000 and the Quality Movement

At the turn of the century, England was the most advanced nation in the world in terms of quality standards. During World War I, England led the charge and during World War II was at least the equal of the United States—with one exception. England did not have Shewhart, Deming, and the other American quality gurus. It was not until the Common Market accepted the firm touch of Prime Minister Margaret Thatcher that the European quality movement was galvanized in 1979 with the forerunner of ISO 9000. It was Thatcher who orchestrated the transformation of the British ISO 9000 series for the European community. In less than 20 years, it has become the worldwide quality standard.

REVIEW QUESTIONS

2.1 What is the definition of total quality?

2.2 What dimensions of quality are ideally addressed when manufacturing products? How do those dimensions change when providing services?

2.3 What is the Japanese notion of control and how does it differ from the notion that has traditionally existed in the United States?

2.4 Define bureaucratic, market, and clan control, and describe the environment for which each is best suited.

2.5 How did the Craft Era contribute to the American concept of quality? Might it be possible for us to revive that concept and put it to use in our service-oriented society?

2.6 How did Eli Whitney's experiences, which led to his development of interchangeable parts for muskets, represent a turning point in the development of the factory and technical systems?

2.7 What were Walter Shewhart's most significant contributions in the areas of statistical process control?

2.8 What did Frederick Winslow Taylor contribute to the early development of management systems?

2.9 How did Frank and Lillian Gilbreth mechanize and commercialize Taylorism?

2.10 What did W. Edwards Deming consider to be the real "villain" in Taylorism and the scientific management system? Why?

2.11 Who are considered the quality "gurus" who have most significantly shaped the quality movement since World War II? With what key contributions has each guru been credited?

2.12 Diagram and describe the key concepts of the relational diagram of the theory of total quality management which underlies the Deming management method (see Abstract 2.1).

DISCUSSION QUESTIONS

2.1 Compare and contrast different types of quality leadership. What effects of each have you observed or personally experienced in your own work history?

2.2 Call to mind the "best boss" for whom you have ever worked. Describe his or her characteristics as a quality leader and how he or she treated you as a worker. What impact did this person's leadership style have on your work motivation and commitment?

2.3 "Total quality is too important to take second place to any other goals. Specifically, it should not be subsidiary to profit or productivity." Do you agree with this assertion? Why or why not?

2.4 What lessons for U.S. managers and OD practitioners does a comparison of the history of Japanese and U.S. quality management afford?

2.5 Discuss the positive and negative aspects of Deming's "Theory of Profound Knowledge." Is it easy to grasp? Why might it be important to study this theory in more depth?

ENDNOTES

1. ANSI/ASQC A3-1978. (1978). *Quality Systems Terminology*. Milwaukee: American Society for Quality Control.
2. Dean, James E. Jr. and Evans, James R. (1994). *Total Quality: Management, Organization and Strategy*. St. Paul, MN: West Publishing, p. 7.
3. Rampey, J. and Roberts, H. (1992). "Perspectives in Total Quality." *Proceedings of Total Quality Forum IV*. Cincinnati, OH: Procter & Gamble, November.
4. Garvin, David A. (1984). "What Does 'Product Quality' Really Mean?" *Sloan Management Review*. Vol. 26, No. 1, pp. 25–43.
5. Parasuraman, A., Zeithaml, V., and Berry, L. (1988). "SERVQUAL: A Multiple Item Scale for Measuring Consumer Perceptions of Service Quality." *Journal of Retailing*. Vol. 64, No. 1, pp. 12–40. See also Page, Harold, S. (1983). "A Quality Strategy for the 80's." *Quality Progress*. Vol. 16, No. 11, pp. 16–21; Zeithaml, V., Parasuraman, A., and Berry, L. (1990). *Delivering Service Quality*. New York: Free Press.
6. During the course of the Deming Prize examination at Florida Power & Light in 1988 and 1989, Dr. Kano consistently emphasized this point in his site visits to

various power plants and district customer service operations. The concept of worker self-inspection, while new in the United States, has been a practiced art in Japan over the past 20 years.

7. Whethan, C.D. (1980). *A History of Science*, 4th edition. New York: MacMillan.

8. See endnote 5.

9. Ouchi, William (1980). "Markets, Bureaucracies, and Clans." *Administrative Science Quarterly*. Vol. 25, pp. 125–141.

10. Walton, Richard E. (1985). "From Control to Commitment in the Workplace." *Harvard Business Review*. Vol. 63, No. 2 (March/April), pp. 77–84.

11. Shewhart, W.A. (1931). *Economic Control of Quality of Manufactured Product*. New York: Van Nostrand.

12. *The Craftsman in America*. Washington, DC: The National Geographic Society, 1975, pp. 30–31.

13. Ibid., p. 164.

14. Olmstead, Denison (1972). *Memoir of Eli Whitney, Esq.* New York: Arno Press.

15. George, Claude S. (1968). *The History of Management Thought*. Englewood Cliffs, NJ: Prentice-Hall, p. 60.

16. To paraphrase Walter Shewhart's "go–no-go" concept: If, for example, a design involving the use of a cylindrical shaft in a bearing is examined, interchangeability might be ensured simply by using a suitable "go" plug gauge on the bearing and a suitable "go" ring gauge on the shaft. In this case, the difference between the dimensions of the two "go" gauges gives the minimum clearance. Such a method of gauging, however, does not fix the maximum clearance. The production worker soon realizes that a slack fit between a part and its "go" gauge might result in enough play between the shaft and its bearing to cause the product to be rejected; therefore, the worker would try to keep the fit between the part and its "go" gauge as close as possible, thus encountering some of the same kind of difficulties that had been experienced in trying to make the parts exactly alike.

17. Walter Shewhart was the first to realize that with the development of the atomic structure of matter and electricity, it became necessary to think of laws as being statistical in nature. The importance of the law of large numbers in the interpretation of physical phenomena will become apparent to anyone who even hastily surveys any one or more of the following works: Darrow, K.K. (1929). "Statistical Theories of Matter, Radiation, and Electricity." *The Physical Review Supplement*. Vol. 1, No. 1, 1929 (also published in the series of Bell Telephone Laboratories reprints, No. 435); Rice, J. (1930). *Introduction to Statistical Mechanics for Students of Physics and Physical Chemistry*. London: Constable & Company; Tolman, R.C. (1927). *Statistical Mechanics with Applications to Physics and Chemistry*. New York: Chemical Catalog Company; Loeb, L.B. (1927). *Kinetic Theory of Gases*. New York: McGraw-Hill; Bloch, E. (1924). *The Kinetic Theory of Bases*. London: Methuen; Richmeyer, F.K. (1928). *Introduction to Modern Physics*. New York: McGraw-Hill; Wilson, H.A. (1928). *Modern Physics*. London: Blackie & Son; Darrow, K.K. (1926). *Introduction to Contemporary Physics*. New York: D. Van Nostrand; and Ruark, A.E. and Uray, H.C. (1930). *Atoms, Molecules and Quanta*. New York: McGraw-Hill.

18. To paraphrase Shewhart on the use of the control chart: Whereas the concept of mass production of 1787 was born of an *exact* science, the concept underlying the

control chart technique of 1924 was born of a *probable* science, which has empirically derived control limits. These limits are to be set so that when the observed quality of a piece of product falls outside of them, even though the observation is still within the limits L_1 and L_2 (tolerance limits), it is desirable to look at the manufacturing process in order to discover and remove, if possible, one or more causes of variation that need not be left to chance.

19. Shewhart (endnote 11), pp. 39–45.

20. Shewhart noted that it is essential, however, in industry and in science to understand the distinction between a stable system and an unstable system and how to plot points and conclude by rational methods whether they indicate a stable system. To quote Shewhart, "This conclusion is consistent with that so admirably presented in a recent paper by S.L. Andres in the *Bell Telephone Quarterly*, January 1931, and also with conclusions set forth in the recent book *Business Adrift*, by W.B. Donham, Dean of the Harvard Business School. Such reading cannot do other than strengthen our belief in the fact that control of quality will come only through the weeding out of assignable causes of variation—particularly those that introduce lack of constancy in the chance cause system."

21. See Shewhart (endnote 11), pp. 72–74. As the statistician enters the scene, the three traditional elements of control take on a new meaning, as Shewhart summarized: Corresponding to these three steps there are three senses in which statistical control may play an important part in attaining uniformity in the quality of a manufactured product: (a) as a concept of a statistical state constituting a limit to which one may hope to go in improving the uniformity of quality; (b) as an operation or technique of attaining uniformity; and (c) as a judgment.

22. Deming referred to assignable causes as being specific to some ephemeral (brief) event that can usually be discovered to the satisfaction of the expert on the job and removed.

23. See Shewhart (endnote 11), pp. 92–95. Shewhart used what he called the Ideal Bowl Experiment to physically characterize a state of statistical control. A number of physically similar poker chips with numbers written on them are placed in a bowl. Successive samples (Shewhart seems to prefer a sample size of four) are taken from the bowl, each time mixing the remaining chips. The chips drawn from the bowl are selected due to chance—there are only chance causes of variation. In speaking of chance causes of variation, Shewhart proves, contrary to popular belief, that the statistician can have a sense of humor. If someone were shooting at a mark and failed to hit the bull's-eye and someone asked why, the answer would likely be *chance*. Had someone asked the same question of one of our earliest known ancestors, he might have attributed his lack of success to the dictates of fate or the will of the gods. In many ways, one of these excuses is just about as good as another. The Ideal Bowl Experiment is an abstract means of characterizing the physical state of statistical control. A sequence of samples of any process can be compared mathematically to the bowl experiment and, if found similar, the process can be characterized as being in a state of statistical control. Shewhart states: "It seems to me that it is far safer to take some one physical operation such as drawing from a bowl as a physical model for an act

that may be repeated at random, and then to require that any other repetitive operation believed to be random shall in addition produce results similar to the results of drawing from a bowl before we act as though the operation in question were random."

24. Matthies, Leslie (1960). "The Beginning of Modern Scientific Management." *The Office*. April.

25. Ibid.

26. It may be helpful to think of the three steps in the mass production process as steps in the scientific method. In this sense, specification, production, and inspection correspond, respectively, to forming a hypothesis, conducting an experiment, and testing the hypothesis. The three steps constitute a dynamic scientific process of acquiring knowledge.

27. The following story was related at one of Deming's now-famous four-day quality seminars: "I remember him [Shewhart] pacing the floor in his room at the Hotel Washington before the third lecture. He was explaining something to me. I remarked that these great thoughts should be in his lectures. He said that they were already written up in his third and fourth lectures. I remarked that if he wrote up these lectures in the same way that he had just explained them to me, they would be clearer. He said that his writing had to be foolproof. I thereupon remarked that he had written his thoughts so damned foolproof that no one could understand them."

28. Halberstam, David (1960). "The War Effort during WWII." Lectures, Articles and Notes.

29. George (endnote 15), p. 128.

30. This is a general consensus feeling among many historians and writers as to the inherent "evil" of Taylorism—machine over man. Walter Shewhart, to his credit and genius, tried to marry quality control and scientific management. In the foreword to his 1931 master work, *Economic Control of Manufactured Product*, he writes, "Broadly speaking, the object of industry is to set up economic ways and means of satisfying human wants and in so doing to reduce everything possible to routines requiring a minimum amount of human effort. Through the use of the scientific method, extended to take account of modern statistical concepts, it has been found possible to set up limits within which the results of routine efforts must lie if they are to be economical. Deviations in the results of a routine process outside such limits indicate that the routine has broken down and will no longer be economical until the cause of trouble is removed."

31. Bonstingal, John Jay (1992). *Schools of Quality*. New York: Free Press.

32. Mayo, George Elton (1933). *The Human Problems of an Industrial Civilization*. Boston: Division of Research, Harvard Business School.

33. Voehl, F.W. (1990). "The Deming Prize." *South Carolina Business Journal*.

34. Hopper, Kenneth (1982). "Creating Japan's New Industrial Management: The Americans as Teachers." *Human Resources Management*. pp. 16–17.

35. Deming, W. Edwards (1993). *The New Economics for Industry, Government, Education*. Cambridge, MA: MIT Center for Advanced Engineering Study.

36. Juran, J.M. and Gryna, Frank M. (1988). *Juran's Quality Control Handbook*. New York: McGraw-Hill.

37. Juran, J.M. (1988). *Juran on Planning for Quality*. New York: Free Press, pp. 5–7.

38. Feigenbaum, A.V. (1983). *Total Quality Control*, 3rd edition. New York: McGraw-Hill.
39. See, for example: Crosby, Philip B. (1979). *Quality Is Free: The Art of Making Quality Certain*. New York: Dutton, and Crosby, Philip B. (1992). *Completeness: Quality for the 21st Century*. New York: Dutton.
40. This section was adapted from Evans, James R. and Lindsay, William M. (1996). *The Management and Control of Quality*, 3rd edition. Minneapolis: West Publishing, pp. 59–101.
41. Deming (endnote 35).
42. Ibid.
43. Lewis, Clarence Irving (1929). *Mind and the World*. Mineola, NY: Dover.

ABSTRACT

ABSTRACT 2.1
THEORETICAL MODEL OF TOTAL QUALITY MANAGEMENT

Anderson, John C., Rungtusanatham, Manus, and Schroeder, Roger G.
Academy of Management Review (AMR), Vol. 19, No. 3, July 1994, pp. 472–509

The theoretical essence of the Deming management method uncovers the creation of an organizational system that fosters cooperation and learning to facilitate the implementation of process management practices. This, in turn, leads to continuous improvement of processes, products, and services and to employee fulfillment, both of which are critical to customer satisfaction and, ultimately, survival. The relational diagram of the theory of total quality management underlying the Deming management method is illustrated as follows:

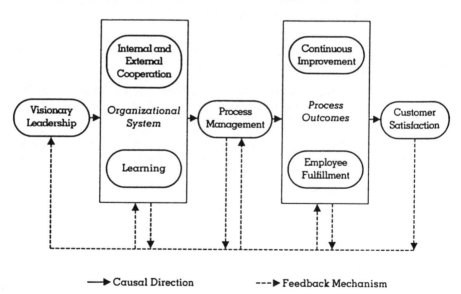

The key concepts underlying the Deming management method are as follow.

Visionary Leadership—The ability of management to establish, practice, and lead a long-term vision for the organization, driven by changing customer requirements, as opposed to an internal management control role. This is exemplified by clarity of vision, long-range orientation, coaching management style, participative change, employee empowerment, and planning and implementing organizational change.

Internal and External Cooperation—The propensity of the organization to engage in noncompetitive activities internally among employees and externally with respect to suppliers. This is exemplified by firm–supplier partnership, single-supplier orientation, collaborative organization, teamwork, organization-wide involvement, systems view of the organization, trust, and elimination of fear.

Learning—The organizational capability to recognize and nurture the development of skills, abilities, and knowledge base. This is exemplified by company-wide training, foundational knowledge, process knowledge, educational development, continuous self-improvement, and managerial learning.

Process Management—The set of methodological and behavioral practices that emphasize the management of process, or means of actions, rather than results. This is exemplified by management of processes, prevention orientation, reduction of mass inspection, design quality, statistical process control, understanding variation, elimination of numerical quotas, elimination of management by objectives, elimination of merit-rating reward systems, understanding motivation, total cost accounting, and stable employment.

Continuous Improvement—The propensity of the organization to pursue incremental and innovative improvements of its processes, products, and services. This is exemplified by continuous improvement.

Employee Fulfillment—The degree to which employees of an organization feel that the organization continually satisfies their needs. This is exemplified by job satisfaction, job commitment, and *pride of workmanship.*

Customer Satisfaction—The degree to which an organization's customers continually perceive that their needs are being met by the organization's products and services. This is exemplified by *customer-driven focus.*

CHAPTER 3

CUSTOMER SATISFACTION: TQ AND OD STRATEGY DIMENSIONS

Chapter 3 focuses on two areas: total quality business strategy and total quality organization development (OD) strategy. The strength of the first pillar of the House of Total Quality depends on strategy development, and the strategic responsibilities of managers in a total quality system require a different approach to business strategy. A total quality business strategy also depends on continuous learning and OD in today's progressive firms. Thus, a successful business strategy requires a successful total-quality-focused OD strategy.

OD professionals need to be aware of their strategic role as organizations attempt to plan for changes in the present while adapting to needs of the future. Several points may be made about the impact of a strategic vision on customer satisfaction, organizational performance, product/service quality, employee treatment and empowerment, and internal and external results from the ethical work culture:

- A vision is the starting point for all total quality initiatives. It should be stated as clearly as possible, thus acting as a beacon to guide and illuminate decision making and actions.

- The OD professional can be the interpreter of the vision when working on organization design or redesign to achieve: (1) customer satisfaction, (2) organizational performance, (3) fair policies for treatment and empowerment of employees, and (4) organizational character development within the ethical work culture framework (previously discussed in Chapter 1).
- The vision can be a powerful force for change, but unless it is carefully monitored, it can also have serious negative consequences.
- The OD consultant can fill a valuable role by keeping an eye out for the emergence of the "daimonic" side of staff (the tendency to introduce change for the sake of change or without regard for possible unintended consequences) which, if it is out of control, can burn an organization out.[1]

TOTAL QUALITY BUSINESS STRATEGY

The first pillar of the House of Total Quality, total customer satisfaction, is based on the cornerstone of strategy planning and the foundation of strategy management, as developed in the previous chapter. We also pointed out in Chapter 1 that total customer satisfaction requires organizations to meet and even exceed customer expectations over time.[2] Customer satisfaction is the **outcome** of sound quality product and process design developed in the cornerstone of *strategy planning* with effective quality implementation delivered in the foundation of *strategy management*, as shown in Figure 3.1.

Figure 3.1 The First Pillar, Foundation, and Cornerstone of the House of Total Quality

Customer focus, and its outcome, customer satisfaction, in fact, has become an umbrella phrase for a range of concepts in successful organizations. Distinctions have been made between **customers** (purchasers of products and services) and **consumers** (the end users of products and services), who both need to be satisfied but who are sometimes the same and at other times different. Distinctions have also been made among product characteristics as being **dissatisfiers** (unstated customer expectations for the product or service that are taken for granted and if absent result in customer dissatisfaction), **satisfiers** (stated customer expectations about the product or service which, if fulfilled, lead to product satisfaction), and **exciters/delighters** (unstated and unexpected consumer desires for products or services which, if met, lead to high perceptions of quality and likely purchase or repurchase of products). Over time, exciters/delighters become satisfiers as customers become used to them, and eventually satisfiers become dissatisfiers, thereby requiring ongoing innovation and customer research to ensure customer satisfaction.

Strategic planning and management are now being substantially re-examined, and traditional models are being questioned[3] in light of global realignment and turbulence in the business environment. In the 1970s, the Arab oil embargo caused strategic planners to realize that "the future isn't what it used to be!" Despite the threats of the Cold War and some intense regional "hot" wars, the United States, Europe, and several countries in Asia experienced fairly predictable, sustained growth from 1945 until 1973. In the 1970s and early 1980s, managers woke up to the fact that in the future, there would be more unpredictable upheavals in the business environment. These could be brought on by economic wars and regional skirmishes and would not be subject to systematic strategic planning processes. Thus, managers must now consider two major approaches to developing business strategy: an "intuitive/inductive" approach and a traditional, rational/analytic one. We will outline the possible impacts of these approaches on strategic quality management and OD.

First, we need to define strategy and total quality strategy in a way that incorporates some of the issues raised by both approaches. A working definition of **strategy** is *the intended, emergent, and realized pattern of organizational guidance and the development of structure and management processes used to achieve an organization's mission and objectives and pursue its vision.* In the traditional view, an effective strategy-making process consists of a planning phase (i.e., environmental scanning and strategy formulation) and a management phase (strategy implementation, evaluation, and control). Similarly, **total quality strategy** is *the intended and realized pattern of organizational guidance and the development of structure and management processes that produce total customer satisfaction.* An effective total quality strategy requires adequate strategic planning and management, whether the inductive/intuitive or the rational/analytic approach is adopted.

Strategic Planning and Management: Intuitive/Inductive Approach

Henry Mintzberg[4] and a few other writers, such as James Brian Quinn,[5] have proposed the view (sometimes called the *intuitive/inductive model*) that strategic planning has more to do with the gradual emergence of direction from strategy implementation than with the grand plans of senior managers. Peter Drucker's definition of the rational approach to planning as "…the continuous process of making present entrepreneurial (risk-taking) decisions systematically and with the greatest knowledge of their futurity"[6] is the opposite of Mintzberg's intuitive/inductive model. Mintzberg spent almost half of a *Harvard Business Review* article[7] taking carefully aimed shots at the conventional planning process. To stress the importance of making full use of the intuitive abilities and operational experience of exceptional managers, Mintzberg contrasts *strategic planners* with *strategic thinkers*. He clearly labels the conventional strategic planning process as the practice of *strategic programming*—"the articulation and elaboration of strategies or visions, that already exist." His concept of strategic thinking[8] is less precise, but more innovative, and seems to encompass: (1) synthesis instead of analysis, (2) use of both soft insights from personal and corporate experience as well as hard data by the intuitive leader/manager, (3) development of a vision or direction, and (4) a willingness by the leader/manager to let others turn the vision into concrete terms needed for "strategic programming."

Mintzberg[9] also put a great deal of emphasis on the "realized pattern" part of the strategy definition above, rather than considering the formal, rational analytical process of planning stressed by the traditional strategists. Using the term "emergent strategy," he signified that analysis may aid managers in understanding their strategic direction by being used more in hindsight than in foresight.

Those who adopt his intuitive/inductive viewpoint must consider the implications of this approach. They must rethink how strategy is developed. Managers must reconsider the role of "professional" planners, determine how they should be involved in the planning process, determine if there are contingencies under which certain strategies may be more successful than others, and consider how to gather and use information from strategy implementation to plan future strategies for their organizations in the face of uncertain strategic direction. There is much to be gained from looking at his alternative approach as it relates to total quality concepts. After considering the rational/analytic planning process, we will revisit the Mintzberg model to explore its implications for OD and total quality management (TQM).

Strategic Planning and Management: Rational/Analytic Approach

In addition to the inductive/intuitive approach, there is the traditional rational/analytic approach, which emphasizes environmental scanning, foresight, and analytic focus in formulating strategy. Once a strategy has been formulated, strategy implementation, evaluation, and control are important in order to successfully carry out the intended strategy. The comprehensive, rational/analytic model of strategy planning and strategy management presented in the next section involves four basic elements: (1) *environmental scanning*, (2) *strategy formulation*, (3) *strategy implementation*, and (4) *evaluation and control*, aspects of all of which are adaptable to total quality strategy. Figure 3.2 shows how the four elements continuously interact.

TOTAL QUALITY BUSINESS STRATEGY PLANNING

The traditional rational/analytic model in Figure 3.2, adapted from Wheelen and Hunger,[10] has four major components SP: SCAN, SP: FOCUS, SM:ACT, and SM:ACT (evaluation and control). These are "shorthand" for strategic planning: environmental scanning, strategic planning: strategy formulation, strategic management: strategy implementation, and strategic management: evaluation and control, respectively. We will look at each module in detail.

Strategy Planning: Environmental Scanning

The first element of the traditional strategic planning process is environmental scanning. It is composed of two major divisions: (1) *external* environment assessment of the opportunities and threats that exist in the natural, social, and industry environments of the organization, and (2) *internal* environment assessment of the strengths and weaknesses that exist within the structure, culture, and resources of the organization. Environmental scanning is used to discover the external opportunities and threats to the organization and to weigh the internal strengths and weaknesses in order to survive and adapt to current reality.

External Environmental Assessment

The external environment includes both a macro- and a micro-environmental view. The macro view considers natural ecological systems, key physical and energy resource constraints, and the social environment (or networks) that influence organizations. Strategic planning processes that ignore the economic limits to the growth of natural ecosystems and neglect to develop

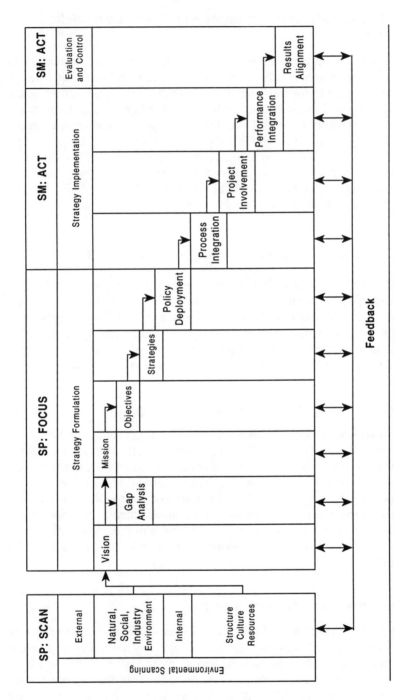

Figure 3.2 The Comprehensive Model of Total Quality Strategy Planning and Management

interorganizational links to reinforce quality efforts will ultimately fail in attempts to develop ecological, sustainable growth and improvement of the firm.[11] The social (socio-economic) environment includes the broad human factors that *indirectly* influence the organization's survival: economic, socio-cultural, political–legal, demographic, labor market, transportation, energy infrastructure, and technological forces. The micro view focuses on the industry environment, which includes those factors that *directly* impact the organization's survival: customers, employees, investors, suppliers, distributors, communities, governments, special interest groups, trade/professional/union organizations, and competitors.

With a total quality viewpoint, an organization's strategic planning process emphasizes external customer–supplier partnerships to reduce the unnecessary market variations in the external environment. The importance of customer–supplier relationships is frequently ignored in traditional strategic planning models. Total customer satisfaction, related to current and future products and services, is **the** primary strategic value. To achieve it, quality strategists recommend extensive, incessant collection and analysis of customer feedback data. Market opportunity analysis tools, including sophisticated measures of buying and use processes, provide refined and useful data on consumer needs and desires which conventional competitors rarely attempt to collect. For example, in an "infomercial" advertisement in *Fortune* entitled "Quality, 1992," Edward C. Johnson, 3rd, CEO and principal owner of Fidelity Investments, pointed out:

> Fidelity was one of the first financial services to embrace computer technology on a large scale, and the company has invested hundreds of millions of dollars in systems design to make the company more responsive to customers. One indication of just how important IT is to Fidelity: the company employs nearly twice as many programmers as it does security analysts.

In addition to frequent and detailed information on the buying process, strategic quality managers must consider the whole use process to better satisfy more customer needs simultaneously. The value of a current or future product or service to a customer is more than the mere act of consumption. Customers have to find, acquire, transport, store, use, dispose of, and stop the ongoing use of a product or service, as indicated below:

1. **Find**—A customer must locate a product or service to fulfill a need. This requires search, recognition, and choice resources.
2. **Acquire**—This process may entail ordering, paying for, financing, transferring, and registering the ownership.
3. **Transport**—Once acquired, the customer may have to move the product from where it is to where it can be further used.

4. **Store**—The customer may have to store the product prior to further use; the storage can be short or long term and may be repeated in different forms.
5. **Use**—At some point, the customer applies the product or service to fulfill an original need or desire.
6. **Disposal**—Once utilized, the customer may have to dispose of the remainder of the product.
7. **Stop**—The customer may decide to stop using the product and need to go through termination procedures.[12]

The acronym FATSUDS has been applied to this sequence of customer use processes.[13] One person may perform all or only some of the FATSUDS activities. In addition, other aspects of the use process, such as ease of availability, quality of the service, and congeniality of supplier, may impact the customer's perception of value, and the astute total quality strategy manager addresses all of these issues as well.

A recent strategic emphasis has been on *delighting* customers, instead of merely *satisfying* them. This generally requires that strategic plans and their execution *anticipate* customer needs by providing features, products, and services that customers may not even know they need but to which they will respond favorably (that is, will be *delighted* to see and buy). This essential requirement in the race for competitive advantage is extremely difficult to systematically plan for in a traditional strategic planning and implementation model.

The traditional approach to industry supplier relations has been one of self-interested adversarial negotiations between customer and supplier, each trying to maximize his or her slice of the pie at the expense of the other.[14] The total quality strategy is to expand the pie rather than argue over its division. Juran's trend framework in Table 3.1 exhibits the total quality difference.[15]

The total quality approach to strategy emphasizes the need for leadership in social responsibility. The Malcolm Baldrige National Quality Award criteria include public responsibility of organizational leaders to the external community. They outline specific responsibilities to the public for health, safety, environmental protection, and ethical business practices as they impact a wide range of stakeholders.

Internal Environmental Assessment

The internal environment includes organizational structure, ethical work culture, and functional resources. The structure is the way the organization is designed and run, including work flows, authority, communication channels, and decision-making processes. Although organization structure may restrict the thinking of strategic managers, influencing them to select one strategy over another, structure should normally follow strategy.[16] Measure-

Table 3.1 Juran on Trends in Supplier Relations

Supplier relations element	Traditional adversary relationship	Total quality partnership relationship
Number of suppliers	Multiple, often many	Few, often single source
Duration of supply contracts	Annual	Three years or more
Criteria for quality	Conformance to specifications	Fitness for use
Emphasis of surveys	Procedures, data systems	Process capability, quality improvement
Quality planning	Separate	Joint
Pattern of collaboration	Arms length, secrecy, mutual supervision	Mutual visits, disclosures; assistance

ment systems relating to financial performance, customer feedback, production efficiency, and employee contributions become key features of internal structure and strategy choice.[17]

The *internal ethical work culture* can be defined as *the collection of beliefs, values, and behaviors regarding organizational integrity that are shared and transmitted by the organization's members.*[18] Shortsighted manipulative organizational ethical work cultures can become major obstacles when the organization most needs to change strategic direction.[19] Few organizations take time to assess internal customer satisfaction or ethical climate levels as inputs to the strategic internal environment analysis, but both are key factors in enhancing the *quality* of strategic input from people in the organization.

Functional resources include *financial, physical, organizational system (including human resources), and technological processes which constitute the raw material for the production of an organization's products and/or services.* Organizations that use a conventional strategic planning approach tend to neglect a thorough analysis of their internal process capabilities and improvement opportunities. The results of such analysis could be valuable in planning for development of a *quality* internal environment. Total quality includes a strong focus on the strategic priority of customer satisfaction, which, in turn, requires a new internal alignment of processes, resources, and performance measures.[20] The traditional U.S. strategic planning approach reinforces top-down authority and gives highest priority to financial measures and resources. In contrast, total quality strategists constantly plan for flatter organizations to enhance total customer satisfaction. Because they regard profit or market share as the outcome of meeting and exceeding customer needs,

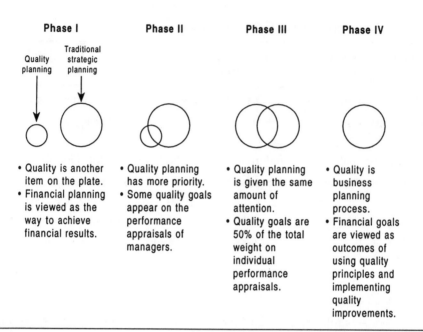

Phase I	Phase II	Phase III	Phase IV

Quality planning   Traditional strategic planning

- Quality is another item on the plate.
- Financial planning is viewed as the way to achieve financial results.

- Quality planning has more priority.
- Some quality goals appear on the performance appraisals of managers.

- Quality planning is given the same amount of attention.
- Quality goals are 50% of the total weight on individual performance appraisals.

- Quality is business planning process.
- Financial goals are viewed as outcomes of using quality principles and implementing quality improvements.

Figure 3.3 The Phased Transition from Traditional Strategic Planning to Total Quality Planning (Adapted from Collins, Brendan and Huge, Ernest (1993). *Management by Policy*. Milwaukee: ASQC Quality Press, p. 138.)

they require full integration of quality into strategic planning, as shown in Figure 3.3.

Recognition of the strategic priority of quality increases the importance of operating measures, customer feedback measures, and employee contribution measures while moderating the influence of traditional financial measures of performance. Sound operating measures are needed to identify and eliminate defects, increase production reliability by meeting progressively higher standards, and reduce cycle time or time to market.[21]

Traditional financial and accounting measures often inadequately represent, or even obscure, operating effectiveness.[22] U.S. financial measures compare unfavorably with similar Japanese measures for reporting critical strategic success factors in the following ways. First, while U.S. firms initially develop a product and price it at whatever level is necessary to turn a profit, Japanese companies reverse the order through "target costing." With target costing, a firm first decides what the consumer will be willing to pay for the new product. It then works backward to drive design, production, distribution, marketing, and supplier costs down to the target figure.[23] Second, rather than using accountants to measure costs, the Japanese tend to use cost engineers who are experienced product developers. These engineers not only measure costs, but also have the expertise and responsibility to reduce them.[24] Third, in order to maintain flexibility across workers and products, Japanese accountants seek to minimize *total* costs (rather than *unit* costs as do U.S. accountants). This keeps staff specialist and other overhead costs to a minimum. These "activity-based" costs focus on the value added at each stage of the production process, including supplier-based stages. Fourth, the Japanese do not make capital investment decisions primarily by anticipated profits or return on investment. They factor in business judgments based on operating, customer, supplier, and employee input. For the most part, internal U.S. business decisions are still driven by processes and data obtained from financial accounting systems designed primarily for external reporting purposes rather than improvement of internal efficiency.[25]

The internal ethical work culture should also be assessed by the total quality strategist. Periodic ethical climate surveys may be used to determine the organization's level of moral development and whether it is at a stage that is hospitable to the House of Total Quality, as described in Chapter 1.[26] Strategic planners who ignore the ethical work culture of an organization may have trouble predicting the kind and degree of employee resistance or support for total quality initiatives. If plans for total quality and organizational ethics development are to mutually reinforce each other, quality leaders must be sure that the organization is structured not around the old paradigm of detection/control, but around the new paradigm of coordination/strategic impact, as shown in Table 3.2.[27]

Table 3.2 Strategic Paradigm Shifts in Total Quality and Organizational Ethics Development

	Old paradigm		New paradigm	
	Detection	Control	Coordination	Strategic impact
Parties responsible for quality management	Inspection department	Engineering, manufacturing, and production departments	All functional departments	All functional departments with strong leadership from top management
Parties responsible for ethics development	Security department	Legal, accounting, and human resource departments	All functional departments	All functional departments with strong leadership from top management

Source: Petrick, Joseph A. and Manning, George E. (1993). *Business Forum.* Vol. 18, No. 4, p. 17.

The sources of low-quality performance and unethical conduct are often due to the prevailing organizational climate and are not simply the result of "rotten apples in an organizational barrel." Therefore, the responsible quality strategic planner will address the ethical work culture as an important element of the internal environment. Quality-oriented and ethical people can be compromised by working in a morally underdeveloped organization, just as people with questionable quality commitment and questionable moral integrity can be uplifted or at least prevented from behaving unacceptably by working in a morally developed organization.[28]

Strategy Planning: Strategy Formulation

The second element of traditional strategic planning, strategy formulation, is composed of six divisions that focus the strategic design: the *enterprise vision*, the *gap analysis*, the *mission*, the *objectives*, the *strategies*, and the *policy deployment* focus steps.

The Enterprise Vision

The enterprise vision is the integrative synthesis, the conceptual crystallization, of the future desired result that both legitimizes and energizes stakeholders.[29] The enterprise vision is not achieved through calculating, quantitative, analytic techniques. To borrow one of Mintzberg's concepts, it is an imaginative, intuitive synthesis that evokes the committed response of stakeholders because it gives voice to their most cherished work aspirations.[30]

Although enterprise visions differ, they should provide directional momentum and key value priorities. Five types of enterprise visions are listed in Table 3.3, with the total quality enterprise vision in bold.[31]

The total quality enterprise vision seeks added value for all stakeholders, but assigns the highest strategic priority to customer satisfaction. Clear visualization, articulation, and endorsement of the vision, however, require strategic leaders who are capable of generating ideas. They must also be skilled in involving people at all organizational levels in the creation and exchange of ideas. The iterative process of creating the vision, requesting and considering input, and thereby developing joint commitment and joint ownership has been called "conceptual catchball," as opposed to isolated, unilateral "conceptual hardball."[32]

In the traditional work environment, the creation of the enterprise vision is an often-neglected strategic task. But it is a litmus test for the type of leadership style required in a total quality environment. Some differences between traditional and total quality leadership styles are indicated in Table 3.4.

Table 3.3 Types and Scope of Enterprise Visions and the Total Quality Enterprise Vision (E-vision)

Type of enterprise vision	Scope of enterprise vision
1. Investor E-vision	The corporation should maximize the interests of investors.
2. Managerial Prerogative E-vision	The corporation should maximize the interests of management.
3. Restricted Stakeholder E-vision	The corporation should maximize the interests of a narrow set of stakeholders such as employees, suppliers, or investors.
4. Unrestricted Stakeholder E-vision	The corporation should maximize the interests of all stakeholders.
5. Unrestricted Prioritized Stakeholder E-vision	**The corporation should optimize the interests of all stakeholders, but should prioritize the interests of some, such as customers, employees, suppliers, investors, communities, society, and natural environments, at appropriate levels.**

Table 3.4 Comparison of Traditional and Total Quality Leadership Styles

Traditional leadership style	Total quality leadership style
Commander, boss ("Do what you're told.")	Coach, facilitator, teacher, mentor
Controller—by insistence on rigid compliance ("People need to be controlled.")	Leader—by shared purpose, vision, values, and beliefs; commitment to the purpose and values provides control
Internally competitive	Internally cooperative, externally competitive
Withholding information and communication	Open communication, always explaining why
Owner mentality ("It's my company. You work for me. I pay your salary. Do what you are told.")	Trustee mentality ("I don't own the company; I've been entrusted with it and am responsible for providing an environment in which people can have a fulfilled life.")
Independent individualist	Interdependent team builder
Says employees are the most valuable asset but acts differently	Consistently says and acts as if employees are the most valuable asset
Plays "conceptual hardball"	Plays "conceptual catchball"

A quality council with wide representation (not only senior management) can demonstrate collaborative rather than controlling leadership, provide a vehicle for generating a shared vision, and maintain participative input into strategic decisions. This helps ensure internal and external customer satisfaction. Leaders who encourage this input of quality council members at the highest levels send a message to stakeholders that participatory leadership with a quality focus should be the norm. An example of the development of an integrated strategic quality planning process is presented in Exhibit 3.1. Texas Instruments Defense Systems & Electronics Group, a Baldrige Award Winner, used a top-management quality improvement team, with input from other levels, to increase participation and guide improvement efforts.

The Texas Instruments Defense Systems & Electronics Group (TI-DSEG) is a Dallas-based maker of precision-guided weapons and other advanced defense technology. At TI-DSEG, quality goals and business goals are one and the same. Executives view TQM as the best approach to accomplish any objective—from increasing market share to controlling employee health costs—and teams as the most effective means to execute the company's quality strategy. TI-DSEG began using teams in 1983 and at the time they won the Baldrige (1992), they had 1900 teams in a network linking top management to individual work teams. The network continues to evolve, with the aim of trimming organizational levels and transferring day-to-day decision-making authority to the workers. Self-managed teams have been highly successful in decreasing defects and production time. As a result, the TI-DSEG Quality Improvement Team (QIT), which is made up of 14 top executives, set a 1995 goal of increasing participation on unsupervised teams to at least half the work force.

Chaired by President Hank Hayes, the TI-DSEG QIT initiates and guides strategic quality planning, beginning with setting company-wide long-term goals and ending with final approval of each division's annual objectives and implementation plans. Evaluations of customer needs drive the entire planning process. These draw on an extensive database assembled from information gathered from a variety of sources, including formal surveys, informal interviews and visits to military offices and laboratories, policy statements, contract specifications, and customer-provided requirements documents. Key requirements are translated into improvement goals and progress toward customer satisfaction is tracked. Clear quality requirements are also set for suppliers, since up to half of TI-DSEG may consist of purchased parts.

Exhibit 3.1 Strategy, Quality, and Customer Focus at TI-DSEG (Source: Baldrige National Quality Award: Profiles of Winners, 1988–1993.)

The Gap Analysis

Once the enterprise vision of the desired future is shared and endorsed, the results of the environmental scanning of the current situation permit comparison between what exists and what should exist. The second focus step, gap analysis, includes recognition, acknowledgment, and treatment of the perceived gap between the current reality and the desired future.

If organizations develop their strategic plans by jumping directly to writing their mission statements after performing the environmental scanning step, they bypass the enterprise vision and gap analysis steps and are likely to encounter strategy resistance from two sources: organizational inertia and organizational defensive patterns.[33]

Organizational inertia occurs when people refuse to acknowledge a performance gap (uncovered by gap analysis) and try to rely on the proven ways of doing things. As Hornstein[34] states: "When in doubt, do what you did yesterday. If it isn't working, do it twice as hard, twice as fast, and twice as carefully."

Organizational defensive patterns occur in a wide variety of forms, but they essentially come down to relying on defensive rather than productive reasoning. Defensive reasoning is used to justify faulty thinking that leads to anticipated or actual failure. Productive reasoning, in contrast, openly acknowledges its premises, inferences, and conclusions in order to responsibly resolve problems.[35] Defensive reasoning can be caused by: (1) lack of personal and organizational virtues (honesty, courage, humility), (2) skilled incompetence in handling embarrassing or threatening situations maturely, (3) pervasive organizational defensive routines to bypass responsibility and cover up performance issues, (4) pervasive organizational "fancy footwork" to protect the defensive routines, (5) emergent organizational malaise (hopelessness, cynicism, distancing, and blaming others), and (6) sustained mediocre performance which is acceptable within an overly tolerant organization. These organizational defensive patterns are diagrammed in Figure 3.4.[36]

Organizational defensive routines are policies and actions that prevent individuals or work units from experiencing embarrassment or threat. The strategic performance gap represents such a threat. Predictably, many managers use face-saving devices and denial to cover up performance gaps and protect their organizational image as winners. Identifying, bringing attention to, and effectively handling organizational defensive routine is a major total quality OD responsibility.

After overcoming these obstacles (many organizations never do and remain "stuck" or regress to institutional mediocrity), the successful gap analysis honestly and adequately provokes several responses: (1) a reassessment and reaffirmation of the vision, (2) a reassessment of current external

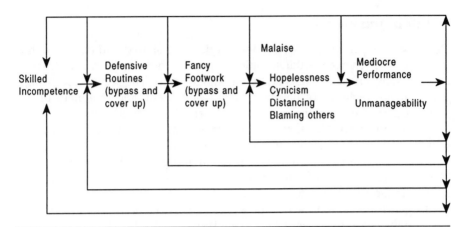

Figure 3.4 Organizational Defensive Patterns to Deny Performance Gaps and to Justify Mediocre Performance (Source: Argyris, C. (1985). *Strategy, Change and Defensive Routines.* Boston: Ballinger, p. 64. Reproduced with permission of the author.)

and internal environments, (3) an assessment of the realistic challenges in bridging the gap between the vision and the current reality, and (4) the development of "trigger themes" that need to be addressed in the mission. Some visions need to be "fleshed out"; others are excessively idealistic or insufficiently motivating and need to be modified. Total quality strategy planners should be aware of the positive dimensions of the tension created by gap awareness. While there is a short-term temptation to "lower the bar," the long-term benefit of "raising the floor" (i.e., adopting challenging performance standards) is preferable to relapsing into mediocrity. If the gap analysis is done properly, it will result in "trigger themes" that the mission will address.

The Mission

The enterprise vision addressed the question "What do we as an organization stand for in the world?" The third focus step, mission, addresses the question "What industry or business are we in and why?" After the vision has determined what is socially worth doing, the mission provides the institutional purpose for the legitimate existence of the firm. The components and corresponding questions that the mission should answer are contained in Table 3.5.[37]

A well-conceived mission statement defines the distinctive purpose which sets an organization apart from others. It identifies the scope of the organization's operations in terms of products/services offered and markets served. Corporations with a unifying set of prioritized values that integrate processes, projects, and people are better able to direct and administer their

Table 3.5 Components and Questions for a Mission Statement

Customers	Who are the enterprise's customers?
Products or services	What are the firm's major products or services?
Markets	Where does the firm compete?
Technology	What is the firm's basic technology?
Concern for survival, growth, and profitability	What is the firm's commitment toward economic objectives?
Philosophy	What are the basic beliefs, values, aspirations, and philosophical priorities of the firm?
Self-concept	What are the firm's major strengths and competitive advantages?
Concern for public image	What is the firm's public image?
Concern for employees	What is the firm's attitude toward employees?
Prioritization of stakeholders	What is the firm's prioritization of stakeholder concerns?

many activities.[38] It is a major challenge to write a mission statement broad enough to facilitate quality growth, yet narrow enough to focus the organization on what it does best.

To develop the sixth component of the mission statement, the philosophy of the organization, an explicit statement of prioritized and shared core values is required.[39] In a total quality organization, service to stakeholders, dedication to continuous improvement, application of scientific tools to system measurement and control, empowerment and respect for people, and personal integrity are core values that form the bases for work community performance. Intense commitment to shared values distinguishes the total quality work community from other workplaces where values are not explicit or are only complied with grudgingly. Total quality organizations are value driven. Their values are created by design and endorsed by participation and consensus, rather than by default.

To meet that challenge, the quality council must provide an open forum to allow diverse individuals and groups to voice their opinions. This will provide valuable input to the council, challenging it to produce a clear and realistic mission statement. The content of the mission statement should factor in the results of the enterprise vision and the gap analysis, clearly prioritizing stakeholder interests for future decision guidance at all levels of the organization. This intense commitment and shared approach to mission and strategic planning and management can be seen in the Zytec case study at the end of the chapter.

Objectives

To fulfill its mission, a total quality organization must complete the fourth step in strategy formulation, stating and achieving its objectives. Objectives

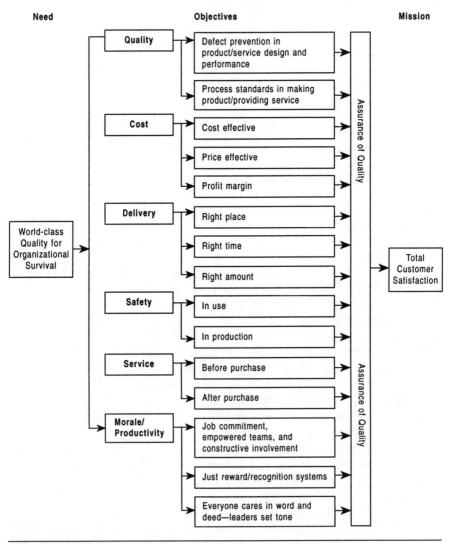

Figure 3.5 Organizational Strategic Objectives of Total Quality

*determine **what** is to be accomplished by **when**, and should be quantified if possible.*[40] In contrast to an objective, a goal is *an open-ended statement of what one wishes to accomplish, with no quantification of what is to be achieved and no time criteria for completion.*[41] Goals for quality firms vary but often include: product quality/service, employee commitment, stakeholder welfare, market share, profitability, growth, research and development, financial stability, and efficiency. It should be noted that Mintzberg[42] criticizes the lack of agreement on definitions and practical uses of both goal and objectives.

The ten major quality objectives to achieve total customer satisfaction are shown in Figure 3.5. Each of these ten objectives will require an individual "champion," a process improvement team, or a committee to monitor progress and/or sustain improvement for each of the areas represented by the objectives.

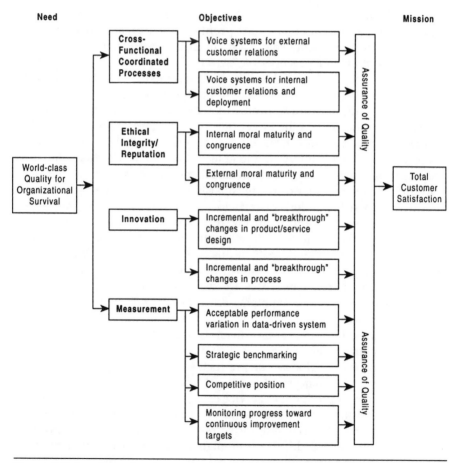

Figure 3.5 (continued) Organizational Strategic Objectives of Total Quality

Normally, the interdependence rooted in the enterprise vision and the mission requires cross-functional attention, by a committee or team, to each of the major objectives that affect total customer satisfaction. The cross-functional *quality* objective focuses on two areas: product/service design and meeting process standards in making products and/or providing services. Quality design dimensions in products (performance, features, reliability, conformance, durability, serviceability, aesthetics, and perceived quality) and quality design dimensions in services (time, timeliness, completeness, courtesy, consistency, accessibility and convenience, accuracy, and responsiveness) were mentioned in Chapter 2. The quality objective is concerned with emphasizing and documenting prevention rather than subsequent inspection and rework in obtaining defect-free performance. Both quality design and quality process standard performance are necessary to monitor in order to ensure total quality.

The aim of the *cost* objective is to ensure the right price for the customer and appropriate market share and profits for the organization. The cost control and improvement "champion" must be positively oriented toward the new theories and practices of "activity-based costing" (ABC). Target costing (a concept compatible with ABC systems) first determines what customers are likely to pay for a new product/service, and this, in turn, drives design, administrative, production, distribution, marketing, and supplier costs down to meet the target figure.[43] Cost targets are developed by subtracting profit margin from the selling price until the desired market share is achieved. It is interesting to note that while the traditional Japanese corporate management style has provided lifetime employment and rewarded seniority, the current glut of white-collar Japanese employees, who are less productive than their blue-collar factory associates, is costing more than many companies can afford during recessionary times.[44] One inevitable result has been the dismissal or "forced retirement" of some inefficient office workers and middle managers.[45] In this case, increasing market share and wealth building through investing in productive resources and reducing inefficient administrative expenses are important aims of the cost objective.

The *delivery* objective maintains schedules by ensuring that the right products/services are delivered to customers at the right times and in the right quantities. Increased responsiveness and flexibility through supply-cycle time reduction is a key international objective.[46]

The *safety* objective focuses on product/service and employee safety and on protection and enhancement of natural/social environment. Legal guidelines pertaining to production/service safety are readily available to safety committees, but the human factors (i.e., employee error, insufficient equipment and/or procedures) that can adversely affect safety need to be properly monitored and addressed.[47] In addition, the potential social/environmental impact of managerial decisions about new products/services requires that a high level of strategic priority be accorded to the safety objective.[48]

The *service* objective is to monitor and ensure continuously improving customer service before and after purchase.[49] External and internal customer perceptions of service can be measured and analyzed continuously to detect and correct undesirable service variations. Multiple teams are needed to focus on this critical objective.

The *morale/productivity* objective addresses the complex relationship between morale and productivity levels.[50] Factors that affect morale and productivity, such as work attitude, job design, group dynamics, team improvement, employee development, and constructive employee involvement in appropriate contexts, should be monitored and addressed.[51] Reward/recognition systems, which balance consistency, competitiveness, contributions, profit/gainsharing, and administration, along with procedural fairness, require the attention of a human resource/OD committee.[52] While changing the way employees are treated may boost productivity more than changing the way they are paid, developing structures to enhance the intrinsic work motivation of employees through team collaboration, meaningful work content, and empowered choice requires human resource/OD committee attention.[53] Finally, managerial leadership practices that demonstrate respectful concern for the welfare of employees, the satisfaction of customers, and the impartial administration of justice, (e.g., avoidance of favoritism), in word and deed, require monitoring and reinforcement.[54]

The *cross-functional coordinated process* (CFCP) objective is to integrate functions by addressing system problems across traditional functional boundaries.[55] Simultaneous engineering, for example, requires coordinated participation in cross-functional processes to ensure that the voices of external and internal customers are heard in a timely and accurate manner. CFCP also ensures that the strategic priority focus has been communicated throughout the organization. Coordinated system flexibility provides competitive advantage. An excellent example of CFPC in pursuit of a difficult strategic objective was demonstrated by the team that redesigned the Ford Taurus (Team Taurus II), profiled in Exhibit 3.2.

The *ethical integrity/reputation* objective is to assess and continually develop an organization that expects, shapes, and supports ethically sound behavior. This strengthens internal customer relationships and builds a solid public reputation for external customer satisfaction and responsible corporate citizenship.[56] While legal compliance of the organizational to all applicable laws and regulations is normally included in this committee's agenda, many corporations are beginning to feel that this approach is less than adequate. In light of the U.S. 1991 Federal Sentencing Guidelines, the intent of the committee must be to promote more responsible conduct within the

The dramatic saga of how "Team Taurus" broke through years of tradition to take a radical approach to the design process in the early 1980s was exciting. For the first time, perhaps with the exception of the Mustang design, Ford approached the Taurus design with the attitude of "delighting" external and internal customers. At the time, the term "delight" had not yet come into general use. The original Taurus was so successful from 1986 until 1995 that Ford was challenged by the question "What do we do for an encore?" The approach that Ford took in redesigning the Taurus for the late 1990s and beyond was equally dramatic, with the extra challenge of an increasing competitive worldwide automotive market.

Richard L. Landgraff was the Ford executive who was named overall project manager for the Taurus redesign. His strategic challenge was to design an American car that truly matched the quality and engineering of its Japanese rivals yet retained its current customer base, while also reaching out to capture part of the market segment of young import buyers to whom the first Taurus had not appealed. This objective, of course, had to be reached "on-time, on cost."

Ford began the design process in 1990 by holding "clinics" with customers and Japanese car owners, looking at nationwide polls by J.D. Power, and conducting its own polls. Team Taurus (II), which consisted of 150 engineers, designers, factory workers, accountants, suppliers, and marketers, was set up in the basement of Ford's Design Center in Dearborn, Michigan. This was the same "Dungeon" that had spawned the original Taurus/Sable design. In the later stages of the design, factory workers were brought into the design center to build 200 prototype cars. They were able to come up with 700 design improvements that would help the car be easier to assemble.

In the quality/cost tradeoff area, some tough decisions had to be made. Engineers wanted each half of the body to be stamped from one piece of steel. This

Exhibit 3.2 Ford's Uneasy Tradeoffs Among Strategy, Design, and Quality Issues (Source: Factual information came from Kerwin, Kathleen, Udike, Edith Hill, and Naughton, Keith (1995). "The Shape of a New Machine." *Business Week.* July 24, pp. 60–66.)

customer chain, rather than just preventing criminal misconduct.[57] Organizational moral maturity reflects the extent of habitual decision making and performance based on principled norms to sustain "organizational character." Over time, organizations of sound character are better able to attract and retain the resources they need to survive and thrive.[58]

The *innovation* objective is to develop and coordinate incremental improvements and innovative "breakthroughs" in products/services, technology, and other processes.[59] To delight customers faster and better than competitors requires cross-functional committee attention to new product development and new service development. A strong TQM organization will pay close attention to the innovation/improvement objective in its strategy.

would make the car stronger, easier to build, and would virtually eliminate customer complaints about unsightly welds, poor door fit, and wind noise. The catch was that a new $90-million, 7000-ton stamping press would have to be purchased. At first, engineers claimed that it could not be purchased in time. This argument proved to be false, but then a skeptical chairman and CEO, Alex Trotman, had to be convinced that the decision was a wise one in the midst of a 1992 cost-cutting campaign. The argument in favor of quality won out over cost.

Meanwhile, the body and interior designers had to deal with the softer issues of aesthetic quality/costs. After 17 exterior design versions and increasingly firm support from the CEO and several Ford family members who were on the board of directors, a radical new design was approved. It featured an oval rear window and a similar contour to taillights, headlights, door handles, and the rear fender. Internally, a special molding process gave the one-piece molded dash a leather-like appearance. Other new exterior and interior features that were added, and would no doubt evoke customer delight, included new or improved V-6 engines that offered a smoother ride; a weld-free, rust-resistant muffler; a versatile central armrest; a slow-release glovebox that would protect passengers' knees; and de-layed power cutoff on standard power windows so that windows could be rolled up after shutting off the engine.

The result was an attractive car with many new features at a base price of $19,150, which provoked the following comment from a Chrysler executive: "I was absolutely flabbergasted by the Taurus price!" For only $2.8 billion (far below the $6.0 billion Ford paid to design the "world-class" Contour), Ford had a design that would compete with comparable models of Honda's Accord and Toyota's Camry in styling, quality, and price. Ford's Trotman said, "Adjusting for the hyperbole you would expect from me anyway, I think it will be sensational."

The *measurement* objective focuses on systematic and continuous quantification and comparison of an organization's products/services and processes against those of global leaders. This is done to gain information which will help the organization continuously improve its performance and enhance its competitive position.[60] The committee monitors use and results of statistical measuring tools to establish improvement targets and to provide precise feedback on current organizational performance and competitive position.

Each of the ten organizational strategic objectives is quantified and assigned time lines (e.g., reduce total manufacturing costs by 20% in five years; improve employee morale survey results by 30% in five years). Priorities that are assigned to objectives depend on mission priorities. They must be clearly communicated throughout the organization.

Critical drivers for prioritizing objectives include: (1) the importance to total customer satisfaction, (2) the opportunity for competitive advantage, and (3) the severity of the areas that have the greatest need for improvement. At times, one of the drivers may assume strategic priority, but a sustained, TQM-focused set of priorities provides the best avenue for coordinated long-term internal effort to achieve objectives.

Strategies

To achieve objectives, the fifth focus step, formulation of strategies must occur. Using the traditional model, strategies are defined as comprehensive master plans that state how an organization will achieve its mission and objectives. They may be divided into grand and generic strategies. Grand strategies refer to an organization's coordinated "macro efforts" to achieve long-term success, whereas generic strategies refer to an organization's "micro efforts" to attain competitive success. Grand strategies may include approaches such as diversification, forward and backward integration, innovation, and joint ventures. For companies in a weak competitive position, market development, turnaround, divestiture of weak products or services, or even liquidation of the firm or a division may be required.

The traditional approach to generic organizational strategies is to divide them into four categories: broad target cost leadership, broad target differentiation, narrow target-focused low cost, or narrow target-focused differentiation.[61] "Broad" and "narrow" targets refer to the competitive scope of business strategies, while "focused" refers to niche segments of quality features (differentiation) or low expenditure (cost leadership). According to Porter, using one of these generic strategies enables a firm to achieve superior competitive position and sustainable competitive advantage, while being "stuck in the middle" (i.e., combining strategies in an industry) lowers performance and may jeopardize survival.

The total quality approach to generic strategies, however, differs from Porter's by advocating the combination of low cost and high quality as a means to integrate generic strategies, as indicated in Figure 3.6.[62]

In quadrant I, the two generic strategies usually recommended for a low-cost, low-differentiation position are cost leadership (broad competitive scope with low expenditure) and/or cost focus (narrow competitive scope with low expenditure).

In quadrant II, combination of cost leadership and differentiation strategies and/or combination of focused cost and focused differentiation strategies is usually recommended by total quality strategists for a low-cost, high-differentiation position. For quality planners, the strategic goal is to simultaneously and continuously lower costs and improve quality, whether a firm is in a broad or narrow competitive arena. Managing external and internal systems by use of statistical process control and empowerment of

Differentiation Positions

		Low			High
C **o** **s** **t**	High	No Competitive Advantage			Differentiation Focused Differentiation
P **o**			IV	III	
s **i**			I	II	
t **i** **o** **n** **s**	Low	Cost Leadership Cost Focus			Focused and Unfocused Cost and Differentiation

Figure 3.6 Total Quality Generic Strategy Selection Matrix (Modified from White, R.E. (1986). "Generic Business Strategies, Organizational Context, and Performance: An Empirical Investigation." *Strategic Management Journal*. Vol. 47, No. 4, p. 226.)

people often results in achieving the best quality and the lowest delivered cost. Inferior input, redesign, scrap, rework, field failures, and customer complaints are eliminated. Superior quality, based on customer feedback and satisfaction, leads to repeat purchases and differentiation in the marketplace. This combination of lowest delivered cost and highest quality usually provides best value to consumers.

In quadrant III, the two generic strategies usually recommended for a high-cost, high-differentiation position are differentiation (broad competitive scope with distinctive features) and focused differentiation (narrow competitive scope with distinctive features).

In quadrant IV, there is no competitive advantage for a firm in a high-cost, low-differentiation position.

The clear, consistent combination of grand and generic strategies helps to integrate an organization's macro and micro efforts and achieve its prioritized objectives. If a firm occupies a generic strategic position at the micro level in quadrant IV, it normally is involved in a grand strategy at the macro level of turnaround, divestiture, and/or liquidation. At a micro level in quadrant III, it normally is engaged in a grand strategy at the macro level of vertical backward integration, vertical forward integration, and/or conglomerate diversification. If a firm's generic position at the micro level is in quadrant II, it is usually engaged in a grand strategy at the macro level of horizontal integration, concentric diversification, joint venture, and/or adaptive innovation. If a firm's generic position at the macro level is in quadrant I, then it normally is involved in a grand strategy of market penetration, market development, product development, and/or indigenous innovation. Congruent, rather than conflicting, grand and generic strategies are most likely to maximize and improve total customer satisfaction.

Policy Deployment[63]

The sixth focus step in strategy formulation is policy deployment, which may be defined as the systematic spreading, integration, and adaptation of organizational resources to support policies.[64] This traditional concept has taken on a major role in the successful development of total quality organizations. After an organization establishes the contours of policy (broad guidelines for decision making throughout the organization), the next step is linking strategy formulation with strategy implementation. This has always been a difficult challenge for corporate executives. Top management requires a method to ensure that its plans and strategies are successfully executed within the organization. This is the equivalent of Mintzberg's inductive/intuitive concept of *strategic programming*. Managers must determine specific responsibility for meeting objectives at lower levels of the organization and provide the resources necessary. The traditional approach to deploying strategy is top-down. With a TQM perspective, subordinates are both customers and suppliers. Therefore, their input is necessary. An iterative process in which senior management asks what lower levels of the organization can do, what they need, and what conflicts may arise can avoid many of the implementation problems that managers typically face. To ensure consistency of direction, quality-focused organizations engage in several deployment processes: catchball analysis; coordination of targets and means; selection/training of functional, cross-functional, process, and project teams; and a technique known as *quality function deployment* (covered in detail as part of strategy implementation in Chapter 7).

The Japanese deploy strategy through a process known as *hoshin kanri*, or *hoshin planning*. In the United States, this is often referred to as *policy deployment*, or *management by planning*. Many companies, most notably Florida Power & Light, Hewlett-Packard, and AT&T, have adopted this process. The literal Japanese translation of *hoshin kanri* is "pointing direction."[65] The idea is to point, or align, the entire organization in a common direction. Florida Power & Light defines policy deployment as "the executive deployment of selected policy driven priorities and the necessary resources to achieve performance breakthroughs." Hewlett-Packard calls it "a process for annual planning and implementation which focuses on areas needing significant improvement." AT&T's definition is "an organization-wide and customer-focused management approach aimed at planning and executing break-through improvements in business performance." Regardless of the particular definition, policy deployment emphasizes organization-wide planning and setting priorities, providing resources to meet objectives, and measuring performance as a basis for improving performance. Policy deployment is essentially a total-quality-based approach to executing a strategy.

Imai provides an example of policy deployment:[66]

> To illustrate the need for policy deployment, let us consider the following case: The president of an airline company proclaims that he believes in safety and that his corporate goal is to make sure that safety is maintained throughout the company. This proclamation is prominently featured in the company's quarterly report and its advertising. Let us further suppose that the department managers also swear a firm belief in safety. The catering manager says he believes in safety. The pilots say they believe in safety. The flight crews say they believe in safety. Everyone in the company practices safety. True? Or might everyone simply be paying lip service to the idea of safety?
>
> On the other hand, if the president states that safety is company policy and works with his division managers to develop a plan for safety that defines their responsibilities, everyone will have a very specific subject to discuss. Safety will become a real concern. For the manager in charge of catering services, safety might mean maintaining the quality of food to avoid customer dissatisfaction or illness.
>
> In that case, how does he ensure that the food is of top quality? What sorts of control points and check points does he establish? How does he ensure that there is no deterioration of food quality in flight? Who checks the temperature of the refrigerators or the condition of the oven while the plane is in the air?
>
> Only when safety is translated into specific actions with specific control and check points established for each employee's job may safety be said to have been truly deployed as a policy. Policy deployment calls for everyone to interpret policy in light of his own responsibilities and for everyone to work out criteria to check his success in carrying out the policy.

With policy deployment, top management is responsible for developing and communicating a vision and then building organization-wide commitment to its achievement.[67] The long-term strategic plan forms the basis for shorter term planning. This vision is deployed through the development and execution of annual objectives and plans. All levels of employees actively participate in generating a strategy and action plans to attain the vision. At each level, progressively more detailed and concrete means to accomplish the objectives are determined. Objectives should be challenging, but people should feel that they are attainable. To this end, middle management negotiates with senior management regarding the objectives that will achieve the strategies and what process changes and resources might be required to achieve the objectives. Middle management then negotiates with the implementation teams the final short-term objectives and the performance measures that are used to indicate progress toward accomplishing the objectives. Measures are specific checkpoints to ensure the effectiveness of individual elements of the strategy. The implementation teams are empowered to manage the actions and schedule their activities. Periodic reviews (monthly or quarterly) track progress and diagnose problems. Management may modify objectives on the basis of these reviews. Top management is responsible for conducting annual reviews to evaluate results as well as the deployment process itself, which serves as a basis for the next planning cycle. One important issue is that top management does not develop action plans; it sets overall guidelines and strategies. Departments and functional units develop specific implementation plans.

The negotiation process is called *catchball*. Catchball analysis is an iterative, two-way communication process designed to actively and openly analyze opportunities and problems in order to assure that they are defined realistically. Managers and employees can enjoy joint commitment and joint ownership of objectives at all organizational levels. Issuing memoranda "from the top" to announce changes in objectives is not the total quality way. Catchball analysis, in effect, is the *plan* step in the PDCA cycle referred to in Chapter 4. For example, top management may state that it wants to have the best quality in the industry for a particular product. For this purpose, it will provide up to $10 million of funding, if needed. This means that achieving the objectives/targets selected by top management becomes the objective/target of middle managers. Middle managers may decide that they must reduce defectives for this product line by 25% in order to meet top management's goal. They decide to use the money that management has provided to improve process capability of equipment and to train line and staff employees in basic and advanced statistical process control techniques. Middle managers, in turn, select the means to achieve their objectives/targets, and these means become the means/targets of lower level managers. The lower level managers must then identify machines and processes to be improved or replaced and must schedule employees for training. Attention to detail and "speaking with facts," rather than blaming and scapegoating, bring focus and alignment to the process of honing strategic objectives and building organizational commitment.

Catchball is an up, down, and sideways communication process as opposed to an autocratic, top-down management style. It marshals the collective expertise of the whole organization and results in realistic objectives that can be achieved and do not conflict. In the spirit of Deming, it focuses on optimizing the system rather than individual goals and objectives. Clearly, this process can only occur in a TQM culture that nourishes open communication. Catchball analysis provides critical concrete data and facts on operational capabilities, key measurement indicators (control points for desired outcomes and checkpoints for process measurement), available support resources, and the list of the causes of problems, by priority. This process is quite different from the traditional "command and control" form of management.

Policy deployment bears some similarity to management by objective (MBO). MBO is "a process by which the superior and subordinate managers of an organization jointly identify its common goals, define each individual's major areas of responsibility in terms of the results expected, and use these measures as guides for operating the unit and assessing the contribution of each of its members."[68] Both approaches are driven by objectives, involve employees, deploy the objectives, emphasize measurement and accountability, and rely on individual participation. However, there are some important differences. First, typical MBO focuses on the management of performance of individual employees rather than improvement of the organization as a whole. Attainment of objectives is closely tied to individual performance evaluation and rewards. This tends to promote actions that optimize the individual's gain, rather than that of the organization. (Think about Deming's philosophy. He was a strong opponent of MBO.) Second, MBO objectives generally do not support the company's vision, but are set independently. MBO usually results in numerous objectives. Activities in policy deployment are aligned with a few critical long-term goals. Third, MBO is primarily used as a means of management control; in practice, most subordinates succumb to their supervisors' wishes. Finally, MBO objectives are often not used in daily work, but are only resurrected during performance reviews, which focus on results. In policy deployment, periodic reviews involve the process as well as results. This is important in identifying and correcting root causes of unsatisfactory results.

The key features of policy deployment are:[69]

- Selected objectives represent the vital few business capabilities that are critical for business competitiveness.
- Annual objectives are tied to the vision and strategic plan.
- Objectives are defined with clear measures at every level of deployment.
- Cross-functional teams are formed to ensure horizontal alignment.
- Bottom-up, top-down negotiations (catchball) are conducted throughout the planning process until all levels reach agreement.
- Decision making is based on facts and data.
- Each level of the management hierarchy is responsible for some project or program that will contribute to one or more objectives.

- Each team participates in regular reviews and diagnosis, using the same language and format.
- Objectives are broken down and deployed in such a way that all employees can see how their individual efforts are aligned with the organizational objectives.

Many different MBO approaches exist in the United States, so one must be cautious in issuing a blanket condemnation. Many small organizations that have good internal communication have used MBO successfully.

TOTAL QUALITY BUSINESS STRATEGY MANAGEMENT

Strategy implementation is where the strategic plan is translated to those who must act on it. This has been one of the most difficult parts of the planning process, as we will see. Some of the total quality approaches for strategy deployment hold the promise of overcoming this historic hurdle and are beginning to prove themselves.

Strategy Management: Strategy Implementation

The first element of the strategy management foundation is strategy implementation. Henry Mintzberg's intuitive/inductive view of strategy implementation contains some valuable insights on how strategic management may evolve and be practiced in "the organization of the future." We will briefly examine his view, but will then develop our own concept of total quality strategy implementation that is built on the rational/analytic concept. We believe that changes in strategic management will tend to be emergent, whether evolutionary or revolutionary, in most organizations.

The Intuitive/Inductive Approach to Strategy Implementation

The intuitive/inductive approach to total quality strategy differs from the rational/analytic approach in its emphasis on the importance of implementation over formulation.

To rethink the way that grand strategy is developed using the intuitive/inductive approach, Mintzberg says that:

> Instead of the formulation-implementation dichotomy so long promoted in the prescriptive literature, we believe that the strategy making process is better characterized as a process of learning—formation in the place of formulation, if you like. People act in order to think, and they think in order to act. The two proceed

in tandem, like two feet walking, eventually converging in viable patterns of behavior. [70]

This approach is not contrary to the concepts of most broad-based total quality advocates. The Deming Wheel, in fact, incorporates continuous learning when it advocates the repeated use of the Plan-Do-Study-Act cycle at every level.

Mintzberg's call to reconsider the role of "professional" planners includes the assumption that analysis, the "stock in trade" of planners, has its place, but that intuition is essential to dealing with the complexities of strategic thinking and strategy making. Thus, Mintzberg argues that strategy formation requires "coupling analysis and intuition."[71]

To determine how managers and planners should be involved in the planning process, Mintzberg redefines the process of formal planning essentially as implementation planning. He states that: "Organizations engage in formal planning, not to create strategies but to program the strategies they already have, that is to elaborate and operationalize their consequences formally." Thus, strategic programming, as he calls it, consists of (1) codifying the strategy, (2) elaborating the strategy, and (3) converting the elaborated strategy.[72] He suggests that managers (and others in the organization) develop the vision and strategic concept of where the organization is heading, and the planners translate (codify, elaborate, and convert) that vision into plans which are then monitored and carried out by operating level people in the organization. He also states that there are three possible roles for planners, all of which are advisory to manager-strategists, who must make the final decisions about what strategy to follow. The planners' roles are: (1) finders of strategy, (2) analysts, and (3) catalysts.

Once again, Mintzberg's concept of the planner can be seen as a "type" or model for the appropriate role of the OD practitioner who has a TQM focus. The OD practitioner is generally an internal or external consultant who must advise the manager-strategist. Manager-strategists need to personally lead the development of a vision for organizational change and revitalization, but they need the assistance of OD planners to assist in (1) finding an appropriate change strategy, and/or (2) analyzing an OD strategy that is under consideration, and/or (3) acting as a catalyst to promote the use of OD and to assist managers in its successful use.

Mintzberg has developed a well-known framework for seven basic types of organizational structures including the entrepreneurial, the machine, the diversified, the professional, the innovative, the ideological/missionary, and the political organizations.[73] Entrepreneurial organizations are small, young organizations led by one or a few owner-managers, with a strong vision of the business and where it needs to grow. Machine organizations generally are relatively mature, larger organizations with highly developed, functional line-staff or divisional organization structure. Diversified organizations generally are organized around semi-autonomous market-based divisions or subsidiary corporations. Professional organizations are often (not always) partnership organizations in the private sector or collegially structured organizations in the public sector. Innovative organizations are highly decentralized, use project management and teams built around the skills of their employees, and depend on constant output of creative products or services to compete in rapidly changing market niches. Missionary organizations may either be public or private organizations that are strongly focused on one or a few values, often articulated by a charismatic founder-leader. Political organizations are based on power and are organized around loose coalitions to attain goals. Examples of each type, respectively, are Ben and Jerry's Homemade Ice Cream Company, the Internal Revenue Service, General Electric, Ernst and Young Consultants (or virtually any university, hospital, or law firm), Microsoft Corporation, the Girl Scouts of America, and the Democratic Party. Based on these organizational forms, Mintzberg argues that there are, indeed *must be*, contingency approaches to strategy formation. He indicates that the traditional strategic planning model is most applicable to the highly structured, often inflexible, machine or diversified forms of organization, such as GE and General Motors, whose environments change relatively slowly. It is least appropriate for innovative organizations, such as Microsoft, which have difficulty making structured plans and must be constantly innovative or risk failure.

Hamel and Prahalad warn of the dangers of seeing strategic planning and OD as consisting of the two current "hot topics": restructuring and reengineering. They point out the while downsizing and process reengineering are important tasks, they merely shore up current businesses, while ignoring the vital task of creating tomorrow's businesses. If a business does not pay attention to creating core competencies and future products and services, it will be forced to run faster and faster, chasing improvements to declining products and seeing margins and profits erode.[74]

To consider how implementation of strategy for various types of organizations takes place in the face of uncertainty of strategic direction, in the absence of future plans, Mintzberg suggests that two types of planners are needed within organizations: "right-brained," creative types and "left-brained" analytical types. Tying this to the need for developing a TQM approach to strategy implementation suggests that different kinds of planners are necessary for implementing and renewing TQM within various types of organizations. Relating this to the work of OD practitioners suggests a need for "right-brained" and "left-brained" OD consultants to do the work of organizational transformation.

To fall back on a more systematic frame of reference, we now return to the development of a TQM model for strategy implementation. We will assume, of course, that the target organization is operating in a somewhat stable environment, thus permitting systematic and sustained efforts at strategy development, process improvement, and integration of operations in order to implement the proposed strategy. We must remain constantly aware of the fact that strategic planning that is overly structured, routine, and "cut and dried" can prevent top managers from developing and exercising strategic vision.

Total Quality Strategy Implementation

Total quality strategy implementation is the operational system by which strategies and policies are put into action through customer focus, process integration, project involvement, and individual performance integration. The goal of customer focus is, of course, customer satisfaction. The goals of process integration, project involvement, and completion of individual activity are, respectively, continuous improvement, speaking with facts, and respect for people (including self-respect). These three goals constitute the remaining three pillars of the House of Total Quality. Since each will be given detailed treatment in later chapters, only a preliminary overview is offered here. Note, however, that in total quality organizations, there is a stronger emphasis on strategy implementation and feedback than in most traditional organizations.

Process Integration and Quality Function Deployment

Process integration is the identification, coordination, measurement, and systematic development of linked organizational activities. A *process* is any set of linked activities that take an input and transform it to create an output.[75] Processes can be physical, involve paperwork, occur within computers, or simply be a logical or standard operational sequence of events. The resulting flow of products, information, and other "deliverables" from their processes is the focus of efforts to continuously improve organizational performance. Structuring ongoing programs and projects around processes that correspond to core organizational objectives strongly aligns strategy formulation and implementation. A new way of visualizing organizations is to see them as a collection of interrelated processes, rather than as compilations of functions.

Process integration is driven by three different improvement goals: internal incremental cost reduction, external competitive renewal, or external breakthrough dominance.[76] Simple process integration with a cost-reduction focus on noncore processes (i.e., the Japanese term is *kaizen*) can lead to incremental advantages over time.[77] Process integration that is more comprehensive focuses on external competitive renewal to accomplish either parity or "best in class" objectives for the company.[78] This effort requires process improvement and integration to match or exceed the processes of those who have set the competitive standards and made the rules in the past. Finally, external breakthrough dominance can only be attained by using reengineering or other breakthrough methods. It requires organization change agents (such as OD practitioners) to rewrite the rules and create a new definition of best in class for all others to achieve in the future.[79] The extensiveness of the process often parallels the improvement goal. Managers must determine which of these goals apply when setting strategic priorities. Ideally, objectives should be set for process improvements at every level. However, not all companies are able or willing to invest in external breakthrough dominance. The cross-functional coordinated process (CFCP) committee and the innovation committee must collaborate to determine the appropriate direction of efforts.

To manage process integration, a variety of process assessment and improvement tools are available. Some of the key process integration management tools that competent strategy implementers need to master are: process mapping, data modeling, flowcharts, cause-and-effect diagrams, Pareto charts, scatter diagrams, histograms, run charts, and control charts. They are treated in detail in Chapter 4.

Process integration should result in clear ongoing program designations, cross-functional coordination for system flexibility, realistic budget estimates, and feedback to strategy formulators about the process capacities of the firm. Process integration clarifies system dynamics and prepares the way for team projects.

Quality function deployment (QFD), mentioned earlier, can help managers focus on designing, streamlining, and measuring processes in order to create more customer value with less effort, rather than focusing on reducing the size of functions in order to simply cut costs.[80] It represents a new way to link planning with doing at the implementation stage of strategic management. QFD is a philosophy and set of planning tools that focuses on customer requirements in coordinating the design, manufacture, and marketing of goods and services. QFD permits translation of "the voice of the customer" into technical requirements that allow the product or service to have the features that the customer desires. For example, if the customer wants a shampoo that leaves his or her hair manageable but neither dry nor sticky, how will the chemist know what ingredients are required? QFD makes the connection between the customer characteristics and the chemical and physical properties of a blend of esters, hydrocarbons, and other ingredients that must go through numerous processes before the finished product stage.

A major benefit of QFD is to improve communication between various functional areas that historically were only "loosely linked" in the design process. This includes market researchers and product designers; design engineers, manufacturing engineers, and hourly shopfloor employees; and purchasing agents and suppliers. Many of the automotive firms have become heavy users of QFD. The process that Ford used to design and redesign the

Taurus (see Exhibit 3.2) was a QFD type of process. Cadillac, the only automobile company to win the Baldrige Award, used QFD to plan and design its 1992 model. Other U.S. companies that are using QFD include Motorola, Xerox, Kodak, IBM, Procter and Gamble, Hewlett-Packard, and AT&T. A more detailed discussion of the QFD technique and how it was applied at Florida Power & Light is given in Chapter 7.

Project Involvement

The second step in quality strategy implementation is project involvement. While process integration deals with the design of the stream of linked activities, project involvement focuses on the single process, set of processes, or definable problem within the work flow. *Projects* are normally regarded as single, nonrecurring events that implement organizational changes through structured phases and specified outcomes and which require teamwork for successful completion.[81] Projects are forms of nonroutine implementation work required to meet new challenges posed by complex changes in today's environment. Routine or repetitive implementation work is best addressed through ongoing programs, standardized processes, and uniform procedures. *Project involvement* is the team assessment and resolution of single, nonrecurring problems, or process design opportunities, through the development of employee involvement.[82]

The relationship of project leaders to functional and executive leaders often determines the success of project initiatives. Sometimes the project originator is either a functional or executive leader, and formal authority and informal influence are joined in project involvement. Generally, however, there are different project and functional structures, which requires strong influencing skills from the project leader. Studies have shown that traditional executives in companies developing new products tend to favor the *functional* matrix structure. Project managers are given limited authority, while functional managers retain responsibility and authority for their specific segments of the project.[83] On the other hand, in companies developing new processes or services, project managers prefer the *project* matrix structure, which grants them primary responsibility and authority for project completion, while functional managers provide personnel and technical expertise as needed.[84]

Quality unit or project teams usually occur in three forms: steering committee team, problem-solving teams, and self-managed teams.[85] They are fully discussed in Chapter 5, but it is important to note that project teams come in various forms. They are needed to enhance the multifunctional, objective, factual implementation of strategy. They must also be part of the integrated processes of the organization and use prioritized objectives as guides. In addition, project management teams need to master project scheduling, work breakdown, operational estimation, progress monitoring, and control tools to monitor and control project work. By developing the capability to use quality management tools, such as affinity diagrams, interrelationship digraphs, tree diagrams, matrix diagrams, prioritization matrices, process decision program charts, and arrow diagrams, team leaders can provide organizational stakeholders with the reliable factual bases for effective strategy implementation, OD, and accurate feedback.[86] These tools are also examined in Chapter 5.

Performance Integration

The third step in quality strategy implementation is performance integration. *Performance integration* is the daily implementation of continuous improvement in personal task and relational activity within an employee's own scope of responsibility.[87] Performance integration occurs at the intrapersonal and interpersonal levels. At the intrapersonal level, it requires individuals to demonstrate both task and relational skills in job performance. It is not enough to be technically competent but rudely uncommunicative in a total quality firm. At the interpersonal level, performance integration requires respectful and sincere relations between persons so that commitment to constantly improving the process rather than mere compliance with system rules and demands occurs in daily activities. The organization's motivational system must be support high individual and group performance, but it must also nurture each person's self-respect and work pride, which grow with competent performance in meeting unit and company quality objectives. In turn, respect for other people who are committed to excellent performance will build and team project involvement will escalate.

Strategy implementation, therefore, requires process, project, and personal coordinated activities. Personal performance integration is enhanced through the use of two tools: performance planning by using Voehl's five-step Personal Improvement Process and performance management by using Roberts and Sergesketter's Personal TQM practices. The former tool outlines a personal mission planning and implementation process using a total quality focus. The latter tool permits individual improvement objects to be set, uses basic quality tools for detailed measurements, provides for self-analysis to detect the causes of the problem, charts the results of corrective actions, and offers numerous opportunities for individual process improvement. These tools will be expanded on in Chapter 6.

Strategy Management: Evaluation and Control

Total quality evaluation and control is the strategic stage in which organizational activities are monitored so that alignment of actual results can be compared with planned results. *Results alignment* is the process of measuring and comparing organizational and societal results to determine the extent to which formulated and implemented strategies are adequate or in need of corrective intervention, as indicated in Figure 3.7.[88]

Organizational results include both enroute results, such as products or services, and *outputs*, the finished products of the system that are delivered or deliverable to society. External societal results include *outcomes*, the effects of outputs in and for society and the community. Evaluation and control systems measure and determine the strength of the "results chain" that extends from organizational inputs and processes to organizational and societal consequences. Without results alignment, organizations could get better and better at doing what should not be done at all, thereby missing the main objective—to meet customer needs.

Regular process reviews and audits ensure that quality strategy remains focused on priority objectives, reduces duplication of effort, limits nonvalue-added activities, and streamlines work processes.

For quality evaluation and control to be effective, however, managers must obtain clear, prompt, and unbiased feedback on an ongoing basis from all sectors of the strategic planning and management system, as indicated previously in Figure 3.2. The ongoing feedback, detailed progress reviews, process indicator measurements, and audit reports warrant continual attention by organizational leadership in order to attain strategic success.

TOTAL QUALITY ORGANIZATION DEVELOPMENT STRATEGY

In total quality OD strategy development, the primary role of the OD practitioner is to be a "change agent," or catalyst, in the process of interpreting organizational vision and improving the organization. The overall objective is to enhance organizational system performance. A constant source of frustration for OD change agents is that they can never "make things happen," except when actually leading a group of OD practitioners in their immediate work processes. Thus, we should briefly look at who the OD practitioners at the upper levels of organizations may be and how they may influence the decision makers to actually make the recommended strategic changes happen.

Who Are the Top-Level Organization Development Practitioners?

Top-level OD practitioners are successful only if they are capable of exerting influence. OD is primarily focused on "breakthrough" types of change. A successful top-level OD practitioner acts as a consultant to influence top-level

	Inputs (raw material)	Processes (how to do it)	Products (enroute result)	Outputs (the aggregated products of the system that are delivered or deliverable to society)	Outcomes (the effects of outputs in and for society and the community)
Examples	Existing human resources; existing needs, goals, objectives, regulations, laws, money, values, societal & community characteristics; current quality of life; natural resources	Means, methods, procedures; searching for "excellence," teaching; learning; human resource development, training, managing	Course completed; competency test passed; competency acquired; learner accomplishments; instructor accomplishments; production quota met; the performance "building blocks"	Delivered automobiles, sold computer systems; program completed; job placements; certified licenses	Safety of outputs; profit; dividends declared; continued funding of agency; self-sufficient, self-reliant, productive individual; socially competent and effective, contributing to self and to others; no addictive relationship to others or to substances; financial independence
Scope	Internal (Organization)			External (Societal)	
Cluster	Organizational Efforts		Organizational Results		Societal Results/Impact

Figure 3.7 Organizational Efforts and Results Model (Source: Reprinted from Kaufman, Roger (1988). "Preparing Useful Performance Indicators." *Training and Development Journal.* Vol. 10, No. 4, p. 81. Copyright ©1988 by the American Society for Training and Development. Reprinted with permission. All rights reserved.)

decision makers to implement "organizational breakthroughs," such as starting a TQM "journey" or making significant organizational changes in their part of the organization. This does not necessarily mean that the OD practitioner can do the work of planning for organizational change and then step out of the picture. Change must be facilitated at every level and is generally a long-term process. As we will see in later chapters, it involves use of TQM tools and techniques, project management, and understanding and application of change management at the organizational, team, and individual levels as well. This suggests that OD practitioners may come to the top-level decision makers from several different directions. They may be external consultants, internal high-level staff, or even lower level line or staff.

External consultants often have "instant credibility" because they have worked in and with many organizations, usually have had in-depth training in the process and background of TQM or OD problems, cost lots of money, and come from far away. As such, they often have access to top managers that others inside the organization do not have. They also frequently have superior training in how to sell their ideas. There are many success stories involving outside consultants in the quality literature. Donald Petersen at Ford Motor Company brought in W. Edwards Deming as his quality "guru." At Xerox, David Kearns became aware of the company's quality problems through internal means, but brought in David Nadler[89] to help guide the process of organizational change that was necessary for turnaround. Even in relatively healthy organizations, such as Johnsonville Foods,[90] owner and CEO Ralph Stayer had a "vision" of empowering the employees in his firm, but he brought in James Belasco as a "sounding board" and change agent to help him implement the process. The danger is that outside consultants will have difficulty knowing (or sometimes obtaining information) about internal processes, history, norms, and cultural factors that may be critical to actually implementing organizational change processes. Thus they may conduct their study, apply their "canned solution," deliver a stellar plan, collect their fee, and fly out on the next plane, leaving the organization to cope with the problems of implementation.

Internal consultants may be of a "formal" or "informal" variety. Formal internal OD consultants may be part of the human resources organization or may have their own OD organization. In very large firms, there may even be a vice president of OD. Formal OD practitioners have been given the "stamp of approval" by top managers and have the additional advantage of being "insiders." Thus, in contrast to outside consultants, they may be permitted to have full access to people at every level of the organization without fear that they will discover trade secrets and take their knowledge to the next organization. However, this can also be a hindrance if line managers and employees do not trust the OD insider and fear that he or she will reveal their hidden problems to top management. Gary E. Jusela,[91] the corporate manager for OD at Boeing Corporation, described a large-scale strategic planning process which he facilitated in the 27,000-person Boeing Aerospace and Electronics Division, beginning in 1989. By bringing together managers from different levels in a phased approach over a concentrated time period, consensus was reached on mission, goals, and objectives, where previously there had been misunderstanding and mistrust. There was a TQM emphasis as managers used the Malcolm Baldrige Quality Award criteria as a framework for establishing objectives and benchmarked planning processes from Ford Motor Company, Motorola, and Hewlett-Packard. Various organization leaders and stakeholders were surveyed after the process had been established and checked out. They reported increased teamwork across functional boundaries and with suppliers and customers, accelerated implementation of systems and programs, and a broader understanding of the needs of customers, as well as extensive understanding of the goals and objectives at all levels within the organization.

The concept of lower level organizational consultants is typically seen as impossible, or perhaps dysfunctional, in the traditional machine (bureaucratic) organization. Although Ford Motor Company is now gaining a reputation for enlightened organization development and design, this was not always the case. A review of the history of the company under the autocratic management of Henry Ford in the 1930s and 1940s shows how the founder depended upon his personal confidant, Harry Bennett,[92] for advice or "organization development." Traub noted:

> Henry never turned to Edsel [his son, and president of the company in the 1930s] for support and advice. Instead he began to look to a man named Harry Bennett for comfort. Ford liked Bennett because, unlike Edsel, he was a yes-man and a bully, a thug who knew nothing about cars but did know how to please his boss: by simply never questioning him.

This type of idiosyncratic, power-dominated organizational advising may still occur in closely held firms. However, a more functional type of lower level organizational consultant is beginning to appear as a result of empowerment of employees, enlightened management, and movement toward a TQM focus. For example, in April 1989, the Air Force Logistics Command[93] issued a document entitled "Quality Bill of Rights," which was designed to empower employees at every level to make quality a top priority. At the Sacramento Air Logistics Center, Wayne Hayes, a F-15 repair line mechanic, was not satisfied with the fit of a cap for the vertical stabilizer that came as part of a repair kit. The base commander sustained the employee's challenge, resulting in a nine-day shutdown of the repair line during a critical workload period. Hayes helped to redesign the part so that it could be easily fitted as the repair was done, thus saving rework costs and resulting in a better product for customers. This example shows that even lower level employees can be powerful "change agents" who can influence the development and implementation of organizational designs and processes.

TOTAL QUALITY ORGANIZATION DEVELOPMENT STRATEGY PLANNING

Total quality OD strategy planning is also reciprocally interdependent with business strategy planning. This insight is probably the most important contribution of the quality orientation to OD practitioners. Organization design input, interventions at implementation and evaluation stages, and application of total quality processes to the OD unit performance are ways that enhance the strategic role of OD and distinguish total quality OD programs from traditional ones. The role of implementation is so significant that the identity of total quality OD units is shaped by the statement: "We implement fully, therefore we are." Traditional OD programs, on the other hand, often follow the Cartesian statement: "We think (design OD policies), therefore we are." OD strategy planning that is not immediately followed by OD strategy management will likely result in a flashy launch of a quality initiative without the concrete follow-up that is critical to the success of the quality OD approach.

Total quality organizations require a different design than traditional hierarchies in order to be effective. In general, they organize around processes, not tasks, flatten hierarchies, use teams to manage everything, let customer satisfaction drive output, reward team results, maximize supplier and customer contact, and inform and train all employees. The interdependence of organization design and OD strategy management, as well as the dramatic differences between total quality company/OD configurations and others, are indicated in Table 3.6.[94]

The three types of organization structures (pyramid, delayered restructured pyramid, and networks/alliances) indicate corporate strategic priorities and require integrated OD strategy implementation for success. The last alternative approximates the ideal total quality organization structure. Therefore, it requires different OD strategy management activities than the traditional pyramid-based OD approaches. OD practitioners who want total quality to have a strategic impact must be willing to engage in organization redesign at the implementation stage.

Juran[95] warns top managers that they must be involved in performing certain types of strategic activities *themselves*, as opposed to delegating them to subordinates. He says that upper managers must develop and implement an *action plan*. Development of the plan requires:

- Provide personal leadership through membership on the quality council
- Adopt the "Big Q" concept

Table 3.6 Organization Design and Organization Development
Strategy Implementation

Organization structure	Strategic priorities	OD strategy implementation
Pyramid	• Command and control	• Hierarchical, specified career paths • Specific, detailed job descriptions • Pay supports, merit promotions, and commitment • Training is job specific • Information in hands of top managers
Delayered restructured pyramid	• Remove layers • Enrich jobs • Team focus • Empower employees	• Limited career paths, horizontal promotions • Share career responsibility with employee • Generic job descriptions • Pay emphasizes individual and team performance • Training emphasizes generalist and flexibility • Information shared with teams on need-to-know basis
Networks/ alliances	• Recreate boundaries to suppliers and customers • De-emphasize functional specialties • Emphasize customers • Teams as basic building blocks	• Careers primarily individual responsibility • Generic job descriptions • Training options at individual discretion • Pay emphasizes individual knowledge and team performance

Source: Adapted from Milkovich, G.T. and Boudreau, J.W. (1994). *Human Resource Management*, 7th edition. Burr Ridge, IL: Irwin, p. 122.

- Train managers and specialists, at all levels, in how to plan for quality
- Put quality goals into the strategic plan
- Replan selected existing processes and products
- Mandate participation in quality planning by those impacted
- Mandate the use of structured quality planning to replace empiricism

To implement the plan he suggests:

- Deploy the strategic quality goals to lower levels in the hierarchy so as to identify clearly the projects to be carried out and the resources needed

- Provide the resources
- Assign clear responsibility for carrying out these projects (such assignments are usually made to teams)
- Revise the reward system to reflect the new priorities given to quality and to include new responsibilities of helping the teams to complete their projects
- Establish measures of progress, and then review progress regularly
- Mandate participation in quality planning by those impacted
- Mandate the use of structured quality planning to replace empiricism

TOTAL QUALITY ORGANIZATION DEVELOPMENT STRATEGY MANAGEMENT

Total quality OD strategy managers, especially those who have the "ear" of top line, staff, and human resource management executives, must be willing to engage in the *shaping, introduction, maintenance,* and *review* of total quality initiatives.[96]

Total quality OD strategy managers *shape* TQM by being actively involved in the following activities:

1. Networking and synthesizing reports from other organizations that have experience in TQM, in conjunction with the management team
2. Assisting with choices about which TQM approach to adopt and, in particular, helping to identify which, if any, internal and external consultants may be able to offer appropriate advice
3. Shaping the type of organizational structure, culture, and ethical climate appropriate for introducing and sustaining TQM
4. Designing and delivering senior management development courses that set the proper tone for TQM

Total quality OD strategy managers *facilitate the introduction and adoption* of TQM by being actively involved in the following activities:

1. Designing communication events and vehicles to publicize the launch of TQM and early successes and consulting with employees about the introduction and development of TQM
2. Promoting and supporting the norm of training all formal leaders (including union officers) in the principles of TQM, advising them of the best means of developing a process of continuous improvement within their areas of influence, encouraging them to persuade everyone to take personal responsibility for their own quality assurance, and being prepared to seek improvements
3. Providing guidance on what is necessary for the successful employment of teams that focus on quality improvement and how these fit into the organizational structure

4. When required, being available to train and coach facilitators, mentors, and team members in interpersonal skills and how to manage the improvement process, and institutionalizing organizational ethics development programs

Next, total quality OD strategy managers *maintain and reinforce* TQM within the organization by being actively involved in the following activities:

1. Encouraging human resource managers to adopt selection processes that target and screen for conceptual, technical, ethical, and social skills that support a TQM environment
2. Recommending to top managers and human resource directors that training in quality management tools, techniques, and processes continues to be provided within the organization and that the knowledge imparted in such training is being used in the workplace
3. Recommending and assisting in redesigning appraisal procedures so that they contain criteria relating to specific TQM objectives, appropriate social relations skills, and support personal responsibility, self-assessment, and 360° performance feedback
4. Promoting special newsletters or team briefs on TQM and improvement initiatives and the successful outcome of quality improvement team projects

Finally, total quality OD strategy managers *review* TQM implementation progress by being actively involved in the following activities:

1. Assessing the effectiveness of the TQM infrastructure, including steering committees, quality councils, quality improvement teams, improvement facilitators, project teams, and individual performance
2. Benchmarking the effectiveness of the organization's TQM with that of competitors and global best practices
3. Facilitating the operation of internal quality and ethics reviews using criteria such as ISO 9000, the Malcolm Baldrige National Quality Award, the Deming Prize, or an ethics audit
4. Identifying organizational strengths and weaknesses and assisting in the design and implementation of action plans to address improvement issues within specific time lines

Total quality OD strategic management would not be complete if OD practitioners do not *review their own activities* as they do all other areas. Some of the more typical self-review total quality activities include:

1. Undertaking a department mission analysis of OD's functional contribution to the organization. This could include the following:
   • Identifying internal customers and suppliers
   • Agreeing to performance measures as part of service-level agreements

- Tracking such measurements
- Identifying nonvalue-added activities
- Taking part in cross-functional project teams to resolve interface problems with customers and suppliers

2. Selecting new OD employees with peer and customer involvement
3. Appraising and rewarding OD staff for teamwork, ethical integrity, and customer satisfaction
4. Training and developing OD employees on a regular basis
5. Surveying and distributing the results of OD staff satisfaction and ethical climate surveys
6. Providing advice on quality and ethical problem analysis and conflict resolution within a specified and agreed-upon time period
7. Benchmarking OD policies and processes with world-class models

In summary, total quality OD strategic management expands the strategic responsibilities of OD practitioners and challenges them to change from "professional whiners" (because they are excluded from strategy input) into "total quality winners" as part of the strategy team.

ENDNOTES

1. May, Rollo (1969). *Love and Will*. New York: W.W. Norton, pp. 30–40.
2. See Horovitz, J. and Panak, M.J. (1994). *Total Customer Satisfaction*. Burr Ridge, IL: Irwin; Barsky, Jonathan D. (1994). *World-Class Customer Satisfaction*. Burr Ridge, IL: Irwin; Whiteley, Richard C. (1991). *The Customer-Driven Company*. Reading, MA: Addison-Wesley.
3. There are at least five approaches to strategic planning and management: (1) the *rational/analytic* approach relies on a conscious, top-down, linear flowchart model (Pearce, John A. II and Robinson, Richard B. Jr. (1994). *Strategic Management*, 5th edition. Burr Ridge, IL: Irwin; Thompson, Arthur A. Jr. and Strickland, A. III (1993). *Strategic Management*, 6th edition. Homewood, IL: Irwin; Wheelen, Thomas L. and Hunger, J. David (1992). *Strategic Management and Business Policy*, 4th edition. Reading, MA: Addison-Wesley); (2) the *intuitive/inductive* approach emphasizes a more imaginative, empirical, incrementally emergent bottom-up model (Quinn, J.B., Mintzberg, Henry, and James, R.M. (1988). *The Strategy Process*. Englewood Cliffs, NJ: Prentice-Hall); (3) the *political/behavioral* approach emphasizes the power and influence factors in strategic decision making (Cyert, R.M. and March, J.G. (1963). *A Behavioral Theory of the Firm*. Englewood Cliffs, NJ: Prentice-Hall); (4) the *customer value* approach relies on detailed market opportunity analysis that emphasizes a customer-driven rather than competition-driven model (Bounds, G., York, L., Adams, A., and Ranney, G. (1994). *Beyond Total Quality Management*. New York: McGraw-Hill); and (5) the *unconscious/drift* approach focuses on individual and/or collective unconscious factors that lead to strategy utilization (Kets de Vries, M.F. and Miller, D. (1984). *The Neurotic Organization*. San Francisco: Jossey-Bass; Mitroff, I. (1983). "Archetypal Social

System Analysis: On the Deeper Structure of Human Systems." *Academy of Management Review*. Vol. 9, No. 2, pp. 207–224). The authors' approach is a creative hybrid version of these five approaches.

4. Mintzberg, Henry (1994). *The Rise and Fall of Strategic Planning*. New York: Free Press.

5. Quinn, J.B. (1980). *Strategies for Change: Logical Incrementalism*. Homewood, IL: Irwin.

6. Drucker, Peter F. (1974). *Management: Tasks, Responsibilities, Practices*. New York: Harper and Row.

7. Mintzberg, Henry (1994). "The Fall and Rise of Strategic Planning." *Harvard Business Review*. Vol. 72, No. 1, pp. 107–114.

8. Ibid., pp. 107–109.

9. Ibid., pp. 46–49.

10. This model is adapted from Wheelen and Hunger (endnote 3), p. x.

11. Willig, J.T., Ed. (1994). *Environmental TQM*, 2nd edition. New York: McGraw-Hill; Shrivastava, P. (1996). *The Greening of Business*. Cincinnati, OH: Thomsen Executive Press.

12. Bounds G.M. and Dobbins, G. (1993). "Changing the Managerial Agenda." *Journal of General Management*. Vol. 8, No. 3. pp. 77–93.

13. Bounds et al. (endnote 3), p. 182.

14. Tenner, Arthur R. and DeToro, Irving J. (1992). *Total Quality Management: Three Steps to Continuous Improvement*. Reading, MA: Addison-Wesley, p. 197.

15. Juran, J.M. (1989). *Juran on Leadership for Quality: An Executive Handbook*. New York: MacMillan.

16. Frederickson, J.W. (1986). "The Strategic Decision Process and Organizational Structure." *Academy of Management Review*. April, pp. 280–297. See also Miller, D. (1986). "Configurations of Strategy and Structure: Towards a Synthesis." *Strategic Management Journal*. May–June, pp. 233–249.

17. Primozic, K., Primozic, E., and Leben, J. (1991). *Strategic Choices*. New York: McGraw-Hill, pp. 83–108.

18. Hofstede, Geert (1991). *Cultures and Organizations*. New York: McGraw-Hill.

19. Lorsch, J. (1985). "Strategic Myopia: Culture as an Invisible Barrier to Change." In R.H. Kilmann, M.J. Saxton, and R. Serpa, Eds. *Gaining Control of the Corporate Culture*. San Francisco: Jossey-Bass, pp. 84–102. See also Petrick, Joseph A. and Wagley, Robert A. (1992). "Enhancing the Responsible Strategic Management of Organizations." *Journal of Management Development*. Vol. 11, No. 4, pp. 57–72.

20. Olian, Judy D. and Rynes, Sara L. (1991). "Making Total Quality Work: Aligning Organizational Processes, Performance Measures, and Stakeholders." *Human Resource Management*. Vol. 30, No. 3, pp. 303–333.

21. Stalk, G. Jr. and Hart, T.M. (1990). *Competing Against Time: How Time-Based Competition Is Reshaping Global Markets*. New York: Free Press.

22. Johnson, T.S. and Kaplan, R.S. (1987). *Relevance Lost*. Cambridge, MA: Harvard Business School.

23. Sakurai, M. (1992). "Target Costing and How to Use It." In B.J. Bunker, Ed. *Emerging Practices in Cost Management*. Boston: Warren, Gorham and Lamont, pp. 65–72.

24. Olian and Rynes (endnote 20), p. 319.

25. Cooper, R. and Kaplan, R. (1991). *The Design of Cost Management Systems: Text, Cases and Readings.* New York: Prentice-Hall.
26. Petrick, Joseph A. and Wagley, Robert A. (1992). "Enhancing the Responsible Strategic Management of Organizations." *Journal of Management Development.* Vol. 11, No. 4, pp. 57–72. See also Paine, Lynn Sharp (1994). "Managing for Organizational Integrity." *Harvard Business Review.* Vol. 72, No. 2, pp. 106–117.
27. Petrick, Joseph A. and Manning, George E. (1993). "Paradigm Shifts in Quality Management and Ethics Development." *Business Forum.* Vol. 18, No. 4, p. 17.
28. Driscoll, D., Hoffman, W.M., and Petry, E. (1995). *The Ethical Edge.* New York: Mastermedia.
29. Anthony, W., Maddox, T., and Wheatley, M. (1988). *Envisionary Management.* New Haven, CT: Greenwood Press, pp. 10–15.
30. Mintzberg (endnote 7), pp. 107–115.
31. Modified from Freeman, R. Edward and Gilbert, Daniel R. Jr. (1988). *Corporate Strategy and the Search for Ethics.* Englewood Cliffs, NJ: Prentice-Hall, pp. 72–73. See also Ansoff, H. Igor (1984). *Implanting Strategic Management.* Englewood Cliffs, NJ: Prentice-Hall, pp. 129–151.
32. Collins, Brendan and Huge, Ernest (1993). *Management for Policy: How Companies Focus Their Total Quality Efforts to Achieve Competitive Advantage.* Milwaukee: ASQC Quality Press, pp. 83–84.
33. Argyris, Chris (1990). *Overcoming Organizational Defenses: Facilitating Organizational Learning.* Boston: Allyn and Bacon, pp. 5–25.
34. Hornstein, Harvey (1986). *Managerial Courage.* New York: John Wiley, pp. 18–19.
35. Argyris, Chris (1985). *Strategy, Change and Defensive Routines.* Boston: Ballenger, pp. 6–40.
36. Argyris, Chris (endnote 33), p. 64.
37. Modified from David, Fred R. (1989). *Concepts of Strategic Management,* 2nd edition. Columbus, OH: Merrill Publishing, pp. 104–105.
38. Ansoff, H.I. (1988). *The New Corporate Strategy.* New York: John Wiley and Sons, pp. 75–77; Snyder, N.H., Dowd, J.J. Jr., and Houghton, D.M. (1994). *Vision, Values and Courage.* New York: Free Press, pp. 153–204.
39. Wheelen and Hunger (endnote 3), p. 15.
40. Richards, M.D. (1987). *Setting Strategic Goals and Objectives,* 2nd edition. St. Paul, MN: West Publishing, p. 12.
41. Ibid., p. 18.
42. Mintzberg (endnote 4), pp. 52–54, 192–195.
43. Sakurai, M. (endnote 23), pp. 66–68.
44. Schlender, Brenton R. (1994). "Japan's White-Collar Blues." *Fortune.* Vol. 129, No. 6, pp. 97–104.
45. Ibid., p. 98.
46. Northey, Patrick (1993). *Cycle Time Management: The Fast Track to Time-Based Production.* Portland, OR: Productivity Press, pp. 5–85; Stalk, George and Hout, Thomas (1990). *Competing Against Time: How Time-Based Competition Is Reshaping Global Markets.* New York: Free Press, pp. 10–70.
47. Scherer, Robert F., Brodzinski, James D., and Crable, Elaine A. (1993). "Human Factors in Workplace Accidents." *HR Magazine.* Vol. 21, No. 4, pp. 92–97.
48. Buchholz, Roger A. (1993). *Principles of Environmental Management.* Englewood Cliffs, NJ: Prentice-Hall, pp. 15–35.

49. Albrecht, Karl and Zemke, Ronald E. (1985). *Service America*. Homewood, IL: Dow Jones-Irwin, pp. 10–24; Band, William A. (1991). *Creating Value for Customers*. New York: John Wiley and Sons, pp. 14–40.

50. Lindsay, William M., Manning, George E., and Petrick, Joseph A. (1992). "Work Morale in the 1990's." *SAM Advanced Management Journal*. Vol. 57, No. 31, pp. 43–48; Petrick, Joseph A. and Manning, George E. (1990). "How to Manage Morale." *The Personnel Journal*. Vol. 69, No. 10, pp. 82–88.

51. Lawler, Edward E. (1994). "Total Quality Management and Employee Involvement: Are They Compatible?" *The Academy of Management Executive*. Vol. 8, No. 1, pp. 68–76; Lawler, E.E. (1992). *Employee Involvement and Total Quality Management*. San Francisco: Jossey-Bass, pp. 14–74; Katzenbach, Jon R. and Smith, Douglas K. (1993). *The Wisdom of Teams: Creating the High-Performance Organization*. Boston: Harvard Business School Press, pp. 212–293; Scholtes, Peter (1988). *The Team Handbook*. Madison, WI: Joiner Associates, pp. 5–44.

52. Milkovich, George T. and Newman, Jerry M. (1992). *Compensation*, 4th edition. Homewood, IL: Irwin, pp. 2–30; McCaffery, Robert M. (1988). *Employee Benefit Programs: A Total Compensation Perspective*. Boston: PWS-Kent, pp. 14–37; Lawler, E.E. (1990). *Strategic Pay: Aligning Organizational Strategies and Pay Systems*. San Francisco: Jossey-Bass, pp. 25–60; Sheppard, Blair H., Lewicki, Roy J., and Minton, John W. (1992). *Organizational Justice: The Search for Fairness in the Workplace*. New York: Lexington Books, pp. 109–138.

53. Blinder, Alan S., Ed. (1990). *Paying for Productivity: A Look at the Evidence*. Washington, DC: Brookings Institution, pp. 5–60; Kohn, Alfie (1993). *Punished by Rewards*. Boston: Houghton Mifflin, pp. 179–198.

54. Yukl, Gary (1994). *Leadership in Organizations*, 3rd edition. Englewood Cliffs, NJ: Prentice-Hall, pp. 252–462; Cohen, Allan R. and Bradford, David L. (1990). *Influence without Authority*. New York: John Wiley and Sons, pp. 1–25; Block, Peter (1992). *Stewardship: Choosing Service Over Self-Interest*. San Francisco: Berrett-Koehler, pp. 2–23.

55. Ishikawa, K. and Lu, D. (1985). *What Is Total Quality Control? The Japanese Way*. Englewood Cliffs, NJ: Prentice-Hall, pp. 40–60; Hammer, M. and Champy, J. (1993). *Reengineering the Corporation*. New York: Harper Collins, pp. 5–49; GOAL/QPC Research Committee (1991). *Cross-Functional Management*. Methuen, MA: GOAL/QPC, pp. 1–15; Akao, Yoji, Ed. (1991). *Hoshin Kanri: Policy Deployment for Successful TQM*. Cambridge, MA: Productivity Press, pp. 10–70; Withey, M.J. and Cooper, W.H. (1989). "Predicting Exit, Voice, Loyalty and Neglect." *Administrative Science Quarterly*. Vol. 34, No. 11, pp. 521–539.

56. Petrick, Joseph A. and Manning, George E. (1990). "Developing an Ethical Climate for Excellence." *The Journal for Quality and Participation*. Vol. 14, No. 2, pp. 84–90; Paine (endnote 26), pp. 106–117; Cohen, Deborah Vidaver (1993). "Creating and Maintaining Ethical Work Climates." *Business Ethics Quarterly*. Vol. 3, No. 4, pp. 343–358.

57. Sigler, Jay A. and Murphy, Joseph E. (1988). *Interactive Corporate Compliance: An Alternative to Regulatory Compulsion*. New York: Quorum Books, pp. 169–199; Fiorelli, Paul E. (1992). "Fine Reductions Through Effective Ethics Programs." *Albany Law Review*. Vol. 56, No. 2, pp. 403–440; Paine (endnote 26), p. 113.

58. Petrick and Manning (endnote 56), p. 88; Wilkins, A.L. (1989). *Developing Corporate Character*. San Francisco: Jossey-Bass, pp. 10–60; Weber, James (1993). "Institutionalizing Ethics into Business Organizations." *Business Ethics Quarterly*. Vol. 3, No. 4, pp. 419–436.

59. Imai, Masaaki (1986). *Kaizen: The Key to Japan's Competitive Success*. New York: Random House, pp. 15–66; Foster, Richard (1986). *Innovation: The Attacker's Advantage*. New York: Summit Books, pp. 165–285; Hammer and Champy (endnote 55), pp. 148–214. Utterback, James M. (1994). *Mastering the Dynamics of Innovation*. Boston: Harvard Business School; Main, Jeremy (1994). *Quality Wars: The Triumphs and Defeats of American Business*. New York: Free Press; Boulton, William R. (1993). *Resource Guide for Management of Innovation and Technology*. Auburn, AL: AACSB and Auburn University.

60. Watson, Gregory H. (1993). *Strategic Benchmarking*. New York: John Wiley and Sons; Camp, Robert C. (1989). *Benchmarking: The Search for Industry Best Practices That Lead to Superior Performance*. Milwaukee: Quality Press/American Society for Quality Control, pp. 25–75; Liebfried, K.H. and McNair, C.J. (1992). *Benchmarking: A Tool for Continuous Improvement*. New York: HarperCollins, pp. 40–77.

61. Porter, Michael (1980). *Competitive Strategy*. New York: Free Press, pp. 40–45.

62. Reitsperger, Wolf D., Daniel, Shirley J., Tallman, Stephen B., and Chisman, William G. (1993). "Product Quality and Cost Leadership: Compatible Strategies?" *Management International Review*. Vol. 33, No. 5, pp. 7–22; Porter, M.E. (1985). *Competitive Advantage: Creating and Sustaining Superior Performance*. New York: Free Press, pp. 80–95.

63. Portions of this section were adapted from Evans, James R. and Lindsay, William M. (1996). *The Management and Control of Quality*, 3rd edition. St. Paul: West Publishing.

64. Sheridan, Bruce M. (1993). *Policy Deployment: The TQM Approach to Long-Range Planning*. Milwaukee: ASQC Quality Press, pp. 25–35.

65. King, Bob (1989). *Hoshin Planning: The Developmental Approach*. Methuen, MA: GOAL/QPC.

66. Imai, M. (1986). *Kaizen: The Key to Japan's Competitive Success*. New York: McGraw-Hill, pp. 144–145.

67. The Ernst & Young Quality Improvement Consulting Group (1990). *Total Quality: An Executive's Guide for the 1990s*. Homewood, IL: Dow Jones-Irwin.

68. Odiorne, G. (1979). *MBO: A System of Managerial Leadership for the '80s*. Belmont, CA: David S. Lake Publishers.

69. AT&T Quality Steering Committee (1992). *Policy Deployment*. Indianapolis: AT&T Bell Laboratories, p. 10.

70. Mintzberg (endnote 4), p. 286.

71. Mintzberg (endnote 4), p. 324.

72. Mintzberg (endnote 4), p. 336.

73. Mintzberg, Henry (1989). *Mintzberg on Management: Inside Our Strange World of Organizations*. New York: Free Press, pp. 10–90.

74. Hamel, Gary and Prahalad, P.K. (1994). *Competing for the Future*. Boston: Harvard Business School Press, p. 5.

75. Johansson, Henry J., McHugh, Patrick, Pendleburg, A. John, and Wheeler, William A. III (1993). *Business Process Reengineering*. New York: John Wiley and Sons, pp. 210–212.

76. Ibid., pp. 61–65.

77. Imai, Massaki (1986). *Kaizen: The Key to Japan's Competitive Success*. New York: Random House, pp. 12–32.

78. Watson, Gregory H. (1992). *The Benchmarking Workbook: Adapting Best Practices for Performance Improvement*. Cambridge, MA: Productivity Press, pp. 15–25; Balm, Gerald J. (1992). *Benchmarking: A Practitioner's Guide for Becoming and Staying Best of the Best*. Schaumberg, IL: Quality and Productivity Management Association, pp. 6–18.

79. Hammer and Champy (endnote 55), pp. 31–65; Moody, Patricia E. (1993). *Breakthrough Partnering*. Essex Junction, VT: Oliver Wight, pp. 3–33; Wallace, Thomas F. and Barnard, William (1994). *Quantum Leap: Achieving Strategic Breakthroughs with QFD*. Essex Junction, VT: Oliver Wight, pp. 25–60.

80. Akai, Yoji, Ed. (1990). *Quality Function Deployment*. Cambridge, MA: Productivity Press.

81. Leavitt, Jeffrey S. and Nunn, Philip C. (1994). *Total Quality Through Project Management*. New York: McGraw-Hill, pp. 47–50.

82. Lawler (endnote 51), pp. 68–76; Lawler, E.E., Mohrman, S.A., and Ledford, G.E. (1992). *Employee Involvement and Total Quality Management: Practices and Results in Fortune 1000 Companies*. San Francisco: Jossey-Bass. Evidence from their research supports the view that the most effective organizations are those that have integrated or coordinated TQM and employee involvement programs.

83. Gobeli, D.H. and Larson, E.W. (1987). "Relative Effectiveness of Different Project Structures." *Project Management Journal*. Vol. 18, No. 2, pp. 82–83.

84. McCollum, J.K. and Sherman, J.D. (1993). "The Matrix Structure: Bane or Benefit to High Tech Organizations?" *Project Management Journal*. Vol. 23, No. 2, pp. 44–46.

85. Cameron, K. and Freeman, S. (1991). "Cultural Congruence, Strength and Type: Relationships to Effectiveness." *Research in Organization Development*. Vol. 5, pp. 23–58; Katzenbach, Jon R. and Smith, Douglas K. (1993). *The Wisdom of Teams*. New York: Harper Business, pp. 27–84; Wellins, Richard S., Byham, William C., and Wilson, Jeanne M. (1991). *Empowered Teams: Creating Self-Directed Work Groups That Improve Quality*. San Francisco: Jossey-Bass, pp. 10–90.

86. Leavitt and Nunn (endnote 81), pp. 50–53; Klein, Ralph L. and Ludin, I.S. (1992). *The People Side of Project Management*. Brookfield, VT: Gower Publishing.

87. Roberts, Harry V. and Sergesketter, Bernard F. (1993). *Quality Is Personal: A Foundation for Total Quality Management*. New York: Free Press, pp. 1–27; Schultz, Louis (1991). *Personal Management: A System for Individual Performance*. Minneapolis: Process Management International.

88. Kaufman, Roger (1988). "Preparing Useful Performance Indicators." *Training and Development Journal*. Vol. 10, No. 4, pp. 80–83; Stone, D.L. and Eddy, E.R. (1996). "A Model of Individual and Organizational Factors Affecting Quality-Related Outcomes." *Journal of Quality Management*. Vol. 1, No. 1, pp. 21–48.

89. Kearns, David and Nadler, David (1992). *Prophets in the Dark: How Xerox Reinvented Itself and Beat Back the Japanese*. New York: HarperCollins.

90. Belasco, James A. and Stayer, Ralph C. (1993). *Flight of the Buffalo: Soaring to Excellence, Learning to Let Employees Lead*. New York: Warner Books.

91. Jusela, Gary E. "Meeting the Global Competitive Challenge: Building Systems that Learn on a Large Scale." Cited in Wendell L. French, Cecil H. Bell, Jr., and Robert A. Zawacki (1994). *Organization Development and Transformation: Managing Effective Change*, 4th edition. Burr Ridge, IL: Irwin, pp. 378–391.

92. Traub, Eric (1991). *Taurus: The Making of the Car that Saved Ford*. New York: Dutton/Penguin Books, p. 29.

93. Air Force Logistics Command (1991). *Application for the President's Award for Quality and Productivity Improvement, 1991*. Dayton, OH: Wright Patterson AFB, p. 44.

94. Adapted to fit OD responsibilities from Milkovich, George T. and Boudreau, John W. (1994). *Human Resource Management*, 7th edition. Burr Ridge, IL: Irwin, p. 122.

95. Juran, J.M. (1992). *Juran on Quality by Design: The New Steps for Planning Quality into Goods and Services*. New York: Free Press, pp. 496–497.

96. Adapted to fit OD responsibilities from Dale, B.G. and Cooper, C.L. (1992). *Total Quality and Human Resources*. London: Blackwell, pp. 10–60; Wilkinson, A., Marchington, M., and Dale, B. (1993). "Enhancing the Contribution of the Human Resource Function to Quality Improvement." *Quality Management Journal*. Vol. 1, No. 1, pp. 42–44.

ABSTRACTS

ABSTRACT 3.1
MEETING WHICH CUSTOMERS' NEEDS?

Linden, Russell
The Public Manager, The New Bureaucrat, Winter 1992–1993, pp. 49–52

This article examines the TQM emphasis on customer satisfaction. It defines and describes four major dilemmas in dealing with customers and offers suggestions for solving these dilemmas.

The first problem examined is defining the customer. This is easy for, say, shoe salesmen, but gets more complicated for public services. "If you manage a group home for the retarded for a local government, who is your customer? The resident? The resident's parents? Or the government officials that grant funds for the program? Each has a claim to being the customer and each would have somewhat different needs." The article offers the "3 Cs approach" to segment customers into three groups: (1) clients (who pays for the services?), (2) consumers (who uses the services?), and (3) constituents (who has a vested interest in the service's work?). Segmenting customers in this manner gives public managers a structure to weigh competing demands and assign priorities.

The second problem examined is determining unarticulated customer needs. Customers often have difficulty articulating their needs, and some customer needs are not even recognized until a new product or service remedies them. As Deming says, nobody asked Edison to invent the light bulb. How then do we determine the customer's need for something that has not been requested? One role of the agency's representative is to probe, to go beyond the stated request and determine underlying needs. It is also often appropriate to shape consumer needs and expectations. We do this by pointing out the available options, describing the consequences of each, recommending options, and explaining the tradeoffs involved (i.e., high speed may mean higher prices). The key in shaping expectations is to help customers, to make them more self-sufficient and less dependent on your company.

The third problem examined is what happens when the customer is not right, when needs expressed are inappropriate, unethical, or counter to the public interest (e.g., a request to stop construction of public housing by neighbors who don't like the people moving in). Here, we should remember what the mission and priorities, or even the code of ethics, are in our agency, determine which of the various interests take priority, and then look for a creative way to ethically meet the request. If the request is unethical or counter to the agency's purpose, we should refuse it with no apologies. If the refusal is due to an outdated company policy, we should look into changing the rule. Whatever the answer, we must make sure we follow through to enact the final promise.

The final problem examined is customers with complementary or conflicting needs—customer one wants less of A and more of B, and customer two wants more B and more A. The article suggests negotiations between conflicting customers to try to find a common ground. Failing that, the article suggests using the "3 Cs" model to establish priority groups and studying the interests and preferences of clients and consumers to determine a compromise.

ABSTRACT 3.2
RIGHTSIZING, NOT DOWNSIZING

Messmer, Max
Industry Week, August 3, 1992, pp. 23–24

This article argues against downsizing in a slow economy. To achieve top quality using the TQM approach, company work forces must demonstrate efficiency, productivity, and contentment with the work at hand. These qualities are very hard to achieve when employees' jobs are in danger of termination. In addition, the downsizing company may be damaging itself, excusing skilled workers who may be needed but unavailable when the economy picks up again. The article explores the alternative of "rightsizing," which entails analyzing a department's personnel needs based on its long-term objectives and those of the overall company—and finding a combination of permanent and temporary employees with the best skills to meet those needs.

In the last decade, the pool of available talent has grown among temporary assignment workers. Interim work provides flexibility and family time for two-career couples, as well as a chance to "sample" companies with which the temporary worker might wish to seek permanent employment. The field of temporary personnel includes everyone from account managers to doctors and lawyers. In addition, companies are more likely today to use temporary workers for specialized positions.

There are several critical steps involved in "rightsizing." The first step is a careful investigation of the day-to-day duties and responsibilities in every function of each and every job department. The article suggests investigating and identifying simple and complex functions and giving simple tasks to less experienced workers and more complex tasks to more highly trained people.

The article states that departments with fluctuating workloads, chronic overtime, and high turnover or heavy absenteeism are ideal rightsizing targets. These departments may have seasonal workloads, for instance, or highly repetitive or boring tasks. Temporary workers are a healthy choice here, since they are retained only when needed.

After analysis of the corporate staffing needs, projections of personnel levels can be quickly and accurately assembled. Budgets and other planning activities can then be pursued. Companies should also consider intangible actions to further enhance quality delivered by employees, such as performance-based pay and employee involvement and responsibility programs.

CASE STUDY

MALCOLM BALDRIGE NATIONAL QUALITY AWARD—ZYTEC CORPORATION: 1991 AWARD WINNER*

From its beginning in 1984, Zytec Corporation fixed its sights on quality, service, and value. By continuously improving these product and service attributes and working to establish a close partnership with customers, the Minnesota firm has risen to the top tier of the hundreds of manufacturers of power supplies for electronic equipment.

Organizing its quality improvement efforts around the concepts of W. Edwards Deming, Zytec has achieved double-digit annual growth in productivity over the last three years. New revenues increased severalfold since 1984, making Zytec the fifth largest U.S. manufacturer of AC to DC power supplies. Sales per employee approached $100,000, as compared with an industry average of only $80,000. Underlying these gains, since 1988, were a 50% improvement in manufacturing yields, a 26% reduction in manufacturing cycle time, a 50% reduction in the design cycle, and a 30 to 40% decrease in product costs—savings that are passed on to customers.

Building on these accomplishments and using the Baldrige Award principles, Zytec began to realign its continuous improvement system, invest in computer-integrated manufacturing technology, and further employee training, all with the aim of advancing to a new threshold of quality performance—six sigma quality in most facets of its operations by 1995.

ZYTEC: A SNAPSHOT

Formerly a unit of Magnetic Peripherals, Inc., a joint venture subsidiary of four electronics firms, Zytec makes power supplies for original equipment manufacturers of computers as well as electronic office, medical, and testing equipment. Sales of the customized power supplies account for 90% of revenues. Zytec also repairs cathode-ray tube monitors and power supplies, including those of its manufacturing competitors. The company is headquartered in Eden Prairie,

Taken from Malcolm Baldrige National Quality Award: Profiles of Winners, 1988–1993. NIST, Department of Commerce.

Minnesota, about 154 kilometers (96 miles) from its manufacturing and repair facilities, which employ 654 of its 748 workers.

When it began operating independently in 1984 following a leveraged buyout, Zytec depended almost entirely on orders from one of its former owners, which now accounts for less than 1.5% of revenues. In 1990, product sales to 20 customers—18 of which have made Zytec a sole-source supplier—totaled $50 million. The repair business, the largest of its kind in the United States, generated $5.8 million in additional revenues.

"TOTAL QUALITY COMMITMENT"

As the foundation for continuous improvement, Zytec senior executives chose Deming's 14 Points for managing productivity and quality. Followed by many Japanese firms, the concepts defined the core values of quality improvement that executives sought to instill throughout the organization. Progress in achieving this cultural transformation is monitored through an annual survey of employees—one of several methods for assessing the quality commitment and the satisfaction of workers.

To foster a common quality focus and to ensure that all 33 of its departments move in step to meet ever more demanding customer requirements, Zytec has adopted an interactive "Management by Planning" process that involves employees in setting long-term and annual improvement goals.

At an annual two-day meeting, about 150 employees, representing all types of personnel, shifts, and departments, review and critique five-year plans prepared by six cross-functional teams. Zytec executives then finalize the long-term strategic plan and set broad corporate objectives to guide quality planning in the departments, where teams develop annual goals to support each corporate objective. In face-to-face meetings with teams or representatives, Zytec CEO Ronald D. Schmidt first reviews departmental goals and, subsequently, action plans, including performance measures and monthly progress targets.

Concurrent with the internal process, the company invites selected customers and suppliers to scrutinize the long-range plan, leading to further refinement. Through these and other steps in the iterative planning process, Zytec helps ensure that it is setting the right goals and following up with the most appropriate actions, supported by adequate resources.

Coordination and integration also are hallmarks of the way Zytec carries out its plans. Design and development of new products, for example, are carried out by interdepartmental teams, which are assigned to projects from start to finish. Working closely with customers, the same cross-functional management teams review performance at four key stages: predesign initiation, prototype delivery and testing, and preproduction certification. The teams are empowered to address all issues of suppliers and processes, including critical parameters for measurement and control.

Zytec is a data-driven company, developing meaningful, measurable criteria for evaluating performance at all levels. In addition, benchmarking competitors' products and services as well as the practices of acknowledged quality leaders in other industries provides Zytec with a clear picture of what it takes to achieve industry- or world-best status in key areas, from employee involvement to just-in-time manufacturing to supplier management.

To realize the full advantage of its employees, Zytec trains them in analytical and problem-solving methods—a major focus of the 72 hours of quality-related instruction received by most Zytec employees. Workers are expected to use this knowledge as their authority and responsibilities grow.

Several departments are directed by self-managed teams of workers. Zytec's production workers are encouraged to improve their knowledge and flexibility through an innovative employee and evaluation reward system called MFE—Multi-Functional Employee program. Through MFE, employees are rewarded for the number of job skills that they acquire.

By aligning all elements of quality improvement—human, technological, and informational—with customer priorities, Zytec has made the most significant performance gains in the areas that count the most. Product quality, as derived from customer-supplied data on failures, has risen to the four sigma range, putting it on track for six sigma quality by 1995. Since 1988, the mean time between failure of a Zytec power supply has increased to over 1,000,000 hours as measured by actual field data and reliability testing, and from 1989 to 1990, the company's on-time delivery rate improved from 85 to 96%.

QUESTIONS FOR DISCUSSION

1 How does Zytec perform its strategic planning process? Would you say that it is more of a rational/analytic or intuitive/inductive approach? Why?
2 How does Zytec use teams to achieve both strategic and operational goals and objectives?
3 Do you think that Zytec has effectively achieved *results alignment* with its strategic and operational management systems as described in the case?

EXERCISE

EXERCISE 3.1 PRACTITIONER ASSESSMENT INSTRUMENT: ORGANIZATIONAL QUALITY AND SUSTAINABLE PRODUCTIVITY ASSESSMENT

Use the following scale to indicate your answers to the statements below.

1	2	3	4	5	6
Strongly disagree	Disagree	Somewhat disagree	Somewhat agree	Agree	Strongly agree

There are no right or wrong answers. Write the number (1, 2, 3, 4, 5, or 6) that best indicates the extent of your agreement with the statement.

1. People are aware of the top priority accorded quality strategy. _____

2. People in the organization are aware of how their jobs contribute to the organization's quality mission. _____

3. Meeting and exceeding customer expectations is accorded a higher strategic priority than short-term financial gain. _____

4. People in the organization try to plan ahead for changes (such as customer expectations) that might impact the organization's future performance. _____

5. People in the organization try to plan ahead for technological changes (such as new developments in computer software) that might impact the organization's future performance. _____

6. People in the organization regularly work together to plan for the future. _____

7. Creativity is actively encouraged in the organization. _____

8. Innovators are the people who get ahead in the organization. _____

9. The quality of work produced is the primary focus of the organization. _____

10. People in the organization see the continuing improvement of work produced as essential to the success of the organization. _____

11. The organization emphasizes doing things right the first time. _____

12. People in the organization live up to high ethical standards. _____

13. The organization has an ethics development system in place. _____

14. People in the organization are used to fair treatment at work. _____

15. Leader(s) in the organization ask people about ways to improve the work produced. _____

16. Leader(s) in the organization encourage people to voice their concerns. _____

17. Leader(s) in the organization follow up on suggestions for improvement. _____

18. Leader(s) in the organization set examples of quality performance in their day-to-day activities. _____

19. Leader(s) in the organization regularly review the organization's progress toward meeting its goals and objectives. _____

20. Leader(s) in the organization attempt to find out why the organization may not be meeting a particular goal or objective. _____

21. People in the work unit turn to their supervisors for advice about how to improve their work. _____

22 People in the work unit know that their supervisors will help them find answers to problems they may be having. _____

23. People in the work unit are challenged by their supervisors to find ways to improve the system. _____

24. Supervisors in the work unit provide guidance to make the continuous improvement of the work produced top priority. _____

25. Supervisors in the work unit regularly ask the customers about the quality of work they receive. _____

26. Supervisors encourage people in the work unit to share their opinions and ideas about work improvement. _____

27. The structure of the organization makes it easy to focus on improving processes. _____

28. People know how the processes in their work unit fit in with the processes of other work units. _____

29. People in the work unit can describe the organization's quality and sustainable productivity policies. _____

30. People in the work unit know how to define the quality of work they produce. _____

31. People in the work unit take pride in their work and rarely demonstrate cynical attitudes. _____

32. People in the work unit share responsibility for the success or failure of the work produced. _____

33. People in the work unit believe that their work is important to the success of the organization. _____

34 There are good working relationships between work units in the organization. _____

35. Rapid feedback reduces the cycle time for improvement in all parts of the system. _____

36. The organization has good working relationships with other organizations. _____

37. People in the work unit encourage each other to work as a team. _____

38. People in the work unit hold each other accountable for work produced. _____

39. The work unit has few bureaucratic barriers to getting the job done properly. _____

40. Work expectations for the work unit are fair. _____

41. People in the work unit are committed to producing high-quality work. _____

42. People in the work unit demonstrate cooperative behavior. _____

43. People in the work unit treat each other fairly and respectfully. _____

44. The right tools, equipment, and material are available in the work unit to get the job done. _____

45. The distribution of work among the people in the work unit is well balanced. _____

46. There is ample time for people in the work unit to perform jobs in a professional manner. _____

47. The pay scale is fair for people in the work unit. _____

48. The reward/recognition policies contribute to a stable quality system with widespread satisfaction. _____

49. People in the work unit receive promotions because they earn them. _____

50. There is quick recognition of people in the work unit for outstanding performance. _____

51. The organization rewards the people in the work unit for working together. _____

52. People in the organization know who their internal and external customers are. _____

53. People in the organization care about meeting or exceeding their customers' expectations. _____

54. In general, all customers know that the organization cares about what they think. _____

55. The organization's customers are asked for their opinions about the work (services, products) they receive from the organization. _____

56. Effective communication channels exist within and between work units in the organization. _____

57. People in the work unit are involved in decision making and listen to what others have to say. _____

58. The facts and information needed to do a good job are available to the people in the work unit. _____

59. Key processes in the organization are regularly measured and qualified. _____

60. Key processes in the work unit are regularly measured and qualified. _____

61. Key processes in the organization are regularly benchmarked and undergo quality auditing. _____

62. Key processes in the work unit are regularly benchmarked and undergo quality auditing. _____

63. People in the work unit are delighted with their supervisor. _____

64. People in the work unit are delighted with other persons in their work group. _____

65. People in the work unit are delighted with their jobs. _____

66. People in the organization experience moderate stress (rather than feeling overstressed or understressed) in meeting workload responsibilities. _____

67. People in the organization are encouraged to experience a healthy balance between work and life obligations. _____

68. In this organization, the natural environmental impact of strategic decisions is regarded as important. _____

69. Sustainable development rather than unmanaged growth or stagnation is typical of this organization's approach to nature. _____

70. There are numerous "greening" (i.e., recycling) policies and practices in this organization to promote ecological sustainability. _____

71. I know the amount of work I produce is within the approved/expected range of variation for anyone in my position. _____

72. I know the quality of work I produce is within the approved/expected range of variation for anyone in my position. _____

73. I know the efficiency of my work habits is within the approved/expected range of variation for anyone in my position. _____

74. My work unit peers know the amount of work our unit produces is within the approved/expected range of variation for any comparable work unit. _____

75. My work unit peers know the quality of work our unit produces is within the approved/expected range of variation for any comparable work unit. _____

76. My work unit peers know the efficiency of their work habits is within the approved/expected range of variation for any comparable work unit. _____

SCORING: ORGANIZATIONAL QUALITY AND SUSTAINABLE PRODUCTIVITY ASSESSMENT

In all cases, carry out division to two decimal places.

Add response numbers from **questions 1–3** and divide by 3. Enter total in last line.
Awareness of Quality Strategy _____ ÷ 3 = _____

Add response numbers from **questions 4–6** and divide by 3. Enter total in last line.
Future Enterprise Vision _____ ÷ 3 = _____

Add response numbers from **questions 7 and 8** and divide by 2. Enter total in last line.
Innovation _____ ÷ 2 = _____

Add response numbers from **questions 9–11** and divide by 3. Enter total in last line.
Quality Policy/Guidance _____ ÷ 3 = _____

Add response numbers from **questions 12–14** and divide by 3. Enter total in last line.
Ethical Work Culture _____ ÷ 3 = _____

Add response numbers from **questions 15–17** and divide by 3. Enter total in last line.
Leader's Quality Involvement _____ ÷ 3 = _____

Add response numbers from **questions 18–20** and divide by 3. Enter total in last line.
Leader's Visible Commitment to Quality Goals _____ ÷ 3 = _____

Add response numbers from **questions 21–23** and divide by 3. Enter total in last line.
Supervisor's Supportive Role in Quality Improvement _____ ÷ 3 = _____

Add response numbers from **questions 24–26** and divide by 3. Enter total in last line.
Supervisor's Support for Improvement _____ ÷ 3 = _____

Add response numbers from **questions 27 and 28** and divide by 2. Enter total in last line.
Quality Process Alignment _____ ÷ 2 = _____

Add response numbers from **questions 29 and 30** and divide by 2. Enter total in last line.
Awareness of Productivity/Quality Issues _____ ÷ 2 = _____

Add response numbers from **questions 31–33** and divide by 3. Enter total in last line.

    Attitudes/Morale   _____ ÷ 3 = _____

Add response numbers from **questions 34–36** and divide by 3. Enter total in last line.

    System Feedback Coordination   _____ ÷ 3 = _____

Add response numbers from **questions 37 and 38** and divide by 2. Enter total in last line.

    Peer Team Support   _____ ÷ 2 = _____

Add response numbers from **questions 39–41** and divide by 3. Enter total in last line.

    Quality Culture Perceptions   _____ ÷ 3 = _____

Add response numbers from **questions 42 and 43** and divide by 2. Enter total in last line.

    Social/Moral Maturity   _____ ÷ 2 = _____

Add response numbers from **questions 44–46** and divide by 3. Enter total in last line.

    Quality Task Resources   _____ ÷ 3 = _____

Add response numbers from **questions 47–51** and divide by 5. Enter total in last line.

    Quality Rewards/Recognition   _____ ÷ 5 = _____

Add response numbers from **questions 52–55** and divide by 4. Enter total in last line.

    Customer Satisfaction Sensitivity   _____ ÷ 4 = _____

Add response numbers from **questions 56–58** and divide by 3. Enter total in last line.

    Communications/Information Sharing   _____ ÷ 3 = _____

Add response numbers from **questions 59 and 60** and divide by 2. Enter total in last line.

    Process Measurement/Qualification   _____ ÷ 2 = _____

Add response numbers from **questions 61 and 62** and divide by 2. Enter total in last line.

    Process Benchmarking/Quality Auditing   _____ ÷ 2 = _____

Add response numbers from **questions 63–65** and divide by 3. Enter total in last line.

    Work Unit Delight   _____ ÷ 3 = _____

Add response numbers from **questions 66 and 67** and divide by 2. Enter total in last line.

    Organizational Health/Work Stress   _____ ÷ 2 = _____

Add response numbers from **questions 68–70** and divide by 3. Enter total in last line.

Total Quality Ecological Sustainability _____ ÷ 3 = _____

Add response numbers from **questions 71–73** and divide by 3. Enter total in last line.

Personal Performance Perception/System _____ ÷ 3 = _____
Stability Results

Add response numbers from **questions 74–76** and divide by 3. Enter total in last line.

Peer Performance Perception/System _____ ÷ 3 = _____
Stability Results

INTERPRETATION: ORGANIZATIONAL QUALITY AND SUSTAINABLE PRODUCTIVITY ASSESSMENT

Score	Interpretation
5.0–6.0	Stable Quality System to Be Maintained
3.5–4.9	System in a State of Moderate Quality Risk
2.0–3.4	System in a State of Severe Quality Risk
0.0–1.9	System in Need of Major Improvement

If any score is lower than or equal to 3.50, this area presents a quality risk. Focus on these prioritized risk areas. Using the text materials, devise appropriate action plans for each area.

CHAPTER 4

CONTINUOUS IMPROVEMENT: TQ AND OD PROCESS DIMENSIONS

In the previous chapter, we linked mission and vision with strategy. Total quality requires integration of planning and objectives with processes that are capable of carrying out the objectives. Thus, process design and implementation is a vital link between planning and doing. Organization development (OD) practitioners have unique abilities that can be used to plan and support the organization's efforts to change and improve its processes. Many people are uncomfortable with the rapidity and amount of change that is occurring in the business environment. OD professionals can help to guide and smooth those transitions, which now seem to be constantly occurring in most organizations.

The focus of Chapter 4 is in two areas: total quality business processes and total quality OD processes. Both are crucial in determining the strength of the second pillar of the House of Total Quality and clarifying the expanded process responsibilities of employees in a total quality system. Both total quality business process improvement and total quality OD process improvement need to be considered to ensure organizational effectiveness and efficiency.

TOTAL QUALITY BUSINESS PROCESS IMPROVEMENT

The second pillar of the House of Total Quality, continuous improvement, is based on the cornerstone of process planning and the foundation of process management. In Chapter 3, a process was defined as a set of linked activities that take an input and transform it to create an output.[1] To elaborate on this, process designers must realize that resources such as materials, equipment, time, labor, data, etc. constitute the inputs to the process. The transformation activity adds more resources (and ideally more value) to the product or service being processed. The result is a "product" that is passed on to a "customer," who may or may not be the ultimate user of the product. The pillar of continuous improvement is the outcome of the sound design developed in the cornerstone of process planning with effective implementation delivered in the foundation of process management, as shown in Figure 4.1.[2]

Key points for total quality OD practitioners to keep in mind when making process improvements are:

- When working together to create a process map for complex processes that are candidates for major or incremental change, senior managers on the team may require several attempts and need help (intervention by a facilitator) to get the process diagram sufficiently correct for department heads to buy into the model and the improvement process.

Figure 4.1 The Second Pillar, Foundation, and Cornerstone of the House of Total Quality

- Some organizations fail to regard their shareholders and/or holding company as customers, which can prove fatal for process change projects. Paying close attention to the needs of directors is part of the OD role of clarifying and influencing decision makers.
- Value analysis is a powerful approach to helping managers and staff understand how much waste is involved in poorly designed processes. Graphical analysis of the present versus proposed processes can often open eyes to the benefits of process improvements. Care must be taken to avoid judgment and blame.

The first step in strategy implementation in Chapter 3 was process integration. This strategy implementation step can now be explored through the process dimensions that ensure continuous improvement. *Total quality continuous improvement* is the range of system innovation designed and implemented to produce total, ongoing customer satisfaction. The three types of continuous improvement, *kaizen*, competitive parity, and breakthrough dominance are listed in Table 4.1.[3]

Continuous improvement, also known as *kaizen*, has been used extensively and for a long time in Japan.[4] This approach requires individuals, process and project teams, and cross-units (interorganizational cooperative networks) to incrementally improve procedures in order to reduce costs and increase efficiency. Perhaps even more than quality control circles, it has been the key to understanding the "Japanese miracle." *Kaizen* has been far less successful in the United States because it requires patience, long-term commitment, and attention to detail, which are not prevalent in our culture but can be acquired if the right attitude and incentives exist in the workplace. This has been demonstrated over a number of years by companies such as Honda, Toyota, Nissan, Sony, and others that use a modified "Japanese" type of work system in their U.S. manufacturing operations.

The second type of continuous improvement, competitive parity, involves a strategy for becoming at least the equal of the "best in class" of existing market leaders. Consider the story about two hunters who were being pursued by a bear. The first hunter sat down by a tree and began to put on running shoes. The second hunter gasped, "John, you can't outrun a bear with those running shoes." John replied, "I don't have to outrun the bear. I just have to outrun you!" The first hunter had to achieve "competitive parity" with the second hunter. Then, it was necessary to have a "breakthrough" (discussed next) in order to win the contest with the bear.

The third type of continuous improvement, breakthrough dominance, is oriented toward outdistancing competitors by reengineering or restructuring processes to achieve quantum breakthrough advantages. OD practitioners can and should play a key role in designing and facilitating breakthrough dominance. Many times incremental changes are inadequate because the rate at which they allow a company to improve is far less than the rate enjoyed

Table 4.1 Types of Continuous Improvement

	Kaizen: cost reduction	Competitive parity	Breakthrough dominance
Effect	Long term and long-lasting, but undramatic	Short term, but dramatic to match best in class	Long term and long-lasting to rewrite the rules
Pace	Small steps to cut costs	Big steps to catch up	Quantum leaps to outdistance
Time frame	Continuous and incremental	Continuous and nonincremental	Intermittent and nonincremental
Change	Gradual and constant	Abrupt and externally focused	Revolutionary restructuring
Involvement	Driven by everybody	Driven primarily by external competition scanning "champions"	Driven primarily by R&D, leadership from the top, and process change agents
Approach	Individual and group efforts, collective systems approach	Strategists and key business process "owners"	R&D and key business processes, cross-functional collaboration and accountability
Mode	Maintenance and improvement	Scrap and rebuild to catch up	Start over, create from scratch
Spark	Conventional know-how and state of the art	Competitor challenges, technological breakthroughs, matching market changes	Reinvent to meet envisioned future needs using technology as the essential enabler
Practical requirements	Requires little investment but great effort to maintain	Requires large investment but little effort to maintain	Requires large investment and great effort to maintain
Effort orientation	People and current daily practices	Competitive benchmarking processes	Reengineering breakthrough business processes
Evaluation criteria	Process and efforts for better results in reducing costs and improving efficiency	Results demonstrated by competitive process parity in the marketplace	"Order-of-magnitude" performance improvements—in key business indicators (cost, timeliness, quality)
Advantage	Works well in slow-growth economy	Better suited to fast-growth economy where keeping pace is crucial	Used when radical redesign is necessary to rapidly outdistance the competition

by the market leader. Therefore, OD practitioners must be able and willing to analyze and, if necessary, help create an entirely new nature and set of interactions in a system. For example, the difference between the U.S. Post Office and Federal Express is an important case; improving the former incrementally will never allow it to catch up with Federal Express, because the latter is based on a completely different breakthrough distribution system.

An appropriate warning was sounded by Long and Vickers-Koch:[5] process planners must beware of "false dichotomies." They point out that there is a tendency by managers and their process improvement advisors (such as outside and even internal OD consultants) to take an "either–or" stance in process improvement. *Either* we engage in *kaizen or* we engage in breakthrough dominance type process improvement. The authors point out that the best companies should engage in *all three* types of improvement simultaneously, in appropriate contexts and times, as shown in Figure 4.2.

The basis of world competition is changing. It now requires reduced time to market, flexibility, service, and market differentiation via value metric

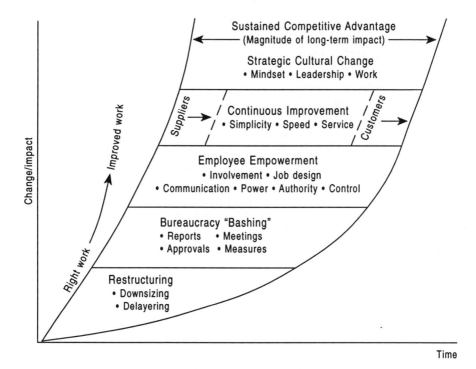

Figure 4.2 The Role of Continuous Improvement in Achieving Sustained Competitive Advantage (Source: Reprinted by permission of the publisher from Beatty, Richard W. and Ulrich, David O. (1991). *Organizational Dynamics*. Vol. 25, No. 4, p. 22. ©1991 American Management Association, New York. All rights reserved.)

excellence. Since the price of admission to world-class status is constantly increasing, business process improvement is essential for global competitive success. Making work processes effective (producing desired results), efficient (minimizing the resources used), and adaptable (able to flexibly meet changing customer and business needs) reduces costs, achieves competitive parity, and eventually provides the basis for sustained competitive advantage.

In the organizational life cycle (from entrepreneurial birth to growth, maturity, and eventual decline), renewal is necessary to sustain competitive advantage. Five steps to achieve that advantage are restructuring, bureaucracy "bashing," employee empowerment, continuous improvement, and strategic cultural change.

- **Step 1: Restructuring**—Through downsizing and delayering using early retirement, reorganization, consolidation, plant closings, and greater spans of control, leaders focus on the right work (essential processes that add value to an internal and/or external customer) to be done.
- **Step 2: Bureaucracy "Bashing"**—Unnecessary reports, procedures, and other bureaucratic barriers to meeting customer needs are eliminated. To facilitate this step, a work process audit containing at least two questions is conducted: (1) To what extent does this work activity add value to the product for customers? (2) To what extent are these activities performed as effectively as possible?[6] Leaders need to encourage and reinforce, rather than punish, risk taking among employees who initiate bureaucracy-bashing activities.
- **Step 3: Employee Empowerment**—Empowerment results in part from bureaucracy bashing, since bureaucracies primarily empower top managers. Real empowerment, however, occurs when position, status, and seniority are no longer the bases of power and authority in a firm, but rather competency relationships, trust, and solid expertise are. Enlarging the horizontal communication channels, dialogue opportunities, and employee involvement processes assists leaders in sharing power in order to build widespread organizational capacities for commitment to change. PepsiCo, for example, has involved and empowered employees by announcing profit-sharing benefits for everyone and challenging its employees to assume a corporate responsibility mindset. Federal Express guarantees all employees access to weekly senior management meetings. Other public and nonprofit organizations have cost-saving and gainsharing programs to align employee and organizational empowerment interests.
- **Step 4: Continuous Improvement**—Work process integrations that simplify, speed up, and increase service to internal and external customers represent effective continuous improvement activities. Restructuring increases productivity, bureaucracy bashing increases flexibility, and em-

ployee involvement increases empowerment; continuous improvement is the integration of the outcomes of these prior steps.

- **Step 5: Strategic Cultural Change**—The cultural change required by continuous improvement ushers in a new employee mindset, leadership style, and work design. The psychological transitions that are required for such mindset shifts in moving from the traditional organizational to the new process focus are discussed later in this chapter.

A completely different thought pattern must emerge, with a view toward improving the effectiveness of all processes in an organization to achieve customer satisfaction. Assessment, resolution, and prevention of strategic and operational problems become easier when the new process focus is used rather than the traditional organizational focus. For example, a *Business Week* article[7] told of the changes made in the previously centralized organizational structure and computer systems used at the Federal National Mortgage Association (Fannie Mae), a quasi-governmental financial corporation head-quartered in Washington, D.C. Until the early 1990s, Fannie Mae's departmentalized organization and mainframe computer systems had been adequate to service its customers. However, it became apparent that they were becoming bogged down in paperwork. Management realized that it had to redesign the organization and began to replace rigid departmental structures with process teams that combined financial, marketing, and computer experts working together on projects. Essential computing power was decentralized by building a computer network, at a cost of some $10 million, that tied together 2000 personal computers with "user-friendly" software that made it easy for employees to access needed information in a timely manner. The real test of the system and its superior productive capability came with the falling interest rates in 1992. Fannie Mae handled $257 billion in new loans—almost double its 1991 volume—while adding only 100 employees to its 3000-employee work force. The increased productivity allowed Fannie Mae to increase profits by 13% to $1.6 billion.

Note that the changes at Fannie Mae incorporated all of the five steps listed above. It restructured, bashed the bureaucracy, instituted continuous improvement, empowered employees, and went through a strategic cultural change in a space of approximately two years.

TOTAL QUALITY BUSINESS PROCESS PLANNING

Business process planning must begin with a clarification of the meaning of relevant concepts. These include *process, system, structure,* and *technique*. A *process* is any set of linked activities that takes an input, adds value to it, and provides an output to an internal or external customer. A *system* is an interrelated set of plans, policies, processes, procedures, people, and technology needed to reach the objectives of an organization. Thus, a *set of processes* may be seen as making up a system. Usually a process will cross organizational boundaries within an operating unit and require coordination across those boundaries. A *structure* is a formal or informal organizational entity that is developed to perform a certain process or set of tasks which are part of a process. Functional structures are common in both manufacturing and service organizations at all levels. From the total quality perspective, however, functional structures are undesirable for at least three reasons: (1) they distance employees from customers and insulate them from customer expectations, (2) they promote complex and wasteful processes and inhibit cross-functional process improvement, and (3) they separate the quality function from the rest of the organization, providing employees with an excuse not to worry about quality. Finally, a *technique* is a systematic approach, procedure, tool, and/or associated technology required to carry out a task.[8]

To use the analogy of an airplane, a *system* is seen at the 35,000-foot level as a "big picture" view of the organization and its processes. Zooming in to the 5000-foot level enables us to see the details of *process*, which may cross some organizational boundaries. At the 500-foot level, the *structure* of organizational departments and groups that carry out processes or tasks becomes clear. Finally, at the 50-foot level, the *techniques* used by individuals and small groups to accomplish work (and sometimes to improve processes) can be easily seen.

Process planning is the cornerstone of continuous improvement, as shown earlier in Figure 4.1. According to Voehl, the purpose of process planning is to ensure that all key processes work in harmony to maximize organizational effectiveness and efficiency.[9] The goal is to achieve a competitive advantage through superior customer satisfaction. A principal activity at this level is to develop a continuous improvement *process* (frequently labeled total quality improvement, TQI) that uses effective and efficient problem-solving *techniques*. If effectively implemented, three major outcomes typically result: (1) a common language for documenting and communicating activities and decisions for key TQI processes is established, (2) an organization-wide system of linking TQI indicators is developed, and (3) both initial and long-term gains due to the elimination of waste, rework, and bottlenecks are realized.

Reengineering and Its Relation to Business Process Planning

Reengineering has become a buzzword, a management trend, and a source of fear and misunderstanding that has affected thousands of corporations across the United States and thousands of others across the world. James Champy, one of the originators of reengineering, cited a 1994 survey conducted by his firm, CSC Index. Of 6000 of the largest firms in North America and Europe surveyed,[10] 69% of the 497 U.S. firms that responded and 75% of the 124 European respondents reported that they were already engaged in one or more reengineering projects, and over 50% of the remainder of the sample had plans to do so.

Reengineering is defined by Hammer and Champy[11] as:

> The fundamental rethinking and radical redesign of business processes to achieve dramatic improvements in contemporary measures of performance, such as cost, quality, service and speed.

Within this definition, there is nothing that represents a major difference in perspective from total quality management (TQM). In fact, many TQM experts would argue that reengineering (or *business process reengineering,* BPR) is part of the accepted philosophy (with roots going back to Juran's concept of *breakthrough* quality improvement and even earlier to Taylor's work [see Exhibit 4.1]) as well as a logical extension of TQM. Thus, it must be the method by which TQM is carried out that results in its lack of reported success in reengineering/downsizing initiatives. Whether they use the banner of "total quality management," "reengineering," "downsizing," or "reinventing government," organizations are facing massive pressure from customers, competitors, and stockholders to perform *significant* process and structural changes, and if not done right the first time to redo it. Unfortunately, reengineering has been equated by many people with downsizing.

Stowell[12] pointed out that downsizing (a label that Hammer and Champy hold is *not* synonymous with reengineering) contains numerous pitfalls for

---

Charles Handy gave an example that tends to show that Frederick W. Taylor, "The Father of Scientific Management," was probably "The Father of Reengineering" as well. Taylor studied the process of shoveling coal at Bethlehem Steel Company in Pennsylvania. He observed that the workers were provided with only one size shovel, which they used to shovel coal with densities of 3.5 to 38 pounds per shovel. After much experimentation, Taylor discovered that the optimum load for worker efficiency was 22 pounds per shovel. Therefore, he made a process improvement by substituting a larger shovel for the less dense coal and smaller shovels for the denser grades. Taylor's studies allowed Bethlehem Steel to reduce its work force from 600 to 140 and pay each worker 60% higher wages. This example has all the elements of Hammer and Champy's definition of reengineering.

Exhibit 4.1 Frederick W. Taylor—Father of Reengineering (Adapted from Handy, Charles (1993). *Understanding Organizations.* New York: Oxford University Press, p. 21.)

which managers frequently do not prepare or recognize as significant hazards. Numerous studies show that downsizing rarely accomplishes the goals that managers have set for the effort. For example, a 1993 American Management Association study reported that only half of the companies surveyed increased profits and only one-third improved their productivity by downsizing. Employee morale was reported to be lower in 80% of the firms. However, in spite of the poor results, two-thirds of the companies were planning further cuts. Basically, Stowell's argument is that most managers do not understand the long-term "system" effects of downsizing. Consequently, they take the "slash and burn" approach, which frequently ends up making things worse rather than better. When the system is not considered, job cuts result in temporarily positive changes, such as lower costs and higher stock prices. However, because such programs tend to "overshoot" their targets for personnel reduction, companies end up with higher costs for rehiring and training people for essential positions and head count "creep" (more people than ever on board within a short period of time), accompanied by lower morale, lower productivity, lower quality, and lower stock price.

It has been noted that successful implementation of TQM depends on several key concepts:[13] a long-term perspective, customer focus, top management commitment, systems thinking, training and tools, participation, measurement and reporting systems, communication, and leadership. The same can be said for process changes that are implemented to achieve *breakthrough dominance* or the other two forms of continuous improvement. A key to effective implementation is how the organization views the system within which it operates and how well it commits to and carries out change. Thus, OD practitioners, working within the framework of the ethical work culture paradigm, have a role to play in acting as the "corporate conscience" and system integration experts. If managers cannot turn to internal and external experts with appropriate experience in BPR, their instinctive approach is to use the "slash and burn" approach to deal with immediate environmental threats and pressures.

TOTAL QUALITY BUSINESS PROCESS MANAGEMENT

Business process management is a systematic approach to helping organizations carry out their plans for making significant advances in the way their business processes operate.[14] The rationale is to ensure that the organization has business processes that:

- Eliminate errors
- Minimize delays
- Maximize the use of assets

- Promote understanding
- Are easy to use
- Are customer friendly
- Are adaptable to customers' changing needs
- Provide the organization with a competitive advantage
- Reduce excess head count

Harrington's widely used model for managing business process improvement (BPI) was conceived in the context of a relatively stable external competitive environment. It identifies five specific phases: organizing for improvement, understanding the process, streamlining, measurement and control, and continuous improvement.[15] Thus, it is most appropriate for either *kaizen* or competitive parity types of projects, although it may be applied with modifications to breakthrough dominance types of projects. Figure 4.3 illustrates these five phases.

The first phase of BPI (organizing for improvement) has the objective of ensuring success by building understanding, leadership, and commitment. To achieve this aim, Harrington recommends a detailed list of ten activities, ranging from (1) establishing an executive improvement team to oversee BPI to (2) selecting the process improvement team cross-functional members to participate in, conduct, and implement BPIs in designated areas.

The second phase of BPI (understanding the process) has the objective of understanding all the dimensions of the current business process. To achieve this aim, ten additional activities are recommended, beginning with defining the process scope and mission in light of strategic objectives and ending with updating process documentation in order to conform to new findings.

The third phase of BPI (streamlining) has the objective of improving effectiveness, efficiency, and adaptability of business processes. To achieve this objective, 13 activities are recommended, including such representative examples as: (1) providing for team training in process improvement sequencing, streamlining by eliminating waste, then preventing errors by pro-

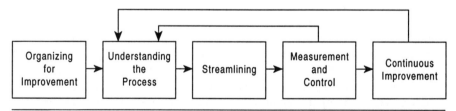

Figure 4.3 Five Phases of Business Process Improvement (Source: Harrington, H. James (1991). *Business Process Improvement*. New York: McGraw-Hill, p. 23.)

cess redesign, then correcting specific problems only after the basic process design is stable and prevents most problems, and finally, excelling in setting up processes to sustain customer delight; and (2) selecting, training, and/or retraining the employees who are implementing the business process. The intermediate steps, as in phases 1 and 2 above, are designed to ensure careful definition, analysis, coordination, and implementation of the process improvement project.

In the case of reengineering, which seeks to achieve a radical process redesign without being limited to the approach currently in place, phases 1 and 2 may still be used to determine the context for change. The detailed steps in phases 1, 2, and 3, however, would be modified to enable breakthrough thinking through a "clean sheet of paper" approach to process design. This approach essentially ignores the existing process and asks the question: "If we were to design this process today, given what we know about our customers, our market, and the technology that is available, how would we design it?" The OD practitioner may play a key role in reframing and restructuring processes in order to overcome dysfunctional organizational resistance to radical change.

The fourth phase of BPI (measurement and control) has the objective of implementing the system to control the process for ongoing improvement. To achieve this objective, the following six activities are recommended: (1) develop appropriate in-process measurements and targets by answering the "11 W's" (which consist of several why, where, what, when, and who questions);[16] (2) establish a process and ethics system for timely positive and negative feedback, utilizing improvement chart indicators; (3) utilize statistical process control procedures whenever possible to identify upper control limits and lower control limits for critical business processes; (4) perform process and ethics audits periodically; (5) establish a poor-quality cost system to detect and control direct and indirect costs to the organization; and (6) establish a routine correction procedure that includes awareness, desire to eliminate errors, training in problem solving, failure analysis, follow-up practices, and liberally giving credit and recognition to all who participate.

The fifth phase of BPI (continuous improvement) has the objective of implementing a continuous improvement process. To achieve this objective, the following six activities are recommended: (1) certify individual contributors and qualify the entire business process and ethical work culture development systems; (2) perform periodic qualification reviews; (3) continuously find, define, and eliminate process problems; (4) evaluate the impact of the change on the business and on customers; (5) benchmark the process over time and across competitor/industry/political boundaries; and (6) provide ongoing advanced team training.

Harrington also developed a six-level process qualification procedure that provides an effective assessment guide for BPI activities. These levels

Table 4.2 The Six Levels of Business Process Qualification

Level	Status	Description
1	Unknown	Process status has not been determined.
2	Understood	Process design is understood and operates according to prescribed documentation.
3	Effective	Process is systematically measured, streamlining has started, and end-customer expectations are met.
4	Efficient	Process is streamlined and is more efficient.
5	Error-free	Process is highly effective (error-free) and efficient.
6	World-class	Process is world-class and continues to improve.

Source: Harrington, H. James (1991). *Business Process Improvement.* New York: McGraw-Hill, p. 206. Numerical order reversed by the authors.

lead process improvement teams (PITs) from an unknown process status to world-class status, as indicated in Table 4.2.[17]

Until the BPI methodology has been applied, all business processes are considered to be at level 1. As the process is improved, it progresses logically up to level 6 as long as the ethical work culture is simultaneously developed. This qualification system enables the organization to quickly evaluate its business process status and determine the stage of ethical work culture that would sustain it.

Business Process Management and the Ethical Work Culture

All processes in all organizations may not need or be able to progress through all six levels. Often, considerable costs are involved in becoming the best. In most cases, organizations have many business processes that need to be improved. Because of the magnitude of this job, it may be wise to use PITs to bring some of the key prioritized processes under control and then direct the limited remaining resources to secondary critical business processes. Once all the critical processes are under control, PITs and other types of teams can be assigned to bring other processes up to level 6.

When the executive team decides that something less than a world-class performance level is acceptable, it should communicate this information to the PIT immediately. Ideally, this decision should be made prior to forming the PIT. When management decreases its expectations late in the process cycle, it can negatively impact the PIT's morale by being interpreted as management's loss of faith.

Table 4.3 Parallels Between Levels/Stages of Business Process and
Ethical Work Culture

Level/stage	Business process status	Ethical work culture status
1. House of Manipulation	Unknown	Social Darwinism
2. House of Manipulation	Understood	Machiavellianism
3. House of Compliance	Effective	Popular Conformity
4. House of Compliance	Efficient	Allegiance to Authority
5. House of Integrity	Error-free	Democratic Participation
6 House of Integrity	World-class	Principled Integrity

The obvious parallel between the six business process levels and the six
ethical work culture stages treated in Chapter 1 needs to be emphasized since
the quality process context can either inhibit or support ethical conduct and
vice versa, as indicated in Table 4.3.

Organizations that want a level 6 world-class business process status to
operate in the House of Integrity require an institutionalized ethical work
culture operating at stage 6, Principled Integrity. Important processes to
institute in designing an organizational ethics development system include
initial ethical work culture assessments, honesty testing in its selection
process, explicit ethical conduct expectations for employee performance,
ethics training and development, ethical impact of employee conduct in
appraisals, protection of whistleblowers from retaliation, vehicles for reporting ethics violations, organizational justice processes for ethics offenders,
commendation rituals for exemplary ethical behavior, and ethical audits for
system improvement processes if world-class principled integrity is to become an organization performance standard.

Organizations that settle for a level 4 Efficiency business process status
to operate in the House of Compliance only require an institutionalized
ethical work culture operating at stage 4, Allegiance to Authority. The traditional hierarchy in most organizations, which relies on the chain of command, legal compliance and control measures, and rapid dismissal for any
ethical offense, can obtain short-term employee compliance. Nevertheless,
process and ethics compliance is not commitment; people may abide by the
letter of the law, but the spirit of community dedication to creating and
improving a world-class workplace will be absent.

Organizations that are mired at level 1, the Unknown business process
status, operate in the House of Manipulation and are stagnating in an ethical

work culture operating at stage 1, Social Darwinism. Organizations that have unknown processes rely upon fear to control behavior, and in the absence of direct or indirect power, employees will resort to unethical and dysfunctional work behavior. Driving fear out of the workplace is essential for total quality implementation.[18] Attempting to introduce total quality processes in such an ethical work culture is doomed to failure.

TOTAL QUALITY ORGANIZATION DEVELOPMENT PROCESS IMPROVEMENT

To implement system-wide total quality continuous improvement, the OD practitioner must simultaneously focus on six certification levels and measure their impact on at least six key organizational stakeholders: external customers, employees, investors, managers, suppliers, and society.[19]

The OD practitioner's challenge is to provide the appropriate input to divide the limited improvement resources among the six levels to get the maximum results. The highest performing organizations do an excellent job of distributing their improvement resources, shifting emphasis at the correct time. Most of the marginal organizations adopt one approach and hold dogmatically to it, while ignoring the others. The losers shift randomly among each approach, without explaining to their employees why they are changing direction. Consequently, employees are left with a feeling that they can wait out any organizational transformation "program." Why change when the next time top management attends a conference, they will come back with another approach that will completely change the organization's direction? OD practitioners need to understand their processes and levels to be able to make correct diagnoses and to assist in resisting the temptation to frequently change direction.

TOTAL QUALITY ORGANIZATION DEVELOPMENT PROCESS PLANNING

Total quality OD process planning requires competence in assessing, interpreting, designing, transforming, and sustaining an organization's stable system processes. OD professionals need to statistically distinguish between common and special causes of process variation. The former are inherent in the process and account for over 80% of variation; the latter arise from external sources. A system governed only by common causes is stable. Tampering with a stable system will increase variation; neglecting special causes by assuming that the system is not controllable, however, may result in a missed opportunity to eliminate unwanted process variation.

Total Quality Organization Development Process Planning and Types of Processes

W. Warner Burke suggested that there are eight processes of interest to OD practitioners and about which more needs to be known. These processes happen to fit the TQM paradigm extremely well, which indicates the potential for developing a fit between processes, needed improvements, and traditional OD versus total quality problem-solving approaches, as summarized in Table 4.4.

Planning for total quality OD processes involves the eight key elements listed in Table 4.4: organization leadership; organization structure (and associated strategy); organization change; appraisal, rewards, and pay; teams and teamwork; training and development; organization size; and organization performance. The total quality OD processes are the result of the business strategy involvements and paradigm shifts referred to in Chapter 3 applied across and within organizations.

Organization Leadership—The prescribed role of managerial change leaders (including both line managers and supporting OD managers and advisors) defines the learning and developmental needs of their human resources. For example, managing for incremental improvement of organizational systems through the study and understanding of variation in systems means that change leaders must develop skills for, and learn about, variation through studying statistical methods. In addition, managerial leaders should convey that part of their role is to continuously improve the systems of the organization for internal and external customer value. They do so by role modeling, coaching, asking process questions in progress reporting meetings, and creating appropriate appreciation and reward systems for the organization. For example, in the early stages of Motorola's quality journey, the CEO would often go to an executive committee meeting to receive reports on quality. After the reports were given, he would often leave, before any financial or operating matters were discussed. This sent a clear signal to the executives that if quality matters were attended to, other things would take care of themselves.

Organization Structure (and Associated Strategy)—It is a managerial axiom that "structure follows strategy." One of the major reasons that massive "breakthrough" organizational redesign has to take place is because the overall system has not been continuously modified to meet strategic shifts. There are numerous organization structural configurations that can be adopted to fit strategic and environmental conditions.

An organization chart shows the *apparent structure* of the formal organization. However, some organizations *refuse* to be tied down by a conventional organization chart, with the result that employees do not take titles seriously. For example, Semco, Inc., a radically unconventional manufacturer of industrial equipment (mixers, washers, air conditioners, bakery plant units) located in Sao Paulo, Brazil, has what is called a "circular" organization chart, with four concentric circles (Semco avoids the use of the term "levels"). The titles used are counselors (CEO and the equivalent of vice presidents), partners (business unit heads), coordinators (supervisory specialists and functional leaders), and associates (everyone else). Anyone who chooses to can think up a title for external use that describes his or her area or job responsibility. As owner and CEO Ricardo Simler explains:[20]

> Consistent with this philosophy, when a promotion takes place now at Semco we simply supply blank business cards and tell the newly elevated individual: "Think of a title that signals externally your area of operation and responsibility and have it printed." If the person likes "Procurement Manager," fine. If he wants something more elegant, he can print up cards saying, "First Pharaoh in Charge of Royal Supplies." Whatever he wants. But inside the company, there are only four options. (Anyway, almost all choose to print only their name.)

Although thousands of different organization structures exist, most conventional ones are variations or combinations of three basic types: (1) the line organization, (2) the line and staff organization, and (3) the matrix organization. The line organization is a functional form in that it has departments that are responsible for marketing, finance, and operations. In this type of organization, quality planning and assurance usually are part of the responsibility of each operating manager and employee at every level. In all likelihood, in a pure line organization, the quality function would be "invisible" in the organization chart, since no one would have the full-time job of quality manager.

The line and staff organization is the most prevalent type of organization structure for medium-sized to large firms. In such organizations, line departments carry out the functions of marketing, finance, and production for the organization. Staff personnel, including quality managers and OD specialists (among many others), assist the line managers in carrying out their jobs by providing technical assistance and advice. In this traditional form of organization structure, quality managers and inspectors may take on the role of guardians of quality, instead of technical experts, who assist line managers and workers in attaining quality.

The matrix type of organization is a relatively new form that was developed for use in situations where large, complex projects are designed and carried out, such as defense weapons systems or large construction projects. Firms that do such work have a basic need to develop an organization structure that will permit the efficient use of human resources while maintaining control over the many facets of the project being developed. In a

Table 4.4 Traditional and Total Quality Organization Development Process Planning by Types of Processes

Processes	Kaizen		Competitive parity		Breakthrough dominance	
	Trad. OD	TQ OD	Trad. OD	TQ OD	Trad. OD	TQ OD
Organization leadership	Cost conscious	Entrepreneurial	Bold, risk taker	Promotes champions	Charismatic visionary	Transcendent
Organization structure (& strategy)	Line & staff	Flat, team based	Expert-led task forces	Champion-coordinated project groups	Expert-led venture analysis groups	Cross-functional, cross-unit structure
Organization change	Technical experts	Executive improvement team driven	OD dept. focus	Cross-functional team	Outside consultants	Facilitated groups
Appraisal, rewards, pay	Individual, money	Team & individual	Individual, MBO, increased pay	Team/individual, enhanced responsibility	Individual, MBO, bonus	Team/individual, equity
Teams & teamwork	Information to experts	Team develops expertise	OD team members with mgmt.	Cross-functional team with experts	Consultants with internal experts	Multiple teams and groups

Training & development	Limited to management or staff	Team members & management	Advanced training for OD people	Advanced needs-based training	Consultants provide limited training	Open-system training
Organization size	Line departments	Line or service departments	Division or geographic unit	Strategic business unit or processes	Company or subsidiary	Cross-unit structure
Organization performance	Productivity or cost	Quality, customer service, cycle time, cost	Relative profit margin or market share	Quality, customer service, market share, profits	Dominant profit margin or market share	Long-term quality, customer service, environmental factors, market share, profits

Source: Adapted from Burke, W. Warner (1995). "Organization Change: What We Know, What We Need to Know." *ODC Newsletter, Academy of Management.* Winter, pp. 1, 9–11.

matrix-type organization, each project has a project manager and each department that is providing personnel to work on various projects has a technical or administrative manager. Thus, a quality assurance technician might be assigned to the quality assurance department for technical and administrative activities but would be attached to project A for day-to-day job assignments. When project A is completed, the technician might be reassigned to project B under a new project manager. He or she would still report to the "technical boss" in quality assurance, however. More will be said about the matrix structure and project management in the next chapter.

Organization Change—Beckhard and Harris[21] have recently developed a phased model of large system change that shows the organization moving from its "present state" through a "transition state" to a "future state." This general model applies regardless of the degree of change (*kaizen* through breakthrough dominance). Change management assists individuals in making the transition from meaninglessness to purpose, powerlessness to control, isolation to interaction, and alienation to community. Bridges approaches change from the perspective of the process.[22] He feels that it is not the changes that are difficult, but rather the transitions. Changes are not the same as transitions. He describes change as being situational: a new boss, a new site, or a new team. In contrast, *transition* is the psychological process that people go through when they must come to terms with a new situation. Even when changes are good, as in situations where processes are improved but no jobs are lost, there are transitions, which begin with having to let go of something. The single largest problem for organizations in transition is the failure to identify and prepare for the endings and losses produced by change.[23] To assist individuals with change and the transition process, there should be a clear understanding of what is over and what is not over. Endings should be marked in such a manner that it is clear that they have occurred. Following this, the past should always be treated with respect. Although these actions take considerable time, implementing them can divert future complications which can take much longer to correct.[24] The psychological transitions that are required are shown in Table 4.5.[25]

Appraisal and Reward Processes—One of the most difficult areas in changing from the traditional OD perspective to the total quality OD philosophy is coming to grips with human performance. *Performance is the contribution both individuals and systems make to the accomplishment of the objectives of the organization.* We will defer detailed treatment of performance factors until the next section in order to deal with the issues of performance appraisal and rewards.

Appraisal is the feedback process of evaluating and improving individual and system performance. Traditional performance appraisal systems tend to rely on an appraisal system, with unilateral flow of information from a single source,

Table 4.5 Comparison of Traditional Organization and New Process Psychological Transitions

Traditional organization mindset	New process mindset
Employees are the problem	The process is the problem
Doing my job	Help to get things done
Understanding my job	Knowing how my job fits into the total process
Measuring individuals	Measuring the process
Change the person	Change the process
Can always find a better employee	Can always improve the process
Motivating people	Removing barriers
Controlling employees	Developing people
Don't trust anyone	We're all in this together
Who made the error?	What allowed the error to occur?
Correct errors	Reduce variation
Bottom-line driven	Customer driven

wherein the immediate superior passes judgment and informs the subordinate. By contrast, Deming argued that individually based appraisals are fundamentally harmful and unfair because if the system in which people work is predictable, then over time, most employees will perform at about the same level. The influence of variation is such that it is impossible to accurately measure the overall performance of individuals within a variable process. In fact, it is impossible to separate the performance of the individual from that of the system.[26] The need to factor in both system and individual inputs into appraisals is a key obligation of both total quality OD professionals, who may be process designers, and human resource (HR) professionals, who administer the processes.

The difference between a traditional and a total quality approach to appraisal is similar to the difference between the traditional approach to quality control through inspection and quality improvement through the statistical study of variation. The orientations and attitudes that accompany these two approaches are very different. Total quality appraisal is more like the statistical approach to continuous improvement, rather than the inspection-oriented approach to quality control. The inspection-oriented approach spends too much time trying to screen out defects or sub-par performers (that is, individuals who do not pull their weight). With this orientation, inspectors miss the opportunities to continuously improve and develop all employees and the systems within which they contribute to customer value.

For behavioral feedback and development, 360-degree appraisals should be gathered from peers, subordinates, internal and external customers, and superiors (plural). Each of these sources possesses strengths and weaknesses, but the biases in one will be balanced by the others. Multiple perspectives give a more accurate and comprehensive appraisal. In addition, self-feedback and self-appraisal should be used. Individual self-assessment is somewhat automatic in an organization in which the managers use statistical methods to monitor and improve their processes and systems.[27]

Reward systems are an important element in this total quality process. *Rewards are all forms of financial and nonfinancial returns to individuals, teams, and the system for contributions as part of the employment relationship.* Rewards have traditionally been distributed exclusively in an individually contingent manner (i.e., rewards are given to individuals on the basis of individual merit or judged individual performance), and individuals come to expect extrinsic rewards for any contribution. They have typically been in the form of *monetary compensation (pay).* Unfortunately, when rewards are administered to individuals, competition between individuals for limited rewards results, rather than the collaboration crucial for quality team and system performance. In addition, when rewards are viewed as extrinsic returns for instrumental work activities, the intrinsic motivation to take pride in a job well done is jeopardized.[28]

The challenge for total quality OD/HR managers is to design a reward system that takes advantage of the extrinsic and intrinsic motivational effects of rewards, satisfies norms for equity, meets external market competitiveness challenges, complies with appropriate laws and regulations, is consistently and efficiently administered, and encourages collaboration for team and system success.

The extrinsic and intrinsic reward system includes the full range of financial and nonfinancial returns: direct and indirect compensation, benefits, and recognition. On the side of extrinsic financial rewards for individuals and teams, progressive firms support quality achievements and employee involvement through profit-sharing and cost-saving/gainsharing plans. For example, Nucor Steel has implemented profit sharing plus a variety of small group incentives, and PepsiCo provides stock options for all of its roughly 100,000 permanent employees to involve everyone in the fate of the company.[29] On the side of extrinsic nonfinancial rewards for individuals and teams, quality approaches to recognition/appreciation systems are verbal, visible and public, have a strong next-and-final-customer bias, focus on teams first and individuals second, are active and frequent, and ensure consistency.[30] For example, Milliken, the Baldrige Award-winning textile manufacturer, has "Alcoves of Excellence," "Walls of Fame," and a company news magazine filled with recognition stories and photos of both individuals and teams. At Xerox, Team Celebration Day is a major event, with over

12,000 employees, customers, and suppliers attending a huge quality fair at one of four U.S. or international locations, all linked via satellite.[31]

Reward systems also need to exhibit visible vertical and horizontal remuneration equity.[32] Companies such as Nike, Herman Miller, and Ben and Jerry's limit the number of pay grades in the hierarchy, as well as the ratio of executive to lowest level employee pay. Other companies (e.g., Mars, Inc.) have increased horizontal equity by not differentiating the pay of same-level managers in different functions or teams. Excessive executive rewards not linked with skill acquisition, quality performance, and/or increased customer satisfaction are rightly perceived as equity problems and should be eliminated by total quality OD/HR professionals.[33] Equitably sharing burdens (downsizing, restructuring, dismissals) at all organizational levels also enhances the perception of systemic, procedural, and outcome justice that operates in a total quality firm dedicated to moral integrity in the workplace.[34]

Furthermore, both Conference Board and KPMG Peat Marwick surveys show that as companies mature along the total quality cycle, they increasingly shift their reward and recognition practices toward teams and broader workplace units, as indicated in Table 4.6.[35]

Rewarding collaboration and community-building choices provides the system incentives needed in a total quality organization.

Teams and Teamwork—The importance of teams and teamwork is reinforced in a number of ways. First, in many companies, ongoing teams play a large (or even solo) role in new employee recruitment and selection. Interpersonal skills, moral maturity, and willingness to be a team player also form a large part of the interviewing and testing procedures. These characteristics are often reinforced through general orientation and socialization, which often lasts several months even for production workers. At Mazda, line workers receive several days of general philosophy training, followed by five to seven weeks of technical skills training, followed by three to four weeks of supervision when first placed on the assembly line. Thus, recruitment, selection, and orientation all work in concert to produce dedicated, team-oriented, and highly skilled employees.

Table 4.6 Frequency of Distributing Rewards to Individuals, Teams, and Broader Work Units

Years TQ process in place	To individuals		To teams		Unit-wide	
	Cash	Noncash	Cash	Noncash	Cash	Noncash
8 or more	10%	58%	10%	53%	10%	53%
1 or less	15%	23%	8%	31%	4%	11%

Teams can also play a major role in massive organizational reengineering projects when used by enlightened firms that are attempting to achieve breakthrough dominance. A *Business Week* article[36] pointed out the use of task teams for a major restructuring effort. It was reported that Levi Strauss spent over $12 million to develop a plan to restructure its manufacturing, marketing, and distribution activities. After getting input from more than 6000 employees, the company brought together a task force of almost 200 managers at corporate headquarters in San Francisco for a year to develop the design. The restructuring, which began in the summer of 1994, is expected to cost about $500 million.

Training and Development—Individual performance involves both task completion and relationship development for individuals in a total quality environment. Balancing both conceptual competence to complete technical tasks with moral/emotional process competence to build the work community is a dual performance responsibility for total quality employees. Moral/emotional competence is exhibited by sincere communication styles that nurture trust and respect, compassionate interactions that sustain a human solace system when adjusting to technical systems that threaten the team stress threshold, and engaging in pain sharing in meetings. Pain sharing builds community at work, because after resolving technical problems in a meeting, it is important for all employees to see who is paying a price and who is not in any new work initiative. This acknowledgment of differential quality of work life effects builds the work unit social memory of who is sacrificing and who is benefiting, which is later used as an informal organizational justice process in balancing the books among employees in future work decisions.[37]

According to the General Accounting Office of the U.S. government (1990), total quality training is typically a two-stage process.[38] The first stage consists of general awareness training to create a common frame of reference and a sense of the leadership commitment. The second stage focuses on concrete skill-based training designed to prepare individuals to become effective members of quality improvement teams. For example, in a small convenience sample of Fortune 199 firms, Olian and Rynes (1991) found the most common training content to be (in descending order of frequency): personal interaction skill, quality improvement process and problem solving, team leading, team building, running meetings, statistical process control, supplier qualification training, and benchmarking.[39]

Development is the other facet of this total quality OD process. *Development is the ongoing process of planned and structured activities designed to improve individual, team, and organizational performance.* Total quality OD normally includes individual and team training and development, organization development, and career development.[40] The identification and nurturing of potential is a never-ending enabling responsibility of total quality OD/HR professionals. Since systems and processes both constrain and enhance the performance of individuals and teams, they are thus an important part of total quality performance. Total quality professionals must attend to various aspects of system development, such as structure, policies, methods, procedures, and ethical work culture.

Formal quality training appears to be the most common technique for initiating and sustaining employee involvement and meeting OD objectives, at least during the early stages of total quality implementation. According to the Conference Board (1991), 90% of manufacturing companies and 75% of service corporations report using some sort of training in their total quality efforts.[41] However, a KPMG Peat Marwick survey (1991) found that while training was the most important initiative in the early stages of total quality implementation, cross-functional quality teams and work process redesign became relatively more important in more mature implementations.[42] Across companies that practice total quality, the median number of hours devoted to quality training (per employee) was 20, with a larger commitment in corporations just launching their total quality efforts.

Career development is an increasingly important component of OD. Career development is the process by which individuals progress through a series of work-related stages, each of which is characterized by a relatively unique set of issues, themes and tasks.[43] Career development activities in a total quality firm run the spectrum from person centered (self-directed workbooks and tapes) to team centered (team enrichment exercises) to organization centered (corporate succession planning). Total quality OD professionals need to be sensitive to the job insecurity and career gridlock concerns of many contemporary U.S. employees.

Organization Size—Organization size is an issue for OD practitioners, because there is evidence that smaller, more focused organizational units may be more effective for certain types of work. Burke states the questions about size that researchers need to answer:[44]

> We need to know more about (1) how to maximize the advantages of large and small simultaneously, (2) provide boundary-spanning activities that mitigate the negative consequences of "silos" in large organizations, and (3) determine when a unit becomes too large and needs to be subdivided.

Organization Performance—Organizational performance has traditionally been measured primarily in terms of cost, market share, profits, and other financial measures. While these measures will always be important for "keeping score" (to use Peter Drucker's phrase), other measures of organizational performance are being requested or demanded by other organizational stakeholders. For example, the awareness of quality is at an all-time high among customers in every country. Environmental issues have caused a "green revolution" in Europe, and explicit environmental quality requirements have been built into the latest revisions of ISO 9000. Workplace diversity, health, safety, and security advocates all can bring pressure to bear on organizations for new performance measures, processes, and accountability for quality efforts. For example, total quality OD professionals need to demonstrate awareness and control of the adverse impacts to health, safety, and security generated by inadequate processes/procedures, equipment insufficiency, and employee error. The aftermath of the Exxon Valdez oil spill incident indicates the extent to which company patterns of overscheduling work and systemic pressures to meet unrealistic deadlines contribute to poor performance which can damage the health, safety, and security of multiple stakeholders

These shifts from a traditional to a total quality OD approach require changes in the approaches used by OD practitioners which reflect the total quality emphasis.[45]

Total Quality Organization Development Interventions During Process Transitions

During process transitions, as organizations struggle to change from old paradigms to new ones, total quality OD practitioners can provide the expertise to deal with multiple issues that face the changing organization. As they focus on major organizational categories such as leadership, the business–customer relationship, work force relationships and processes, and organization systems, total quality OD practitioners can help sort out the transition issues and propose interventions to carry the organizational change through to a point of equilibrium, as shown in Table 4.7.

TOTAL QUALITY ORGANIZATION DEVELOPMENT PROCESS MANAGEMENT

Total quality OD process management involves the systematic implementation of the eight OD processes. To accomplish this, total quality OD professionals need to master a wide range of new process improvement tools.[46] While the number of such tools runs into the hundreds, seven "higher level" process management and planning tools are provided in this section. The term "higher level" planning is not meant to imply that only top managers should be involved in the use of such tools, nor does it mean that the tools are only applicable to corporate-wide change efforts. However, these tools are most useful where reorganization, process changes, or improvements involve several groups or departments, require coordination with other or-

Table 4.7 Focus, Transition Issues, and Total Quality Organization Development Interventions

Focus	Transition issues	Interventions
Leadership	Walking the talk	• Operating agreements • Third-party coaching • Choose new leaders
	Exhibiting new behavior	• Operating agreements • Third-party coaching • Team coaching • 360° feedback
	Committing to success	• Individual choice • Commitment to success—a choice
Business and customer	Remembering the customer	• Instill customer-mindedness (banners, notices, reminders) • Measurement system • Customer "hit squad" • Full-value contracting • Realistic expectations
	Frustration with slow buy-in	• Dual-track operations • Visible successes • Put the hierarchy to rest • Road map for change • Chart progress
	What do we do with the hierarchy?	• Everyone on a team • Basic skills training • Redesign appraisal/compensation systems • Measure effectiveness • Celebrate milestones
Work force relationships and processes	"I'm from Missouri" Doing real work Building tolerance for ambiguity Developing new skills	• Senior management walks the talk • Define the new covenant • Redefine the work culture • Real work in real time by real teams • Create collaborative teams • Operating agreements • Establish milestones • Implement new roles and responsibilities • Identify skills needed • Provide collaborative skills training
Organization systems	Becoming focused on the internal customer	• Customer engagement process • Meet the immediate customer needs • Full value contracts • Mindset and behavioral change

Table 4.7 (continued) Focus, Transition Issues, and Total Quality
Organization Development Interventions

Focus	Transition issues	Interventions
Organization systems (continued)	Moving from control to contribution	• New work processes • Evaluate and realign systems • No sacred cows
	Realigning organization systems	• Open up discussion • Realign all systems • Cross-functional team assessment
	Creating a healing culture	• Values review • Delegate management responsibilities to teams • 360° feedback • Results-based performance • Integrated skills-development process • Customer-driven information system

Source: Frank W. Voehl, Strategy Associates.

ganizations or partners, and are beyond the small project level in size and scope.

The seven major process improvement tools include *affinity diagram/KJ method, interrelationship digraph, tree diagram, matrix diagram, arrow diagram, process decision program chart (PDPC), and matrix data analysis.*

1. Affinity Diagram/KJ Method—Organizes pieces of information into groupings based on the natural relationships that exist among them. Used when large numbers of ideas, issues, and other items are being collected.

The affinity diagram/KJ method was developed in the 1960s in Japan by Kawakita Jiro (the "KJ" is a registered trademark owned by the Kawayoshida Research Center). For a human resource management (HRM) application, it may be extremely helpful to use this tool in the early stages of a large-scale process or reengineering project to consider responses and ideas generated by questions such as: What are our *essential* products or processes? How might departments be rearranged if we went from a functional to a process orientation? What system might we use for assessing individual and group effectiveness if we eliminate performance reviews?

2. Interrelationship Digraph—Displays the cause-and-effect relationship between factors relating to a central issue. Factors that have a high number of relationships (arrows going into and emanating from) are usually the most fundamental or critical. A HRM application would be delineating the mul-

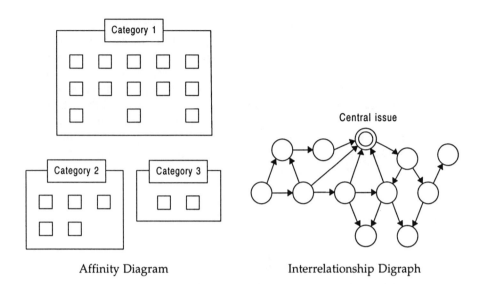

Affinity Diagram   Interrelationship Digraph

tiple causes for turnover and diagramming responses to the question "Why is this happening?" The diagram above shows both the strength (indicated by the boldness of the arrow) and direction of causes.

3. Tree Diagram—Shows the complete range and sequence of subtasks required to achieve an objective. Tree diagrams have been used for many years in decision analysis. They have been called "decision trees" in operations research literature. One of the best-known models of leadership, the Vroom Jago model,[47] uses a decision tree to show the degrees of participation that leaders can and should use in making decisions. This model is referenced in many organization behavior and TQM texts today.

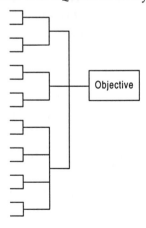

4. Matrix Diagram—Shows the relationships among various pieces of data. For example, quality function deployment (QFD) is a process to understand the voice of the customer and to translate it into technical design parameters, subsystems, parts, components, processes, and process controls. The House of Quality matrix used in QFD is shown below. It depicts the relationship between primary, secondary, and tertiary customer needs and the technical design parameters or substitute quality characteristics which, if met, would ensure that the customer's needs will be satisfied. This type of diagram could be used by OD practitioners in planning collective bargaining sessions by anticipating and soliciting initial union demands.

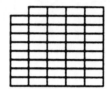

5. Arrow Diagram—Used to develop the best schedule and appropriate controls to accomplish an objective and answers "when" questions. It is very similar to the program evaluation review technique (PERT) and the critical path method (CPM).

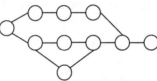

6. Process Decision Program Chart (PDPC)—Used to plan the implementation of new or revised tasks that are complex. The PDPC maps out all conceivable events that can go wrong and contingencies for these events. HRM applications are evident in forecasting contingencies for labor shortages, downsizing effects, and/or new compensation and benefits plans.

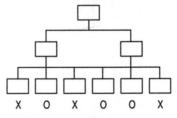

X   O   X   O   O   X

X = Impossible/difficult to do
O = Selected events

7. Matrix Data Analysis—Mathematical analysis of numerical data arranged as matrices (e.g., "Where in the data do we find various patterns?"). There are many methods, often called multivariate analysis, including cluster, multiple regressions, and principle component analysis. Matrix data analysis can be applied to all five of the major HRM processes to quantitatively detect and analyze patterns; it is a useful check on qualitative intuitions about problem identification and causal analysis.

$$w_j = \sum_{i=1}^{p} [i_j \, x]_j$$

In addition to the seven major process management tools, six supplemental process tools include *competitive benchmarking, flowcharts, nominal group technique, structured surveys, trend charts, and Excelerator.*

1. Competitive Benchmarking—Measures process, product, and/or service against those of recognized leaders. Helps establish priorities and targets which lead to a competitive advantage.

The concept of benchmarking was developed and has been used extensively by Xerox.[48] When Xerox was attempting to regain market share that it had lost to Japanese copier manufacturers in the late 1970s and early 1980s, it undertook a study of competitors' products in terms of quality, features, and costs in comparison with Xerox products. Xerox was shocked to learn that its unit manufacturing costs were equal to the Japanese makers' selling price in the United States, the number of suppliers used by Xerox was nine times the number used by the best competitors, assembly line rejects were ten times higher, product lead times were two times longer, and defects per 100 machines were seven times higher. After a second benchmarking study confirmed the results of the first one, Xerox assembled the top 25 managers in the company to begin planning its HRM/TQM efforts which eventually brought about its turnaround.

2. Flowchart—A pictorial diagram of the steps in a process. It is useful for finding out how a process works.

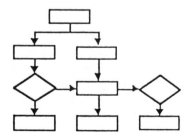

Flowcharting is actually a term that may be used to describe a "family" of useful techniques which can be applied at many levels within an organization. A comprehensive approach was developed by Harrington,[49] who advocates using flowcharting as the basic tool for *business process improvement.* In addition to being used to "map" existing processes, flowcharts can also be used to develop proposed new systems and processes within organizations. OD managers and practitioners frequently use flowcharts during their process of examining current systems and proposing new ones for implementation in organizations.

3. Nominal Group Technique (NGT)—A structured group decision-making process used to assign priorities or rank order groups of ideas.

The nominal group technique is used where agreement about a decision is lacking or where group members have incomplete knowledge about the details of a problem. It was developed by Delbecq and his colleagues in the 1970s[50] and has been used for a wide variety of OD and HRM improvement activities since then. For example, one of the authors used it to obtain responses from a focus group of business faculty on the type and relative importance of changes that were needed in a comprehensive revision of an MBA program at a state university.

The process for performing the NGT is as follows:

- Silent (written) generation of ideas in response to a focused question
- Round-robin recording (usually on a flip chart) of one idea at a time from each group member by a designated recorder
- Clarifying ideas through questions from group members on the meaning of various listed items
- Voting on ideas to prioritize importance; uses a one- or two-stage process
- Closure around a decision of what to do about the prioritized items

4. Structured Surveys—Written questionnaires in which survey questions are designed to address anticipated quality problems.

As pointed out in Chapter 1, one of the earliest tools used by OD practitioners was survey research. There are many standardized survey instruments that can be used to assess organizational climate, morale, leadership characteristics, and other measure of organizational health and performance. These can be extremely valuable in pinpointing the need for organization change and quality improvement, and they can point to the direction in which the change should take place. The survey questionnaire generally has a number of questions, followed by a point scale that usually ranges from low to high, indicating some perceived degree of disagreement to agreement for each item. It is easy to quantify the results of such an instrument, but difficult to determine whether they reflect the true opinions of the respondents.

5. Trend Chart—Used to monitor shifts in long-range averages and graph results of a process such as defect reduction, admissions increases, machine downtime, or phone calls.

Trend charts have also been used for many years to graphically depict data. HR practitioners can use them in planning for organizational interventions by observing the trends in survey results from period to period and perhaps comparing them on the same graph with changes in grievances or employment levels over a period of months or even years. The advantage of doing this is that it allows HR specialists and managers to have a common basis for understanding and to "speak from facts."

6. Excelerator—A personal computer software tool for systems analysis, design, and documentation. Available from Index Tech Corp., 1 Main Street, Cambridge, MA 02142.

This computerized software package contains various tools, which make it easy for an analyst to enter data and to have that data summarized in chart, graph, or other form so that it can be distributed and discussed and conclusions on courses of action drawn.

A survey of 40 firms (Baldrige Award winners or finalists, Deming Prize winners, or nationally recognized leaders in quality) using basic and advanced quality tools was made by Janice Ceridwen of Ventana Corporation.[51] Of the seven "new tools" of quality, she found that the four that were used most included arrow diagram (49%), prioritization matrix (39%), structure tree (22%), and affinity diagram (14%). She reported that managers found the tools extremely powerful but were difficult to use.

In summary, it should be pointed out that at every level of process improvement, from *kaizen* to breakthrough dominance, the objective is not merely to correct problems, but to creatively improve the process. Therefore, process problems need not be considered "out of control" situations to be brought back under control and "fixed," but opportunities for creative invention and change.

REVIEW QUESTIONS

4.1 List the three types of continuous improvement, along with some of their characteristics.

4.2 What are the five steps of organizational renewal that lead to sustained competitive advantage?

4.3 How do traditional and process mindsets differ? Why is it important for managers and OD practitioners to make the psychological transition from the former to the latter?

4.4 Give a brief definition of systems, structures, processes, and techniques, and tell how they are interrelated.

4.5 Define reengineering and compare the concept with TQM.

4.6 Why might Frederick W. Taylor be considered the "father of reengineering"?

4.7 List Harrington's five phases of business process improvement. Can this be considered a "process" for process improvement? Why or why not?

4.8 List the eight organizational processes with which OD practitioners are (or should be) concerned. What are some of the characteristics that they possess under different contingencies of continuous improvement approaches and how do they differ from a traditional OD philosophy?

4.9 How does performance appraisal differ in a total quality environment from the appraisal that has occurred traditionally in organizations?

4.10 Cite some of the appropriate total quality OD interventions to bring about the transition from the traditional to the total quality focus in (1) leadership, (2) business and customer, (3) work force relationships and processes, and (4) organization systems.

4.11 Define each of the seven major process management tools, and demonstrate how each could be used in OD process problem solving.

DISCUSSION QUESTIONS

4.1 The three types of total quality continuous improvement are *kaizen*, competitive parity, and breakthrough dominance.
  A. In what competitive situations would each one be most beneficial for a corporation to pursue?
  B. What internal organizational capabilities must be present in order to achieve success with each one?

4.2 Harrington developed a six-level process quality certification model to suggest the degree to which processes approach or meet "world-class" standards. Discuss how this classification scheme might be of use to OD practitioners.

4.3 Drawing on your own experience, what difficulties might an organization encounter in shifting from an evaluative approach to an improvement approach in its appraisal of performance? Would managers find it more or less difficult to make the shift than employees? Why?

4.4 What major barriers and opportunities would need to be addressed in order to successfully move from a level 1 to a level 6 ethical work culture while simultaneously doing so for related organizational processes?

4.5 Do you think that small or large organizations are more effective, quality minded, and efficient today? Give reasons for your answer.

4.6 What do you consider to be the *essential* requirements needed for an OD practitioner, department, or consulting organization making the "paradigm shift" from a traditional OD focus to a total quality OD focus?

ENDNOTES

1. Harrington, H. James (1995). *Total Improvement Management*. New York: McGraw-Hill; Harrington, H. James (1991). *Business Process Improvement*. New York: McGraw-Hill, pp. 9–14; Lillrank, P. and Kano, N. (1989). *Continuous Improvement*. Ann Arbor, MI: University of Michigan Press, pp. 15–26.
2. Voehl, Frank W. (1992). *Total Quality: Principles and Processes within Organizations*. Pompano Beach, FL: Strategy Associates, pp. 4–7.
3. Imai, Masaaki (1986). *Kaizen: The Key to Japan's Competitive Success*. New York: Random House, pp. 10–70; Hammer, Michael and Champy, James (1993). *Reengineering the Corporation*. New York: Harper Business, pp. 31–158; Moody, Patricia E. (1993). *Breakthrough Partnering*. Essex Junction, VT: Oliver Wight, pp. 49–132.
4. Imai (endnote 3), pp. 20–40; Kume, Hitoshi (1985). *Statistical Methods for Quality Improvement*. Tokyo: AOTS Press, pp. 10–60.
5. Long, Carl and Vickers-Koch, Mary (1995). "Is it Process Management and, with or instead of TQM?" *The Journal for Quality and Participation*. June, p. 71.
6. Mills, Charles A. (1989). *The Quality Audit: A Management Evaluation Tool*. New York: McGraw-Hill, pp. 20–64; Mills, David (1993). *Quality Auditing*. New York: Chapman and Hall, pp. 30–71.
7. Gleckman, Howard with John Carey, Russell Mitchell, Tim Smart, and Chris Roush (1993). "The Technology Payoff." *Business Week*. June 14, p. 57.
8. Evans, James R. and Lindsay, William M. (1993). *The Management and Control of Quality*. Minneapolis: West Publishing, p. 14.
9. Voehl (endnote 2), pp. 20–25.
10. Champy, James (1995). *Reengineering Management*. New York: HarperCollins, p. 2.
11. Hammer and Champy (endnote 3), p. 32.
12. Stowell, Daniel M. (1994). "Innovative Approaches to Quality and Downsizing." *Quality Digest*. April, pp. 46–52.
13. Pfau, Loren D. (1989). "Total Quality Management Gives Companies a Way to Enhance Position in Global Marketplace." *Industrial Engineering*. Vol. 21, No. 4, pp. 17–21.
14. Johansson, Henry J. et al. (1993). *Business Process Reengineering: Breakpoint Strategies for Market Dominance*. New York: Wiley, p. 10.
15. Harrington, 1991 (endnote 1), p. 23; Harrington, H.J. (1989). *The Quality/Profit Connection*. Milwaukee: ASQC Quality Press, pp. 38–59.
16. Harrington, 1991 (endnote 1), pp. 164–165.
17. Harrington, 1991 (endnote 1), p. 206. Order reversed by the authors.
18. Ryan, Kathleen D. and Oestreich, Daniel K. (1991). *Driving Fear Out of the Workplace*. San Francisco: Jossey-Bass, pp. 3–102.

19. Harrington, 1995 (endnote 1), p. 39.
20. Simler, Ricardo (1993). *Maverick*. New York: Warner Books, p. 196.
21. Beckhard, R. and Harris, R.T. (1987). *Organizational Transitions: Managing Complex Change*, 2nd edition. Reading, MA: Addison-Wesley.
22. Bridges, William (1991). *Managing Transitions*. New York: Addison-Wesley.
23. Ibid., pp. 3–6.
24. Ibid., pp. 19–30; Fried, Y. (1995). "TQM and the Legal Environment in the United States: A Neglected Issue in the TQM Literature." *Academy of Management Review*. Vol. 20, pp. 15–17; Morgan, R.B. and Smith, J.E. (1996). *Staffing the New Workplace*. Milwaukee: ASQC.
25. Shiba, Shoji, Graham, A., and Walden D. (1993). *A New American TQM: Four Practical Revolutions in Management*. Cambridge, MA: Productivity Press, pp. 107–188; Tenner, Arthur R. and DeToro, Irving J. (1992). *Total Quality Management*. Reading, MA: Addison-Wesley, pp. 97–124.
26. Cardy, R.L. and Dobbins, G.H. (1996). "Human Resource Management on a Total Quality Organizational Environment." *Journal of Quality Management*. Vol. 1, No. 1, pp. 5–21.
27. Knouse, S.B. (1995). *The Reward and Recognition Process in Total Quality Management*. Milwaukee: ASQC; Masterson, S. and Taylor, M. (1996). "Total Quality Management and Performance Appraisal: An Integrative Perspective." *Journal of Quality Management*. Vol. 1, No. 1, pp. 67–91; Kohn, Alfie (1993). *Punished by Rewards*. Boston: Houghton Mifflin, pp. 183–186.
28. Kohn (endnote 27), pp. 49–67, 270–276.
29. Petrick, Joseph A. and Furr, Diana S. (1995). *Total Quality in Managing Human Resources*. Delray Beach, FL: St. Lucie Press, pp. 146–148.
30. Schonberger, R. J. (1990). *Building a Chain of Customers*. New York: Free Press, pp. 95–107.
31. Schonberger (endnote 30), pp. 86–87.
32. Greene, R.T. (1993). *Global Quality: A Synthesis of the World's Best Management Methods*. Milwaukee, WI and Homewood, IL: ASQC Quality Press/Business One Irwin, pp. 137–140; Sheppard, B.H., Lewicki, R.J., and Minton, J.W. (1992). *Organizational Justice: The Search for Fairness in the Workplace*. New York: Lexington Books, pp. 9–108; Olian, J. and Rynes, S. (1991). "Making Total Quality Work: Aligning Organizational Processes, Performance, Measures and Stakeholders." *Human Resource Management*. Vol. 30, No. 3, p. 312.
33. Crystal, G.S. (1992). *In Search of Excess: The Overcompensation of American Executives*. New York: W.W. Norton, pp. 15–70.
34. Sheppard, Lewicki, and Minton (endnote 32), pp. 109–201; Withey, M.J. and Cooper, W.H. (1989). "Predicting Exit, Voice, Loyalty and Neglect." *Administrative Science Quarterly*. Vol. 34, No. 4, pp. 521–539.
35. The Conference Board (1991). *Employee Buy-in to Total Quality*. New York: The Conference Board, Report No. 974, pp. 11–17; KPMG Peat Marwick (1991). *Quality Improvement Initiatives Through the Management of Human Resources*. Short Hills, NJ: KPMG Peat Marwick, pp. 15–20.
36. Mitchell, Russell with O'neal, Michael (1994). "Managing by Values." *Business Week*. August 1, pp. 47–49.
37. Greene (endnote 32), pp. 215–216.

38. General Accounting Office (1990). *Management Practices—U.S. Companies Improve Performance Through Quality Efforts.* Washington, DC: U.S. General Accounting Office, pp. 7–12.

39. Olian, J.D. and Rynes, S.L. (1991). "Survey of U.S. Quality Practices." Unpublished manuscript. College of Business and Management, University of Maryland.

40. Harris, David M. and De Simone, R.L. (1994). *Human Resource Development.* New York: Dryden Press, pp. 430–450; McCormack, S.P. (1992). "TQM: Getting It Right the First Time." *Training and Development Journal.* Vol. 41, No. 1, pp. 25–27; Schonberger, R.J. (1992). Total Quality Management Cuts a Broad Swath Through Manufacturing and Beyond." *Organizational Dynamics.* Vol. 20, No. 4, pp. 16–28; Bowen, D.E. and Lawler E.E. III (1992). "Total Quality-Oriented Human Resources Management." *Organizational Dynamics.* Vol. 20, No. 4, pp. 29–41; Tollison, P. (1992). "Assessing TQM Training Needs." *Journal for Quality and Participation.* Vol. 15, No. 1, pp. 50–54.

41. The Conference Board (endnote 35), pp. 15–17; Blackburn, R.S. and Rosen, B. (1994). "Human Resource Management Practices and Total Quality Management Paper." Paper presented at the Annual Meeting of the Academy of Management, Dallas, August. Argues that nonexecutive quality training is the most effective utilization of quality training expenditures.

42. KPMG Peat Marwick (endnote 35), pp. 29–32.

43. Hall, D.T. and Richter, J. (1990). "Career Gridlock: Baby Boomers Hit the Wall." *The Executive.* Vol. 14, No. 4, p. 19.

44. Burke, W. Warner (1995). "Organization Change: What We Know, What We Need to Know." *ODC Newsletter, Academy of Management.* Winter, p. 10.

45. Jackson, Susan (1995). "Special Topic Forum on Ecologically Sustainable Organizations." *Academy of Management Review.* Vol. 20, No. 4, pp. 873–1090; Blackburn, R. and Rosen, B. (1993). "Total Quality and Human Resources Management: Lessons Learned from Baldrige Award-Winning Companies." *Academy of Management Executive.* Vol. 7, No. 3, pp. 49–66; Schmidt, W.H. and Finnigan, J.P. (1993). *TQ Manager.* San Francisco: Jossey-Bass, pp. 45–138; Schuler, R.S. and Harris, D. (1992). *Managing Quality.* Reading, MA: Addison-Wesley, pp. 89–140; Lawler, E., Mohrman, S., and Ledford, G. (1992). *Employee Involvement and Total Quality Management: Practices and Results in Fortune 1000 Companies.* San Francisco: Jossey-Bass; Olian and Rynes (endnote 32), pp. 303–333.

46. Gitlow, H., Oppenheim, A., and Oppenheim, R. (1995). *Quality Management: Tools and Methods for Improvement.* Burr Ridge, IL: Irwin.

47. Vroom, V.H. and Jago, A.G. (1988). *The New Leadership: Managing Participation in Organizations.* Englewood Cliffs, NJ: Prentice-Hall, pp. 20–65.

48. Watson, Gregory H. (1993). *Strategic Benchmarking.* New York: John Wiley and Sons, pp. 31–77.

49. Harrington (endnote 15), pp. 40–49.

50. Delbecq, A.L., Van de Ven, A.H., and Gustafson, D.H. (1975). *Group Techniques for Program Planning: A Guide to Nominal and Delphi Processes.* Glenview, IL: Scott Foresman.

51. Ceridwen, Janice (1992). "Using Quality Tools: What's Working Well?" *The Journal for Quality and Participation.* March, pp. 92–99.

ABSTRACTS

ABSTRACT 4.1
REENGINEERING WORK: DON'T AUTOMATE, OBLITERATE

Hammer, Michael
Harvard Business Review, July–August 1990, pp. 104–112

This article looks at the less-than-adequate results of process rationalization and automation—two common methods for boosting organizational production. Hammer argues that these methods, which are based mainly in heavy investments in information technology, have not been up to par because they are usually used in attempts to mechanize and speed up old processes and techniques. Thus, these old job designs, work flows, control mechanisms, and organizational structures are outdated relics of the eras of efficiency and control and are not geared for today's world of innovation, speed, service, and quality. They should be completely thrown out and business processes "reengineered" to achieve improvements.

The author cites the example of Mutual Benefit Life (MBL). Prior to reengineering its process for approving insurance applications, paperwork had to go through a 30-step, 5-department journey involving credit checking, quoting, rating, underwriting, etc. The process of passing applications around took anywhere from 24 hours to 25 days, but the work time itself was clocked at only 17 minutes. The president of MBL demanded a 60% improvement in productivity. The management team in charge of reengineering the process found that shared databases and computer networks could make different kinds of information available to a single person, and expert systems could help people with limited experience make sound decisions. A new position, the case manager, was created. Each has total responsibility for an application from the time it is received to the time the policy is issued. They are supported by PC-based workstations that run an expert system and connect to a range of automated systems on a mainframe. Senior underwriters or physicians are on hand to counsel and advise. MBL can now complete an application in four hours, and average turnaround takes two to five days.

Reengineering involves the notion of discontinuous thinking—of recognizing and breaking away from the outdated rules and fundamental assumptions underlying operations. New technologies, demographics, and business objectives have left behind the old methods of organizing work into a sequence of separate tasks, at the same time employing complex mechanisms to track progress. These control-and-discipline patterns of organization are so ingrained that it is hard to conceive of work being done any other way. Managers who try to adapt their processes to new circumstances usually just end up creating more problems.

Reengineering requires examining the fundamental processes of the business from a cross-functional perspective. This is done by assembling a team representing the functional units involved in the process being reengineered. The team must scrutinize the existing process until it really understands the objective of the process. It should then determine which steps really add value and search for new ways to achieve the result. The team should keep asking *why* and *what if* questions. (Why do we need the manager's signature on a requisition? What if we give it to this other guy to sign?)

There are several principles of reengineering, including:

1. Organize around outcomes, not tasks. This requires having one person perform all the steps in a process. Designing that person's job around an objective or outcome instead of a single task opens up new possibilities for improvement.
2. Have those who use the output of the process perform the process. To capitalize on the benefits of specialization and scale, companies often establish special departments to perform specialized processes. Departments do only one type of work and are "customers" of other groups' processes. Now computer technology, such as in-house and supplier databases and catalogs and customer service help lines, allows each "customer" to interact and get what it needs from other departments and companies at a faster pace. With proper coordination, the process runs smoothly.
3. Subsume information-processing work into the real work that produces the information. In the past, people who produced information did not have the time or were not trusted to process it. They were required to pass it on to the department that had the "authority" to approve an expenditure or action. Thus, under the old approach, the receiving department checked materials from a vendor, then sent it to accounts payable, which authorized payment and sent it to data processing, which cut and mailed the check. Ford Motor Company reengineered its accounts payable process and now has the receiving clerk check a database to see if a purchase order exists for the materials. If so, receipt is acknowledged, and a check is automatically issued by the computer. Needless to say, the accounts receivable department has a lot fewer people than before.
4. Treat geographically dispersed resources as though they were centralized. Decentralizing resources (people, equipment, or inventory) gives better service to those who use it, but the cost of redundancy, bureaucracy, and missed economies of sale generally outweighs the service improvements. Databases and telecom networks now give scale economies and improved coordination while maintaining flexibility and service.
5. Parallel activities should be linked instead of having their results integrated. When separate units perform the same function, or different functions that eventually come together, connections should be formed and functions coor-

dinated to save time and effort. Communication networks, shared databases, and teleconferencing can bring independent groups together so that coordination is ongoing.

6. The major decisions and control structure for each process should be placed with the workers who perform it. In this way, management layers can be compressed and the organization leveled. Information technology can collect and process data, and expert systems can to some extent supply knowledge, so people can make their own decisions. As workers become self-managing and self-controlling, the slowness and bureaucracy of hierarchy vanish.

7. Incoming information should be collected at the source, and collected only once. Previously, each department or unit had its own requirements which had to be fulfilled and its own forms to be filled out. Waiting for all the necessary forms and requirements was just part of the routine. Now with on-line databases, bar coding, and electronic data interchange, we are saved from having to enter the same data time and time again.

The concept of reengineering encourages us to "think big." In Hammer's words: "We have the tools to do what we need to. Information technology offers many options for reorganizing work. But our imaginations must guide our decisions about technology, not the other way around. We must have the boldness to imagine taking 78 days out of an 80-day turnaround time, cutting 75% overhead, and eliminating 80% of the errors. These are not unrealistic goals. If managers have the vision, reengineering will provide a way."

ABSTRACT 4.2
WORLD-CLASS PRODUCTIVITY AT STANDARD AERO

Sharman, Paul A.
CMA Magazine, April 1991, pp. 7–12

Major changes in productivity followed the adoption of TQM at Standard Aero (SA), a Winnipeg company employing 700 workers, one of the largest suppliers of airline engine repair and overhaul. Where the process of airline engine repair and overhaul normally takes up to two months, Standard Aero has set itself the objective of cutting the two months down to 15 days. Faster turnaround requires the elimination of inefficient activities and waiting time.

The driving force behind the change has been Bob Hamaberg, president of SA, who joined the company in 1985. In July 1987, SA was acquired in a leveraged buyout by Avcorp. Hamaberg, then general manager, was assigned to sell off the distribution portion of the business. During this time, he examined the necessity of all purchases made by the company and discovered that poor forecasting was causing millions of dollars to be spent on purchasing and storing unnecessary inventory. Hamaberg set about improving forecasting accuracy by establishing an initial target of 75%, providing incentives to SA distribution customers to examine and improve their forecasting accuracy, and imposing penalties on them if they failed to do so.

Task forces to reduce company inventory were set up to examine each of the company's six business units. Each multifunctional group was comprised of an accountant, a buyer, an inspector, and a mechanic from the shop floor. By identifying overstocked or obsolete inventory, and by selling existing stock or canceling unnecessary orders, SA was able to reduce $30 million of projected material requirements off its own 12-month rolling forecast which it provides to suppliers. It also demanded that suppliers deliver 100% against its new forecasts. The result is that the current inventory investment dropped 50%, with considerable attendant cash flow benefit.

In 1989, the British conglomerate Hawker Siddeley purchased SA on advice from Hamaberg. Hamaberg met Dr. Alan K. Watkins, recently appointed managing director and chief executive of Hawker Siddeley, formerly of Lucas Industries. Watkins introduced Hamaberg to the TQM concept by reviewing its success at Lucas Industries. Hamaberg returned to SA and crash-started a series of TQM programs. The first, through examination of reports and practices, eliminated 20% of the company's annual paper consumption. The next target was the accounting office. Accounting employees were introduced to TQM, and their supervisors were introduced to the concept of employee empowerment. The six most senior finance managers were reassigned to operations, reporting directly to the business unit managers. The business unit accountants were now responsible for the accuracy of transactions of all kinds associated with their operations. Within a short time, accounting record accuracy improved substantially. Other organizations within the company quickly followed suit on TQM.

In 1990, SA's largest unit, the T56 Allison Engine Overhaul, began a joint venture with Lucas Industries and Hawker Siddeley to redesign the entire business according to TQM standards. The target was the aforementioned reduction of 75% turnover time for engine overhauls. The task force assigned to the program was to be headed up full time by a Lucas facilitator and would run the business once the project phase was complete.

The team went through the five-step process of (1) identifying the business, its players, markets, and competition; (2) interviewing customers to determine their needs and establish a new rapport; (3) analyzing customer complaints to determine strengths and weaknesses; (4) determining which customers and business it wanted; and (5) redesigning the business unit, relative to the criteria identified, to meet the established goal. This meant evaluating every step of the business, eliminating waste activities, and identifying a brand new set of performance measurements to focus on flow of work in order to meet customers' needs.

At the time of publication of this article, the 15-day turnaround target had been reached and, through the continuous improvement policy, will soon be surpassed. Company results show earnings up 45% in the last year on sales increases for the same period of 4.5%. Cash flow exceeded profits by 50%, thanks to the improvements of TQM.

CASE STUDY

MERCY HOSPITAL'S EXPERIENCE: TRANSITION FROM A FUNCTIONAL TO A PROCESS ORGANIZATION*

In the health care field across the nation, mergers, alliances, consolidations, physician practice acquisitions, physician–hospital organizations, and a number of other organizational forms have developed in preparation for the day when a single check will be received from a sponsor to cover health care needs of the enrolled population in a managed care environment. In response to this demanding environment, the Mercy Health System has developed an integrated community health system in the greater Cincinnati, Ohio, region. This system is comprised of four facilities, described below.

MERCY HEALTH SYSTEM NETWORK

The Mercy Health System (MHS), Cincinnati Regional Community, has developed a position paper, similar to a mission statement, to assist its member organizations in developing integrated community health systems. This "system" is defined as an organized group of health care providers who cover the continuum of health needs. They act in concert to continually improve the effectiveness and efficiency of services. Energy is directed at optimizing the health of enrolled populations and, ultimately, entire communities. An ideal local or regional system will have the following characteristics:

- Optimize community health, not maximize medical procedures
- Maintain incentives for efficiency and effectiveness
- Eliminate unnecessary duplication, yet promote beneficial competition
- Maintain continuity between all providers
- Hold itself accountable for outcomes and value

While many health care organizations have approached integration using the traditional business model of vertical and horizontal integration, MHS has defined integration primarily in terms of goal, incentive, and values integration, not structural integration. It has recognized that merger and acquisition is not the only method to meet this definition. MHS also believes that it is possible for

---

*Adapted with permission from a term paper of the same title by Ms. Barbara Dickison, Vice President of Operations, Mercy Hospital Anderson, Cincinnati, Ohio.

otherwise wholly independent organizations to share common goals, incentives, and values and to therefore achieve a symbiotic relationship. Under these guidelines and definition, the Mercy Health System–Greater Cincinnati Region was developed with four hospitals, including such services as a long-term care facility, a freestanding surgery center, and home care and hospice entities, under a single umbrella.

MERCY HEALTH SYSTEM–GREATER CINCINNATI REGION

The Mercy Health System–Greater Cincinnati Region (MHS-GCR *or* the Region) has been developing its identity for the past two years. Figure MH-1 shows a conceptual model of the structure of the Region. The system's stakeholders, including sponsors and trustees, payers, medical staff, the work force, and most important, the customers, are placed at the center of the model. Support systems for the customer are the physician and the product line manager subsystems. The product line manager must assure that the customer receives coordinated, cost-effective, quality service designed specifically to fit his or her needs. This service is provided through the coordinated interactions of the clinical nurse specialist, case manager, support services, and care providers. The outer circle identifies all the support services required to deliver quality health care in the Region. These services include human resources, information systems, legal services, etc.

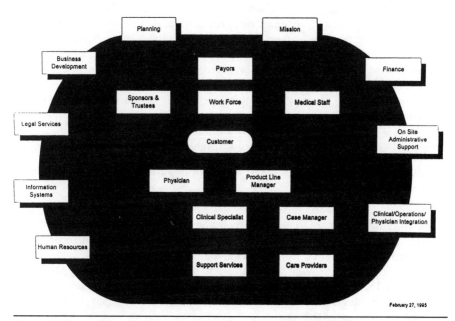

Figure MH-1   Mercy Health System–Greater Cincinnati Region

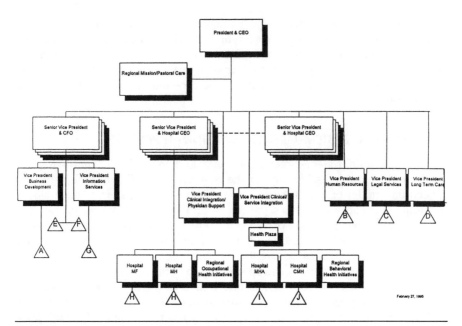

Figure MH-2 Mercy Health System–Greater Cincinnati Region Organization Chart

A traditional organization chart is shown in Figure MH-2. The regional president and CEO has three senior vice presidents as direct reports. Two of these are the CEOs for the four acute care facilities. The other senior vice president is also the regional chief financial officer (CFO) and has responsibility for all regional financial activity, business development, and information services. There are five other vice presidents who report directly to the regional CEO. Two of these positions were recently developed specifically to assist in physician and clinical integration across the Region.

Regional Goals and the Regional Quality Program

In 1995, the Region set four goals in which all regional units were expected to participate, including:

- Quality standards and measurement—The targeted result for this goal is that quality measures are to be developed and standardized across the network and that not less than a 5% overall improvement in the baseline scores that have been established must be achieved.
- Clinical and functional integration—The targeted result for this goal is that at least 15 of 20 identified projects will be complete by the year's end.
- Physician integration—Completion of at least eight out of ten projects is the targeted result for this goal.

- Profitability—With a targeted result to achieve a combined net operating income of 7%. However, it is to be achieved without compromising any of the first three goals.

To achieve the first goal of quality, a task force was formed to develop quality measures to be used throughout the Region. Data collection and reporting forms were developed for each measure. The patient is identified as the center of all quality activity. Seven quality measures were identified, including customer service (e.g., patient satisfaction), waiting time required to access care, revenue enhancement through a Diagnostic Resource Group (DRG) Options program, completion rate of performance appraisals within HRM, reduction of internal cycle times, outcome measures (e.g., unscheduled readmissions), and decrease of length of stay and average charges for six selected DRGs.

DRGs selected for regional focus in the last item have characteristics of high volume and high cost. Five of the DRGs were selected by the task force for evaluation, and each acute care facility selected one DRG. Baseline measurements of regional average length of stay and total charges were established. The goal was to reduce both of these by 5% by the end of the year.

A pool of facilitators was trained and educated in team training and problem-solving methods. These facilitators assist teams working with each quality measure and ensure the development of a consistent approach in the regional quality program.

An incentive compensation program was implemented for individuals at the director level and above throughout the Region. Compensation is based on the achievement of the four goals as previously described. The scope of participation was initially limited to a particular level of management, although a proposal has been made to include all employees in such a program in the future.

MERCY HOSPITAL ANDERSON

Mercy Hospital Anderson (MHA), a member of the regional network, has integrated these goals into its quality improvement program. In addition, MHA has implemented other activities to start the evolution from a functional to a process organization.

The organization's new CEO, an individual who firmly believes that organizations should be quality driven, took office in April 1994. She has made significant efforts to break down the functional "silos." Although some efforts regarding continuous quality improvement (CQI) and a focus on processes had been previously implemented at MHA, there were significant barriers created by the existing strong functional organization. The new CEO stated that her vision was to bring MHA from a functional model to a process model, and her goal was for the organization to be quality driven and customer focused.

One of the first actions taken was to change the quality assurance (QA) model that existed in the organization. Under the original structure, clinical and nonclinical activities were completely separated both functionally and through reporting mechanisms. The clinical areas, including clinical departments and medical staff departments, reported to a combined CQI/QA Committee which met monthly. Reports from this committee were subsequently taken to the medical executive committee and finally to the hospital board of directors. The nonclinical areas report to the CQI Advisory Committee, a conduit for information to flow to administration and the hospital board. This committee was formed when the hospital CQI program was developed, with the assistance of an outside consultant. The purpose of the committee was to guide the CQI process for the hospital, but it became more of a barrier to the process than a facilitative body. "Permission" had to be obtained from this group before any process improvement activity could take place. This was cumbersome and actually reduced commitment to CQI in the organization.

Figure MH-3 shows the performance improvement model that has been adopted. A multifunctional and multilevel team-focused approach to improving organizational performance has been developed. The process is based on the mission, vision, and values of MHS-GCR and is shaped by strategic plans and supported by the leadership of the Region. Priorities are established using pre-selected criteria and teams are chartered to guide performance improvement. The team focuses on quality improvement through the development, implementation, and analysis of critical pathways such as chest pain, pneumonia, and total joint replacement. This team receives statistical data from the individuals coordinating the critical pathways and from the clinical information center. The clinical information center is the source of clinical data that can be obtained through concurrent review, discharge planning, etc. A computer software system named MIDAS is used to collect data and place it in a meaningful format. Activities of these teams are reported at both the Operations Quality Forum and the Medical Staff Quality Forum. Both clinical and nonclinical individuals are members of the Operations Quality Forum. Activities from both of these forums are reported to the Hospital Board QI Committee.

The change from a QA model to a performance improvement model, plus the development and use of a number of multifunctional teams, focused on addressing specific standards related to the hospital accrediting body (JCAHO), has done more to break down barriers in the organization than any other activity to date.

One other change was made that will impact functional barriers in the future. In the past, MHA has attempted to develop a product line concept in the organization. The conceptual model of the regional organization showed that product line management is the element that helps drive the customer-focused approach. This concept is being emphasized at MHA. Figure MH-4 illustrates a matrix approach to product line management at MHA. There are four lines which have been identified: women's health, orthopedics, oncology, and cardiology. A distinction has been made with the concept of "service lines." The emergency department, surgery, and general medical/surgical services have been identified as "service" areas which supply services to the product lines. However, because

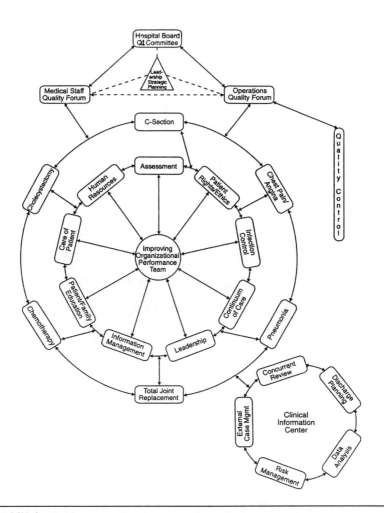

Figure MH-3 Performance Improvement Process

each is important to the profitability of the organization, it was felt that emphasis should be placed on them, as well.

Many of the activities of the new CEO at MHA are reflected in the proposed structures. She has made it a point to develop energy and commitment in the organization. Initial discussion with all levels of staff were focused on breaking down the silos that exist in the organization. Entrepreneurial ideas were invited from all levels, and "wisdoms" of the past were subject to scrutiny. Her behavior as a change leader has developed an openness and trust that had not previously been seen in the organization.

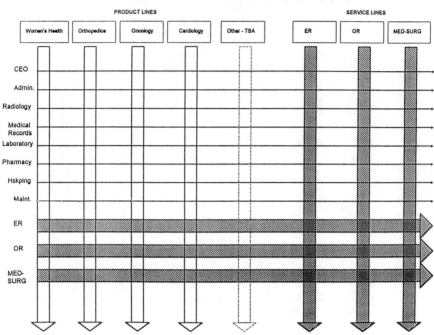

Figure MH-4 Matrix Approach to Product Line Management

Assisting the Organization Change Process

Administrators at MHA realized that to assist individuals with change and the transition process, there should be a clear understanding of what was over and what was not over. Endings should be marked in such a manner that it was clear that they had occurred. Following this, the past should always be treated with respect. Although these actions take considerable time, implementing them can avoid complications in the future which can take much longer to correct. The new beginnings at MHA involved new understandings, new values, new attitudes, and new identities. The purpose of the change had to be real, not abstract, and understood by all. Both the local CEO and the Region have strived to follow these concepts. This required:

- Explaining the basic purpose behind the outcome
- Painting a picture of what the outcome will look and feel like
- Establishing a step-by step plan for phasing in the outcome
- Giving people a part to play in both the plan and the outcome

The efforts made by top management at MHA to explain the need and purpose of the change, paint what the future will look like, provide a plan, and allow individuals to participate have greatly assisted in the transition process.

Quality Improvement at MHA

MHA's mission statement focuses on continuing the healing ministry of Jesus and bringing better quality to life for all, especially to the poor, vulnerable, and underserved. Enhancement of quality of life is sought for patients and their families, the community, and members of the hospital and medical staff by creating an environment responsive to their physical, spiritual, social, and emotional needs.

MHA has followed a CQI process that was introduced approximately three years ago by a consultant. The staff was trained on how to apply the concepts of this program and the tools of total quality management (e.g., brainstorming, sampling, survey, flowcharting, and cause-and-effect diagramming). The organization has developed many outcome measures, and process improvement and continuous improvement activities are ongoing. Most of these activities are related to DRGs within the identified product/service lines. One example of process improvement that was accomplished involved patients having pre-surgical testing (PST) for total joint replacement (TJR).

Patients having TJR surgeries are known to have better outcomes if they are thoroughly educated regarding what to expect following their surgery. The PST process at MHA was examined, and it was found to be complex and tiring for the patient. A multidisciplinary team consisting of the orthopedic service line director, schedulers, physical therapists, nursing, and social work/discharge planning was organized to study the process and determine if improvements could be made. The team mapped the PST process from scheduling through the PST visit, as shown in Figure MH-5. Opportunities for improvement were identified, including:

- Delays in PST procedures, especially in transportation.
- Patients travel around much of the hospital during PST visits.
- Instructions are given to individual patients, when this might be done in groups.
- Nurses are scheduled to see patients at the time that they arrive, but this may be delayed for as much as three hours. Also, nursing assessments are not being done when required.
- The PST visit may last up to four hours.

The team realized that there were scheduling conflicts and that the patient education program needed to be redesigned. The team had the freedom to make the improvements without dealing with any significant barriers, and neither large dollars nor facility restructuring was necessary. Even individuals who had to "change the way they were doing things" were supportive of the new process.

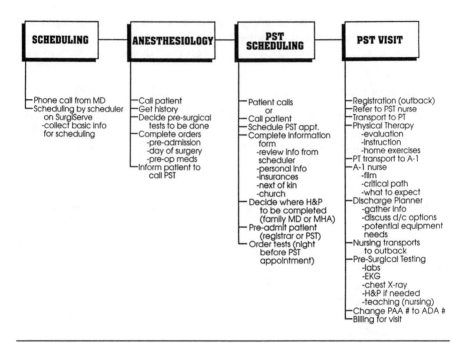

Figure MH-5 Pre-Surgical Testing Continuum of Care–Patient Flow

This probably occurred because they had the opportunity to participate and they understood how complex the PST visit had become for the patient. Some opportunities for improvement were resolved rapidly, such as the transportation and scheduling issues. Restructuring the PST visit to include an educational session for patients using a classroom format required a significant amount of planning. Patient satisfaction for the first session was rated 4 to 5 on a 5-point scale, indicating that the improvement was significant.

An important aspect of the quality improvement plan is assuring that the organization is aware of the activities that have taken place and what outcomes have been achieved. MHA now communicates the information at department meetings, general staff meetings, medical staff meetings, and the hospital and medical staff Quality Forum committee meetings. One technique that has proven to be very effective in delivering the message is storyboards. All of the activities, data collection, and outcomes of multidisciplinary teams' efforts are concisely displayed on a large folding board that can easily be taken from one meeting to the next. After the committees have viewed the storyboards, they are displayed in the cafeteria so that staff and the public are aware of the quality improvement activities.

MHA underwent tremendous change in less than a year, yet there seemed to be a general sense that the changes have been for the best and that further evaluation and work was warranted. How well the staff can function under the new organization design remains to be seen.

QUESTIONS FOR DISCUSSION

1 How has the Mercy Health System–Greater Cincinnati Region and MHA used total quality management principles to restructure the organization(s)?

2 Is it possible for staff that have to go through the chaos of "reengineering" the organization to accept (or even enjoy) the changes? What might be done to bring about this outcome?

3 How does the product line management concept at MHA streamline the process? What costs (in people, time, etc.) might have to be incurred in moving from a departmental approach to a product line approach?

EXERCISE

EXERCISE 4.1   PRACTITIONER ASSESSMENT INSTRUMENT: ORGANIZATION PROCESS CLIMATE

DIRECTIONS

Read each dimension of organization process climate and consider the descriptions at both ends of the scale. Circle the number on the scale that reflects your evaluation of conditions in your organization at this time (1 is the lowest evaluation possible and 20 is the highest evaluation possible).

1. **Reward System:**   The degree to which employees, as individuals and as teams, feel they are being recognized and rewarded for good work rather than being ignored, criticized, or punished when something goes wrong.

Rewards are not in line with effort and performance				Employees are recognized and rewarded positively
1 2 3 4 5	6 7 8 9 10	11 12 13 14 15	16 17 18 19 20	

2. **Standards of Performance:**   The emphasis placed upon quality performance and achieving results, including the degree to which employees feel meaningful and challenging goals are being set at every level of the organization.

Performance standards are low				Performance standards are high
1 2 3 4 5	6 7 8 9 10	11 12 13 14 15	16 17 18 19 20	

3. **Warmth and Support:**   The feeling that friendliness is a valued norm and that employees trust, respect, and offer support to one another. The feeling that good human relationships prevail in the day-to-day work of the organization.

There is little warmth and support in the organization				Warmth and support are characteristic of the organization
1 2 3 4 5	6 7 8 9 10	11 12 13 14 15	16 17 18 19 20	

4. **Leadership:**   As needs for leadership arise, people feel free to take leadership roles and are rewarded for shared successful leadership. The organization is not dominated by or dependent upon just one or two individuals.

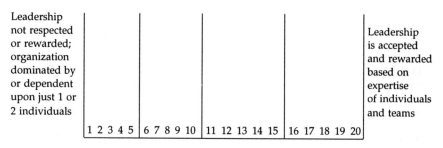

Leadership
not respected
or rewarded;
organization
dominated by
or dependent
upon just 1 or
2 individuals

Leadership
is accepted
and rewarded
based on
expertise
of individuals
and teams

| 1 2 3 4 5 | 6 7 8 9 10 | 11 12 13 14 15 | 16 17 18 19 20 |

5. **Organizational Clarity:**   The feeling among employees that things are well organized and goals and responsibilities are clearly defined rather than being disorderly, confused, or chaotic.

The
organization
is disorderly,
confused, and
chaotic

Organization is
well organized,
with clearly
defined
goals and
responsibilities

| 1 2 3 4 5 | 6 7 8 9 10 | 11 12 13 14 15 | 16 17 18 19 20 |

6. **Communications:**   Important information is shared quickly and accurately—up, down, and sideways—in the organization.

Information is
wrong,
censored, or
unavailable

Information is
accurate, open,
and available

| 1 2 3 4 5 | 6 7 8 9 10 | 11 12 13 14 15 | 16 17 18 19 20 |

7. **Creativity:**   New ideas are sought and used in all areas of the organization. Employee creativity is encouraged at every level of responsibility.

The organiza-
tion is closed
and unrespon-
sive to change

The organization
is innovative
and open
to new ideas

| 1 2 3 4 5 | 6 7 8 9 10 | 11 12 13 14 15 | 16 17 18 19 20 |

8. **Job Stress:** Employees are neither overworked nor underworked. Stress levels are appropriate for the job.

Stress levels are harmful					Stress levels are optimum
	1 2 3 4 5	6 7 8 9 10	11 12 13 14 15	16 17 18 19 20	

9. **Ethics:** The emphasis the organization places upon high standards of moral behavior at all levels of responsibility.

Double standards exist; ethics are low					High standards of conduct are expected at all levels
	1 2 3 4 5	6 7 8 9 10	11 12 13 14 15	16 17 18 19 20	

10. **Tolerance:** The degree of open-mindedness that exists toward different people, ideas, and customs in the organization.

Prejudice and discrimination are the norm					Nonprejudice and nondiscrimination are the norm
	1 2 3 4 5	6 7 8 9 10	11 12 13 14 15	16 17 18 19 20	

11. **Feedback and Controls:** The use of reporting, comparing, and correcting procedures, such as employee evaluations and financial audits.

Controls are used for policing and punishment					Controls are used to provide guidance and solve problems
	1 2 3 4 5	6 7 8 9 10	11 12 13 14 15	16 17 18 19 20	

12. **Resources:** Sufficient financial and physical resources are available to accomplish the job.

Insufficient funds, equipment, and supplies					Supplies, equipment, and funds are sufficient
	1 2 3 4 5	6 7 8 9 10	11 12 13 14 15	16 17 18 19 20	

13. **Employee Growth:** Personal and professional development is emphasized at all levels and in all classifications in the organization.

Employee growth is a low priority in the organization				Employee growth is a high priority in the organization
1 2 3 4 5	6 7 8 9 10	11 12 13 14 15	16 17 18 19 20	

14. **Physical Working Conditions** (lighting, space, heat, washroom facilities, etc.): Safe and comfortable working conditions exist throughout the organization.

Working conditions are poor				Working conditions are good
1 2 3 4 5	6 7 8 9 10	11 12 13 14 15	16 17 18 19 20	

15. **Teamwork:** The amount of understanding and cooperation between different levels and work groups in the organization.

Teamwork is poor				Teamwork is high
1 2 3 4 5	6 7 8 9 10	11 12 13 14 15	16 17 18 19 20	

16. **Employee Pride:** The degree of pride that exists—pride of individual workmanship and pride of organization goals and accomplishments.

Pride is low				Pride is high
1 2 3 4 5	6 7 8 9 10	11 12 13 14 15	16 17 18 19 20	

17. **Employee Involvement:** Responsibility for decision making is broadly shared in the organization. Employees are involved in decisions that affect them.

Low employee participation in decision making				High employee participation in decision making
1 2 3 4 5	6 7 8 9 10	11 12 13 14 15	16 17 18 19 20	

SCORING
Total all the scores you gave to all the dimensions of organization climate and divide by 17. Place this number on the following scale:

Types of Organization Process Climates

1 2 3 4 5	6 7 8 9 10	11 12 13 14 15	16 17 18 19 20
Exploitive	Impoverished	Supportive	Total Quality

INTERPRETATION

Exploitive (1–5.9):   Organizational process climate is autocratic and hierarchical, with virtually no participation by employees. Managers show little confidence or trust in employees, and employees do not feel free to discuss job-related problems with their managers. Exploitive climates rarely survive for any length of time because employees avoid them as much as possible. Where they do exist, they are characterized by a lack of employee loyalty, substandard performance, and recurrent financial crises.

Impoverished (6–10.9):   Organizational process climate attempts to avoid being completely autocratic, but power remains at the top and employees are given only occasional opportunities for participation. Impoverished process climates fall into two categories: benevolent autocracy, in which those at the top of the organization have genuine concern for the welfare of their employees, and neglectful autocracies, in which concern for employees and worker participation are perfunctory. Impoverished process climates rarely excel because employees are never encouraged to do so. Managers may invest only in what will keep employees minimally contented and avoid investments in employee empowerment.

Supportive (11–15.9):   Organizational process climate maintains power in the hands of managers, but there is good communication, encouragement, and participation throughout the organization. Employees understand the goals of the organization, feel free to discuss job-related problems with their managers, and are committed to achieve organization goals as long as the external reward and recognition system compensates them adequately. There is no sense of employee ownership of process and/or product improvement, nor is there a sense of autonomous interdependence between fully mature parties. Supportive process climates create productive but dependent followers and underutilize the intellectual capital of an organization relative to total quality organizations.

Total quality (16–20):   Organizational process climate is one in which a high degree of work empowerment maturity exists in all parties. Employees have a high degree of autonomy to initiate, coordinate, and implement plans to accomplish goals. Communication between employees and managers is open and honest; employees are treated with trust and respect rather than suspicion. Employees have a sense of process ownership and pride in continually improving and learning. Power resides in the logical focus of interest and concern for a process problem rather than in the hierarchical chain of command. Total quality process climates result in the highest work productivity for an organization and the highest quality of work life for responsible employees.

Source: Adapted from Likert, Rensis (1967). *The Human Organization*. New York: McGraw-Hill, pp. 119–125; Manning, George and Curtis, Kent (1988). *Morale: Quality of Work Life*. Cincinnati: South-Western Publishing, pp. 74–81.

CHAPTER 5

SPEAKING WITH FACTS: TQ AND OD PROJECT DIMENSIONS

The focus of Chapter 5 is on two key areas of implementing systems: total quality business projects and total quality organization development (OD) projects. Both are crucial in determining the strength of the third pillar of the House of Total Quality and clarifying the expanding team project responsibilities of employees in a total quality system. Quality projects can be developed for many reasons, including *kaizen,* competitive parity, or breakthrough dominance, as discussed in the previous chapter. They can include product, service, or process design, improvement, or reengineering.

In Chapter 3, a project was defined as a single, nonrecurring event that implements organizational changes through structured phases and specified outcomes, requiring teamwork for successful completion.[1] The major *tasks* in project planning and management include developing the project-centered vision; identifying critical success factors; developing control, estimating, scheduling, and tracking *processes*; and identifying the skills and performance indicators that are required.[2] Total quality tools (described in Chapter 3 and partially detailed in Chapter 4) are used extensively at this level for effective data collection and analysis. Tools that are especially appropriate for use by project teams are explained in greater detail at the end of this chapter. Application of these tools to the tasks of project teams enables the organization to make its processes operational and to "speak with facts."

TOTAL QUALITY BUSINESS PROJECTS

As discussed in Chapter 1, the third pillar of the House of Total Quality, **speaking with facts**, is based on the cornerstone of **project planning** and the foundation of **project management**. The pillar of speaking with facts is the outcome of a process of sound design, developed in the cornerstone of project planning, and reinforced by a process of effective implementation, delivered in the foundation of project management, shown in Figure 5.1.[3]

Quality project involvement is undertaken for many reasons, such as monitoring and maintaining existing processes, new product development, service or process design, assessing and improving standards, process certification, quality audits, and/or breakthroughs via reengineering. To achieve world-class quality project success, teams and entire organizations must learn to *speak with facts*. To speak with facts means that the organization has the resources and methods to determine what is factually true and structures itself to ensure that members give voice to the truth.

To appreciate the importance of speaking with facts, it is useful to consider it in the context of four alternatives: (1) speaking without facts, (2)

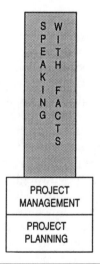

Figure 5.1   The Third Pillar, Foundation, and Cornerstone of the House of Total Quality

not knowing the facts and not speaking with facts, (3) knowing the facts but not speaking with facts, and (4) speaking with facts. With the first option, individuals or groups make themselves heard in the traditional organization through various ways of voicing their opinions (e.g., committees, policy meetings, newsletters, open-door policies, training sessions, and suggestions).[4] Voice mechanisms promote organizational loyalty and vitality.[5] They normally preserve and protect the power of those who currently manage the organization.[6] Being allowed to voice ideas is a form of empowerment, and some persons delight in the use of voice power, even when they "do not know what they are talking about." Persuasive personalities and powerful groups that speak without facts (and either intentionally or unintentionally deceive or make decisions with inadequate factual justification) put the organization's survival and success at risk for their own benefit.

With the second option, individuals and/or groups do not know the truth, do not have adequate statistical documentation, or do not speak up. Generally, these individuals and groups flounder and eventually fail; their personal fears and the climate of fear in the workplace paralyze them and prevent them from obtaining the facts and assertively voicing them.[7] Sometimes, they intuitively know what needs to be done, but they do not have the self-esteem or the training in statistical methods to transform their intuition into knowledge that decision makers would regard as credible.[8]

With the third option, individuals or groups may know the truth and have adequate statistical documentation, but there is no voice mechanism in the organization for them to be heard. Often, line employees who are close to the operations know what causes problems and how to fix them, but their knowledge is discounted by those with more voice power.[9] In fact, in many organizations "shooting the messenger" is routine, and the fear of confronting those who have more voice power with the truth, based on facts, inhibits any expression of dissent from stated policy.[10] Again, the organization's survival and success are put at risk because its internal voice systems do not empower those who could help it the most.

In the final option, speaking with facts is recognized as being essential to successfully carrying out total quality business projects. It requires the disciplined use of tools and techniques to obtain facts and the responsibility to voice those findings, whether they be good news or bad news. It requires elimination of barriers to fact-finding; accurate, honest, and timely reporting; and a proactive dedication to placing relevant voice mechanisms at the disposal of those who are ready to speak with facts. In other words, it means that incompetent fact-finding, unwillingness to use statistical tools, dishonest reporting, hoarding of information, and uncooperative relations with internal and/or external customers will not be tolerated. When employees are routinely empowered to use a variety of voice mechanisms, valuable learning from successes and failures occurs. Employees can expect a total quality firm that wants the facts to provide ongoing training in technical, teamwork, and communication skills and provide a reward and recognition process that reinforces that aim.

The importance of speaking with facts was emphasized by a recent nationwide survey of human resource management practice and total quality management.[11] The survey found that firms with higher levels of total quality commitment and effectiveness can be distinguished from firms with lower levels of commitment and effectiveness based on substantive communication practices and changes in job design.[12] Firms reporting higher levels of total quality commitment and effectiveness tended to use more and different types of multidirectional voice systems, do more to empower employees to obtain facts, and make more changes in a number of human resource key processes rather than changing only one or two such key processes.[13]

Measurement as a Part of Speaking with Facts

The topic of measurement is often thought to be synonymous with total quality by novices who are just becoming aware of the field. It is undoubtedly true that measurement is essential to a total quality process, but it will not suffice either as a definition or as a stand-alone activity in total quality. A thorough treatment of measurement is beyond the scope of this text, but numerous examples of the importance of measurement and the systems that are used can be found in texts that feature case studies of Baldrige Award winners. In fact, the Baldrige Award criteria specify two categories out of a total of seven in which measurement **must** take place. Category 2 (right after leadership) is "Information and Analysis" and Category 6 is "Business Results."

In the "Information and Analysis" category, applicants are expected to document the fact that they have processes in place to gather and analyze data. These essential measurement processes are critical to proving that applicants have attained a superior competitive position, have benchmarked and implemented best practices, and that they use information to drive improvement of key processes.

In the "Business Results" category, Baldrige applicants are expected to have collected and analyzed data related to current trends and levels of internal product and service quality, results and trends in processes and process improvement, customer satisfaction, and operational and financial performance of the organization. Measurement of external indicators such as levels and trends of supplier performance and comparative performance against competitors and other external benchmarks is also required.

Motorola, one of the first Baldrige Award winners, is an example of a company that has comprehensive and excellent measurement processes. The company regularly measures virtually all of its processes, from product design to order entry to marketing, clerical, and even cafeteria operations. The benchmark standard for acceptable quality in the firm at this point is "six sigma," a statistical term that represents approximately 3.4 defects per million opportunities for occurrence. Some of Motorola's plant operations have exceeded that and now measure some of their processes in terms of defective parts per *billion*! The story is told of the manager for worldwide cafeteria operations who was in a training session where he was introduced to the six sigma concept. He asked how it could be applied to his cafeteria operations. The instructor told him that it meant one piece of burned toast every four years, worldwide!

Next, we will see how the work of total quality OD professionals can enhance total quality business process planning, measurement, and implementation.

TOTAL QUALITY BUSINESS PROJECT PLANNING

Total quality OD professionals can play a key role in linking team members and managers in business project planning and implementation. Some key points related to the uses of OD in project planning include:

- Projects are an important strategy for ensuring continuous improvement and breakthrough by involving everyone in the organization.
- For projects to be successful, they need to be supported by the formal organization through a structure of quality teams at both the corporate and department or activity levels.
- A project team is not a permanent group; it is a task team brought together to solve a particular problem and then is disbanded. Thus, it is a parallel organizational entity, co-existing alongside the "normal structure."
- A total quality project team normally goes through the stages of: (1) defining the symptoms of a problem, (2) making a project proposal and obtaining approval to proceed, (3) data collection, (4) submitting proposed solution for approval and implementation planning, (5) communication and training, and (6) implementation and follow-up.
- The role of total quality OD practitioners in projects is to encourage and enable others to successfully carry out the projects. Care must be taken not to undermine someone else's responsibility, no matter what. In other words, total quality OD people cannot do the job of the project team leader, unless that is their assignment.
- Managers often believe that their role is to provide answers to all the questions. The total quality OD consultant's role is to help managers adapt to new ways of working with teams.

- The project proposal is a critical document. The quality council will generally either approve or stop projects based on the proposal. Total quality OD experts should spend time helping project leaders write the proposal so as to express themselves clearly and precisely.
- Before a project begins, effective *pre-planning* must be performed (elaborated on in greater detail in the discussion of consulting practices later in this chapter). Pre-planning involves getting to know the client of the project and his or her needs ("value equation"), searching for keys to root causes of problems, assessing the limits and potential costs for the project, preparing the consulting team and client counterparts for the engagement, building quality measurements, obtaining and providing feedback on progress, and seeking buy-in from the client before and after the engagement begins.

Since speaking with facts is the purpose of business project planning, a total quality business project plan must be developed to identify how and what facts are needed and how they may be obtained. In a total quality environment, the process of obtaining facts and implementing a measurement process is as important as the facts themselves. Table 5.1 identifies the steps, key fact-finding cycles, and appropriate measurement tools to speak with facts.

In column A of Table 5.1, the seven quality control (QC) steps provide the procedure for fact-finding. The first step is to select a theme. A problem has to be perceived (a difference between "what is" and "what ought to be" must be noticed), the situation must be explored, and the problem must be formally stated. One of the most difficult requirements is to honestly acknowledge any perceived weaknesses (e.g., defects, mistakes, delays, waste, accidents/injuries, performance gaps) and to use the appropriate management and planning tools in column C (which were treated in Chapter 4) to define the boundaries of the problem. The second and third steps require collecting and analyzing data and analyzing causes without jumping to conclusions. Teams can make use of the appropriate tools from among the seven QC project tools in column D (which will be treated at the end of this chapter). The remaining steps, assisted by the use of appropriate tools, follow to arrive at a solution with sufficient process documentation to standardize it.

To achieve and maintain quality project success, alternating cycles of process control, standardizing routine daily work, structured improvement activities, and measurement recording processes must be performed, as indicated in Figure 5.2.

A Japanese approach to understanding the basic process control cycle for maintaining routine daily work is called the SDCA cycle. In the SDCA cycle, there is a standard (S), and it is used to do the process (D). Results of the process are checked (C), and appropriate action is taken (A). If the results are within specification, the appropriate action is to continue to use the standard

Table 5.1 Fact-Finding Steps, Cycles, and Tools

(A) 7 QC steps	(B) PDCA/SDCA cycles	(C) 7 process management/ planning tools	(D) 7 QC project tools
1. Select theme		KJ method, matrix data analysis, relations diagram	Check sheet, display graphs, Pareto chart, histogram, scatter diagram, cause-and
2. Collect and analyze data	Plan	Matrix diagram, flowcharting	effect diagram, control chart
3. Analyze causes		Flowchart analysis	
4. Plan and implement solution	Do	Tree diagram, matrix diagram, arrow diagram, PDPC diagram	
5. Evaluate effects	Check		Check sheet, display graphs, Pareto chart, histogram, scatter diagram, cause-and- effect diagram, control chart
6. Standardize solution		Arrow diagram, PDPC diagram	*Poke yoke*
7. Reflect on process (and next problem)	Act	KJ method	
(Provides steps)	(Provides repetitions)	(Provides tools)	(Provides tools)

Source: Adapted from *A New American TQM: Four Practical Revolutions in Management* by Shoji Shiba, Alan Graham, and David Walden. Copyright ©1993 by Center for Quality Management, p. 159. Published by Productivity Press, Inc., PO Box 13390, Portland, OR 97213-0390, (800)394-6898. Reprinted by permission.

and repeat the cycle. If the results are beginning to drift or are out of specification (i.e., not meeting customer needs), standard corrective actions are to be taken.

However, from time to time, project teams may decide that the specifications are not stringent enough and that they must improve the process (reduce the variance) so that tighter specifications can be met. When this happens, they use a form of PDCA (Figure 5.2) to find the source of the greatest natural variation and to improve the process by eliminating it. This

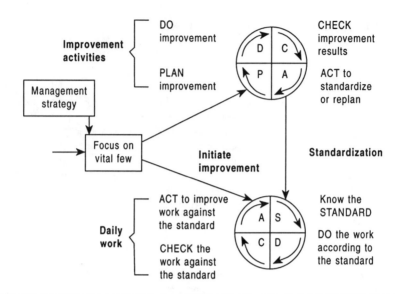

Figure 5.2 Alternation of SDCA and PDCA Process Control Cycles (Source: From *A New American TQM: Four Practical Revolutions in Management* by Shoji Shiba, Alan Graham, and David Walden. Copyright ©1993 by Center for Quality Management, p. 67. Published by Productivity Press, Inc., PO Box 13390, Portland, OR 97213-0390, (800)394-6898. Reprinted by permission.)

alternating interaction between the SDCA cycle and the PDCA cycle for initiating improvements can be depicted in the following scenario:

SDCA   Run an existing process for a while. Compute the natural variation, thus highlighting uncontrolled variation.

PDCA   Find and eliminate the sources of uncontrolled variation.

SDCA   Continue running the new or now accurately followed process. Eliminate the source of any out-of-control condition that begins to occur.[14]

PDCA   Use the seven QC steps to find and reduce the largest source of controlled variation.

SDCA   Continue running the new process. Eliminate the source of any out-of-control condition that begins to occur.

Speaking with facts, therefore, is different from speaking with feelings or speaking with power. Speaking with facts requires disciplined application of quality control steps, cycles, and tools to the system itself.

As pointed out in the last chapter, both incremental and breakthrough improvement must frequently take place simultaneously. The approaches used by project teams are similar, but generally vary in terms of objectives and tools. Thus, the design of new products and processes or reengineering tasks requires project teams to use the "clean slate" approach. Certification, troubleshooting, and incremental improvement of existing processes often require that teams use problem-solving techniques and proven improvement strategies to identify and "fix" problems.

Once a method of fact-finding is mastered, project teams can determine which facts to obtain and in what order. Engaging in a quality audit is one form of determining which facts to address where a more structured process environment exists. A *quality audit provides a comprehensive and systematic examination of the extent to which formulated plans and implemented processes are successful.*[15] There is obviously a wide range of fact-finding in which quality project teams must engage to complete a quality audit. The focus of project attention must be on the system, not persons. Project teams are focused on improving the system, not scapegoating people. In organizations that do not speak with facts, special project teams are often formed to justify a predetermined executive decision or build a case of incompetence against personnel whom a manager wishes to demote or dismiss. While domestic or international award criteria (Baldrige, Deming, or ISO 9000) provide a convenient checklist for a quality audit, project teams are often expected to certify system processes.

Project Planning for *Kaizen* and Competitive Parity

Six levels of system processes were identified by Harrington and outlined in Chapter 4. Although not exclusively focused on *kaizen* or competitive parity, his approach suggests incremental improvement of processes in order to reach world-class status. At some point, when the gains from projects become more and more difficult to achieve, it may be necessary for planners to address how "breakthroughs" may be achieved in order to attain "dominance" required for world-class processes.

Harrington provides a road map for process improvement via project teams. To determine whether each process has evolved to the next level, project teams need to ascertain the facts in eight major change areas:[16]

- End-customer-related measurements
- Process and/or performance measurements
- Supplier partnerships
- Documentation
- Training
- Benchmarking
- Process adaptability
- Continuous improvement

Harrington addresses each of the levels in detail as the processes move from meeting customer requirements to expectations and, finally, latent desires. The following is a condensed list of project team tasks to obtain factual documentation for each level:

Factual Requirements to Be Qualified at Level 2—All processes are classified as level 1 (*unknown status*) until sufficient data have been collected to determine their true status. Normally, processes at qualification level 1 can be moved to qualification 2 level (*understood status*) by gathering some basic process data. Qualification level 2 signifies that the process design is understood by the process improvement team and is operating according to the prescribed documentation. To be qualified at level 1, all the criteria in each of the eight major change areas (for example, supplier partnerships, process measurements, and/or performance) must be met and factually documented.

Factual Requirements to Be Qualified at Level 3—When a process is qualified at level 3, it is called an *effective process*. Level 3 processes have a systematic measurement system in place that ensures end-customer expectations are met. Streamlining of the process has been started. Project teams will have helped document the overall process, develop customer-related measures, establish feedback systems with critical suppliers, and been involved in appropriate training, benchmarking, and improvement activities. To be qualified at level 3, the process must be able to meet all the requirements for qualification level 2, plus additional requirements.

Factual Requirements to Be Qualified at Level 4—When a process evolves to qualification level 4, it is called an *efficient process*. Streamlining activities for processes qualified at level 4 have been completed, and there has been a significant improvement in the efficiency of the process. To be qualified at level 4, the process must be able to meet all the requirements for qualification levels 2 and 3, plus additional requirements. At this level, project teams will have ensured that customer requirements were being consistently met, process controls and OD measures were showing steady improvement, critical supplier requirements were being achieved, and training, benchmarking, and continuous improvement targets were being met and new goals developed.

Factual Requirements to Be Qualified at Level 5—When a process has reached qualification level 5, it is called an *error-free process*. Processes qualified at level 5 are highly effective and efficient. Both external and internal customer expectations are measured and met. Rarely is there a problem within the process. Schedules are always met, and stress levels are low. To be qualified at level 5, the process must be able to meet all the requirements for the previous qualification levels, plus additional requirements. Project teams at his point have assisted in making the processes consistently excellent. End-customer expectations are consistently met and updated, process and performance measures are generally performed by people on the job and show consistent improvement, suppliers meet requirements and are expected to improve on both product and process dimensions, and documentation, training, and continuous improvement are conducted at a high level, with targets in place to move to world class (level 6).

Factual Requirements to Be Qualified at Level 6—Qualification level 6 is the highest level. The process is one of the ten best processes of its kind in the world or it is in the top 10% of like processes, whichever has the smallest population. Processes that reach level 6 are called *world-class processes.* These processes are often benchmark target processes for other organizations. Few processes ever get this good. Processes that reach level 6 truly are world class and must be continuously improved so that they keep their world-class status. To be qualified at level 6, the process must be able to meet all the requirements for the previous levels, plus additional requirements.

Note that the ultimate goal for level 6 processes is to go beyond world-class to become the *best-of-breed process.* Although some processes become best-of-breed for short periods of time, it is very difficult to stay in first place. It requires sustained work and creativity, but the personal, team, and organizational satisfaction is well worth it.

Project Planning for Breakthrough Dominance and Reengineering

Obviously, when project teams are used to attain level 6 qualification, a "breakthrough" has to be attained. This often requires major changes in corporate culture, infrastructure, and the way projects are conceived and carried out in the organization. Specialized team skills and project teams composed of employees, suppliers, and/or customers must often be established. In the case of massive reengineering projects, teams must often learn to work with consultants for periods of time and must often deal with complex issues of consolidation of functions, downsizing, realignment of job skills, automation of processes, and relocation of facilities.

An article about the San Diego Zoo and Wild Animal Park (SDZ/WAP)[17] showed how management and employees worked together to develop new procedures and organization structures through participative team approaches to total quality OD and placed the organization on the path to reaching level 6, world-class, processes. The SDZ/WAP began with traditional quality circles in 1984. Steady progress was made so that by 1990, approximately 25% of the work force of 1200 was involved in quality circles. However, more was needed in order to meet the two main goals of the organization: (1) providing quality care for the animals in the collection and (2) providing a thoroughly pleasant and rewarding experience for the guests (customers) of the zoo and park. It was felt that this could only be attained by including a third objective of *developing the best possible work environment* for employees. To accomplish this, two areas were the focus of project teams: developing high-quality training and developing a prototype cross-functional semi-autonomous team in one area.

To develop high-quality keeper training, goals were established by a cross-functional team. An instructional design company was hired to create materials for a comprehensive curriculum. Content specialists from each SDZ/WAP area were involved in development of modules such as communication skills, nutrition and feeding, animal training and behavior modification, veterinary medicine, etc. The classes are taught by in-house personnel and involve some 474 hours of training for each participant. The program involves approximately four hours of classroom time and eight hours of on-the-job training per week. The program is constantly being improved, and increasing numbers of inquiries about the program from other zoos indicate that it is destined to become the world-class benchmark in the field.

The development of the prototype semi-autonomous team required a complete restructuring of job tasks using a sociotechnical systems approach. This was necessary because of a change of physical structures at SDZ/WAP from moated "second-generation" zoo design to "third-generation" bioclimatic zones. This made the traditional functional departments for cleaning, repairs, horticulture, mammals, birds, reptiles, etc. cost prohibitive and virtually obsolete. Thus, when a new area, called Tiger River, was in the design stage, a project team had to be put together to redesign the work processes as well. This team was composed of the best people from the former departments and was screened by the SDZ/WAP's executive director, human resources director, and an outside consultant. This project team was to become the new work force for the Tiger River exhibit. After going through team training and team-building processes, the team established goals, received cross-training, and began work in the new area before it was opened to the public. This led to development of a sense of mutual responsibility and ownership, with keepers washing windows, grounds attendants cutting food, and vacations and days off negotiated between equals according to need, and not on the basis of seniority. A before-and-after survey of the team members showed that job satisfaction, attitude toward animal care and exhibits, perception of guest experience, and cross-training/job enrichment/shared responsibility all went from negative or neutral to highly positive ratings.

TOTAL QUALITY BUSINESS PROJECT MANAGEMENT

After successfully carrying out the steps of business project planning, effective *project managers* must gather facts from across organizational subcultures. The savvy project management leader must be aware of the four basic subcultures in most organizations: clan subculture, adhocracy subculture, market subculture, and bureaucratic subculture.[18] These subcultures and

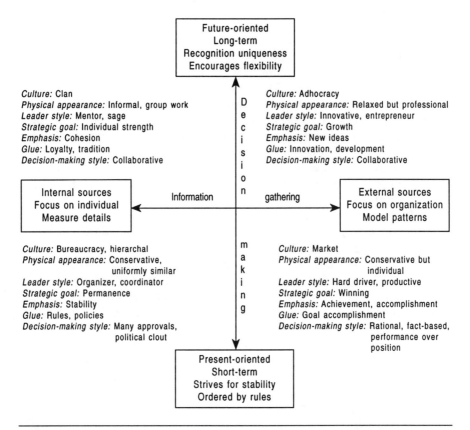

Figure 5.3 Organizational Subcultures and Project Leadership Styles for Information Gathering (Source: Cameron, K. and Freeman, S. (1991). "Cultural Consequence, Strength, and Type: Relationships to Effectiveness." *Research in Organization Development*. Vol. 5, p. 33.)

their features are shown in Figure 5.3. Leadership roles required to successfully direct a project and gather accurate information for decision making may differ, depending on the subculture that is encountered.

The clan, adhocracy, market, and bureaucratic subcultures are the organizational "homes" for employees who will become involved in quality project teams. Good project leaders recognize these differences and attempt to develop a project team culture that will not violate the norms of the team members' home organization subcultures. The natural goals and emphases of team members from adhocracy and market cultures make it easy for them to adapt to participation in project teams. On the other hand, team members from clans and bureaucracies normally have greater difficulty in joining project teams because of their focus on individual performance. *Information-*

gathering activities tend to separate members from the various subcultures by their focus on individual details and organizational patterns, and *decision-making activities* tend to separate such team members into short-term and long-term thinkers. Project leaders need to integrate diverse skills, personalities, and subcultural orientations into a focused, fact-finding unit able to weather attacks from functional departments wary of possible team infringement on their domains.[19] A key objective of project management is to reduce the organizational impact of the bureaucratic subculture over time. This is a natural consequence of working in cross-functional teams, where team members come to appreciate the diverse skills and viewpoints of people from other parts of the organization. Trust tends to grow and suspicion diminishes in such a setting.

Effective total quality project management also requires competence in coordinating the phases and stages of the project life cycle, shown in Figure 5.4.[20] Lack of coordination may lead to either the premature death of a worthwhile project or, at the least, the inefficient use of resources. In a competitive business environment, where there is a need to make the best use of limited resources, effective project managers must orchestrate internal and external support to complete worthwhile projects on time and under budget. Committed project teams that invest a great deal of time and energy in worthwhile projects only to find them underfunded become frustrated. On the other hand, if organizational leaders external to the project team are not kept informed, they may overtly or covertly resist supporting a project because they fail to see how the project will contribute to meeting the organization's objectives.

The *phases* of a project life cycle show the *internal* momentum of the project. They represent all of the processes and practices required for the

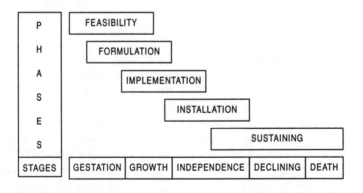

Figure 5.4 The Phases and Stages of a Project Life Cycle (Source: Kleim, Ralph L. and Ludin, Irwin S. (1992). *The People Side of Project Management*. Brookfield, VT: Gower Publishing, p. 40.)

successful planning and implementation of the project by the leader and/or the team and include feasibility, formulation, implementation, installation, and sustaining the changes. The *stages* of a project life cycle show the kind and degree of assistance provided to the project by key external stakeholders. The stages (a type of project life cycle), which include gestation, growth, independence, decline, and death, represent the *external* organizational and/or extra-organizational support for the project over time.

Project stages typically lag behind project phases because the project team is closer to and more familiar with the needs of the project and what can and cannot be done. Therefore, the team's challenge is to speak with facts about the probability of the project's success in such a way as to develop and sustain support from key stakeholders over time. A competent project leader should keep internal phases and external stages aligned to ensure a successful outcome for the project leader, the project team, and the target organization(s).

When phases and stages become misaligned, the responsible project leader must diagnose the cause(s) and take appropriate action. A project, for example, may exist in the gestation stage for a long time but may need to be in the implementation phase in the project leader's agenda. That may be because of a lack of support for the project, either by senior management or even the client department. The project manager must assertively justify the project to key external parties.

A project may be in the growth stage while simultaneously in the implementation phase. In this case, senior management recognizes the importance of the project and is willing to allocate whatever resources are required for its successful completion. They may even expand the project's scope. This can be both an opportunity and a threat. The project may take on all the features of a standing program, due to its level of magnitude relative to other projects. It may receive more than the minimum resources it needs to succeed, while other projects are neglected.

Again, a project may be in the independence stage while in the sustaining phase. Because the project was so successful, senior management and the client department are willing to treat the continued support of the project in the sustaining phase as an ongoing endeavor that has the same level of status as a project in the earlier phases.

A project may actually be in the decline stage regardless of phase. Senior management may feel that more important projects exist which demand attention. They may also decide to trim existing resources. The project quickly loses legitimacy. This requires prompt action by the project leader to regain legitimacy and momentum. In addition, a project may be in the death stage during any phase. Senior management may make the decision to cut all support and the project becomes nonexistent. Premature project death is a tragedy that every project leader wants to avoid and requires steady communication, interim progress reports, and sustained advocacy of the merits of the project.

Project Management and Teams

The people involved with and responsible for project management are the managers, supervisors, and operations level workers in manufacturing and service organizations. This is where plans become operational in the total quality process. It is at this level that "the talk is walked"; leaders must lead, and followers must be empowered to carry out their ideas as individuals and group members. Projects are created by managers or suggested by individual employees or employee groups. They are then delegated for solution to groups of managers, technical experts, supervisors, and/or workers. A growing trend is to identify these groups as teams. A closer look at the importance of teams is necessary.

To overcome the tendency to fight "turf battles" and benefit from the synergistic results that are possible from project teams, a project leader must form a strong project team. A *team* (or a **real team**, as discussed below) is a small number of people with complementary skills who are equally committed to a common purpose, goals, and working approach for which they hold themselves mutually accountable. Teams can generally outperform individuals acting alone or in larger organizational groupings, especially when performance requires diverse skills, broad experience, informed judgment, complex coordination, and multiple accountabilities.

Consider the rewarding experience of working on a project team where a strong sense of unity and commitment toward accomplishing a highly motivating goal prevail. Most people have at some time had the opportunity to enjoy the experience of participating in a team effort that was highly focused and driven by a shared vision. Every team member spent countless hours working on the task, and the result possibly surpassed the original goal. Some examples include the achievements of putting a man on the moon, the defeat of the Russians by the U.S. Olympic hockey team, or writing and publishing a book, to include an immediate example.

The story of "Team Taurus," which designed the original model of the Taurus/Sable automobile at Ford Motor Company, is one total quality OD example of how superb teamwork in a product design project contributed to total quality within a business organization.[21] According to various accounts, the unique approach of gathering together representatives from design, engineering, purchasing, marketing, quality assurance, sales, and service had never been done at Ford until Team Taurus was formed in 1980. From this effort came innovations for over 1400 significant design improvements that were culled from suggestions by customers, employees, and suppliers. Engineers tore down over 50 comparable cars, seeking the "best-in-class" features. Of some 400 such features, Ford claimed that the final Taurus/Sable product met or exceeded 80% of them in design quality. The final result of this team effort was that Taurus and Sable were the number one and number two choices for *Motor Trend's* Car of the Year award in 1986. Later versions of the Taurus outsold the Honda Accord to recapture first place in the mid-sized car market in the United States in 1993.

Such experiences are very fulfilling, but may be short-lived. It is the goal of quality-centered project management to create these or similar experiences within organizations by empowering each person to exercise and continuously develop his or her skills and talents within the framework of effective teams.

The basic ingredients of teams are shown graphically in Figure 5.5. Teams normally consist of fewer than 25 people with complementary tech-

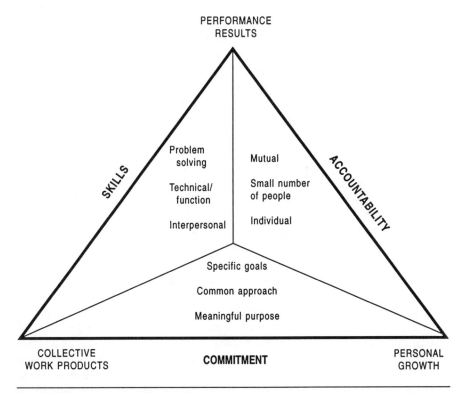

Figure 5.5 Basic Ingredients of Teams (Source: Reprinted by permission of Harvard Business School Press from *The Wisdom of Teams: Creating the High-Performance Organization* by Jon R. Katzenbach and Douglas K. Smith, New York: HarperBusiness, 1994, p. 8. Copyright ©1993 by McKinsey & Company, Inc. Originally published by Harvard Business School Press, Boston, 1993.)

nical/functional, problem-solving, and interpersonal *skills*. Technical/functional skills might include marketing and engineering skills for new product development. Problem-solving skills might include quantitative analysis skills to assess computer printouts of company progress reports and decision-making skills regarding new practices to follow in light of the statistical data. Interpersonal skills might include helpful criticism, risk-taking, objective feedback, active listening, giving the benefit of the doubt, emotional encouragement, respecting the needs of others, and celebrating the achievement of others.

Teams must also develop a **commitment** to a shared, meaningful purpose. They must own and translate that purpose into specific and action-oriented goals. Groups that fail to become teams often do not identify with a challenging purpose for various reasons (i.e., insufficient focus on performance, lack of effort, or poor leadership). Specific goals that define the team's proposed work products are essential. These must be recognizably different from both organization-wide goals and the sum of individual objectives. Well-stated group goals facilitate clear communication, constructive conflict, and have a democratic leveling effect since all members are working toward the same end. If the team celebrates small "wins" when intermediate goals are reached, it can build renewed membership commitment and a sense of meaningful purpose. In addition, well-structured teams are committed to a common approach. They must agree on who will do particular jobs, how schedules will be set and adhered to, what skills need to be developed, how continuing membership is to be earned, and how the group will make and modify decisions. The approach that delegates all the real work to a few members (or staff outsiders) and thus relies only on review and discussion meetings for a semblance of "working together" cannot be used by a real team.

Finally, teams require individual and joint **accountability** for performance. Basically, team accountability is about sincere promises made to each other for which there is a pledge of committed action. When promises are followed through, the team preserves and extends the trust upon which it is built.

Members earn the right to express their own views about all aspects of the team's efforts and to have their judgments receive a fair, respectful, and constructive hearing. Specific performance goals and agreed-upon approaches provide clear yardsticks for mutual accountability.[22] The success of every total quality organization rests on the effectiveness of each work group and each team. *A group* is a collection of individuals who are in an interdependent relationship with one another.[23] A *nonworking group* is simply a loose affiliation of individuals without a task focus. A *working group* is one for which there is no significant incentive for shared activity or opportunity that would require it to become a team. The members interact primarily to share information, best practices, or perspectives and to make decisions to help each individual perform within his or her area of responsibility. Beyond that, there is no realistic or truly desired "small group" common purpose, shared performance goals, or joint work products that call for either a team approach or mutual accountability. Groups can be productive, but it is evident that just bringing a group of people together to complete specific tasks is often unproductive and ineffective. Members of *real teams* (defined below) develop strong feelings of allegiance that go beyond the mere grouping of individuals. The productive outcome is synergistic, and team accomplishments often can exceed even the original goals of the group or its sponsor.

As groups progress through four phases—pseudo teams, potential teams, real teams, and high-performance teams[24]—performance tends to increase significantly.

A *pseudo team* is a group for which there could be significant, shared performance goals or opportunities, but it has not focused on group performance and is not trying to achieve it. It has no interest in shaping a common purpose or set of performance goals, even though it may call itself a team. Pseudo teams almost always contribute less to company performance than effective working groups because their interactions detract from each member's individual performance without delivering any joint benefit. In pseudo teams, the sum of the whole is less than the potential of the individual parts.

The *potential team* is a group for which there are significant, shared performance goals and which really is trying to improve its performance impact. It typically lacks clarity about its purpose, goals, or work products. It generally needs more discipline in hammering out a common working approach. It has not yet established collective accountability. Potential teams abound in most organizations.

A *real team* is a small number of people with complementary skills who are equally committed to a common purpose, goals, and working approach for which they hold themselves mutually accountable. Real teams are the basic operating units of performance in total quality organizations. They exhibit task, psychosocial, and moral maturity. Real project teams are the models to which pseudo and potential teams aspire. Members of pseudo and potential teams may demand empowerment as a right; members of real teams deserve empowerment because they have the capability to use it successfully and are the backbone of any successful total quality organization. The ability to determine empowerment readiness of individuals, groups, and teams is a crucial skill in making managerial decisions to share power. Diversion of valuable scarce resources to "squeaky wheel" groups that are unable or unwilling to shoulder the responsibilities of power deprives real teams of the fuel they need to continue productive contributions.

High-performance teams meet all the conditions of real teams and have members who are also deeply committed to one another's personal growth and success. That commitment usually transcends the team. The high-performance team significantly outperforms all other like teams and outperforms many expectations that managers reasonably have for real teams. It is as powerful as it is rare, but it remains an excellent model for all real teams.

TOTAL QUALITY ORGANIZATION DEVELOPMENT PROJECTS

The thrust of OD projects in most organizations has traditionally been focused on organization structures, not teams. Thus, organizational change project assignments, opportunities, and rewards for OD practitioners have been designed around structural change, not teams. This contributes to power plays, competition, favoritism, and self-centeredness, which collectively counter the focus of two of the most important functions of quality organizations: customer satisfaction and continuous improvement.

The central role of teams, and the need for team skills such as cooperation, interpersonal communications, cross-training, and group decision making, represents a fundamental shift in how the work of public and private organizations is performed in the United States and many other countries. Presently, *cooperation* between departments, such as design and manufacturing in automotive firms, doctors and administrators in hospitals, and business managers and orchestra conductors, is not the norm. Predominant practices encourage *individual* advancement through management processes such as management by objectives, individual performance evaluation, professional status and privileges, and individual promotion.

To counter these mainstream practices, total quality OD projects need to be focused on fact-finding regarding key system processes. These processes typically have to be coordinated with human resource (HR) processes in order to be effectively carried out. These processes include selection, performance, appraisal, rewards, and development. Through the use of the seven QC scientific procedure steps, the alternating SDCA/PDCA cycles, and appropriate total quality tools, the certification of all business/OD processes can take place. If the selection process in the OD domain, for example, is at stage 4 (efficient) and it needs to be at least at stage 5 (error-free), facts need to be gathered in the eight process subcategories (end-customer-related measurements, process measurements and/or performance, supplier partnerships, documentation, training, benchmarking, process adaptability, and continuous improvement). The best way for OD departments to lead quality project initiatives is to make sure that their own function has certified and is improving its own processes using the total quality steps, cycles, and tools. How many OD departments, for example, systematically benchmark their own policies and procedures with the best practices in their industry, nation, or the world? For most OD professionals, this would mean additional training in statistics, certification procedures (such as ISO 9000 quality certification), and applying quality practices to OD processes.

Audits and Organization Development Applications

Organizations frequently use audits to assess the financial health of the firm. An *audit* is simply an independent, unbiased assessment of work practices. The ANSI/ASQC definition of a *quality audit* is: "a systematic and independent examination and evaluation to determine whether quality activities and results comply with planned arrangements and whether these arrangements are implemented effectively and are suitable to achieving objectives."[25] Audits are now being used to assess policies, practices, and products within quality-focused organizations, as well as for the suppliers of such firms.

A HR audit is one way for OD professionals to assess current HR policies and practices.[26] It provides a means to keep up with changes, avoid litigation, and incorporate new techniques to improve performance. Supplementing the HR audit with both an OD quality audit and an ethics audit[27] would provide the organization with valuable information regarding its current stage of organizational process certification and its current level of ethical work culture development.[28] If, for example, current OD audit procedures are primarily geared to regard the organization as only a House of Compliance (i.e., assessing policies and practices to avoid litigation), whereas the rest of the organization has reached a quality process stage and an ethical work culture level ready for the House of Integrity, the OD function might well be perceived as unable to provide leadership in total quality initiatives.

An article in *The Wall Street Journal*[29] shows how difficult it may be to ensure that quality processes and policies relating to ethical work culture values are being adhered to in an increasingly chaotic global marketplace. Many companies, such as J.C. Penney, Wal-Mart, and Levi Strauss, have ethical codes of conduct that apply to relations with foreign suppliers in developing companies. For example, J.C. Penney's code provides for specific wording in contracts with suppliers that forbids violations of local labor laws, including employment of underage workers. However, in visits to supplier plants in Guatemala City, Guatemala, a *Journal* reporter quickly found evidence of underage workers, workers being paid less that the $2.80 per day minimum wage, and workers being forced to work unpaid overtime for 15-hour work days. There were even rumors of threats of bodily harm to union organizers if they did not cease their activities and resign from a supplier company. Indications are that the inspectors from J.C. Penney and other U.S. companies that visit their suppliers are more interested in checking on product quality, cost, and delivery targets than working conditions. Even Levi Strauss, which has a reputation for social responsibility and hires inspectors expressly to check on working conditions, admits that inspectors frequently miss violations because they do not want to probe too deeply for fear of angering owners. One Wal-Mart vice president, when told that a reporter had found evidence of employment of underage workers at a supplier's plant in Guatemala City, immediately promised to cancel its contract and "make an example" of the delinquent supplier. The supplier immediately required his 1200 workers to produce proof of age and fired those who could not do so. The decision by Wal-Mart was not rescinded, however, and the business was shifted to the Dominican Republic. This resulted in the delinquent supplier having to fire 300 people and shut down 5 of his factory's 12 production lines.

To avoid the organizational perception of being a group that is reactive, rather than proactive, OD professionals can capitalize on their traditional strengths in delivering quality training and development programs. The proactive approach would require shifting the emphasis of training and development efforts from the traditional, hierarchic supervisory approach toward one of participative leadership and still further toward team leadership within a total quality context.[30]

The movement toward team leadership is essential in a total quality firm, and OD has an important role to play in that transition. It is possible to offer training in both team building and team development; the former would emphasize intense, short-term attention to remedial relationship issues to unblock performance, whereas the latter would emphasize diffused, long-term attention to positive growth opportunities for sustaining superior team performance.[31] Effective real teams improve quality within a reasonable time frame and strengthen working relationships both inside and outside the team.[32] In light of current progressive organizational trends, it would appear to be in the best interest of OD departments to contribute to building and developing effective real teams by facilitating the transition from supervisory leadership to team leadership.

TOTAL QUALITY ORGANIZATION DEVELOPMENT PROJECT PLANNING

To respond to the quality project planning challenge, OD practitioners should concentrate on three areas: development of a team structure, team empowerment, and personal development of consultant–client process skills. The first is necessary because of the unprecedented movement of organizations to teams. As a result, "networks" of teams must be developed. Managers do not "naturally" know how to work in teams or to use teams to best advantage. They must be taught how to coach teams and assisted in carrying out team development processes and projects. The second requirement is needed because teams do not "naturally" understand or appreciate the need for empowerment. They must be taught new skills and learn to become comfortable in a new role. The third requirement for development of client–consultant process skills may seem to be unnecessary to some OD professionals who have had years of internal or external consulting experience. However, the environment is changing rapidly and these skills must be modified and updated, as discussed below.

Total Quality Organization Development Planning and Types of Teams

OD practitioners need to be aware that in most total quality firms, there are at least four types of teams, which generally correspond to organization levels and tasks. The four types of teams are *lead teams, functional teams, cross-functional teams, and task teams.*

The highest team level is the lead team, which is sometimes called the *quality council.* This team is responsible for the strategic management of the quality process (discussed in Chapter 4). It acts as a steering committee to set policy, establish guidelines, and handle overall logistics and communications for teams that it coordinates. Membership of the lead team may differ according to the general structure of the organization and the team's position in it. A company-wide lead team might be formed at the executive level and consist of the president of the firm and his or her vice presidents. In some organizations, a divisional lead team might be composed of an executive vice president and vice presidents or directors reporting to him or her. In an organization that is organized around activities (such as a university or hospital), one or more lead teams might be composed of the vice president or director and immediate subordinates or staff. It might provide leadership and guidance for specific activities, such as academic affairs, admissions, or business office activities. In a geographically oriented organization, a location-centered lead team, led by a zone manager, plant manager, or other local executive, might be formed. It provides the same type of leadership at the local level as an executive-level team provides for the whole organization.

Lead teams coordinate, and generally review and approve, the activities of the other three types of teams. *Functional* teams are composed of members from a single work or functional area. They are the same as, or similar to, traditional quality circle or employee involvement groups. Membership is generally voluntary, and the team operates continuously over an extended period of time. Functional teams generally average about eight members. *Cross-functional* teams consist of people from more than one work area, function, or department. As the name implies, they work on projects that cut across functional lines. Like functional teams, membership is generally voluntary and the team is ongoing. *Task* teams generally include people from one or more functional areas. They are generally formed to solve a specific problem or group of problems and are then disbanded. Members of these teams are selected based on their skills, background, and experience. Membership and tasks are generally selected by management (the lead team). Examples of teamwork are seen in the case study at the end of the chapter.

An OD team development project will necessarily entail balancing empowerment and responsibility/authority issues in the organization as a whole, as well as within the evolution of each team. In fact, there is a team empowerment continuum with specific responsibilities to determine how much empowerment each team is able and willing to assume.[33] Teams may progress through levels of empowerment, progressively taking on more responsibility and authority.

Total Quality Organization Development Planning and Factors in Team Empowerment

The process of responsible team empowerment does not occur automatically and in isolation; rather, it is the result of the OD-managed convergence of two factors: (1) the micro and macro stage of system development along the team involvement/empowerment continuum and (2) the matching of leadership styles with follower maturity (task, psychosocial, and moral) levels to promote team empowerment. The first factor is shown in Table 5.2.[34] The second factor is discussed below.

At the micro-system level, process involvement steps that project teams need to take, from defining problems through implementing solutions and conducting evaluation, can entail different ranges of employee involvement and ownership, from awareness with low involvement to empowered ownership. Patterns of business process improvements become part of the micro-system decision-making tradition, and they determine at the operational level whether empowered ownership becomes a daily work reality for line employees.

At the macro-system level, the organizational dimensions of structure, focus, authority, idea sources, and stakeholder intensity can also entail different ranges of employee involvement and ownership, from compliant involvement to empowered ownership. The macro-system structure and dynamics determine at the strategic design level whether empowered ownership will be supported. Responsible team empowerment, therefore, is the managed alignment of micro- and macro-system support for empowered ownership. Without this alignment, the gap between empowerment rhetoric and reality will widen, leading to a form of organizational cynicism that erodes the ethical work culture necessary for world-class productivity. Responsible managers cannot preach teamwork without providing and monitoring the actual micro and macro systems that support it.

The second factor in responsible team empowerment is matching leadership styles with empowerment readiness as demonstrated by the task, psychosocial, and moral maturity levels of followers (see Exercise 5.1).[35] As followers mature, the leader's behavior is normally characterized by a decreasing emphasis on task structuring and an increased emphasis on consideration. As the followers continue to mature, there should be an eventual decrease in consideration. *Work empowerment maturity is a condition characterized by high task competence and wide experience, high psychosocial motivation to achieve and ability/willingness to accept responsibility, and high moral commitment to use power to enhance justice, trust, and care in the workplace.* Premature empowerment of leaders and/or followers can lead to poor business decisions being made more quickly and more often—a recipe for disaster.

To avoid premature team empowerment, the situational leadership style grid in Figure 5.6 provides a road map. It shows four appropriate leadership styles—managerial directing, coaching, participating, and delegating—in order to promote responsible team empowerment.[34] The four leadership styles are placed within a two-dimensional grid of contexts under which each style is appropriate. The vertical dimension shows supporting actions of the leaders, while the horizontal dimension shows directive actions. A time line starts at the top left (low supportive and high directive actions) and works its way through all four styles, ending at the top right quadrant (low supportive and low directive actions). Total quality associates should progress along this time line, which is a measure of training effectiveness and ownership of the total quality process as time progresses. In fact, total quality leadership and team empowerment must be a blend of both situational (system) adaptability and transformational leadership styles.[35]

The second line on the chart places the four leadership styles along the time line. This shows the expected progression of people in their interactions with their leader-managers, from their initial introduction into any work situation. Associates and their managers should expect to begin employment in a new company or process under the directing style, move through the stages of coaching, to participating, and to the ultimate payoff afforded by the delegation stage. In the directive stage, a high level of support either is not required or there is not time. The coaching stage is a natural progression as training and awareness of need take hold. In the participating stage, high-level direction is not needed and may interfere with the team's initiative. When the delegating stage is reached, the team is willing and able to handle the situation facing it with little support or direction. Either action would generally be undesired by empowered teams. Since the greatest performance potential exists under the delegating style, the leader's goal must be to bring the team up to speed rapidly so it can effectively operate in this self-directed, delegative mode.

The third line shows the power position that accompanies each of the

Table 5.2 Micro- and Macro-System Phases of the Involvement/Empowerment Continuum

Micro-system improvement phases	Awareness with low involvement	Some involved commitment	Empowered ownership
1. Define problem	Manager defines customers, requirements, and necessary processes	Group proposes opportunity; manager approves	Team defines opportunity as next stage in improvement
2. Identify and document process	Manager or staff documents processes	Group works with staff to document	Team documents and flowcharts processes
3. Measure performance	Manager collects data but shares little	Manager defines data for group to collect	Team determines what data to collect and obtains them
4. Understand why	Manager analyzes data and draws conclusions	Manager suggests causal factors and group confirms	Team analyzes data, determines root causes, and understands variation
5. Develop and test ideas	Manager defines improvements	Manager suggests alternatives for group to evaluate	Team identifies and tests alternative solutions
6. Implement solutions and evaluate	Manager drives implementation and evaluates outcome	Group implements solution and shares evaluation with manager	Team has responsibility and authority to implement solution and track results
Macro-system organizational phases	**Compliant involvement**	**Participative involvement**	**Empowered ownership**
7. Structure	Hierarchical Precise job descriptions Functional units	Less hierarchical Loose job descriptions Matrix management	Flat No job descriptions Self-directed teams

8. Focus	Internal targets Preservation Costs Problem solving Find-and-fix	Competition Adaptation Quality and productivity Product service improvement Detection	Customers' needs Flexible, responsive Customer satisfaction Process improvement Prevention
9. Authority	Top-down command Inflexible Controlling Rank and title	Special assignments Open to challenge Sharing Committee	Consensus Seeks challenge Trusting Knowledge
10. Idea sources	Work measurement Suggestion systems Occasional morale assessment	Staff studies Quality circles	Work teams Customers and employees
11. Morale	Acceptance of low morale levels as long as system objectives achieved	Regular morale assessment Acceptance only of moderate morale levels as long as system objectives are achieved	Regular morale assessment and development Acceptance only of high morale levels and achievement of system objectives
12. Stakeholder intensity	Apathetic compliance No ownership	Participative involvement Some ownership	Committed dedication Full ownership

Source: Adapted from AK Tenner/DeToro, *Total Quality Management: Three Steps to Continuous Improvement*, ©1992 by Addison-Wesley Publishing Company, Inc. Reprinted by permission of Addison-Wesley Publishing Company, Inc.

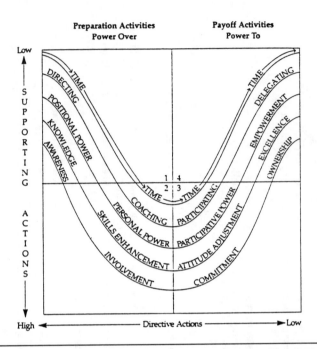

Figure 5.6 Total Quality Situational Leadership Styles and Team Empowerment (Source: Johnson, Richard S. (1993). *TQM: Leadership for the Quality Transformation.* Milwaukee: ASQC Quality Press, p. 92.)

leadership styles. Positional power is generally the prime mover during the directing stages. Initial relationships with new employees do not produce personal power to any great degree. The deployment of new processes requires the leader to create and sell his or her vision of work excellence. When the followers have progressed long enough for coaching to be used, the skilled coach usually has gained considerable personal power. This becomes the motivating force, in contrast to the earlier power resulting from "do it because I'm the boss." A leader's indirect influence is enough in most cases in stage 3, when participative leadership style is employed. Full empowerment fuels the delegative style in stage 4.

The fourth line illustrates the progression of training and development that supports the various leadership styles. Knowledge acquisition introduces the participants to the task at hand and provides them with the basics to begin their efforts in that tasking in the initial phase of training. This is followed in stage 2 by skills enhancement, which helps people become productive. In this stage, with proper leadership, most people are willing to perform as their ability increases. This leads to the need in stage 3 for social, psychosocial, and moral attitude adjustments; organization citizenship behavior; and teamwork skills for maximum effectiveness. To achieve a high degree of excellence in stage 4, fine-tuning the process requires a delegative style and demands even more attention to task, psychosocial, and moral dimensions of the work environment.

The fifth line exhibits employee attitudes and contributions to the total quality management (TQM) process in part and the organization as a whole. In stage 1, people are basically aware of organizational needs and quality processes. As they progress in their knowledge and skill development and work with solid leaders, they become involved at stage 2 in TQM and the organization. Commitment to excellence, participation, and the organization is required at stage 3 if there is to be a payoff. The ultimate psychic reward comes as teams are empowered through the delegating leadership style to "own" their TQM and organizational processes. Responsible team empowerment, therefore, is the result of empowerment maturity along task, psychosocial, and moral dimensions. It can only occur if leaders and followers are both developed and mature in their respective roles. The Empowerment Readiness Assessment instrument in Exercise 5.1 can be of use in this determination.

The situational leadership flow from quadrant 1 to quadrant 4 depends on the empowerment maturity of leaders and employees in the first quadrant. Leaders who have positional power without commensurate empowerment maturity (i.e., inadequate task competence and experience, low psychosocial motivation to achieve, inability or unwillingness to accept responsibility, or low moral commitment to use power to enhance justice, trust, and care in the workplace) will impede employee empowerment. Employee reactions to leaders with low work empowerment maturity are likely to include: (1) lack of respect for leadership direction, position, knowledge, and awareness; (2) active or passive resistance; (3) compliance accompanied by resentment; or (4) exit from the organization. To avoid these possible negative outcomes, employees must be able to speak with facts (i.e., be permitted to voice the truth about leadership inadequacies without fear of negative consequences).

The flow of empowerment in this model is not leader controlled, as it is in a traditional organization. Employee empowerment readiness may exceed the leader's readiness to delegate and share power. Leaders may react to employees with high empowerment maturity in the following ways: (1) lack of willingness to acknowledge obvious employee capability, (2) active or passive resistance to employee empowerment, (3) resignation and abdication of the responsibility required at each stage, or (4) exit from the organization. To avoid these possible negative outcomes, leaders must adjust to new role responsibilities, relinquishing some of their traditional position power prerogatives. Empowerment requires a reallocation of responsibilities for both leaders and employees. If work force empowerment does not result, both parties have failed.

Rath & Strong, a Lexington, Massachusetts-based management consulting firm, polled almost 200 executives from Fortune 500 companies about activities that foster superior performance results for an organization.[36] The survey revealed that *personal initiative*, when combined with a customer-focused orientation and *employee involvement*, has a positive impact on business success and sales growth rate. However, although 79% of all respondents indicated that employees are increasingly expected to take initiative to bring about change in the company, 40% of the respondents replied that most people in their company *do not believe* that they can make a personal contribution to the company's success. Alan Frohman, senior associate with the firm, stated: "These results are significant because they suggest that although people are being expected to take personal initiative, most organizations have not figured out how to translate those expectations into positive behaviors."

Project Planning for Organization Development Consulting[37]

The current total quality literature emphasizes the growing importance of improving *service* quality. In addition to project development skills, the total quality OD practitioner must learn to apply total quality concepts to his or her consulting intervention style.

Increasingly, OD practitioners are having to "sell" their services, whether they are part of an internal department or are in an external consulting firm. Thus, service quality dimensions (mentioned in Chapter 1) apply to OD consultant service delivery, as well as to retail and other service operations. The stages in the consulting process, and a comparison and contrast of the practices of "conventional" consultants and clients with those that take a total quality focus, can provide guidance in planning successful total quality OD consulting interventions. The consulting process, as depicted in Figure 5.7, consists of the following four stages:

1. Recognition of a business need
2. Client/consultant engagement
3. Client/consultant performance
4. Completion, follow-up, or termination

Stage 1: Recognition of the Business Need—The initial stage of an engagement occurs when a client or consultant recognizes that a change must occur and there is a business need for consultative assistance. From the consultant's perspective, understanding client needs (where "understanding" includes knowing the client's business, suppliers, competitors, external issues, and,

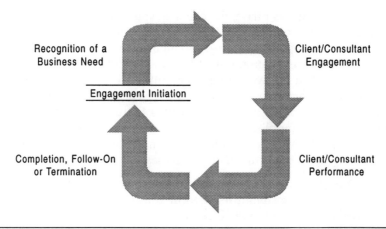

Figure 5.7 The Consulting Process

most importantly, the client's value equation) is the foundation of a good client/consultant relationship. Determining the client's value equation means determining the benefits that the client expects to derive from the engagement. Note that "value" may contain either monetary and/or nonmonetary attributes.

Stage 2: Client/Consultant Engagement—After a client recognizes the business need, an engagement process aimed toward developing a contract with a consultant begins. The client often chooses the consultant based upon: (1) selecting a consultant with whom the client had a previously successful relationship (the most common) or (2) choosing from a group of potential consulting organizations, usually by submitting requests for proposals (RFPs) to them. Consultants' proposals, in response to the RFP, may contain services offered by the organization, the objectives and scope of the engagement, a methodology to be used, benefits and deliverables to the client, names of team members, and the estimated duration, fees, and expenses for the engagement. The RFP is used by the client to "qualify" and eventually select the consulting organization. The consulting organization will usually try to "qualify" *itself* by assessing the risks in the proposed project. It may consider such questions as: Does this organizational group or firm have the necessary resources and core capabilities to meet the client's needs? Do we understand the value we can add to the client's situation? Can we differentiate the product enough to win the engagement?

Stage 3: Client/Consultant Performance—After winning the engagement, tasks leading to deliverables for the client must be performed. Successful performance of the tasks requires participation by both the client and the consultant. Early in this phase, the client's expectations of the deliverables, the consultant's role, and "buy-in" on these deliverables must be established. Buy-in includes agreement on the goals and objectives of each deliverable by executive management, commitment to providing client resources (such as staff) to accomplish the work plan, and full participation by joint client/consultant work teams. Status meetings are typically used to communicate to the client the value of the consulting services. Status meetings may be used to present recent accomplishments, track planned versus actual project milestones, clarify issues or barriers to task completion, assess project-to-date performance, and discuss upcoming activities.

Stage 4: Completion/Follow-up/Exit—Upon project completion, the client may either ask the consultant to perform additional work (not necessarily unsolicited) or the consultant will exit the project without follow-up, which does not imply that the relationship has ended.

After completing the engagement, the consulting team usually assesses its performance in the project and follows up on the results and the impact of the deliverables. Many consultants do not assess client satisfaction or performance at the initial stage (*recognition of a need*), but rather wait until the final stage (*completion*) to do so. This is equivalent to trying to inspect for quality in a manufactured product, rather than building it in throughout the production process.

A TQM Perspective on the Client/Consultant Engagement

Total quality principles can be directly applied to the client/consultant process. Based on the four stages of the client/consultant engagement above, there are some key contributors to TQM of an engagement:

- Development of performance measurements at the beginning of the engagement
- Acquiring the appropriate training for the (internal and external) consulting team
- Facilitating knowledge transfer of the client, industry, products, and business issues
- Constant communication with the client on project status and deliverables
- Development of a high-performance and empowered team
- Communicating value-added to the client organization
- Obtaining feedback on engagement performance (at every opportunity)

A TQM perspective of the client/consultant engagement can be summarized by the following components:

1. Maintaining a customer focus
2. Pre-planning

3. Establishing measurement and control
4. Employee involvement and empowerment
5. Continuous improvement

Each of these components should be enhanced by *information technology* tools to facilitate client customization; enhance knowledge storage, retrieval, and rapid transfer; assist in repeatability of quality; facilitate consultant/client communication; improve accuracy; and provide just-in-time (JIT) training for new techniques to both consultant team members and client participants.

Maintaining a Customer Focus—Maintaining a customer focus is essential in the total quality philosophy. The consulting organization must know its clients, their value equations, how to build quality measures into each deliverable, and how to continuously obtain feedback on engagement performance. Consultants should also view each other as customers, since tasks, knowledge, and portions of deliverables are often transferred from one consultant to another. Maintaining a "right the first time" attitude toward all customers is part of the process of "building in quality" in the customer-focused organization.

Pre-Planning—Pre-planning includes thorough prior planning of all engagement deliverables, facilitating the necessary training and/or knowledge transfer to the client/consultant team (especially the consultant team members), and building performance measurements around each proposed deliverable based on a deep understanding of the client's value equation.

Measurement and Control—The total quality consulting approach requires measuring engagement participants (including client and consultant team members), the engagement as a whole, and the quality of the deliverables. Control tools must be developed to measure engagement performance and quality and to minimize "scope creep."

Employee Involvement and Empowerment—Involving client personnel in the engagement process is essential for success. Even if the consulting organization is supplying 100% of the support staff to the engagement (as in total outsourcing of a development project), buy-in and participation by the client are critical to a high-quality deliverable. Involvement of client staff assures better overall buy-in to the process and enhances the client/consultant relationship. Empowerment is another critical element in a high-performance team. The team must be empowered to perform the agreed-upon process and change mid-stream if required. Political barriers must be removed, the goals and objectives of the consulting project clearly communicated, and the team must be empowered to develop its own recommendations and to making its own decisions (sometimes with the approval of upper-level management).

Team Building—Building a high-performance team is another critical requirement in the total quality consulting approach. High-performance teams will progress through four stages in their development: forming, norming, storming, and performing. Only the high-performing teams will reach the performing stage. The progression from one stage to the next can be expedited through team-building exercises, facilitating necessary communication between team members, and the acquisition of specific team skills in order to perform at a highly functional level. Conflict may be channeled into focused creativity, driving problems down to their root causes, formulating innovative solutions, and implementing a far superior system. High-performing team members are aware of personality differences and work to build confidence and trust in each other. They must forego egos and titles for the sake of capitalizing on the contributions of each member.

Continuous Improvement—An infrastructure that supports continuous improvement is the final essential element in the total quality consulting approach. Continuous improvement is facilitated through performance feedback (follow-up), communicating improvement recommendations to the other members in the organization (consulting team or organization-wide), developing an action plan for improvement, and incorporating the action plan.

Like instruments in an orchestra, each total quality component has its purpose in this consulting approach, and each is equally important in achieving the end result—continuously improving the services to clients.

The Conventional versus the Total Quality Approach

To identify quality "gaps," it is helpful to examine the contrasts between the conventional and the total quality approaches, as viewed by consultants and their clients. Each "partner" comes to the engagement with different perspectives as to what each wishes to obtain from their joint efforts. The conventional versus total quality perspective of consultants' views of clients will be considered next. The "gaps" that arise from taking a conventional view of the engagement will lead to suggestions on how the total quality approach may be of benefit to both the client and the consultant.

A client may pursue engaging a consultant, OD group, or firm for a myriad of reasons, but primarily will look to the relationship to fulfill a business need. Consultants who have training in identifying clients and understanding the engagement from the client's perspective will realize that they have multiple clients to deal with in an engagement. During selection and upon engagement, the consultant may be viewed by client executive management and lower-level management in both positive and negative ways. The split between positive and negative client views typically occurs between upper-level client management and lower-level management and client staff. This frequently occurs because upper-level management has had more experience with consulting relationships and understands that there is usually a great deal of valuable knowledge and experience that can be obtained from the consulting team. Lower-level client management and client staff who will participate on teams are usually less knowledgeable about these relationships, are not aware of the benefits that consultants provide, are threatened by the existence of the consultants, and are uncertain as to what roles they must play while working with the consultants.

Table 5.3 contrasts the conventional versus the total quality OD perspectives of consultants and their views of clients at each stage of the consulting engagement. It should be pointed out that a similar table could be constructed to contrast clients' views of consultants. This table shows many of

Table 5.3 Comparison of Conventional Consultant Approaches versus Total Quality Approaches

Stages of the consulting engagement	Selected conventional consultant approaches	Selected total quality OD consultant approaches
Recognition of business need	• Focus on consulting needs • Emphasis on consultant values • Ignoring baseline variables • Short-term perspective on engagements	• Focus on customer needs • Emphasis on client values • Planning on baseline variables • Long-term perspective on engagements
Client engagement	• Tendency to overlook need to qualify clients • Loss of a bid is a failure • Tendency for teams to be underprepared for engagements • Inadequate client understanding and buy-in on deliverables • Lack of empowerment of team members • Little or no access to client work areas/staff • Limited use of information technology to transfer knowledge	• Recognizing importance of qualified clients • Loss of a bid is a learning opportunity • Fully prepared team members on engagements • Clear client under standing and buy-in on deliverables • Full empowerment of team members • Free access to client work areas or staff • Extensive use of information technology to transfer knowledge

Table 5.3 (continued) Comparison of Conventional Consultant Approaches versus Total Quality Approaches

Stages of the consulting engagement	Selected conventional consultant approaches	Selected total quality OD consultant approaches
Consultant performance	• Lack of communication with client on project status, value added, and issues • Inadequate assistance to client in making interim decisions • Lack of a means of keeping track of issues and their resolution • Emphasis on just meeting the client's needs	• Frequent communication with client on project status, value added, and issues • Timely assistance to client in making interim decisions • Use of issue logs to keep track of issues and their resolution • Emphasis on "delighting" the client, not just meeting needs
Completion/ follow-up/exit	• Failure to identify follow-up projects • Inadequate follow-up on project results • Failure to seek client feedback on projects • Waiting until final stage to assess quality	• Continuous effort to identify follow-up projects • Timely follow-up on project results • Use of established client feedback methods on projects • Measures used to continually assess quality all during the engagement

the "gaps" that exist in conventional client approaches and may be used to infer how these gaps may be closed using the basic total quality concepts outlined in earlier chapters.

A detailed point-by-point analysis of the table will not be undertaken. It is sufficient to say that the "gaps" that are apparent can be traced to the differences in values of conventional versus total quality OD-focused consultants. The total quality OD-focused consultant understands an attempts to practice customer focus and concern, team-based problem analysis and problem solving, and continuous assessment and improvement of the process. The conventional approach is focused on the technical capabilities of the consultant(s), a short-term perspective, "command and control" of participants, and an inadequate understanding of customer-focused quality. While expertise is often sufficient to land an initial engagement, only an understanding of human dynamics will be adequate for follow-up business and process improvement.

TOTAL QUALITY ORGANIZATION DEVELOPMENT PROJECT MANAGEMENT

In total quality OD project management, practitioners have an opportunity to use both development tools and structured problem-solving tools to improve quality. The development tools can permit individuals and groups to focus on improving their own problem-solving processes to yield higher quality results in decision making. Use of structured tools can help to make analysis more systematic and objective, thus contributing to the goal of bringing about "management by fact." First, we will look briefly at the use of a development tool that is growing in importance—simulation. Then we will look at structured project-related tools that can contribute to "management by fact."

Simulation as a Development Tool[38]

A simulation (in its total quality OD applications) is an interactive exercise which involves a real-life type of problem that a team works to solve, in most cases, first as individuals and then in groups. An important objective of this type of simulation process is to help people understand and practice the behaviors and skills that contribute to effective group problem solving, consensus, and superior decision making.[39]

The "living laboratory" atmosphere created by simulations provides an opportunity to identify, explore, and analyze aspects of group behavior. Through simulation processes, teams may explore group dynamics, which are the ways that team members interact as they work together to solve problems and achieve consensus. In so doing, group members experience a sense of "synergy," in which the "whole is greater than the sum of the parts" in group decision making. When reflection and inquiry exercises are included, the laboratory becomes a "mental model practice field" where people can develop skills to talk about assumptions at the moment they are dealing with real issues. "To talk coherently about attitudes and beliefs, to allow others to point them out, to hear comment about them with involvement but without rancor, and to look more clearly at the sources of our own actions—these capabilities all improve with practice, and particularly with well-structured, supported team practice."[40] Thus, simulations provide participants with a wealth of sound information, group process techniques, and insights into the value of participative management and consensus.

Structured Total Quality Project Tools

OD practitioners need to develop competence in the following major structured total quality project tools: *cause-and-effect diagrams, check sheets, display*

Table 5.4 Problem-Solving Steps and Useful Quality Control Tools

Problem-solving step	Useful QC tools
Understanding the mess	Flowcharts
Understanding facts	Check sheets
Identifying problems	Pareto chart Histograms Force-field analysis
Generating ideas	Cause-and-effect diagrams
Developing solutions	Scatter diagrams Prioritization matrix
Implementation	Control charts

Source: Evans, James R. and Lindsay, William M. (1993). *The Management and Control of Quality*, 2nd. edition. Minneapolis: West Publishing, p. 251. Modified by the authors.

graphs, histograms, Pareto charts, scatter diagrams, and control charts. Another tool that is extremely versatile is the *flowchart*, which was discussed in Chapter 3.

To facilitate the appropriate application of the QC process and project tools that have been introduced and efficient, creative problem solving, Table 5.4 suggests a practical format to link problem-solving steps with useful QC tools.[41] These QC tools, which are useful for project management and team problem solving, are briefly defined below. For more detailed coverage, see *Introduction to Modern Statistical Quality Control and Management.*[42]

1. Cause-and-Effect Diagram—Problem identification tool that organizes potential causes of a desirable or undesirable effect. It assists in identifying root causes by asking, five times, why a cause exists.

To identify and solve a problem, it is important to know the real causes and the interrelations among causes. One can then identify the major causes to solve the problem. A cause-and-effect diagram is used to guide data collection and analysis to find the root cause of a problem. A cause-and-effect diagram shows an effect at the right and the main causes of that effect off the horizontal axis. These main causes are in turn effects that have subcauses, and so on, down many levels. This is not basically a statistical tool; it enumerates the variety of causes rather than the frequency of events. However, it is a useful tool for noting the frequency of events once one has the data.

The cause-and-effect diagram was developed by Dr. Kaoru Ishikawa in Japan in the 1960s.[43] By diagramming a relatively simple problem, one may find that there are a number of factors that contribute to the problem but have not been carefully considered. For example, callers to an OD group office may be upset by the fact that they cannot reach someone to discuss the impact of a proposed reengineering project. Instead, they either get a busy signal or are switched to a recorder. Initially, a problem-solving team can meet and discuss the factors that contribute to this problem of "unsatisfactory handling of phone calls to the OD group." Factors might include the number of OD representatives that are available at specific times, the number of phone lines available and in use, peak period calls, printed information that is available to be sent out, etc. A cause-and-effect diagram clarifies which factors of materials (printed information, etc.), personnel (number of representatives), methods (training in handling questions and problems, messages on recorders, etc.), and "machinery" (telephone lines and recorders, etc.) contribute in a negative way to the problem.

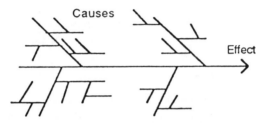

2. Check Sheet—Form used for easy collection of data is called a check sheet. To analyze problems, the total quality OD practitioner must collect data that represent the facts. Check sheets are used to take data systematically regarding the frequency of various effects (e.g., racial, gender, and age data for all organizational employees or work accidents reported by causes). They are much like a set of tally marks on the back of an envelope. However, they are usually marked on forms prepared in advance, according to expected effects. Also, they are calibrated so that when someone takes the data, a running plot of frequency of effects is created; the check marks create a histogram.

Check sheets are simple forms that have been used to record and categorize data for many years. Extending the OD group telephone problem mentioned above, check sheets could be used to classify the nature of the calls to an OD office according to how they were handled (by machine or human operator) and/or how they were resolved, according to several predetermined categories listed on the sheet.

```
A| x x
B| x x x x
C| x x x
D| x x
E| x
```

3. Display Graphs—Display graphs visually delineate data. There are many kinds of display graphs: bar graphs, line graphs, circle graphs, and radar graphs, among others. Most people are familiar with the first three types of graphs (see sample line and radar graph below)·[44]

A *radar graph* compares several items on multiple dimensions. Suppose that for three competitive products, *e1* is performance, *e2* is cost, *e3* is reliability, and *e4* is delivery; in all four dimensions, the good direction is out from the center. The following example shows that one of the products is inferior in all dimensions. Of the other two products, one wins slightly in performance, and the other wins slightly in all other dimensions. This is useful for total quality OD/HR practitioners who compare vendors of benefit packages.

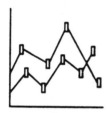

4. Histogram—Shows dispersion of the data. From this graph, the characteristics of the data and the cause of dispersion can be analyzed. Typically, a histogram is a bar graph that shows the statistical distribution over equal intervals of some measure of quality, such as computer literacy skills, high moral maturity ratings, and/or gaps in technical training. Histograms are used in analysis for *stratification* to create hypotheses for why defects are occurring. For example, when a piece of computer equipment used in an OD office has too much dispersion (i.e., uneven quality indicators) and it was made from two machines, it is possible to stratify or segregate the data corresponding to each machine. Thus, it is possible to find the difference between machine A and B and easily make adjustments.

A histogram could be used to display the data taken from a check sheet on the frequency of calls received by a total quality OD group according to time of day or day of the week. After analysis of the data, it might suggest that a possible solution would be to increase the staff available to answer the phones for peak periods of the day, such as lunchtime.

5. Pareto Chart—Organizes causes by frequency. By using it, the significant few causes that account for most of the effect can be identified.

At any given time, there are many kinds of problems surrounding the total quality OD practitioner. It is not feasible to attack all these problems at the same time. Therefore, arranging the problems in order of importance and attacking the bigger problems first is important. A bar graph that shows the biggest problem on the left followed by the lesser problems is called a Pareto chart. Pareto charts help one focus on the vital few effects or causes.

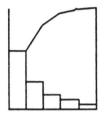

Use of the Pareto concept of "the significant few items and the insignificant many" for quality problem analysis was first suggested by "quality guru" Joseph Juran. The Pareto principle is sometimes called the 80–20 rule and suggests that 80% of the items are accounted for by 20% of the causes or issues. A Pareto chart is simply a histogram in which frequency data are shown by "bars" on the chart which are arranged from highest to lowest, in order by cause. For the OD office telephone problem, data from a check sheet on the most frequent questions that are asked by callers could be displayed. If the phones are overloaded by calls, the problem-solving team might recommend that printed materials listing frequently asked questions and their answers could be distributed to all employees who would be interested.

6. Scatter Diagram—Depicts the relationship between variables. Thus, it helps to substantiate whether a potential root cause is related to the effect.

The relationship between cause and effect (e.g., between illumination level at a worksite and inspection mistakes at the worksite) may be drawn on a graph called a *scatter diagram*. A scatter diagram plots many data points, typically with a measure of quality on one axis and a variable hypothesized to influence quality on the other axis. Used in analysis to test hypotheses on cause-and-effect relations, a scatter diagram is a visual representation of a two-dimensional correlation. A diagram such as this is often very useful because it illustrates patterns of data that are not otherwise obvious.

The scatter diagram might be set up to show the relationship between the number of hours of training for a total quality OD telephone representative and the average number of minutes required to respond to each call. The premise that would be tested by this diagram would be that the more training (up to a certain point) that the representative received, the faster she or he would be able to respond to questions received from callers.

7. Control Chart—Shows whether variation is due to common or special causes. Upper and lower control limits are easily calculated using the averages and ranges of the data observed. Control charts are used only to determine the nature of variation. They are much more precise than run charts relative to indicating whether variation is due to common or special causes.

Once training had been completed, and the "system" was stable, the average time to complete phone calls to the OD group should be stable and could be plotted on a control chart to determine if there have been significant changes in the average time to handle a call.

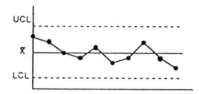

In addition to the seven major quality project management tools (plus flowcharting), six supplemental tools include *force-field analysis, prioritization matrix, run charts, block diagram, customer/supplier relations checklist, and quality mapping.*

1. Force-Field Analysis—Used to identify problems, their causes, and the driving and restraining forces that affect the problem.

Problem causes are shown as arrows restraining or opposing the driving forces needed to successfully accomplish a task or project. For example, a company may wish to develop a total quality process in one of its divisions. The driving forces would be such things as leadership, competitiveness, cost, and need for greater employee involvement and commitment. The restraining forces might be a hostile union environment, lack of familiarity with total quality principles and processes, perceived high start-up costs, and employee skepticism over the benefits versus the efforts required. The political strength of the respective forces can be quantified and analyzed.

2. Prioritization Matrix—Uses a diagram of alternatives and a list of weighted criteria to quantitatively determine the preferred option. Prioritization matrices are used to reduce the number of alternatives to those that are most significant in a structured, quantitative way. In OD settings, disciplinary alternatives for employees could be determined, evaluated, and justified.

This tool can be computerized and input solicited and collectively tallied prior to a meeting to determine the level of support for an option *before* meeting face to face.

3. Run Chart—Shows the results of a process plotted over time. It is useful to see the dynamic aspects of a process and identify cyclical patterns.

Again, data on the frequencies of calls to the OD group might be plotted day by day on a run chart. If the printed materials mentioned above were distributed, a run chart would help to show if the calls concerning frequently asked questions declined after the materials reached the affected employees.

4. Block Diagram—Traces the paths that materials and/or information take between the point of input and final output.

A block diagram can frequently be used in the preliminary stages of process analysis to classify the system. For example, the major activities of a purchasing system could be shown on a block diagram. They might include issuing requests for proposal from potential vendors, receiving proposals, selecting the vendor, developing and signing the contract, receiving the goods, assuring compliance, closing out the contract, and verifying payment. If the purpose of the study was to simplify and/or improve the system, each of these activities, or the entire process, might be studied by one or more project teams.

5. Customer/Supplier Relations Checklist—Used to assess the relationship with customers and suppliers within and outside the organization.

This is a specialized form of check sheet that may be used to classify customers or suppliers into categories. For example, although it is not certain that such checklists were used, Hewlett-Packard (HP) may have, or could have, done so in a case study reported in a recent article. HP was experiencing a large number of defects of a critical computer component that it received from a vendor. Instead of replacing the vendor, it formed a three-person project team to investigate the feasibility of eliminating incoming inspection and establishing direct shipments of the parts from the vendor. By gathering and analyzing data, it was determined that the reasons for the vendor's problems were: (1) a misinterpretation of the product specifications, (2) lack of consistency in the vendor's production and quality assurance capabilities, and (3) need for the development of a system to eliminate the need for HP to perform incoming inspection on the parts. Eventually the vendor was able to meet all of HP's requirements, thus retaining the HP account, while HP received the benefits of lower costs, shorter lead time, and elimination of 100% inspection and associated rework returns.

6. Quality Mapping—Refers to Q-Map (Quality Map), a personal software program for developing measures of process and project performance, available from Pacesetter Software, P.O. Box 5270, Princeton, NJ 08540. This proprietary software makes charting and analysis of various processes/ projects easier and faster, once a total quality OD analyst becomes familiar with how to use the package.

REVIEW QUESTIONS

5.1 Distinguish "speaking with facts" from three alternatives, and describe how each impacts project success.

5.2 List some ways in which projects are playing an increasingly important role in organization design.

5.3 Identify the major steps, key fact-finding cycles, and appropriate tools to speak with facts in a total quality environment.

5.4 Describe how the factual requirements of an "efficient" process (level 4) differ from those of an "effective" process (level 3). How do they both fall short of creating a *total* quality environment?

5.5 Elaborate on the skills a total quality project manager must have in order to deal with organizational subcultures and the phases/stages of project life cycles.

5.6 Describe the basic ingredients of teams in detail, and distinguish real teams from pseudo, potential, and high-performance teams.

5.7 Define a quality audit and describe its importance for total quality and OD improvement projects.

5.8 Define and elaborate on the four types of teams and how they are structurally related in a total quality organization.

5.9 How can total quality OD professionals develop, use, and share their internal and external consulting skills to strategically and operationally contribute to project management?

5.10 Define and apply the seven major total quality project management tools to an OD issue.

5.11 Using a real OD issue, elaborate on Evans and Lindsay's problem-solving sequence and the total quality tools linked to each step.

DISCUSSION QUESTIONS

5.1 Drawing on your own experience, make a case for the importance of "speaking with facts" in an organization. Discuss the challenges and obstacles that may be present in successfully creating an organization that speaks with facts.

5.2 Compare and contrast four basic subcultures found in most organizations and the implications of these subcultures for information sharing and fact-based decision making.

5.3 Discuss the process of responsible team empowerment, considering it from three points of view: the organization, the employee, and the OD professional. From each point of view, what factors might "disable" empowerment, and how might these disablers be overcome?

5.4 Identify at least one current business example of a real team *and* a high-performance team. Distinguish each team's characteristics and how those characteristics contributed to the team's results. Discuss what you think is required—from team leaders and team members—to make each kind of team work.

5.5 Discuss the ways in which traditional HR/OD-developed systems or practices have tended to reinforce only individual effort, not team effort. Using real-case examples, identify system, policy, or practice innovations you believe will be required to foster cross-functional team collaboration. Drawing on both the successes and failures in your case examples, what advice would you offer as "keys to success"?

5.6 Discuss the ways in which OD practices contribute to the micro- and macro-system phases of the involvement/empowerment continuum (see Table 5.2).

5.7 What would (should) you do if you are offered a high-paying leadership position in a Machiavellian ethical work culture and are expected to lead a group with very low empowerment readiness? What would (should) you do if you are an employee with a high level of empowerment readiness, but your immediate manager is overdirecting you?

ENDNOTES

1. Leavitt, Jeffrey S. and Nunn, Philip C. (1994). *Total Quality Through Project Management*. New York: McGraw-Hill, pp. 45–46; Kleim, Ralph L. and Ludin, Irwin S. (1992). *The People Side of Project Management*. Brookfield, VT: Gower Publishing.

2. Goetsch, D.L. and Davis, S. (1995). *Implementing Total Quality*. Englewood Cliffs, NJ: Prentice-Hall.

3. Voehl, Frank F. (1992). *Total Quality: Principles and Practices within Organizations*. Coral Springs, FL: Strategy Associates, pp. 5–7.

4. Gordon, W.I., Infante, D.A., and Graham, E.E. (1988). "Corporate Conditions Conducive to Employee Voice: A Subordinate Perspective." *Employee Rights and Responsibilities Journal*. Vol. 1, No. 3, pp. 101–111; Saunders, D.M., Sheppard, B.H., Knight, V.E., and Roth, J. (1992). "Employee Voice to Supervisors." *Employee Rights and Responsibilities Journal*. Vol. 8, No. 4, pp. 85–94.

5. Minton, J.W. (1988). "Justice, Satisfaction and Loyalty: Employee Withdrawal and Voice in the Din of Inequity." Unpublished doctoral dissertation. Durham, NC: Duke University; Spencer, D.G. (1986). "Employee Voice and Employee Retention." *Academy of Management Journal*. Vol. 29, No. 3, pp. 488–502.

6. Sheppard, B.H., Lewicki, R., and Minton, J.W. (1992). *Organizational Justice: The Search for Fairness in the Workplace.* New York: Lexington Books, pp. 154–155.
7. Ryan, Kathleen D. and Oestrich, D.K. (1991). *Driving Fear Out of the Workplace.* San Francisco: Jossey-Bass, pp. 29–102.
8. Alexander, Phil (1992). "Self-Esteem and Empowerment." *Journal for Quality and Participation.* Vol. 12, No. 6, pp. 26–28.
9. Rusbelt, C.E., Farrell, D., Rogers, G., and Mainous, A.G. (1988). "Impact of Exchange Variables on Exit, Voice, Loyalty, and Neglect: An Integrative Model of Responses to Declining Job Satisfaction." *Academy of Management Journal.* Vol. 31, No. 2, pp. 599–627.
10. Sheppard, Lewicki, and Minton (endnote 6), pp. 156–158.
11. Blackburn, Richard and Rosen, Benson (1994). "Human Resource Management Practices and Total Quality Management." Paper presented at the 1994 Academy of Management Meetings, Atlanta.
12. Ibid., pp. 12–15.
13. Ibid., pp. 9–11. For precursor of the survey instrument used in the most recent study, see also Seraph, J., Benson, P., and Schroeder, R. (1989). "An Instrument for Measuring the Critical Factors of Quality Management." *Decision Sciences.* Vol. 20, No. 5, pp. 810–829.
14. Shiba, Shoji, Graham, A., and Walden, D. (1993). *A New American TQM: Four Practical Revolutions in Management.* Cambridge, MA: Productivity Press, p. 65.
15. Mills, Charles A. (1989). *The Quality Audit: A Management Evaluation Tool.* New York: McGraw-Hill, pp. 10–70; Mills, David (1993). *Quality Auditing.* New York: Chapman and Hall, pp. 25–81.
16. The material in this section relies heavily on Harrington, H. James (1991). *Business Process Improvement.* New York: McGraw-Hill, pp. 206–215.
17. Glines, David, Ledder, Diane, Kling, John, and Tahmahkera, Virginia (1990). "Quality Service for People and Animals." *The Journal for Quality and Participation.* July/August, pp. 90–95.
18. Cameron, K. and Freeman, S. (1991). "Cultural Consequence, Strength and Type: Relationships to Effectiveness." *Research in Organizational Development.* Vol. 5, pp. 23–58; Phillips, M.E., Goodman, R.A., and Sackmann, S.A. (1992). "Exploring the Complex Culture Milieu of Project Teams." *PM Network.* Vol. 6, No. 8, pp. 79–88; Ouchi, William (1987). "Bureaucratic, Market and Clan Control." *Academy of Management Journal.* Vol. 24, No. 5, pp. 120–129.
19. Leavitt and Nunn (endnote 1), pp. 48–53.
20. Kleim and Ludin (endnote 1), pp. 38–42.
21. Evans, James R. and Lindsay, William M. (1993). *The Management and Control of Quality,* 2nd edition. Minneapolis: West Publishing, pp. 490–491.
22. The material in this section relies heavily on Katzenbach, J.R. and Smith, D.K. (1993). *The Wisdom of Teams.* Boston: Harvard Business School Press, pp. 43–92. Also Reddy, Brendan W. (1994). *Intervention Skills: Process Consultation for Small Groups and Teams.* San Diego: Pfeiffer and Company.
23. Mears, P. and Voehl, F. (1994). *Team Building: A Structured Learning Approach.* Delray Beach, FL: St. Lucie Press, p. 62; Earley, P.C. (1993). "East Meets West Meets Midwest: Further Explorations of Collectivistic and Individualistic Work Groups." *Academy of Management Journal.* Vol. 36, pp. 319–348.

24. Katzenbach and Smith (endnote 22), pp. 87–129.
25. ANSI/ASQC (1987). A3-1987, "Quality Systems Terminology." Milwaukee: ASQC.
26. Hartsfield, William E. (1990). *HR Audit: How to Evaluate Your Personnel Policies and Practices.* Madison, CT: Business and Legal Reports.
27. Reidenbach, R.E. and Robin, D.P. (1989). *Ethics and Profits.* Englewood Cliffs, NJ: Prentice-Hall, pp. 200–203; contact Organizational Ethics Associates in Cincinnati, Ohio (513-984-2820) for additional information.
28. Ibid.; Rothwell, W.J., Sullivan, R., and McLean, G.N., Eds. (1995). *Practicing Organization Development: A Guide for Consultants.* San Diego: Pfeiffer and Company; Kirkpatrick, D.L. (1994). *Evaluating Training Programs.* San Francisco: Barrett-Koehler.
29. Ortega, Bob (1995). "Conduct Codes Garner Goodwill for Retailers, But Violations Go On." *Wall Street Journal.* July 3, pp. A1, A4.
30. Zenger, J., Musselwhite, E., Hurson, K., and Perrin, C. (1994). *Leading Teams: Mastering the New Role.* Burr Ridge, IL: Irwin, pp. 27–53.
31. Aubrey, C.A. and Felkins, P.K. (1988). *Teamwork: Involving People in Quality and Productivity Improvement.* Milwaukee: ASQC Quality Press, pp. 10–40.
32. Dean, James W. Jr. and Evans, James R. (1994). *Total Quality: Management, Organization, and Strategy.* Minneapolis: West Publishing, p. 182.
33. Wellins, R.S., Byham, W.C., and Wilson, J.M. (1991). *Empowered Teams.* San Francisco: Jossey-Bass, pp. 24–63.
34. Hersey, P. (1984). *The Situational Leader.* New York: Warner Books.
35. Johnson, Richard S. (1993). *TQM: Leadership for the Quality Transformation.* Milwaukee: ASQC Quality Press, pp. 88–99.
36. Rath & Strong Executive Panel, Winter 1994 Survey on Personal Initiative, Summary of Findings.
37. Adapted from Droder, George R. and Lindsay, William (1995). "A Model for Client Satisfaction in the Global Consulting Industry: A TQM Focus." Paper abstracted in the Proceedings of the 1995 Association on Employment Practices and Principles Annual Convention, New Orleans.
38. This section is adapted from materials provided by Frank W. Voehl of Strategy Associates, Inc.
39. For the development and use of simulations, see the work of Norman Maier and Clayton Lafferty. Some of the best-known simulations are the Desert Survival Simulation, "Lost on the Moon," The Project Planning Situation, Turnaround, and Envisioning a Culture for Quality.
40. Senge, Peter (1994). *The Fifth Discipline Fieldbook,* New York: Doubleday.
41. Evans and Lindsay (endnote 21), pp. 237–251.
42. Swift, J.A. (1995). *Introduction to Modern Statistical Quality Control and Management.* Delray Beach, FL: St. Lucie Press.
43. Ishikawa, Kaoru and Lu, D. (1985). *What Is Total Quality Control? The Japanese Way.* Englewood Cliffs, NJ: Prentice-Hall, pp. 45–62.
44. Shiba, Graham, and Walden (endnote 14), pp. 102–105.

CASE STUDY

THE MUSTANG RIDES AGAIN AT FORD*

Building on the success of its early 1980s experiment in teamwork which led to the award-winning design of the Taurus-Sable, Ford Motor Company set out in 1989 to revive the Mustang of the 1960s. There were one or two differences that made it unlikely that Ford would duplicate either of its earlier feats. First, worldwide competition had turned up the heat to a fever pitch, placing enormous expectations on any design team for higher quality, faster time to market, and miserly design costs that were unknown even in the early 1980s. Second, Ford was striving to reinvent a legend and to harness the opposing forces of "finance and feelings" that would be in effect from the 1990s and into the 21st century. Against what seemed to be insurmountable odds, a group of 400 people, dubbed "Team Mustang," was assembled to take on the redesign task.

"The danger with the Mustang was that it was so emotional, you had more chances to go off in the wrong direction," says John Coletti, a founding member of the group. Some Mustang stylists wanted a muscle-bound look, nicknamed "Rambo." Others though a milder design nicknamed "Bruce Jenner" would sell better. The compromise: "We sent Bruce back to the gym," says Mr. Coletti. The result was "Schwarzenneger"—rugged but cultured.

The car only arrived in showrooms on December 9, 1993, and it won the coveted *Motor Trend's* "Car of the Year" award for 1994. Thus it matched the design performance of its "big brother," Taurus, which won the award in 1986.

Team Mustang didn't do badly in the competitive design race, either. Although it was projected to cost over $1 billion for the design phase, the team was able to hold the costs down to $700 million and to complete the project in three years. That was 25% less time and 30% lower cost than had usually been required for recent Ford designs. Much of the credit goes to Will Boddie, the engineer who led the Mustang development team, chief engineer Michael Zevalkink, and program manufacturing boss Dia Hothi, as well as Mr. Coletti.

The Mustang project almost didn't get off the ground. The market for the Mustang shrank steadily from a peak of 600,000 in 1966 to just over 86,000 in 1992. In 1989, Ford was facing up to a new federal mandate that said that all vehicles sold after September 1, 1993 would have to have "passive restraints"— airbags. That meant that a redesign would have to be done to accommodate the requirement, or Ford would have to put the Mustang out of its misery.

*Adapted from White, Joseph B. and Oscar Suris (1993). "How a 'Skunk Works' Kept the Mustang Alive—On a Tight Budget." *The Wall Street Journal*. September 21, pp. A1, A12.

Coletti got the go-ahead from management to form a "skunk works" development team and do the redesign project that many said was impossible. Fortunately, Coletti had a strong ally in the form of Alex Trotman, executive vice president of North American automotive operations. Coletti and his small team jetted around the world looking for ideas on how to design the car in the shortest possible time period for the lowest possible cost. After sifting through ideas from partners in Japan, a subsidiary in Australia, and design centers in Germany and Italy, their new product development approach took shape. Their plan would have been simple for a 200-person machine shop, but it mean breaking long-standing policies and customs at Ford.

Coletti proposed, and eventually received approval from Trotman, to put the whole Mustang design team under one roof and to give it unprecedented freedom to make its own decisions without interference from headquarters or other departments. He also boldly proposed to put accountants, draftspeople, engineers, and stylists in the same or adjoining rooms. Finally, he proposed that Dia Hothi, the manufacturing chief, be given veto power over the designers if their proposed changes would force him to make drastic changes in the tools that he was using to manufacture the current Mustangs. This had *never* been done in a previous Ford design project!

Mr. Boddie, the man chosen as program manager, was a well-respected engineer who had worked on previous innovative design and assembly technology projects, but had never managed a car program. He had his own unconventional ways of doing things. The "Mustang Car Company" was set up in an old furniture warehouse in Allen Park, Michigan. He and the team leaders virtually did away with the bidding process for suppliers, selected those that they thought could do the best job, and invited them into the design process at the very beginning. When the design for the convertible version of the Mustang hit a snag because of vibrations, top executives had to hold their breath and keep their promise not to meddle with the design team. It looked like the production and budget targets might be missed, until Boddie assembled a 50-person SWAT team to correct the problem. With about eight weeks of effort and the help of several suppliers, the problem was solved. As an added touch, Boddie wondered about why the new Mercedes-Benz had such a smooth ride, so he had his engineers buy one and take it apart. Based on this "reverse engineering," they found that the addition of a 25-pound cylinder at a strategic spot under the front fender would dampen vibrations very nicely!

The design effort exceeded all expectations, coming in under the variable cost targets for manufacturing, and the investment cost target, and beating the expected time to market by two months.

Although the price tag for the new Mustang will never match the under $2,400 of the 1964 model, it will give its closest rival, the Chevrolet Camaro, fits by undercutting its starting price of $13,399.

EXERCISE

EXERCISE 5.1   PRACTITIONER ASSESSMENT INSTRUMENT: EMPOWERMENT READINESS ASSESSMENT

DIRECTIONS
This rating form considers the total quality empowerment readiness level of individuals and/or groups. It can be used as a personal or group self-assessment instrument, *or* by a manager considering another individual for promotion or group members for a project, *or* distributed for anonymous collective feedback about a prospective individual or group empowerment activity. For each of the dimensions listed below, circle the number that most closely represents your perception of the individual or group under consideration, using the rating scale below. Comments are optional.

High		Moderate				Low	
8	7	6	5	4	3	2	1

Dimensions   **Comments**

1. Job/project knowledge

Has job/project   Does not have job/   _____
knowledge   project knowledge

8   7   6   5   4   3   2   1

2. Achievement motivation

Has high desire to   Has little desire to   _____
achieve   achieve

8   7   6   5   4   3   2   1

3. Honesty

Always honest   Never honest   _____

8   7   6   5   4   3   2   1

4. Total quality problem-solving ability

Solves problems using   Unable to solve problems   _____
total quality tools   using total quality tools

8   7   6   5   4   3   2   1

5. Communication style

Communicates   Does not communicate   _____
effectively at work   effectively at work

8   7   6   5   4   3   2   1

6. Trustworthy

Always trustworthy   Never trustworthy   _____

8   7   6   5   4   3   2   1

7. Past job/project experience

Has relevant experience   No relevant experience   _____

8   7   6   5   4   3   2   1

8. Sense of humor

Always exhibits an   Never exhibits an
appropriate sense of   appropriate sense of
humor   of humor   _____

8   7   6   5   4   3   2   1

9. Justice/fairness

Always fair and just   Never fair and just   _____

8   7   6   5   4   3   2   1

10. Relevant computer literacy

Always uses computer   Never uses computer
effectively at work   effectively at work   _____

8   7   6   5   4   3   2   1

11. Work attitude

Has "can do–enjoy   Has "can't do–thank
making it happen"   goodness it's Friday"
attitude   attitude   _____

8   7   6   5   4   3   2   1

12. Respectfully caring

Always respectfully   Never respectfully
caring   caring   _____

8   7   6   5   4   3   2   1

13. Organization knowledge

Knows the   Does not know the
organization as   organization as a whole
a whole system   system   _____

8   7   6   5   4   3   2   1

14. Interdependent cooperation

Works cooperatively   Does not work cooper-
with others   atively with others   _____

8   7   6   5   4   3   2   1

15. Good judgment

| Always exhibits good judgment | Never exhibits good judgment | _____ |

8   7   6   5   4   3   2   1

16. Takes responsibility for an envisioned future

| Envisions a future and takes responsibility for it | Does not envision a future and take responsibility for it | _____ |

8   7   6   5   4   3   2   1

17. Uses and shares power effectively

| Uses and shares power effectively | Uses and shares power ineffectively | _____ |

8   7   6   5   4   3   2   1

18. Courage

| Always exhibits courage | Never exhibits courage | _____ |

8   7   6   5   4   3   2   1

SCORING

Task maturity: Add the numbers circled for questions 1, 4, 7, 10, 13, and 16 and divide the total by 6.

Psychosocial maturity: Add the numbers circled for questions 2, 5, 8, 11, 14, and 17 and divide by 6.

Moral maturity: Add the numbers circled for questions 3, 6, 9, 12, 15, and 18 and divide by 6.

INTERPRETATION

Average scores for any of the factors:

0–4.0 = Individual or group is not ready for total quality empowerment at this time

4.1–7 = Individual or group is ready for regular participation in total quality teamwork

7.1–8 = Individual or group is ready for self-directed, high-performance total quality teamwork

Use your lowest average factor score as a place to begin preparing yourself or your group for responsible empowerment. Individuals or groups who are prematurely empowered (e.g., individual promoted without being ready to assume the commensurate responsibilities) eventually become problems for themselves, others, and the total quality system (i.e., "The Peter Principle" of institutionalized incompetence).

CHAPTER 6

RESPECT FOR PEOPLE: TQ AND OD PERFORMANCE DIMENSIONS

The focus of Chapter 6 is on two areas: total quality *business* individual performance and total quality *organization development* (OD) individual performance. Both are crucial in determining the strength of the fourth pillar of the House of Total Quality and clarifying the expanded daily performance responsibilities of individual employees in a total quality system. Both total quality business and OD individual performance need to be aligned to ensure organizational effectiveness and efficiency.

TOTAL QUALITY BUSINESS PERFORMANCE

As indicated in Chapter 1, the fourth pillar of the House of Total Quality, respect for people, is based on the cornerstone of individual performance planning and the foundation of individual performance management. In Chapter 3, *individual performance* was defined as the daily implementation of continuous improvement in personal tasks and relational activity within an employee's own scope of responsibility.[1] The pillar of respect for people is

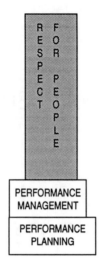

Figure 6.1 The Fourth Pillar, Foundation, and Cornerstone of the House of Total Quality

the outcome of sound design developed in the cornerstone of individual performance planning with effective implementation delivered in the foundation of individual performance management, as shown in Figure 6.1.[2]

While the previous total quality pillars involved system strategy and process and project dimensions, the last pillar focuses on daily personal task and relational performance. Key points to be considered include:

- When considering what behavioral theories may apply to a situation, a useful guide is to (1) diagnose the situation, (2) choose the appropriate theory, (3) explore current behavior, (4) introduce the theory to those who are involved, (5) relate the theory to the organization, (6) relate the theory to individuals in the situation, and (7) perform action planning.
- Many behavioral theories and models are useful in describing OD performance dimensions. Some are simply descriptions of theory and others involve the use of questionnaires and instruments.
- Communication is fundamental to the success of total quality. Everyone in the organization requires a high level of communication skills. These skills should be periodically audited by total quality OD practitioners to identify where barriers exist. Often the barriers are part of the organization's culture, and total quality OD professionals can help confront the issues.
- In the past, OD programs were often undertaken to improve the integration of the goals of individuals with the performance of duties to attain

desired outcomes or objectives of the organization. The "exchange theory" of goal integration, based on the assumption of rational evaluations of costs versus economic outcomes and social benefits between the parties, seems to have been rejected by OD theorists. Thus "accommodation theory," in which each side tries to accommodate the immediate needs and inducements of the other, takes over.

Even with the most innovative and sophisticated approaches to strategy, process and project management will be unable to produce world-class results if respect for people is absent. And respect for people is built—or eroded—every day in organizational planning, task design, and management of individual work performance.

Respect for People and Work Cultures

Quality is *personal*, as Roberts and Sergesketter proclaim in the title of their book.[3] Certainly, teamwork is necessary for quality processes and projects to be designed, maintained, and improved. But if *individuals* do not "buy into" the quality philosophy, learn the quality tools and techniques, develop the ability to work together in teams in order to improve business processes and work designs, and use the new knowledge, skills, and abilities (KSAs) in their daily work, then nothing will happen. Yet Deming said that quality problems are the fault of the *system* 85 to 90% of the time, which only management could correct. The answers to quality problems are not easy, but they *are* subject to analysis and improvement. The bottom line is that if managers and workers do not work as *both* individuals and teams to remove barriers to quality, quality will never improve.

This personal commitment to quality will not come about by default; it must be nurtured by design. The fourth pillar, therefore, goes to the very heart of what makes or breaks total quality in any organization. *Respect for people* is the fundamental *positive* regard we have for ourselves and for one another as people. It plays out in what we expect of ourselves, how we treat ourselves and each other each day, how we view ourselves in relation to others, and how we view the value each person brings to every interaction. Individuals with high self-respect have enough pride in their work to make a strong personal commitment to quality performance. They treat others in such a way that *shared work pride* becomes the norm rather than the exception in an organization. Table 6.1 shows the characteristics of people who respect themselves and others and the implications these factors have in a traditional versus a total quality work culture.[4]

Individuals at work who respect others but not themselves do not relate well to others in a cooperative manner because they undervalue their own worth, do not voice their own opinions, and rely on the approval of others

Table 6.1 Characteristics and Work Culture Implications of Respect for People

People who respect themselves and others	Implications in a traditional work culture	Implications in a total quality work culture
Less interested in seeking approval from others	May be perceived as rebels, mavericks, "loose cannons," self-serving	May be more likely to challenge status quo and take risks
More accepting of others	May be regarded with suspicion ("What's their hidden agenda?")	May foster collaboration and mutual support
Less likely to be driven by feedback from others	May be perceived as a stubborn, closed, ineffective person with "blinders" on	May seek the "best" solution, despite biases of tradition
High internal locus of control	May be perceived as resistant to the rightful authority of others	May hold self more accountable and take personal responsibility
Less likely to model others	May be perceived as devaluing heritage and past strengths	May envision and create needed innovations
Accept and feel good about themselves	May be seen as uncontrollable; may seem threatening to the insecure	May take more initiative to act with confidence even in the face of uncertainty
Driven to meet their own self-set goals which tend to be high and resistant to change	May be seen as troublemakers, making others "look bad"	May "raise the bar" and continuously seek improvement
Expect to succeed regardless of the context	May be perceived as unrealistic, naive	May help others achieve beyond self-imposed limitations
Emotionally well-adjusted	May be perceived as sensible and not easily manipulated or intimidated	May demonstrate emotional balance in handling success and coping with failure
Have humility to learn the truth	May be perceived as indecisive, self-doubting, and/or weak	May openly acknowledge own improvement needs and seek both feedback and help from others in order to learn
Excellent empathic listeners	May be regarded as too considerate (emphasizing feelings over results)	May listen sincerely for genuine understanding of others' concerns or feedback, without being defensive, justifying self, or imposing advice

for validation. An example is a manager or employee who allows others to verbally abuse him or her without setting boundaries for respectful discourse at work. Individuals who only respect themselves but not others alienate co-workers and are unable to learn from others or generate teamwork (e.g., managers who do not solicit input or ignore feedback from knowledgeable employees because they [the managers] are too proud to learn from others). Some persons only feel or show honor for those who have higher rank or status in work organizations and treat peers or direct reports with contempt or neglect. Total quality firms require respect for all people in the organization, regardless of role, since each person is continually empowered to enhance the effectiveness of the organization. Some persons profess respect for others, but act as if they always expect others to defer to their judgment. For example, they often dismiss the contributions of others in conversations and decision-making processes. This gap between the rhetoric and reality of respect for people is what must be, and is, eliminated or severely reduced in a total quality organization because the system cannot improve without sincere respect and integrity.

Respect for people and social tolerance are particularly important in valuing diversity and achieving unity of purpose (Deming's point number 9) in today's workplace.[5] Discrimination against people at work is illegal, violates the principles for which the fourth pillar of total quality stands, and is morally offensive. It reduces the effectiveness of an organization by erecting barriers to equal access to information and training and by fostering prejudice against those who contribute to organizational success. People who respect themselves and others, whether or not they are in a protected class, are more likely to appreciate others' success and emulate it rather than resent it. For example, when a co-worker has been successful, respectful people acknowledge and celebrate that achievement. They are inspired by their co-worker's example to honor their own talents and to do their personal best rather than allege favoritism or feel envy. In total quality organizations, people earn respect through performance, and emulation of success, rather than resentment against achievement, is the norm. Respect for people, therefore, includes both sincere self-respect and sincere respect for others to enhance personal performance integration in a total quality work culture. Exhibit 6.1 shows how the Ritz-Carlton Hotel Company (a division of Marriott Corporation) achieves respect for individuals and quality service at every level.

TOTAL QUALITY BUSINESS PERFORMANCE PLANNING

In planning overall business quality performance, both system and personal factors need to be addressed, as discussed in Chapter 4. However, a more

The Ritz-Carlton Hotel Company (a division of Marriott Corporation) won the Malcolm Baldrige National Quality Award in 1992 based on service excellence. The key to its service excellence is careful selection of employees; respect for individuals; intensive training; individual empowerment; certification of knowledge, skills, and abilities, and pride of accomplishment.

The company's service philosophy is captured in the simple statement, "We are ladies and gentlemen serving ladies and gentlemen." This provides both a customer focus and an employee focus. These words are backed up by management actions.

Employees are carefully selected based on a system of character trait analysis developed for each of about 130 company jobs. The result has been that Ritz-Carlton's turnover rate has been reduced to 48% versus an industry average of over 100%. After selection, employees are given over 100 hours of extensive training in the Ritz-Carlton philosophy, the three steps of service (a warm and sincere greeting, anticipating and complying with guests' needs, and a fond farewell—using the guests' names at all times), and the basics of employee empowerment. One of those basics is that the employees can "move heaven and earth" to satisfy a customer. Front-desk employees are empowered to authorize expenditures of up to $2000 to ensure guest satisfaction. Employees are involved in an annual process of certification of technical skills, with more than 75% of the company's 14,000 employees certified by the end of the first year of the process. Finally, to instill pride of workmanship, top management works side by side with employees in every new hotel opening in what is called the "seven day countdown" before the opening. Here, the CEO, Horst Schulze, and his vice presidents may do anything from change beds to wash dishes, side by side with hotel employees. Mr. Schulze typically introduces himself by saying, "My name is Horst Schulze. I'm president of this company. I'm very important." Then he adds, "but so are you. Absolutely. Equally important."

Exhibit 6.1 Respect for People at Ritz-Carlton (Adapted from Henderson, Cheri (1992). "Putting on the Ritz." *The TQM Magazine.* November/December, pp. 292–296; Bounds, Gregory M. (1996). "The Ritz-Carlton Hotel Company." *Cases in Quality.* pp. 608–623; and various internal documents.)

detailed approach to work performance is required to clarify the best ways to enhance personal contributions in a total quality system.

Work performance can be defined as behavior associated with the accomplishment of expected, specified, or formal role requirements on the part of individual organizational members.[6] Total quality organizations may be described in terms of the norms, values, and reward procedures that emphasize holistic behavior of individuals oriented toward cooperation with fellow organizational members.[7] Work performance in a total quality management (TQM) environment includes accomplishing tasks and taking initiatives above and beyond the call of duty, and sharing information with and helping co-workers. Moorman and Blakely classify these behaviors as organizational citizenship behavior (OCB).[8] In a total quality organization, OCB is both expected and formally rewarded.[9] Support staff in a total quality organization will often phone other departments for work if their own department's work has been completed. This cooperative "helping out" attitude will consequently be recognized and rewarded. Well-engineered technical or business systems are no substitute for achieving total work performance through personal contributions and cooperation.

Four Influences on Work Performance Planning[10]

Work performance will be influenced by four categories of factors: (1) *systematic system*, (2) *random factors* that influence the system, (3) *person*, and (4) *person/system* interaction.[11] Individual performance variation within a system results only from the latter three categories. Systematic system factors are those that affect persons equally (e.g., employees serving milkshakes in a fast-food restaurant use the same equipment and rely on identical procedures). One sales representative may be assigned to a rapidly growing sales territory, while another may not be as fortunate; the first representative benefits from systemic system variation.[12] Although systematic system factors may affect overall worker performance, such as when employees must use obsolete technology, those factors do not explain individual performance variations. Deming held that these "system" causes were under the control of management. Thus, employees could do nothing about them without the direct involvement and approval of management.

Random factors that influence the system, however, affect employees differently. These factors may be of two types: common causes and special causes. Variations that occur in environmental conditions, such as a supplier plant burning down, uncontrollable temperature variations in a process, normal variations in characteristics of materials, and tool wear on a cutting tool, are known as "common causes." They are beyond the control of simple methods of correction and must be tolerated. They may be considered as special cases of systemic factors, outside the immediate control of management as well.

Several factors influence the personal impact on quality that may be exerted in the person–system interaction. These may be considered as questions of control (see Chapter 2 for an introduction to the concept of control). Once a system has been brought under control, if there are breakdowns in the quality of raw materials from a supplier, occasional deviations from established procedures, supplier errors, improper equipment maintenance, or ethical work culture lapses, they may affect individual performance. Both Deming and Juran agree that random system factors (both common and special causes) account for most performance variation. However, certain problems that may be categorized as "special causes" can be detected by an effective, appropriate statistical quality control system and brought back under control by employee action.[13] The extent of random system influence, however, depends on the impact of factor 4 (i.e., the person–system interaction) and, in particular, the work hierarchy level and autonomy of individual performers. Other aspects of the person–system interface, such as autonomy and empowerment, will be considered in greater detail later in this chapter.

While it is necessary to address the systematic and random system factors, OCB work performance will not automatically result from these factors alone. The personal KSAs, as well as the motives possessed by individuals, may make them more or less disposed to support total quality initiatives.[14] These personal factors have been the major concern of traditional OD/human resource management practice. However, continuous training, development, and job redesign required in a total quality firm tend to prevent worker obsolescence, enrich work, and cause it to be intrinsically more motivating, thus disposing people toward OCB.

The person–system interaction is crucial, because even if the system does not vary, people interact differently according to their level in the organizational hierarchy and their autonomy, as shown in Figure 6.2.

Research has already established that managers at higher organizational levels shape and influence internal systems more effectively than lower-level managers. If *autonomy is defined as the degree of freedom or discretion a person has*

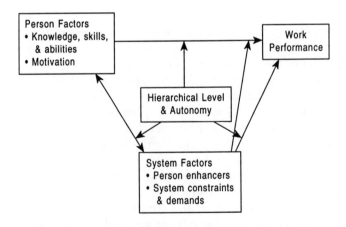

Figure 6.2 The Person–System Interaction Model of Work Performance (Source: Waldman, David A. (1994). "The Contributions of Total Quality Management to a Theory of Work Performance." *Academy of Management Review*. Vol. 19, No. 3, p. 518. Title modified by the authors.)

over the task domain regarding activities such as determining procedures and scheduling, research also demonstrates that increased autonomy varies inversely with powerlessness (i.e., the state of "organizationally induced helplessness"). Many work designs so tightly structure the work process that line employees feel incapable of process improvement. Deming's overattribution of system factors as exclusive causes of individual work performance is due in part to the prevailing lack of autonomy in work design in most industries. When industry workers are empowered, however, as was the case at the NUMMI automobile manufacturing facility in California, significant work changes resulted from personal choices to effectively contribute. In fact, individual factors will outweigh system constraints and demands in the determination of work performance at increasing hierarchical levels of management and when work is designed with a higher degree of autonomy, allowing for choice and personal control.

Figure 6.2 shows the connections between person and system factors as mediated by individual hierarchical level and autonomy to result in work performance. In total quality organizations, as individuals are empowered, their increased autonomy can lead to heightened personal work performance and reciprocally reduce the effects of system constraints and demands. Since the advantages of increased empowerment and enhanced performance are to be maximized by design in a total quality firm, the model used to link individual empowerment and personal leadership becomes crucial for quality planners.

TOTAL QUALITY BUSINESS PERFORMANCE MANAGEMENT[15]

Personal total quality performance management is of particular interest to managers in light of recent research on the productivity of total quality organizations.[16] The most productive total quality firms are those whose employees "personalize" quality practices in their daily work.[17] Employees who believe in their organization's quality standards and daily use of quality procedures contribute significantly to superior work unit and organizational productivity. (See the case study on AT&T Universal Card Services at the end of this chapter.)

Personal quality in daily work can also be assessed and improved by the routine, periodic application of the alternation of SDCA and PDCA cycles as indicated in Figure 5.3. The process and project tools discussed in Chapters 4 and 5 can be adapted from system use to personal use (e.g., check sheets can be used to tally defects in personal work habits, and Pareto charts can be used to identify and prioritize individual task performance steps for personal improvement).

Personal Quality Improvement Process

In addition, business performance management is enhanced through the regular use of a structured personal quality improvement process.[18] This process is similar to ones that organizations use to develop and carry out a quality plan. The process includes the following five steps, which can be repeated for sustained personal improvement:

- Create a personal, energizing vision of a desired future
- Develop a personal mission statement
- Set personal tactical objectives
- Develop personal strategies to achieve objectives
- Tie in cross-functional projects and functional tasks that help to achieve individual, team, and organizational objectives

These steps are the action core for fulfilling an individual plan for continuous growth by establishing an effective relationship between personal vision and mission and professional or career requirements, within the vision, mission, operating objectives, projects, and tasks of an organization. These five steps will now be more fully described.

Step 1. Create a Personal Energizing Vision of a Desired Future*

A plan for personal growth is not new. Creating a personal vision requires a vivid imagination and a willingness to ask yourself what you want to be doing five, seven, and even ten (or more) years from now. Further, it asks the question, "What business (or service) am I in?" This begins to get at Tom Peters' idea of "every employee a businessperson." Through various activities (described below), an individual can develop a strategic picture (or, more accurately, a video) of his or her life as he or she would like to live it (to lead it) in the foreseeable future.

When personalized and truly owned, a vision energizes and provides the incentive—the drive toward fulfillment. It creates the commitment, the motivation, and the drive for initiating the mission, objectives, projects, and tasks necessary to realize the vision. The personal vision addresses the question: "What do I as a person hope for and stand for in the world?" This question may be partially answered in isolated reflection, but it may also be answered by engaging in sustained dialogue (recall the "catchball" process

---

*It is not possible in this book, nor is it the intent, to describe in detail the development and implementation of personal strategies, projects, and tasks. Examples are given here to emphasize the benefit of this process, from the vision to the strategies, specific projects, and tasks that are governed by commitment to the vision.

from Chapter 3), with trusted, insightful significant others. Such people may help a person bridge the gap between his or her vision of the preferred future (what *should* exist) and the current situation (what *does* exist). The guidelines and steps for developing a personal vision are presented in Exhibit 6.2.

The more compelling the vision, the more energy the person is likely to put forth to realize it. The person who can voice his or her most cherished aspirations has a head start on developing a viable personal quality vision.

Step 2. Develop a Mission Statement

If the vision addresses a person's aspirations, the personal mission statement provides the overall direction for achieving the vision. As described by Covey, "It focuses on what you want to be (character) and to do (contributions and achievements) and on the values and principles upon which being and doing are based."

The major challenge is to develop a personal mission statement that is broad enough to encourage quality growth, yet narrow enough to focus one on what he or she does best. Key activities required to frame a mission statement include:

- Clarifying one's basic beliefs about reality, truth, and value (personal philosophy)
- Identifying and prioritizing the major life roles that form one's self-concept
- Acknowledging one's personal strengths and weaknesses
- Acknowledging the gap between one's personal future vision and the current reality
- Prioritizing commitments to one's diverse customers

It is especially important for one to refrain from defensive patterns that deny current performance gaps to avoid embarrassment. The guidelines and steps for developing a personal mission statement are presented in Exhibit 6.3. From this base of a personal vision and mission, practical objectives can be developed.

Step 3. Develop Personal Tactical Objectives

If the vision is the *what* of life and the mission is the *why*, objectives, projects, and tasks are the *hows*. They are the operational benchmarks of the personal action plan. An effective vision is long term (five, ten, or more years) and provides the drive and emotion. The mission statement identifies the activities and roles to be fulfilled over the next two to three years. Objectives are the action statements of the personal plan, identifying specific functions to be

1. **Purpose: What you will be doing**—Putting in writing a personal vision of your life five to ten years from now.

2. **You will know you are done when**—You have created a long-range vision that you "own" and are excited about.

3. **Techniques or instruments you can use for this activity** (refer to Chapters 3, 4, and 5)—The two techniques appropriate from the many listed earlier are affinity diagram and brainstorming. In addition, techniques used in life planning exercises would include daydreaming, journaling, and scenarios.

4. **Reality check: How will I know this vision "fits" me?**—You have a clear picture or "video" of what you will be doing in a typical week five to ten years from now. This will include the "significant others" in your life (as they will be at that time); what and where you will be working; your future healthy lifestyle; your wealth/retirement profile; your character development; your role(s) in nature, society, and community; and your leisure activities. The picture is also based on principled regard for others.

5. **Guidelines/instructions (KISS)—**
   a. If you have not been keeping a journal, begin keeping a brief record of your daily life and activities. Assess your activities, identifying those things you like and don't like to do. If there are some things you don't like but must do *for your growth and development*, are there some changes you can make in order to enjoy them more?
   b. Find an hour of quiet time alone and brainstorm about all the possible images that come to mind of what you want to be doing seven to ten years from now. Put each one on a separate card. Daydream about this list, and then brainstorm again a week or so later. Then put the cards aside for one or two weeks. Let the ideas percolate.
   c. Review the cards and combine similar activities. Then, edit and briefly rewrite any that need to be more personal for you. Feel free to dialogue with significant others.
   d. List at least the following six categories: health, wealth, love, esteem, character, and leisure. You may have other names for these items and additional categories, but keep the number to a minimum. Then place each card (brainstorming statement) under the heading that it best fits. Put this aside for a week, if possible, to percolate some more.
   e. Again, find an hour alone and write a scenario of a typical week seven to ten years from now, using the lists you compiled. If you have time, you might want to write a *best-case* and *worst-case* scenario (synthesis) that appears to be most realistic *at this time*.
   f. Your scenario may serve as a vision statement, but you may want to develop a succinct statement of your vision that you can use as the basis of your mission statement. A vision statement should be something you want to move toward, not move from.

Exhibit 6.2 General Guidelines for Implementing Step 1: Personal Vision

1. **Purpose: What you will be doing**—Develop a personal mission statement that focuses on what you want to be and what you want to do. Like the U.S. (or any other country's) Constitution, it is a personal constitution. It is personal and positive, written in the present tense, and provides a direction for achieving your vision. Finally, it defines the prioritized beliefs, values, and roles you consider important in your life.

2. **You will know you are done when**—You have a fairly brief, but succinct, statement that clearly states who you are, your personal strengths and weaknesses, and your beliefs, values, and the roles important to you and how you plan to fulfill them.

3. **Techniques or instruments you can use for this activity** (refer to Chapters 3, 4, and 5)—The techniques appropriate from those listed in Chapters 3 and 4 are affinity diagram, brainstorming, fishbone diagram, flowcharting, and surveys. In addition, tools used in life planning exercises would include journaling and mindmapping.

4. **Reality check: How will I know this plan "fits" me?**—You have a written statement that represents the best that is within you. It provides direction and purpose upon which you can develop functional objectives. In sum, this prioritized statement guides your investment in all future projects and tasks.

5. **Guidelines for implementation**—
   a. First, review your vision. This is what your mission will be based on—your mission or goal is to actualize your vision. Conduct a mindmap, putting your vision in the center and identifying the strategies you will use to realize the vision.
   b. Continue the journaling started while developing your vision. Record the activities you do over, say, a two- to three-week period. Another way is to identify all the activities you do, with the help of the brainstorming technique.
   c. From this activity list you will begin to identify the beliefs, values, and roles that are important to you. Through the use of an affinity diagram and/or fishbone diagram, group the activities under major roles, such as worker, spouse, parent, citizen. By identifying your life roles, you will gain perspective on your life activities.
   d. After collecting information on role performance, analyze your personal strengths and weaknesses and acknowledge any discrepancies between what you want to be and who you are.
   e. Develop a draft of a personal mission statement by leveraging your strengths, asking the following questions (they should also be asked periodically in order to keep your statement in harmony with yourself):
   (1) Is my mission aligned with my personal vision?
   (2) Does this mission statement represent what is distinctive about me?

Exhibit 6.3 General Guidelines for Implementing Step 2: Personal Mission

(3) Do I obtain a sense of direction, purpose, and challenge when I review this statement?
(4) Am I able to develop operational objectives from this mission statement?
(5) Revise your rough draft based on these questions. Then, keep it for a while to further revise and evaluate. Write a permanent draft, and try to commit it to memory so that you keep your vision and your mission clearly in mind. A second alternative is to keep it on your calendar or in a place where you will frequently look at it.

Exhibit 6.3 (continued) General Guidelines for Implementing Step 2: Personal Mission

accomplished in order to fulfill the mission. They are measurable and designed to be achieved within a maximum of 12 months. The basic question to be answered is whether a specific, observable change or transformation will have occurred when this objective has been completed.

Among the personal objectives to be considered are the following: (1) personal happiness/fulfillment; (2) personal quality standards; (3) personal costs; (4) personal safety standards; (5) personal reliability standards, based on promises made; (6) personal morale and productivity levels; (7) personal communications and relations standards; (8) personal integrity and reputation; (9) personal creativity standards; and (10) personal performance measurement standards.

The guidelines and steps for developing tactical personal objectives are presented in Exhibit 6.4. Objectives reflect the mission statement, using the activities and roles for identifying the objectives to be initiated first. The objectives are action oriented, with a specific time frame, and written in the past tense in order to create a mental image of what is to be accomplished. They should also provide the framework upon which the strategic projects and tasks can be developed and implemented.

Step 4. Develop Personal Strategies

Once your personal objectives are prioritized, it is important to determine what strategy or strategies you will employ to achieve your quality objectives. There are basically four strategy options: (1) maximize personal strengths by acquiring external resources, (2) overcome personal weaknesses by acquiring personal resources, (3) maximize personal strengths by redirecting internal resources, and/or (4) overcome personal weaknesses by redirecting internal resources. For example, if improving punctuality (reliability standards) is a prioritized objective, then redirecting some of your internal resources (money) to purchase a better alarm clock would be a feasible strat-

1. **Purpose: What you will be doing**—Develop performance-based, operational objectives that are based on specific mission statement(s). The objectives are written in the past tense to establish a mindset of their being accomplished. Two examples would be (1) *I developed and pilot tested a survey questionnaire for assessing the managers' perceptions of our training process. This was completed in the fall.* (2) *I coordinated the revision of our project manual, including the development and approval of new guidelines for selection of project managers. This took four months (at four hours per week) to complete.*

2. **You will know you are done when**—You have a prioritized, time-focused statement upon which strategies, projects, and tasks can be developed and which are aligned with personal vision and mission priorities.

3. **Techniques or instruments you can use for this activity** (refer to Chapter 3)—Affinity diagram, brainstorming, competitive benchmarking, flowcharting, nominal group technique, surveys, and trend charts.

4. **Reality check: How will I know this plan "fits" me?**—The objective is clear in what will be accomplished, challenging, and achievable within a given time frame. It enables you to identify specific projects and tasks which you are able to complete, using appropriate strategies.

5. **Guidelines for implementation**—
   a. Your mission statement, described in Step 2, lists the beliefs, values, and roles you wish to fulfill, as well as a statement of how you would most like to be described in each role. You also listed the activities and developed an affinity, or a fishbone, diagram to group the activities within each role. This is the basis for your objectives.
   b. From the above, identify (with the help of brainstorming) the activities that focus on your role statements. With the help of the fishbone diagram, expand on the activities, coding each one if space does not allow an adequate description or statement.
   c. Establish a time frame (e.g., 12 months) and identify those activities you wish to focus on first. If this is the first time you have done this type of activity, select those that have the greatest chance of succeeding.
   d. Develop a draft of specific objectives, using the examples above as guidelines. The objective should be action oriented, aligned with mission priorities, have a specific time frame, and written in the past tense (i.e., you have already completed the objective).
   e. Evaluate this draft, asking the following questions:
      (1) As stated, is the objective aligned with my vision and mission?
      (2) Can the objective be realistically completed within the stated time?
      (3) Is there a clear direction and challenge in this objective?
      (4) Are my objectives prioritized according to mission priorities?
      (5) Am I able to develop specific strategies, projects, and tasks from this objective, as stated?
   f. Revise your draft based on these questions. Then, quickly move on to the development of the required strategies, projects, and tasks.

Exhibit 6.4 General Guidelines for Implementing Step 3: Personal Objectives

egy. The challenge is to devise strategies that achieve the largest number of objectives at the least cost in terms of time, energy, and money. The guidelines and steps for developing personal strategies are presented in Exhibit 6.5.

Steps 5. Implement Personal Projects and Tasks

Once personal strategies have been set, personal projects and tasks are required to implement the strategies. Projects are very specific activities that are necessary in order to move toward accomplishing an objective. Tasks are specific steps to be completed in order to accomplish a project. Each objective usually requires multiple projects, and each project of course requires many tasks.

---

1. **Purpose: What you will be doing**—Develop broad, macro strategies that are aligned with and will achieve your vision, mission, and objectives.

2. **You will know you are done when**—You have an action-oriented set of statements that incorporate personal strengths and weaknesses and rely upon internal and external resources to achieve objectives. These statements will provide a platform for future projects and tasks.

3. **Techniques or instruments you can use for this activity** (refer to Chapters 3 and 4)—The appropriate techniques include brainstorming, flowcharting, competitive benchmarking, surveys, and prioritization matrices.

4. **Reality check: How will I know this vision "fits" me?**—The strategy is clear in what it will accomplish and is feasible.

5. **Guidelines for implementation**—
   a. Your objectives are fully listed and prioritized. Alongside each objective, you should list the strategies you will employ for the four options: (1) maximizing personal strengths by acquiring external resource, (2) overcoming personal weaknesses by acquiring personal resources, (3) maximizing personal strengths by redirecting internal resources, and (4) overcoming personal weaknesses by redirecting internal resources.
   b. Prioritize and align all strategies with vision, mission, and objectives.
   c. Formulate a draft of a personal strategy statement, asking the following questions:
      (1) Are my strategies appropriate for my objectives and feasible?
      (2) Are my strategies prioritized in accordance with my objectives and mission?
      (3) Are my strategies the best way to accomplish my prioritized objectives at minimal costs?

Exhibit 6.5 General Guidelines for Implementing Step 4: Personal Strategies

The guidelines and steps for implementing projects and tasks are presented in Exhibit 6.6. A disclaimer is given regarding the guidelines (i.e., project and task development, implementation, and management require more description and guidelines than is the intent of this book). Specific techniques and a personal project list are presented. Examples of projects and tasks based on the two objectives in Exhibit 6.6 are also presented.

---

1. **Purpose: What you will be doing**—Develop and implement specific projects and related tasks that are based on a single objective. An objective usually requires multiple strategies and numerous projects, which in turn requires numerous tasks. An example based on one objective stated in Step 3 is:

   3 *Start-up project* (a survey questionnaire for assessing the managers' perceptions of our training process--the third of eleven projects for this objective)
     3.1 Develop project schedule (control chart, PERT chart)
     3.2 Develop initial list of project tasks (flowchart, check sheet)
     3.3 Organize meeting of project team
   4 *Gather information* (the fourth of eleven projects)
     4.1 Develop questions for information gathering (brainstorm)
     4.2 Interview selected managers (small survey)
     4.3 Contact other divisions (benchmarking)
     4.4 Summarize data obtained (histogram, Pareto diagram, trend chart)
   2 *Gather information* (revision of the questionnaire—the second of nine projects)
     2.1 Conduct manager focus group (brainstorm, survey)
     2.2 Conduct alumni (training participants) focus group (cause-and-effect diagram, check sheet, survey)
     2.3 Interview managers in other divisions (benchmarking)
     2.4 Prepare summary report (histogram, Pareto diagram, trend chart)
   3 *Pilot study and administer the questionnaire* (the second of nine projects)
     3.1 Review summary data with project team (affinity diagram, cause-and-effect diagram)
     3.2 Brainstorm revised questionnaire with team (brainstorm)
     3.3 Chart proposed survey process (flowchart)
     3.4 Conduct the pilot study
     3.5 Review results with project team, managers, and alumni
     3.6 Accept design, conduct full study, analyze and publish results
     3.7 Modify training programs, based on results

2. **You will know you are done when**—You have developed all the projects and related tasks and are able to design a flowchart that aligns each project and task with designated strategies in order to make them operational.

3. **Techniques or instruments you can use for this activity** (Chapter 3, 4, and 5)— Affinity diagram, block diagram, brainstorming, cause-and-effect diagram, check

---

Exhibit 6.6 General Guidelines for Implementing Step 5: Personal Projects and Tasks

sheet, competitive benchmarking, control chart, histogram, interview, Pareto diagram, run chart, scatter diagram, survey, tree diagram, and trend chart.

4. **Reality check: How will I know this plan "fits" me?**—You are able to "walk" through the project without missing a step (task), fully implement the strategy, and complete the objective within the limits of available time, energy, and costs.

5. **Guidelines for implementation**—As noted earlier, it is not the intent here to describe in detail the development and implementation of all personal projects. It is strongly recommended that you at least read a text or manual on project development and management or, preferably, attend a seminar for your own and your team's benefit. What can be provided here is a personal project checklist as a start in the development of productive projects:
   1. Select a strategy.
   2. Determine an appropriate, feasible project.
   3. Identify tasks related to project completion.
   4. Develop measures for task and project tracking.
   5. Develop a schedule, with milestones and reviews.
   6. Develop a budget, with scheduled project reviews.
   7. Monitor progress against schedules and budgets.
   8. Take corrective action when indicated by excessive variation from goals.
   9. Provide feedback to yourself and significant others.
   10. Test the final outcome for "fit" in meeting personal and customer needs.
   11. Evaluate the project, based on mission, vision, goals, and objectives.
   12. Initiate the next project.

Exhibit 6.6 (continued)   General Guidelines for Implementing Step 5: Personal Projects and Tasks

The potential impact of developing a personal plan cannot be overemphasized. The technique is applicable to every individual, from household manager to custodian to chairman of the board of a Fortune 500 corporation. While the process requires time and energy, the benefit of having a personal vision upon which a mission statement (and related objectives, projects, and tasks) far outweighs the effort needed to complete it.

TOTAL QUALITY ORGANIZATION DEVELOPMENT PERFORMANCE

Total quality OD performance depends on individual motivation and the process of empowerment of employees. Without individual motivation to produce quality work and to make improvements, organizations are lost. "Quality in daily work" has been used in a number of firms to signify the importance of individual quality efforts. At the same time, if traditional command-and-control approaches are used in organizations, the creative capabilities of employees will never be realized. Employees on the "front lines" must be empowered to make decisions, take risks, and innovate in order to meet customer needs.

Motivation and Empowerment

Motivation can be defined as a pattern of factors that initiate, direct, and sustain human behavior over time.[19] An understanding of motivation theory is critical to Deming's concept of "Profound Knowledge," which relates to personal aspects of TQM and self-leadership. Empowerment links motivation and performance to organizational outcomes. In this section, we will present basic concepts of both motivation and empowerment.

Motivation

A complete review of the multitude of motivation theories is beyond the scope of this text. However, a model developed by Wagner and Hollenbeck synthesizes a number of motivation theories and provides a frame of reference for a brief discussion of empowerment. The model is presented in Figure 6.3. It contains six components in five steps and is used to explain four outcomes.

The six components of motivation are represented by circles on the model and include valence, instrumentality, expectancy, ability, accuracy of role perceptions, and equity of reward. *Valence* refers to the preference that a person has for a particular outcome. If two outcomes are to be expected, a person may prefer a specific outcome (a positive valence), prefer *not* to attain that outcome (negative valence), or have no preference between the two possible outcomes (zero valence). Valence does not refer to the *value* that the person places on the outcome, but merely on the *preference* for an outcome. *Instrumentality* refers to the belief that a person has about the relationship between performing an act and receiving an outcome. Thus, an OD specialist must believe that the establishment of employee involvement groups will lead to better quality, if a high degree of instrumentality is to be present to motivate him or her. *Expectancy* refers to the belief that links effort to performance expectancies. For example, a salesperson being paid on a commission basis is more likely to put forth more selling effort if he or she believes that it will definitely result in higher earnings versus someone who is paid a straight salary and will receive no immediate benefit (if any at all) for extraordinary efforts. *Ability* is the capability to perform specific physical, psychomotor, or mental tasks, based on individual characteristics. *Accuracy*

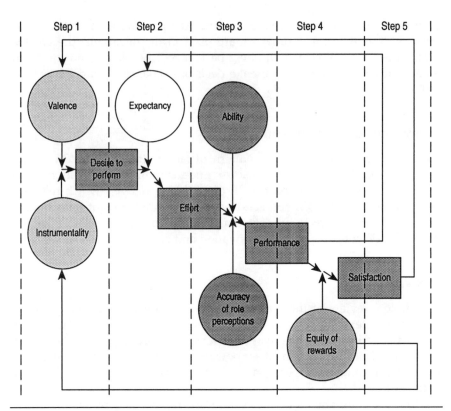

Figure 6.3 Model of Motivation and Performance (Source: Wagner, John A. III and Hollenbeck, John R. (1995). *The Management of Organizational Behavior*, 2nd edition. Englewood Cliffs, NJ: Prentice-Hall, p. 204.)

of role perceptions results from people knowing what needs to be done, how it is to be done, and who has the responsibility to ensure that the task is accomplished. Finally, *equity of reward* is a perception by individuals of the fairness of the reward that they receive, based on their accomplishment of a task.

The five steps of the model show the key places where components combine to influence outcomes. The four outcomes, shown as rectangles, are desire, effort, performance, and satisfaction.

Step 1 shows that the *desire to perform* will be high if valence for the outcome is high and strong personal performance is seen as instrumental in successfully completing the task. Step 2 shows that *effort* is directly dependent on *desire to perform* (which relates back to valence and instrumentality) and *expectancy*. In Step 3, the *performance* outcome is driven by *effort* (linked back to *expectancy*, with a feedback loop) and two components of *ability* and *accuracy of role perceptions.* In Step 4, the *satisfaction* outcome is driven by the *performance* outcome (which relates back to *ability* and *accuracy of role perceptions*) and the *equity of rewards* component. Finally, in Step 5, feedback loops indicate that the *equity of rewards* component will have an effect during later time periods on the perceived *instrumentality* of efforts and that *satisfaction* (or lack of it) with *performance* and *equity of rewards* will have a positive (or negative) effect on *valence* (anticipated satisfaction) in future time periods.

A brief example illustrates how this model could be applied in a quality context. Imagine the designer of an automobile interior at the start of a new design project. She heads up a small team of people who have been given responsibility to complete the project within a specified time frame. She may feel that her efforts to lead the team are highly likely to have a major impact on the design quality (high *instrumentality*). In addition, she also highly values the satisfaction and rewards that she anticipates receiving when the project is completed (high *valence*). This creates a high *desire to perform* and, coupled with a high *expectancy* of success, thus causes her to put in a great deal of *effort* on the project, where she spends many hours with her team members. Knowing the she has the *ability* to lead the team to success, together with *accuracy of role perception* and the previously generated *effort*, the *performance* is outstanding! The design team leader completes her project on time, under budget, and with many features that will *delight the customer* due to innovative design quality. The feedback loop from *performance* to *expectancy* indicates that during the next project, she will feel even more confident that she can perform at a high level. She and the team receive the anticipated *equitable reward*, a bonus and heartfelt thanks from top management, and she reaps the *satisfaction* that she anticipated. With feedback loops to *instrumentality* of efforts and *valence* (anticipated satisfaction), there will be positive effects on those components in future time periods. Of course, unsatisfactory combinations of components could have produced negative outcomes anywhere along the chain.

Individual Empowerment

In total quality organizations, as individuals are empowered, their increased autonomy can lead to heightened personal work performance and simultaneously reduce the effects of system constraints and demands.[20] Since total quality firms seek to gain the maximum advantage by first determining empowerment readiness (see Exercise 5.1) and then increasing empowerment to improve performance, the components of individual empowerment are important to develop.

Individual empowerment has been described as motivation that is "built in" (intrinsic) to tasks. It consists of four components: choice, meaningfulness, competence, and impact.[21] *Choice* involves designing tasks so as to make individuals accountable for their actions and consists of an individual's belief, at a given point in time, in his or her ability to effect a change, in a desired direction, on the environment.[22] Field research has demonstrated that choice and personal control are related to "built-in" task motivation, job performance, and job satisfaction.[23] The central factor in empowerment is choice. *Meaningfulness* concerns the value a task holds in relation to the individual's value system.[24] *Competence* refers to self-efficacy, or the belief that one is capable of successfully performing a particular task or activity.[25] *Impact* represents the degree to which individuals believe that their behavior makes a difference.[26] Thus, the motivation theories labeled as personal control, job design, self-efficacy, and intrinsic theories link the three dimensions of empowerment, work satisfaction, and job performance.[27] Individuals, in turn, usually appreciate organizations that provide them with opportunities for personal control, responsibility, and challenge in their work and will tend to be more committed to the organization.[28] As individuals demonstrate readiness for empowerment, the choice of their personal leadership style will impact their performance (see Figure 5.6).[29]

An example of how empowerment and commitment go hand in hand is reflected in a story about an employee at Disney World. A young girl laid her dental retainer on a picnic table at Disney World while eating lunch.[30] She forgot about it until later in the day. Her family returned to the spot, found the table had been cleaned, and were at a loss as to what to do. They spotted a custodian and told him the problem. The custodian sought permission from his supervisor to have the garbage bags searched by the night crew that evening! Two weeks later, the girl's father received a letter from the supervisor explaining that they had been unable to locate the retainer, despite their best efforts.

TOTAL QUALITY ORGANIZATION DEVELOPMENT PERFORMANCE PLANNING

Total quality OD performance planning that promotes empowerment requires two key components: (1) principle-centered leadership and ethical work culture development and (2) clarification, joint modification, and ensuring the integrity of the psychological contract. The first factor expands upon the total quality OD practitioner's responsibility to keep management abreast of indicators of the organization's climate. In this context, principle-centered leaders or potential leaders may be identified using instruments such as the Empowerment Readiness Assessment (see Exercise 5.1). In addition, by using instruments like the Ethical Work Culture Assessment (Exercise 6.1), total quality OD practitioners may determine the level of organizational support for principle-centered leadership.

The second factor expands the total quality OD practitioner's responsibility to monitor the psychological contract and its impact on the organization. Clarifying, urging joint rather than unilateral modification, and ensuring the integrity of the revised psychological contract are all part of the expanding responsibilities of the total quality OD practitioner.

The approach to principle-centered leadership developed by Stephen Covey suggests ways in which formal, occasional, and informal leaders can develop the trait approach to leadership and direction.

Principle-Centered Leadership and Ethical Work Culture Development

Stephen Covey[31] discusses developing "principle-centered" leadership by using an inside-out perspective, moving from the individual level to interpersonal relations, and then to managerial responsibilities and organizational values. He lists these levels, or key principle "pairs," as:

- Personal—trustworthiness
- Interpersonal—trust
- Managerial—empowerment
- Organizational—alignment

Personal trustworthiness is based on moral maturity and application of his "Seven Habits of Highly Effective People," including:[32]

- Be proactive
- Begin with the end in mind
- Put first things first
- Think win–win
- Seek first to understand…then to be understood
- Synergize
- Sharpen the saw (e.g., exercise balanced self-renewal)

Interpersonal trust is earned when the word of another can be relied on repeatedly without betrayal. On a broader scale, management must empower employees to make organizational improvements and exert self-control. This essential ingredient of self-management is character built around principles. The Empowerment Readiness Assessment instrument (see Exercise 5.1) provides a way to quantify the degree of individual, group, and organizational readiness to take on the responsibilities of empowerment. Finally, organizations must demonstrate integrity, behavioral alignment with their values. Everyone, especially leaders, must "walk their talk." At every level, individuals and groups must break "bad" habits and replace them with "good" ones. As in every case where one tries to break a habit, it is hardly ever easy, as Covey points out in his favorite metaphor, "the law of the farm."

On a farm, you can't "cram" as you may do for exams in school. Covey states:[33] "Procrastination and cramming don't work on a farm. The cows must be milked daily. Other things must be done in season, according to natural cycles." Covey provides a strong philosophical base for personal self-management and a number of practical tips and techniques on how to accomplish it. However, some "applied tools" (you have to write for Covey's forms [tools], since they are not published in his books) can help individuals to apply the new habits they have learned and the self-control that they wish to attain, as we will see in the following section.

Total quality OD professionals know that personal, interpersonal, and principle-centered leadership conduct is not enough to sustain organizational integrity. People move on and leaders change. Organizations must develop an ongoing ethics development system, rather than simply relying on principled conduct of individual employees or leaders alone. If an ethics development system is not implemented, it is like putting good apples into a rotten barrel. The rotten barrel will eventually corrode the good apples, making them unfit to eat. Regular assessment (see Exercise 6.1: Ethical Work Culture Assessment) and active development of a strong ethical work culture will help the organization to sustain its character despite the turnover of associates and leaders. Maintenance of a "good barrel" and selection of "good apples" is a key obligation of the total quality OD practitioner. Good barrels (i.e., strong ethical work cultures) do not "just happen"; they are consciously designed, continuously developed, and rigorously maintained.

A sound ethical work culture infrastructure (described in Chapter 1) can only be developed if the following ingredients are present:

- Strong moral leadership at the top
- Routine ethical work culture assessments
- Consideration of ethics factors in organization strategy and structure decisions
- An ethics steering committee
- A statement of prioritized values and an ethics code of conduct
- Ethics policy and procedure manuals
- Ethics factors considered in all human resource processes, including selection, performance appraisal, reward, and development
- Commendation and rewards for outstanding ethical conduct
- Ethics stressed in formal and informal communications and work attitudes
- Ethics training and education on a regular basis
- Ethics factors considered in decision making
- Organization ethics officers and/or designated role at operating levels
- Reporting of ethics offenses and ethical conflict resolution processes
- Enforcement processes for ethics standards violations

- Ethics audit and evaluation subsystems
- Ethics control and improvement processes

Total quality OD practitioners know that without a sound system of support, unethical and substandard behavior will eventually arise. Neglecting to attend to the "barrel" invites erosion of organization character. A strong ethical infrastructure makes it reasonable to expect that employees at every level will exercise principled leadership. If the organization wants principled leaders, it must develop and sustain a principled ethical work culture. This is where organizational responsibility for understanding and maintaining the psychological contract comes into play.

New Psychological Contract and Organizational Self-Respect

A *psychological contract* is a set of beliefs regarding the terms and conditions of a reciprocal exchange agreement between a person and another party.[34] In the U.S. employment relationship, the old psychological contract between employer and employee was a paternalistic one, with an employee assumption that employment security would be guaranteed in exchange for loyal productivity. In response to global competition and investor demand for short-term profitability, however, a new psychological contract has emerged, primarily unilaterally promoted by employers. This new psychological contract is more of a partnership arrangement, wherein employability security, rather than employment security, is offered by the employer in exchange for loyal productivity.[35]

Naturally, employees regarded this new arrangement as a violation of the previous psychological contract. In 1994, 55% of U.S. employees believed their employment contract had been violated by their employer in the previous two years, and even today, perceptions of violations of the psychological contract have become more the norm than the exception.[36] Five adverse effects have resulted from the widespread perception of psychological contract violations: lowered trust, reduced individual performance, loss of organizational self-respect, increased workplace violence, and reduced OCB, the extra-role employee contribution that is essential for total quality organizations.[37]

In order to maintain self-respect and protect themselves from additional disrespectful treatment in today's workplace, many employees have adopted a careerist mindset and a cynical attitude.[38] Careerists see their current employer as a stepping-stone up the career ladder and are likely to adopt a more "transactional" employment relationship with their employer. Careerists tend to avoid long-term employment relationships, and what is exchanged has a short-term focus—the immediate rewards of pay, training, and credentials—to obtain a better job in either the current or another organization.

However, as job mobility decreases due to oversupply of domestic and foreign labor, frustration leads to cynical attitudes, which may lead to high levels of organizational cynicism (correlated with ethical work culture stage 2, Machiavellianism). In contrast, those low on the careerist scale have a more "relational orientation." Individual career planning and community commitment, therefore, are important dimensions of total quality OD performance assessment planning. Balancing the intrinsic values that appeal to "low careerist" employees with the instrumental values of career mobility that appeal to careerists in the work community are important responsibilities for the total quality OD professional.

The terms of the new psychological contract imply new responsibilities for employees and employers. For employees, it means becoming full-fledged partners in a business for as long as the employment relationship lasts. It means taking the initiative to develop and enhance skills and actively seeking ways to grow the business. For the employer, it means coming through with the building blocks of partnership: meaningful rewards for goals achieved; relevant support for skill development; honest, open communication about mutual objectives and financial data; and reasonable flexibility in the work environment. While many employees are trying to meet the terms of the new contract, recent surveys indicate the following: (1) many employees are being poorly led by managers who are out of touch with the new psychological contract conditions[39] and (2) many employees do not think that employers are holding up their end of the new psychological contract (i.e., cementing their shared financial fate by continuing to provide resources and opportunities for employability security).[40]

Total quality OD practitioners must adjust quality programs developed in the 1980s in the wake of 1990s downsizing to ensure that balanced, sustainable employment relationships and organizational character can endure tough times. This may mean that individuals need to assume more responsibility for their own future employability (e.g., through personal learning programs, professional networking, and gaining broad project experience). It may also mean that organizational self-respect (i.e., the collective pride in the way the business is managed and its people treated) is accorded commensurate attention. Organizations that downsize employees for short-term profits and neglect the impact on future business growth lose organizational self-respect and erode organizational character. When most employees feel ashamed of the way top managers receive excessive compensation and enact callous downsizing policies on the rank and file, the collective readiness to perform well is diminished. Total quality OD practitioners need to assess and develop organizational self-respect as a key to overall performance.

In their professional role, total quality OD practitioners must take steps at strategic and tactical levels to determine the company's level of organizational self-respect. They must encourage top management to develop congruent company policies that demonstrate a reciprocal commitment to an appropriate holistic concern for the total quality employee. Too often, companies raise individual performance standards to the ethical work culture level of the House of Integrity and then develop company policies that treat people with disrespect at the level of the House of Manipulation. If companies want to equip themselves with a committed, versatile, creative, continually learning, sustainable work community that repeatedly generates high performance, they must act to attract, deserve, and keep that high-performance work force. The lack of reciprocity leads to a loss of organizational self-respect.

If the new psychological contract is jointly modified to shift from employment security to employability security, then the total quality OD practitioner needs to secure the resources necessary to preserve the integrity of the new psychological contract (e.g., to obtain the resources to provide ongoing training opportunities to keep employee skills updated and marketable). Also, additional resources may be required during downsizing to provide outplacement services to facilitate employee transitions to new employment. While showing empathy and assisting with the transition of employees who will be laid off as a result of a corporate downsizing, the total quality OD professional must not forget the organizational change survivors. Downsizing survivors normally experience a range of feelings, including fear, frustration, guilt, and unfairness.[41] As a result, most downsized U.S. organizations are trying to compete globally with risk-averse, relatively unproductive and anxious employees.

To counter this situation, total quality OD practitioners need to develop the intervention skills that will help heal the wounds of the survivors and encourage them to revitalize their commitment to high-quality performance. This means that OD professionals may need to learn to facilitate emotional release by acknowledging the legitimacy of grieving, assist in breaking organizational co-dependency habits, and encourage employees to assume responsibility for adjusting to change. The glue that should bond the total quality learning community is the commitment to do good work which adds value to clients' and customers' products and services. In a total quality environment, personal mission should ideally be more aligned with service (e.g., meeting or exceeding customers' real needs) than with self-protection (e.g., keeping one's job).[42] In addition, the terms of the new psychological contract based on employability must be met by providing sufficient resources to fully maintain its provisions. Total quality OD practitioners who actively support *all* employees in a downsizing effort by attending to their needs for emotional healing, retraining, and redeployment demonstrate commitment to total quality principles at the top level of the House of Total Quality. They are preparing for quantum quality.[43]

TOTAL QUALITY ORGANIZATION DEVELOPMENT PERFORMANCE MANAGEMENT

Throughout this text, we have discussed needs for paradigm shifts and ways in which OD professionals can help to bring that about. There is a strong need to bring about a paradigm shift in the way individual workers see themselves and the way that organizations treat them and their contributions. Deming considered it so important that 8 of his 14 points address systemic issues at the system and team levels which management must face and deal with if individuals are to be "empowered" to perform effectively within organizations. Note, however, that a reality in the workplace of today and tomorrow is the need for an accompanying paradigm shift around the issue of what security on the job really means. A recent *Fortune* magazine article[44] confirmed our earlier observation that the contract between individuals and companies has shifted dramatically in the last five years. Previously, employees in large prosperous companies could expect the company to provide a more-or-less paternalistic culture with job security or even "lifetime employment," career paths with steady advancement, defined benefit pension plans, offices with various amenities for each level of the hierarchy, a nine to five workday, and annual performance reviews with standard pay raises. Now, the "best" companies can only provide "opportunities" for their employees in the form of candor and communication on where the business is going and how that may affect job security and careers. Career paths are being replaced by project experiences and lateral moves, defined benefit pension plans are giving way to defined contribution plans, offices are being replaced by telecommuting, the nine to five workday is insufficient for even those who want to keep up let alone get ahead, annual performance reviews are supplemented or replaced by peer reviews and a variety of frequent evaluations, and standard pay raises are giving way to various types of incentive plans, pay for performance, or pay for skill plans. In short, as the *Fortune* article points out: "Employees become far more responsible for their work and their careers: No more parent–child relationships…but adult to adult." This is the reality of the new psychological contract. Total quality OD performance management includes treatment of quantum quality issues and regular use of personal quality checklists.

Quantum Quality

Quantum quality is a term used to describe achieving breakthroughs in customer delight through increased personal motivation and commitment to quality.[45] Employees come to define quality not only through the lack of statistical process variation but also in moral–emotional terms such as pride in craftsmanship and satisfaction in delighting customers. The four dimensions of quantum quality that require total quality OD practitioner attention, support, and respect include *learning, integrity, creativity,* and *sustainability.*[46]

First, respecting individual self-managed learning contributes to performance improvement and creates the learning community necessary for adaptation to changing organizational pressures.[47] In 1991, for the first time, companies spent more money on computing and communications gear than all the funds spent on industrial, mining, farm, and construction equipment. An estimated two-thirds of U.S. employees work in the service sector, where knowledge is the most important "product." By the year 2000, no developed country will have more than one-sixth or one-eighth of its work force in the traditional roles of making and moving goods.[48] This calls for learning different kinds of work, preparing different kinds of workers, and building different kinds of organizations (i.e., continually improving organizations that support workers who engage in self-managed learning activities and design meaningful work to satisfy multiple customers).[49]

As work, workers, and organizations change, OD practitioners must take on new roles. OD practitioners have often functioned as trainers who were working against time to ensure that the work force had the requisite skills. They cannot drop this challenge, but they now must help the work force face an unknown future that is changing unpredictably at unbelievable rates. OD practitioners increasingly recognize that people learn all the time on the job, but that this learning is not necessarily sound or shared. OD practitioners can extend their impact by working with all employees to make *self-managed learning* more effective and by creating ways for people *to share what they learn.* They can work with managers to create and sustain the level of ethical work culture that supports continuous learning in the House of Total Quality. They can help build the infrastructure of a learning system by, for instance, *ensuring that individuals have budgets for self-managed learning* and that the organization has policies that *reward knowledge acquisition and the teaching of others.*

Second, respecting personal and organizational integrity requires that total quality OD practitioners work to develop processes that reinforce OCB, reward continual self- and process improvement, enhance the design of meaningful work, and promote ethical work culture policies and practices that help individuals become better persons. In a total quality culture with these features, employees can feel that they are not only putting in time but also leaving a legacy of work contributions for future generations. To set an example, OD projects must be managed to show that personal standards of integrity (honesty, trustworthiness, and respectful, sincere human interactions) are important and those standards also apply to organization integrity.[50]

Third, respecting personal creativity means not only providing ample resources for R&D innovations, but insisting that individual employees creatively analyze their daily work to eliminate irrationality, waste, and inconsistency.[51] Total quality OD practitioners train both for current work competence and future work improvement; commitment to creatively developing mastery at work becomes a total quality employee obligation.[52]

Fourth, respecting sustainability means considering the personal stage of readiness of employees to absorb and sustain new work changes. If total quality employers want long-term high performance to be sustained, they cannot treat their employees as commodities that can be replaced if proposed work changes are resisted. By introducing total quality work performance changes in a way that respects the personal stages of readiness, a sustainable work community can be built. OD interventions that manage work changes by addressing appropriate personal concerns of workers are more likely to result in significant work improvements and build a sustainable work community. This means a routine total quality OD practice should be surveying employee attitudes toward current and future work changes and avoiding forced change on workers which ignores their concerns. Building a sustainable work community is one of the most important tasks facing workers and leaders today.[53] Empowered workers in a productive work unit recognize when they have lost that sense of community and quickly expend the necessary effort to rapidly regain it.[54] Great companies respect their customers and employees at all levels. "Out of showing respect for others, an organization itself becomes respected. It rises in stature as a role model, and makes a positive impact on the world."[55]

Personal Total Quality Management Tools

As in any area of quality, we once again have the opportunity, if we decide to take advantage of it, to learn from the Japanese. In a recently translated book written by the Japan Human Relations Association, the idea of breaking personal habits of lack of observation and correction of common problems in our workplace was developed. The book points to the need to "notice problems" before they can be solved. According to the text and the model questions shown in Figure 6.4, this is the first step in eliminating irrationality, waste, and inconsistency in everyday work.

Many of the quality tools listed in Chapters 3, 4, and 5 can be used to achieve improvements in personal quality. As discussed earlier, the tools may be divided into categories where they are most useful. This does not prevent them from being used in more than one category, however.

Developing and Using the Personal Quality Checklist[56]

One of the most useful approaches to personal quality management and improvement of "daily work" which has recently come on the scene was

Daily work

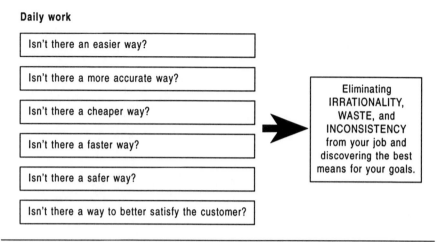

| Isn't there an easier way? |
| Isn't there a more accurate way? |
| Isn't there a cheaper way? |
| Isn't there a faster way? |
| Isn't there a safer way? |
| Isn't there a way to better satisfy the customer? |

Eliminating IRRATIONALITY, WASTE, and INCONSISTENCY from your job and discovering the best means for your goals.

Figure 6.4 Observing Problems in Daily Work

developed by Roberts and Sergesketter, who were quoted at the beginning of the chapter. They present a simple but extremely effective method for personal quality improvement.

Harry V. Roberts, former Sigmund E. Edelstone Professor of Statistics and Quality Management (now Professor Emeritus) at the University of Chicago's Graduate School of Business, and Bernard F. Sergesketter, Vice President, Central Region, for AT&T, developed the concept of a Personal Quality Checklist to keep track of personal shortcomings, or defects, in personal work processes. Since these checklists are kept by individuals, personal control is a paramount feature of this concept. The authors defended the use of a checklist to keep track of "defects" in a note entitled "Why Count Defects?" which includes the following paragraph:

> The word "defect" has a negative connotation for some people who would like to keep track of the times we do things right rather than times we do things wrong. Fortunately, most of us do things right much more than we do things wrong, so it is easier in practice to count the defects. Moreover, we can get positive satisfaction from avoiding defects—witness accident prevention programs that count days without accidents.

Sergesketter plotted defects that he observed during the first 18 months of his use of his own Personal Quality Checklist on a run chart as shown in Figure 6.5. Many of the results were surprising. For instance, he was surprised at the extent to which he was not returning phone calls the same day. He discovered that he had no way to count defects related to correspondence.

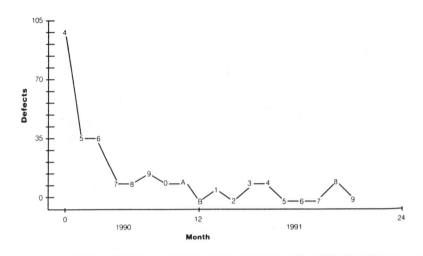

Figure 6.5 Number of Defects per Month

As a result, he started to date-stamp correspondence when it arrives and date-stamp the file copy of the response. None of the items he measured was in the "four minute mile" category, and yet he started out at a rate of 100 defects per month, but dropped drastically simply because he was aware of them. He also observed that when you share your defect list with others, they will help you reduce defects.

Although we cannot develop the concept as fully as the originators did in their text, a sample checklist developed by one of the authors, a business professor, is provided in Figure 6.6 as a starting point. Note that each item on the checklist has a desired result, a way to measure each type of defect, and a time frame. Note also that there are both work and personal defect categories listed on the sheet.

Some of Sergesketter's other observations include:

- Some associates have asked about counting defects related to being on time for meetings. I will be late for a meeting rather than cut short a conversation for a customer, but I will count it as a defect. This has caused me to schedule my calls at times when the probability is low that I will be late for a meeting. If I notify people in advance that I will be late and specify the time I will be there, I do not count a defect unless I miss the specified time without further notification. Arriving for a meeting even one second after the scheduled starting time counts for me as a defect, as you have to draw the line somewhere.

Professor's Personal Total Quality Management Checklist

WEEK OF: _____

DEFECT CATEGORY	M	T	W	TH	F	S	SU	Total
Search for something misplaced or lost (>10 min)								
Failure to discard incoming junk mail (end of day)								
Putting a small task on the "hold" pile (>24 hours)								
Failure to respond to a letter/phone call (end of day)								
Lack of clarity in setting requirements/deadlines								
Excessive "general interest" reading (over 1 hour/day)								
Failure to provide weekly opportunity for feedback from a class								
Less than 2 hours of writing per day, 4 days/week								
Less than 8 hours/night of sleep on a weekday								
Less than 3 exercise sessions per week								
Take spouse out for one meal a week								
Less than 0.5 hr meditation per weekday								

Figure 6.6 Personal TQM Checklist (Source: Roberts, Harry V. and Sergesketter, Bernard F. (1993). *Quality Is Personal: A Foundation for Total Quality Management*. New York: Free Press, p. 13. Adapted with the permission of The Free Press, a division of Simon & Schuster. Copyright ©1993 by Harry V. Roberts and Bernard F. Sergesketter.)

- I encourage and challenge you to start counting defects. It is impossible to reduce defects if we don't count them, and we can't reasonably ask our associates to count defects if we don't!
- I really believe that if several thousand of us here in the Central Region start counting defects, we will reduce them and differentiate ourselves from our competitors in a significant way.

Showing such personal commitment to quality improvement is one of the key signs of leadership that were discussed in Chapter 1 and other chapters.

CONCLUSION

Personal TQM is an essential ingredient to make quality happen in the workplace, yet it has been neglected for a long time in the development of the quality movement. Perhaps there has been too much of a feeling, especially on the part of management, that promoting quality is something that you *do to* your employees, rather than quality as something that you *do with* your employees. Until we come to grips with the personal aspects of quality and make it something that is an everyday consideration and a part of the way we do business, it is in constant danger of becoming a "fad" in every organization where it is tried. Perhaps in your daily attempt to bring about change in your part of the organizational universe, you may find that personal TQM is the key that unlocks the door to a wider understanding of what TQM really is all about.

REVIEW QUESTIONS

6.1 Identify five characteristics of people who respect themselves and others and their five parallel implications in a total quality work culture.

6.2 Define work performance, and detail the four categories of factors that influence it.

6.3 Outline the key components of the model of individual motivation and performance, and discuss how it could be applied to development of an OD project or situation.

6.4 Define and elaborate on the new psychological contract and the need for organizational self-respect.

6.5 Define quantum quality and elaborate on its four dimensions. How do these dimensions impact OD practitioners in a total quality environment?

6.6 Describe the relationship between principle-centered leadership and ethical work culture development.

6.7 Outline the steps in developing a personal development plan. How is such a plan different from those developed by corporations?

DISCUSSION QUESTIONS

6.1 Discuss at least five steps that you could take (or as a consultant recommend for a manager to take) as a total quality OD practitioner to enhance the self-respect of employees for themselves and for others.

6.2 Develop and use a personal TQM checklist based on the model given in Figure 6.6. Were your experiences after three weeks of use similar to Sergesketter's? Why or why not?

6.3 Discuss the theory and application of intrinsic motivation and equity of rewards. Relate their impacts to work performance and satisfaction, using an actual situation or realistic example.

6.4 Discuss the role of an OD practitioner in helping to manage the terms of the new psychological contract and organizational self-respect so that employee and organizational needs are respected.

6.5 Describe the extent to which you have experienced quantum quality in a work situation. List and discuss four ways in which regular implementation of the four dimensions of quantum quality would improve work performance.

6.6 Describe the extent to which you have experienced unprincipled leadership in an unprincipled ethical work culture. Then discuss the ways in which your performance could have been improved by the organization (or your immediate supervisor) adopting personal principled leadership and working to build a principle-centered work culture.

6.7 Have you ever felt ashamed or embarrassed by the way your organization conducts business or treats people? What can you do to improve organizational self-respect?

ENDNOTES

1. Roberts, Harry V. and Sergesketter, Bernard F. (1993). *Quality Is Personal: A Foundation for Total Quality Management.* New York: Free Press, pp. 1–27; Schultz, Louis (1991). *Personal Management: A System for Individual Performance Improvement.* Minneapolis: Process Management International, pp. 2–7.

2. Voehl, Frank W. (1992). *Total Quality: Principles and Processes within Organizations.* Coral Springs, FL: Strategy Associates, p. 5.

3. Roberts and Sergesketter (endnote 1).

4. The authors have selected concepts in column one of Table 6.1 from the following works and have created the rest of the material in the table: Brockner, J. (1988). *Self-Esteem at Work.* Lexington, MA: Lexington Books, p. 144; Weiss, H.M. and Knight, P.A. (1980). "The Utility of Humility: Self-Esteem, Information Search, and Problem Solving Efficiency." *Organizational Behavior and Human Performance.* Vol. 25, No. 3, pp. 216–223.

5. Fernandez, John (1991). *Managing a Diverse Workforce.* New York: Free Press, pp. 15–90; Fernandez, J. and Barr, M. (1993). *The Diversity Advantage.* Lexington, MA: Heath and Company, pp. 10–70.

6. Campbell, J.P. (1990). "Modeling the Performance Prediction Problem in Industrial and Organizational Psychology." In M.D. Dunnette and L.M. Hough, Eds. *Handbook of Industrial and Organizational Psychology,* 2nd edition, Volume 1. Palo Alto, CA: Consulting Psychologists' Press, pp. 687–732.

7. Bushe, G.R. (1988). "Cultural Contradictions of Statistical Process Control in American Manufacturing Organizations." *Journal of Management.* Vol. 14, No. 1, pp. 19–31.

8. Moorman, R.H. and Blakely, G.L. (1993). "Individualism–Collectivism as an Individual Difference Predictor of Organizational Citizenship Behavior." Paper presented at the Annual Meeting of the Academy of Management, Atlanta; Van Dyne, L., Graham, J.W., and Dienesch, R.M. (1994). "Organizational Citizenship Behavior: Construct Redefinition, Measurement and Validation." *Academy of Management Journal.* Vol. 37, No. 4, pp. 765–802.

9. Scholtes, P.R. (1988). *The Team Handbook: How to Use Teams to Improve Quality.* Madison, WI: Joiner Associates; Sashkin, M. and Kiser, K.L. (1993). *Total Quality Management.* San Francisco: Berrett-Koehler, pp. 15–20.

10. This section was adapted from Petrick, Joseph A. and Furr, Diana S. (1995). *Total Quality in Managing Human Resources.* Delray Beach, FL: St. Lucie Press, pp. 237–240.

11. Waldman, David A. (1994). "The Contributions of Total Quality Management to a Theory of Work Performance." *Academy of Management Review.* Vol. 19, No. 3, p. 516; Dobbins, G.H., Cardy, R.L., and Carson, K.P. (1991). "Examining Fundamental Assumptions: A Contrast of Person and System Approaches to Human Resource Management." *Research in Personnel and Human Resource Management."* Vol. 3, pp. 1–38; Robinson, D.G. and Robinson, J.C. (1995) *Performance Consulting: Moving Beyond Training.* San Francisco: Berrett-Koehler.

12. Dobbins et al. (endnote 11), p. 11.

13. Deming, W.E. (1986). *Out of the Crisis.* Cambridge, MA: Massachusetts Institute of Technology, pp. 95–105; Juran, J.M. (1989). *Juran on Leadership for Quality: An Executive Handbook.* Wilson, CT: Juran Institute, pp. 55–60.

14. Campbell (endnote 6), pp. 701–703; Blumberg, M. and Pringle, C.C. (1982). "The Missing Opportunity in Organizational Research: Some Implications for a Theory of Work Performance." *Academy of Management Review.* Vol. 7, No. 4, pp. 560–569.

15. Exhibits and content in this section were adapted from Lewis, Ralph G. and Smith, Douglas H. (1994). *Total Quality in Higher Education.* Delray Beach, FL: St. Lucie Press, pp. 217–226 from a process originally developed by Frank Voehl, CEO of Strategy Associates, Inc.

16. Cameron, Kim (1994). "An Empirical Investigation of Quality Cultures, Practices and Outcomes." Paper presented at the Annual Meeting of the Academy of Management, Dallas.

17. Ibid., p. 5.

18. This section was adapted from Lewis and Smith (endnote 15), pp. 217–226.

19. Wagner, John A. III and Hollenbeck, John R. (1995). *The Management of Organizational Behavior,* 2nd edition. Englewood Cliffs, NJ: Prentice-Hall, pp. 172–176. This subsection of the chapter has been adapted from material from this text.

20. Steel, R.P. and Mento, A.S. (1986). "Impact of Situational Constraints on Subjective and Objective Criteria of Managerial Job Performance." *Organizational Behavior and Human Decision Processes.* Vol. 37, No. 3, pp. 254–265; Bowen, D.E., Ledford, G.E., and Nathan, B.R. (1991). "Hiring for the Organization, Not the Job." *Academy of Management Executive.* Vol. 5, No. 4, pp. 40–42; Sashkin, M. and Kiser, K.J. (1993). *Total Quality Management.* San Francisco: Berrett-Koehler, pp. 140–150; Chatman, J.A. (1989). "Improving Interactional Organizational Research: A Model of Person-Organization Fit." *Academy of Management Review.* Vol. 14, pp. 333–349.

21. Thomas, K.W. and Velthouse, B.A. (1990). "Cognitive Elements of Empowerment: An Interpretive Model of Intrinsic Task Motivation." *Academy of Management Review.* Vol. 15, No. 4, pp. 666–681; McWhirter, E.H. (1991). "Empowerment in Counseling." *Journal of Counseling and Development.* Vol. 69, No. 2, pp. 222–227.

22. Greenberger, D.B. and Strasser, S. (1986). "Development and Application of a Model of Personal Control in Organizations." *Academy of Management Review.* Vol. 11, No. 4, p. 165.

23. Greenberger, D.B., Strasser, S., Cummings, L.L., and Dunham, R.B. (1989). "The Impact of Personal Control on Performance and Satisfaction." *Organizational Behavior and Human Decision Processes.* Vol. 43, No. 2, pp. 29–51.

24. Hackman, J.R. and Oldham, G.R. (1976). "Motivation Through the Design of Work: Test of a Theory." *Organizational Behavior and Human Performance.* Vol. 16, No. 3, pp. 250–279.

25. Bandura, A. (1977). "Self-Efficacy: Toward a Unifying Theory of Behavior Change." *Psychological Review.* Vol. 84, No. 1, pp. 191–215.

26. Herzberg, F., Mausner, B., and Snyderman, B.B. (1959). *The Motivation to Work,* 2nd edition. New York: John Wiley and Sons; Thomas and Velthouse (endnote 21), pp. 666–681.

27. Greenberger, D.B. and Strasser, S. (1991). "The Role of Situational and Dispositional Factors in the Enhancement of Personal Control in Organizations." *Research in Organizational Behavior.* Vol. 13, No. 2, pp. 111–145; Hackman and Oldham (endnote 24), pp. 250–279; Bandura (endnote 25), pp. 191–215; Herzberg, Mausner, and Snyderman (endnote 26), pp. 42–60.

28. Eisenberger, R., Fasolo, P., and Davis-LaMastro, V. (1990). "Perceived Organizational Support and Employee Diligence, Commitment, and Innovation." *Journal of Applied Psychology.* Vol. 75, No. 5, pp. 51–59; Mathieu, J.E. and Zajac, D.M. (1990). "A Review and Meta-Analysis of the Antecedents, Correlates, and Consequences of Organizational Commitment." *Psychological Bulletin.* Vol. 108, No. 2, pp. 171–194; Meyer, J.P. and Allen, N.J. (1991). "A Three-Component Conceptualization of Organizational Commitment." *Human Resource Management Review.* Vol. 1, No. 1, pp. 61–69; Mowday, R.T., Porter, L.W., and Steers, R.M. (1982). *Employee–Organization Linkages: The Psychology of Commitment, Absenteeism, and Turnover.* New York: Academic Press, pp. 15–46; Conner, D.R. and Patterson, R. (1981). *Building Commitment to Organizational Change.* Atlanta: OD Resources, pp. 20–65.

29. Beck, John D. and Yeager, Neil M. (1994). *The Leader's Window.* New York: John Wiley and Sons, pp. 30–32.

30. Armstrong, David (1992). *Management by Storying Around.* New York: Doubleday Currency, pp. 117–119.

31. Covey, Stephen R. (1991). *Principle-Centered Leadership.* New York: Summit Books, p. 32.

32. Covey, Stephen R. (1989). *The Seven Habits of Highly Effective People.* New York: Fireside/Simon and Schuster, p. 63.

33. Covey (endnote 31), p. 161.

34. Schein, E.H. (1980). *Organizational Psychology.* Englewood Cliffs, NJ: Prentice-Hall, pp. 19–29; Rousseau, D. and McLean Parks, J. (1993). "The Contracts of

Individuals and Organizations." In L.L. Cummings and B.M. Staw, Eds. *Research in Organizational Behavior*, Vol. 15. Greenwich, CT: JAI Press, pp. 1–47; Solomon, Robert C. (1990). *A Passion for Justice*. Reading, MA: Addison-Wesley, pp. 149–152. According to Solomon, and the authors concur, any psychological or social contracts originate from and are founded upon a shared sense of justice and caring.

35. Robinson, S., Kraatz, M., and Rousseau, D. (1994). "Changing Obligations and the Psychological Contract: A Longitudinal Study." *Academy of Management Journal*. Vol. 37, No. 5, pp. 137–152.

36. Robinson, S. and Rousseau, D. (1994). "Violating the Psychological Contract: Not the Exception But the Norm." *Journal of Organizational Behavior*. Vol 15, No. 6, pp. 245–259.

37. Moorman, R.H. (1991). "The Relationship Between Organizational Justice and Organizational Citizenship Behaviors: Do Fairness Perceptions Influence Employee Citizenship?" *Journal of Applied Psychology*. Vol. 76, No. 4, pp. 845–855; O'Leary-Kelly, A.M., Griffin, R.W., and Glew, D.J. (1996). "Organization-Motivated Aggression: A Research Framework." *Academy of Management Review*. Vol. 21, No. 1, pp. 225–253.

38. Rousseau, D. (1990). "New Hire Perceptions of Their Own and Their Employer's Obligations: A Study of Psychological Contracts." *Journal of Organizational Behavior*. Vol. 11, No. 4, pp. 389–400.

39. Spitzer, T.Q. (1995). *People and Their Jobs: What's Real, What's Rhetoric*. Princeton, NJ: Kepner-Tregoe.

40. *The 1995 Towers Perrin Workplace Index* (1995). New York: Towers Perrin.

41. Noer, D.M. (1993). *Healing the Wounds: Overcoming the Trauma of Lay-offs and Revitalizing Downsized Organizations*. San Francisco: Jossey-Bass, pp. 24–26.

42. Drath, W.H. and Palus, C.J. (1994). *Leadership as Meaning Making in Communities of Practice*. Greensboro, NC: Center for Creative Leadership, pp. 25–40.

43. Miller, William C. (1994). "Quantum Quality: The Innovative Resolution." *Quality Digest*. Vol. 3, No. 4, pp. 53–57.

44. Wyatt, John (1994). "The New Deal: What Companies and Employees Owe Each Other." *Fortune*. June 13, pp. 44–52.

45. Ibid., p. 56.

46. Ibid., p. 57.

47. Senge, Peter M. (1990). *The Fifth Discipline: The Art and Practice of the Learning Organization*. New York: Doubleday Currency, pp. 139–173; Watkins, Karen E. and Marsick, Victoria J. (1993). *Sculpting the Learning Organization*. San Francisco: Jossey-Bass, pp. 3–23; Howard, Robert, Ed. (1993). *The Learning Imperative: Managing People for Continuous Innovation*. Boston: Harvard Business School, pp. 41–57.

48. Pritchett, Price (1994). *The Employee Handbook of New Work Habits for a Radically Changing World*. Dallas: Pritchett, pp. 1–5.

49. Watkins, K.E. and Marsick, V.J. (1993). *Sculpting the Learning Organization*. San Francisco: Jossey-Bass, pp. 262–278.

50. Petrick, Joseph A. and Quinn, John F. (1996). *Management Ethics and Organizational Integrity*. Thousand Oaks, CA: Sage, pp. 10–17; Paine, Lynn S. (1994).

"Managing for Organizational Integrity." *Harvard Business Review.* Vol. 28, No. 3, pp. 106–113.

51. Roberts and Sergesketter (endnote 1), pp. 5–19.

52. Senge (endnote 47), pp. 150–173; Stewart, Thomas A. (1994). "Your Company's Most Valuable Asset: Intellectual Capital." *Fortune.* Vol. 130, No. 7, pp. 68–74.

53. Conger, Jay A. (1992). *Learning to Lead: The Art of Transforming Managers into Leaders.* San Francisco: Jossey-Bass, pp. 15–61.

54. Senge (endnote 47), pp. 233–270; Daly, Markate, Ed. (1994). *Communitarianism: A New Public Ethics.* Belmont, CA: Wadsworth, pp. 3–345; Etzioni, Amitai (1993). *The Spirit of Community.* New York: Simon and Schuster, pp. 1–207; Etzioni, Amitai (1988). *The Moral Dimension: Toward a New Economics.* New York: Free Press, pp. 10–95; Glendon, Mary Ann (1991). *Rights Talk: The Impoverishment of Political Discourse.* New York: Free Press, pp. 5–85.

55. Collins, James and Lazier, William (1992). *Beyond Entrepreneurship.* Englewood Cliffs, NJ: Prentice-Hall, p. 55.

56. Roberts and Sergesketter (endnote 1), pp. 13–14.

CASE STUDY

AT&T UNIVERSAL CARD SERVICES*

In 1990, AT&T jumped into an already crowded credit card industry with a new card. At that time, there were more than 6000 issuers of MasterCard and Visa cards in the United States. Many had been in business for more than 20 years. AT&T believed that by linking the AT&T Calling Card to a consumer credit card, it could create a product of exceptional value to customers, business, and the credit card industry.

AT&T Universal Card Services (UCS) was launched as a wholly owned subsidiary of AT&T. UCS's strategy was to offer a highly competitive credit card with an extensive set of services. Through a carefully executed plan, it intended to continuously improve internal performance and enhance its product and service offerings. The aim was to both "delight customers" and to ensure that the Universal Card outdistanced competitors' products.

Within six months of its launch, UCS realized its vision. The Universal Card was among the top ten bank credit cards. In 30 months, it was the second largest in the credit card industry. Supported by AT&T Consumer Services Group, UCS developed a business worth more than $9 billion in receivables in less than four years. Its vision—"To be our customers' best service relationship"—made it a major force in the industry.

APPROACH TO PROCESS DESIGN

To serve a worldwide market, UCS built a world-class integrated information and analysis system. UCS determined what constituted world-class quality and set its goals accordingly. Its systems represent a huge financial investment in computer hardware and software. Perhaps more important, its human investments in quality processes affect millions of customer account inquiries, data access capabilities, and information analyses. By continuously improving its systems, it has reduced operating expenses, increased productivity, and led the industry in customer satisfaction. Key processes and suppliers used to service its customers include:

*This case was prepared from numerous sources, including: Evans, James R. and Lindsay, William M. (1996). *The Management and Control of Quality*, 3rd edition. St. Paul, MN: West Publishing, pp. 124–125; Bounds, Gregory M. (1996) *Cases in Quality*. Chicago: Irwin, pp. 508–519; quality profile information available from the Baldrige Award Office of NIST and other sources in the public domain.

Business Processes
- Strategic/business planning
- Total quality management
- Technology management

Support Services
- Customer assistance (collections)
- Constituency management
- Customer acquisition management
- Information management
- Financial management

Product and Services Production and Delivery Processes
- Application processing
- Authorizations management
- Billing/statement processing
- Credit screening
- Credit card protection
- Customer acquisition process management (prospective customer list development)
- Payment processing
- Relationship management (service, communications, program, brand management)

VALUES AT UCS

Top management established UCS quality values that guide the business. A comprehensive plan communicated those values to every level of the organization. By communicating and living its values, UCS has established a vigorous, supportive corporate culture. The values that guide UCS include customer delight, commitment, teamwork, continuous improvement, trust and integrity, mutual respect, and a sense of urgency. Its business strategies are formulated to support its values and reflect its dedication to quality, customer service, and long-term success. UCS has stated a public commitment to an ethical business approach in granting consumer credit. Its consumer affairs group works closely with consumer advocates, regularly reviewing its product offerings and credit policies from its consumer' viewpoint to assess its customers' risk in using credit, as well as its own. This input serves as the foundation of the Pro-Consumer Platform, which earned UCS the reputation as a leading consumer advocate in the credit card industry.

UCS WANTS TO BE A GREAT PLACE TO WORK AND DO BUSINESS WITH

UCS strives to create an environment in which associates enjoy their work and consider UCS the best company to work for. Associates learn the importance of UCS's vision and values through specialized training. The importance of empowerment is emphasized. UCS associates are empowered to do what it takes to delight customers. Recognition and performance systems are linked to quality achievements and encourage associates to seek customer delight.

The total quality approach has been used as a foundation for business operations since UCS was launched. Almost since start-up, it has conducted frequent self-assessments using the Malcolm Baldrige National Quality Award criteria. It uses the findings as the basis for its strategic quality plan. Each time an assessment is conducted, UCS learns more about its business and identifies new ways to improve its quality and customer focus.

UCS partners with key suppliers to help them with quality improvement. UCS provides tools and coaching for self-assessment. Then, UCS quality teams provide assessment feedback.

LEADERSHIP AND INDIVIDUAL QUALITY

One year after launching UCS, its vision and mission, used since its start-up, were revised based on input from its associates. At its first annual strategic quality planning sessions, it also refined its strategic quality direction and objectives based on associate feedback.

UCS promotes quality through high leadership visibility. Its CEO writes columns for the in-house newspaper on quality, *UNIverse*. At least quarterly, UCS executives reinforce quality values at all-associate and organizational meetings. They also give direct reports at daily and semi-monthly meetings, encouraging associates to ask questions.

UCS assesses its leadership in a variety of ways. Monthly and annual associate opinion surveys include questions about management leadership. UCS leadership also identifies the ten quality improvement gaps with highest priority through the annual AT&T Chairman's Quality Award assessments. Executives assume ownership of these gaps, designated the "Ten Most Wanted" quality improvements, and report on progress at leadership meetings.

INFORMATION AND ANALYSIS

Information management and analysis are critical to the success of the business. An integrated five-year Strategic Systems Plan to build a world-class set of information analysis systems is being implemented in order to shorten lead times and improve analysis capabilities.

Each customer account contains more than 1000 elements that provide information about its life cycle. UCS uses standard data entry templates to ensure consistent editing of manually input data. Data collected automatically from interfaces with other systems use standard record formats and edits and are reconciled at each handoff.

Its systems development methods and project management handbook provide guidelines and standards for effective development, maintenance, documentation, and management of data systems. These methods ensure an orderly, efficient system and data improvement cycle, as well as the appropriate allocation of resources.

UCS benchmarks its key business processes, performance indicators, best-in-class companies (top-performing national credit card companies), best current practices, and world-class companies with similar processes. To better understand and improve UCS's processes, its process owners visit the best-in-class and world-class service providers. Teams use this information to formulate action plans and set process improvement goals and objectives. Cross-functional teams use computer technology to continuously evaluate and improve statement cycle times and decision-making capabilities.

HUMAN RESOURCE DEVELOPMENT AND MANAGEMENT

UCS's long-term and short-term human resource plans focus on creating a superior work environment and a highly skilled organization. UCS works to involve every associate in continuous improvement by encouraging personal and group involvement, communicating performance goals, and ensuring that associates develop a broad understanding of the business. Its values encourage empowerment, responsibility, and innovation. These quality values are reinforced at new associate orientations, initial customer-service training sessions, and Passport to Excellence training (the initiation into the UCS vision and values).

Innovation is supported through specific programs such as "Your Ideas, Your Universe" (the UCS suggestion program), improvement teams, and associate action teams. UCS encourages associate innovation by providing a vehicle for offering suggestions and analyzing problems. Universal Card University delivers classroom education and training. Training and education are linked to strategic plans to measure current and future competencies.

Performance needs and analysis, organizational input from individuals or individuals' managers, and the UCS commitment to training determine types and amounts of training. UCS addresses skill and development gaps systematically—with the instructional technology approach—to assess, analyze, and design course curricula.

Recognition and performance programs are linked to UCS quality and financial goals. Associates are given opportunities to participate in development and recognition. The programs have rigorous eligibility requirements designed to encourage outstanding quality and performance behaviors. Awards indicate significant achievement.

UCS routinely assesses overall associate satisfaction using monthly and annual surveys and periodic focus groups.

Customer-contact associates complete an extensive employment screening process. In 1990, staffing demands grew from 100 to 2000 associates, but selection criteria remained uncompromised. Applicants must complete a two-part general aptitude test. Successful candidates then undergo additional testing, including a customer service role-playing exercise where each applicant handles simulated incoming and outgoing calls. If the candidate passes the initial screening tests, he or she must pass a background check, credit check, and a medical examination, including drug testing, before being hired. Customer-contact associates attend a general UCS orientation workshop and an intensive eight-week training program. Additional training is provided in corporate values and innovation, as outlined earlier.

UCS's explicit Service Guarantee represents a unique commitment. Its customers can expect:

> *A Trusted Partner*—Each AT&T Universal Card member will be treated as a trustworthy and respected individual whose problems are legitimate and whose point of view is valued.

Entitlement to Error-Free Service—Our customers are entitled to 100 percent error-free service. No excuses.

Availability When You Need Us—Our service staff is a phone call away, 24 hours a day, 365 days a year.

Quick Action to Protect Your Interests—The solution to any problem with a transaction made with the AT&T Universal Card can be started with a call. We will take immediate action to protect customer billing rights.

More Than Just Plastic—If a cardmember's AT&T Universal Card is lost or stolen, we will immediately replace it and, if requested, deliver the new card within 24 hours anywhere in the United States and in most worldwide locations. In addition, we will provide emergency charge capability, access to cash, and AT&T Calling Card capability until the new card is received.

If at any time a cardmember is not happy with the service provided by UCS, the customer receives a $10 Service Guarantee that can be applied to the account. It's UCS's way of saying "Sorry for the inconvenience."

Customers have learned that the AT&T brand represents another significant commitment from UCS to its customers. The American public trusts AT&T as a company that stands behind its products and services. The public expects no less from the company's credit card products.

QUESTIONS FOR DISCUSSION

1 How does AT&T Universal Card Services empower individuals to promote quality? How does the company attempt to use intrinsic and extrinsic motivation in the design of jobs?
2 From the description given, at what level of ethical work culture might you infer that AT&T Universal Card Services works?
3 How might a total quality OD practitioner have helped to design the systems and processes that are in place at AT&T Universal Card Services? Are there areas that appear to require changes or improvements in order to emphasize OD principles?

EXERCISE

EXERCISE 6.1 PRACTITIONER ASSESSMENT INSTRUMENT: ETHICAL WORK CULTURE ASSESSMENT

PURPOSE
The purpose of this self-assessment instrument is to determine the perceived level of moral development within the organization as a whole and the work unit in particular. Demographic variables may be added before or after the instrument to determine perceptual differences, for instance between individuals in managerial and nonmanagerial roles.

DIRECTIONS
Think about what it takes for you and people like yourself (e.g., your co-workers, people in similar positions) to "fit in" and meet expectations in your organization and in your particular work unit (e.g., department, team, or work group). Select the number correlated with each response option below that best describes the current interpersonal behavioral styles of your organization and work unit. Respond in terms of your perceptions of *"how things are now,"* not *"how you would like them to be,"* in both your organization and your work unit. Place the number that correlates with each option in the appropriate blank spaces below under the columns labeled "Organization" and "Work Unit":

1 = Not at all   4 = To a great extent
2 = To a slight extent   5 = To a very great extent
3 = To a moderate extent

SURVEY INSTRUMENT

Most people at work...	Organization	Work Unit
1. Turn the job into a contest	_____	_____
2. Play "politics" to gain influence	_____	_____
3. Do things to avoid the disapproval of others	_____	_____
4. Focus on pleasing those in positions of authority	_____	_____
5. Involve others in decisions affecting them	_____	_____
6. Trust that conflicts at work will be resolved fairly	_____	_____
7. Appear hard, tough, and intimidating	_____	_____
8. Oppose things indirectly	_____	_____
9. Wait for others to act first	_____	_____
10. Never challenge superiors	_____	_____
11. Resolve conflicts by majority vote	_____	_____
12. Help others to think for themselves	_____	_____

Most people at work...	Organization	Work Unit
13. Compete rather than cooperate	_____	_____
14. Try to avoid appearing as a loser	_____	_____
15. Conform to the "way things are"	_____	_____
16. Treat rules as more important than ideas	_____	_____
17. Encourage and help others to participate in decision making at work	_____	_____
18. Demonstrate sincere caring for others at work	_____	_____
19. Maintain an image of superiority	_____	_____
20. Focus on building and maintaining a power base	_____	_____
21. Make "popular" rather than necessary decisions	_____	_____
22. Accord highest priority to respecting the "chain of command"	_____	_____
23. Think in terms of what would be supported by the majority of people	_____	_____
24. Try to "do the right thing" rather than "take the easy way out"	_____	_____

SCORING

A. Add response numbers from questions 1, 7, 13, and 19   (Social Darwinism)

B. Add response numbers from questions 2, 8, 14, and 20   (Machiavellianism)

C. *House of Manipulation Score* (total of A and B scores) _____

D. Add response numbers from questions 3, 9, 15, and 21   (Popular Conformity)

E. Add response numbers from questions 4, 10, 16, and 22   (Allegiance to Authority)

F. *House of Compliance Score* (total of D and E scores) _____

G. Add response numbers from questions 5, 11, 17, and 23   (Democratic Participation)

H. Add response numbers from questions 6, 12, 18, and 24   (Organizational Integrity)

I. *House of Integrity Score* (total of G and H scores) _____

INTERPRETATION

Step 1: The highest total score among scoring steps C, F, and I indicates the level of moral development perceived by the respondent in both the organization and work unit. If C is the highest total score, the ethical work culture of the House of Manipulation predominates; if F is the highest score, the ethical work culture of the House of Compliance prevails; and if I is the highest total score, the ethical work culture of the House of Integrity prevails. Any level score ties are to be interpreted as indicating the lower (or lowest) work environment level of moral development.

The Organizational House is _____

The Work Unit House is _____

Step 2:   Once the work environment level has been determined (House of Manipulation, House of Compliance, or House of Integrity), the higher of the two scores that led to the level totals indicates the specific ethical work culture stage. Again, any stage score ties are to be interpreted as indicating the lower stage of moral development.

Work Environment Level Scores		Ethical Work Culture Stage	
If A is the higher total within the House of Manipulation	=	Social Darwinism	(Stage 1)
If B is the higher total within the House of Manipulation	=	Machiavellianism	(Stage 2)
If D is the higher total within the House of Compliance	=	Popular Conformity	(Stage 3)
If E is the higher total within the House of Compliance	=	Allegiance to Authority	(Stage 4)
If G is the higher total within the House of Integrity	=	Democratic Participation	(Stage 5)
If H is the higher total within the House of Integrity	=	Organizational Integrity	(Stage 6)

Organizational Ethical Stage is _____

Work Unit Ethical Stage is _____

Step 3:   Note any difference between organizational and work unit scores since these disparities are points of both potential ethical conflict and opportunities for ethical work culture alignment and improvement. Persons caught between conflicting ethical work cultures for long periods of time experience severe work stress symptoms that inevitably impair optimal quality performance. Proactive management of ethical work culture development indicates human resource respect for people and commitment to building community at work.

Source: Petrick, Joseph A. and Quinn, John F. (1994). *Abbreviated Variation Four of Ethical Work Culture Assessment Instrument.* Cincinnati: Organizational Ethics Associates.

CHAPTER 7

TOTAL QUALITY OD IMPLEMENTATION: THE TRANSFORMING PROCESS

The focus of this chapter is on the implementation of total quality within the context of organization development (OD) principles and practices. As was pointed out in Chapter 1, this encompasses a broad domain, including:

- Planned changes
- Organization-wide implementation
- Managed from the top
- Design which will increase organization effectiveness and health
- Carried out through planned interventions in the organization's processes using behavioral science knowledge

The total quality focus is in harmony with all of these, although some have been "discovered" or "reinvented" by practitioners, consultants, or theoreticians who would violently resist being called OD specialists or advocates.

Implementation is about "just doing it" with total quality management (TQM). It is the "bottom line." It is the *results* that are obtained from the marriage of OD and quality that, in the ideal case, cause empowered people to carry out a planned organization design that will result in continuously improved, flawlessly produced products and services, delivered on time and on cost to delight customers. In his recent book, Phil Crosby, who has his own slant on quality, tries to explain why we *don't* "just do it." He puts it this way:[1]

> "What do we do after Total Quality Management?" People ask me that question continually…They forget, or perhaps don't know, that I have never recommended that they fool around with TQM in the first place. They are just a set of initials without definition or formulation that have been used by organizations to avoid the really hard work of managing quality…The problem of quality has always been management's lack of understanding of their responsibility for causing a culture of prevention in their company. That is what quality management is supposed to do. It is a matter of determining exactly what the customers (both internal and external) want; describing what has to be accomplished in order to give that to the customer; and then meeting the requirement every time.

GUIDELINES FOR IMPLEMENTATION

In one sense, Chapters 4 to 6 provided the general strategic implementation guidelines for total quality. The focus of this chapter is on three areas: (1) an integrative operational model for directing the transformational steps needed to systematically implement total quality using OD principles, (2) a current case study of successful (though perhaps fleeting) organization change using a total quality philosophy, and (3) a brief overview of the international total quality practices that are related to total quality OD and already exist in three major regions of the globe.

Guidelines for implementation can be provided, but even this may prove confusing. The overwhelming volume of literature in total quality is primarily focused on techniques, prescriptions, and procedures. However, less attention has been devoted to how total quality has been implemented, the hurdles encountered by organizations, and how they adapted the principles of total quality to existing cultures. Even the leaders in the field cannot agree.

Furthermore, the lack of agreement among the TQM gurus produces contradictions and inconsistent prescriptions that are puzzling to would-be users. Deming says "eliminate slogans," while Crosby uses the slogan of "zero defects." Deming says "drive out fear," while Juran says "fear can bring out the best in people." Deming's process starts at the top and works down, while Juran starts with middle management and works both ways.

From this rich and diverse stew, six models for implementing total quality can be identified:[2]

1. **Total quality element approach**—Uses elements of quality improvement programs rather than full implementation of total quality, such as quality circles, statistical process control, and quality function deployment.
2. **Guru approach**—Uses the writings of Deming, Juran, and Crosby for analysis and implementation. Deming's 14-point model is an example.
3. **Japanese model approach**—Uses the writings of such Japanese writers as Kaoru Ishikawa and the educational guidelines of the Union of Japanese Scientists and Engineers (JUSE).
4. **Industrial company model approach**—Leaders from one organization visit an organization using total quality, identify its system, and integrate this information with their own ideas to create a customized approach. Visiting winners of the Baldrige Award is an example.
5. **Hoshin planning approach**—Focuses on successful planning, deployment, and execution and monthly diagnosis. Developed by the Japanese firm Bridgestone and used successfully by such firms as Hewlett-Packard.
6. **Baldrige Award criteria approach**—Uses the criteria for the Malcolm Baldrige National Quality Award to identify areas for improvement.

All of the approaches work and have been applied in hundreds of organizations. Which approach, or approaches, is most compatible with OD principles? In this book, a variety of total quality principles, practices, and techniques and tools have been described. In Chapters 1 and 3, strategic models and their applications, along with Deming's 14 Points and the seven Baldrige criteria, were described in a form modified for total quality OD/ human resource (HR) application. The managerial levels for implementing total quality were described in Chapter 4, maintaining that total quality can begin at any of these levels. Management models have been used throughout the text to suggest methods and process of analysis and implementation. In sum, the strategy advocated in this book is a hybrid of all of these approaches: taking the best and configuring it into a framework that "fits" the organization's mission, strategy, goals, objectives, and ethical work culture is the best approach to successful management of total quality OD activities.

TOTAL QUALITY INTEGRATED IMPLEMENTATION MODEL FOR MANAGING AN ORGANIZATION DEVELOPMENT CHANGE PROCESS

A model and supportive framework should be developed to assist in a planned total quality OD initiative. The most useful total quality implementation plan would be an integrated blend of all approaches mentioned above.

An integrated model for implementing total quality using a total quality OD change process should meet a number of criteria to incorporate the material in this text and be operational at the same time:

1. It must identify activities, indicators, and time lines required to adopt total quality OD-based improvement approaches at distinct phases in the total quality implementation process.
2. It must address the need to complete assessment (speaking with facts) and ethical work culture diagnoses at critical phases in the OD process.
3. It must identify four levels at which total quality OD efforts may be initiated: *strategy implementation* (Chapter 3), *process implementation* (Chapter 4), *project implementation* (Chapter 5), and *individual performance implementation* (Chapter 6).
4. It must address the need for continual evaluation and control of the total quality OD/HR area and its quality improvement efforts, with the evaluation and control based on facts.

The Total Quality Integrated Implementation Plan[3] in Table 7.1 meets the above criteria and presents a flow of seven operational steps for systematic implementation: (1) goal setting implementation, (2) assessment implementation, (3) strategy implementation, (4) process implementation, (5) project

Table 7.1   Total Quality Integrated Implementation Plan

No.	Action	What	Who
1.0 GOAL SETTING IMPLEMENTATION			
1.1	Commit to transformation. Develop organization change strategy and plan [PLAN]	Explore strategic issues, opportunities, and competitive status; identify business imperatives for change; commit to quality focus; develop mission, vision, guiding principles, and goals for QC	President (head of sponsoring unit) and Executive Management Group, and the QC (or EIT)
1.2	Communications and education plan [DO]	Plan to communicate the organization change process and TQM philosophy to a limited group of managers and staff. Develop plan to introduce the quality principles and strategies.	President and QC (or EIT), EWCT and PIT

implementation, (6) individual performance implementation, and (7) evaluation and control implementation. This integrated approach to implementation is necessary if the goal of a true total quality system that pervades the organization's processes is to be considered. In some organizations, beginning at the initial, organization-wide stages (e.g., goal setting, assessment, strategy, and evaluation and control implementation) may not always be politically advisable. Thus, intervention at other levels, such as process, project, or individual performance implementation, may be most appropriate for initiating total quality improvement. The ideal situation is to systematically incorporate all seven steps into the total quality implementation.

The Total Quality Integrated Implementation Plan consists of actions required to achieve each implementation stage. Each action specifies *what* should be done, *who* should be doing it, *why* this particular action is necessary, *how* the action should be carried out, *when* it should be done, and what *indicators* are required to ensure that it has been completed. While still an operational framework model upon which a specific plan applicable to TQM must be designed and developed, this summary provides an extensive guide for initiating a thorough and possibly more effective and productive total quality transformation plan.

Table 7.1 Total Quality Integrated Implementation Plan

No.	Why	How	When	Indicators
1.0 GOAL SETTING IMPLEMENTATION				
1.1	To ensure top-level commitment to the effort and to develop the framework for the quality improvement effort	Off-site strategy formulation and goal-setting sessions; formation of QC or EIT; application of OD expertise, internal quality champions, and external consulting support	Months 1 and 2	Executive Management Group minutes, QC (or EIT) minutes, and other written documents
1.2	To ensure systematic and consistent communication about the change effort and to initiate the transformation process with all key players of the organization	Appoint a PIT and EWCT to report to the QC (or EIT) for system design and development. Selective publication of the plan, employee meetings, seminars, and workshops.	Month 1 and continuously throughout the effort	QC (or EIT), PIT, and EWCT minutes, written documentation

Table 7.1 (continued) Total Quality Integrated Implementation Plan

No.	Action	What	Who
1.3	Evaluate effects of initial steps [STUDY]	Determine initial response of managers and staff to proposed changes. Assess perceived organizational impacts and threats.	President and QC (or EIT), EWCT, and PIT
1.4	Introduce quality improvement [ACT]	Begin implementation and communicate education plans to set the stage for change and to introduce all members to quality improvement principles and techniques	President and QC (or EIT), EWCT, and PIT

2.0 ASSESSMENT IMPLEMENTATION

No.	Action	What	Who
2.1	Develop assessment plan [PLAN]	Develop a plan to assess the organization and its leadership in terms of quality improvement principles and issues	President and QC (or EIT), EWCT, and PIT
2.2	Conduct assessment [DO]	Conduct the assessment with customers (internal and external) and suppliers; analyze the results	PIT and EWCT
2.3	Prepare and circulate report with gap analysis [STUDY]	Identify gaps between current reality and "desired stage"; identify opportunities for quality improvement. Report recommended actions to close gaps; circulate to the President, QC (or EIT), and key individuals.	President and QC (or EIT), PIT, and EWCT for approval of actions
2.4	Implement action steps to close gaps [ACT]	Begin implementation, using plans to set the critical gaps	PIT and EWCT, including process "owners"

Table 7.1 (continued) Total Quality Integrated Implementation Plan

No.	Why	How	When	Indicators
1.3	To ensure systematic and consistent communication about the change effort and to determine levels of support for philosophy and actions. Begin building team culture with all key players of the organization.	Feedback, using surveys, feedback sessions, and assessments led by members of the PITs and EWCT to report to the QC (or EIT)	Months 2 and 3	Survey results and summaries, QC (or EIT), PIT, and EWCT minutes
1.4	To initiate the transformation process with all members of the organization	Official documents, newsletters, employee meetings, seminars, and workshops	Month 3	QC (or EIT), PIT, and EWCT minutes

2.0 ASSESSMENT IMPLEMENTATION

No.	Why	How	When	Indicators
2.1	To obtain data to assess the current state of "quality" and "ethics" in the organization	Review existing literature for assessment, gather benchmarking data and internal data, obtain services of total quality OD consultants	Month 3	Assessment instruments
2.2	To collect data on quality and ethical work culture in the organization	Surveys, preview of documents, existing databases	Month 3	Completed data files
2.3	To share data, obtain feedback, and involve members and to select target areas for quality improvement efforts	Analysis of report(s), discussions with key members. Formal meetings, written reports, newsletters.	Month 4	Assessment report, other related documents, record of the meetings. List of target opportunities.
2.4	To initiate the transformation process with members of the organization, with specific objective of "closing gaps"	Analysis of report(s), discussions with key members. Formal meetings, written reports, newsletters.	Month 4 and beyond	Assessment instruments and follow-up reports

Table 7.1 (continued) Total Quality Integrated Implementation Plan

No.	Action	What	Who
3.0 STRATEGY IMPLEMENTATION			
3.1	Begin planning the transformation [PLAN]	Develop basic plans for the quality improvement effort at the strategic level	President and Executive Management Group
3.2.1	Determine the charter and composition of the Steering Team: QC (or EIT) [DO]	Appoint QC (or EIT) from key positions in the organization (executive management, operations groups, unions, professional staff, other employee groups)	President and Executive Management Group
3.2.2	Select a business process improvement champion [DO]	Identify one person who will be visible and accountable to lead the effort	President in collaboration with Executive Management Group and QC (or EIT)
3.2.3	Form the PIT and EWCT [DO]	Create the PIT and EWCT	QC (or EIT)
3.3	Top-level education and training [ACT]	Train the QC (or EIT), PIT, and EWCT	Qualified individuals, which may include outside consultants initially

Table 7.1 (continued) Total Quality Integrated Implementation Plan

No.	Why	How	When	Indicators
3.0 STRATEGY IMPLEMENTATION				
3.1	To ensure top-level commitment to the effort	Form QC (or EIT)	Month 1	Minutes of Executive Management Group
3.2.1	To provide ongoing leadership in establishing and maintaining total quality effort	Establish QC (or EIT), plus its parameters and outcome expectations	Month 1	Minutes of Executive Management Group and the QC (or EIT)
3.2.2	To dedicate one person at a senior level, to ensure all foundations are properly laid for the transition to quality and to build commitment and remove barriers to implementation	Select a formal leader with broad-based credibility, total quality competency, clout, and reputation for integrity	Month 1	Minutes of Executive Management Group and the QC (or EIT)
3.2.3	To have a multilevel cross-functional team responsible for developing and monitoring the total quality plan; to encourage everyone to contribute to the quality improvement effort	Select formal and informal leaders from critical divisions and departments; establish parameters and outcome expectations for the team	Month 2	Minutes of the QC (or EIT), PIT, and EWCT
3.3	To increase the understanding of quality and ethical work culture improvement principles and build commitment to the change process	Intensive workshops (a location away from work would be very beneficial); combine initial training with follow-through sessions	Months 1 and 2, with follow-through session continuous during the project	Training designed and delivered; written initial vision, mission, guiding principles, and goals

Table 7.1 (continued)   Total Quality Integrated Implementation Plan

No.	Action	What	Who
3.4	Establish and/ or clarify mission, vision, guiding principles, and goals [ACT]	Conduct meetings (workshops) focused on the organization's vision, mission, guiding principles, and overarching goals	QC (or EIT), PIT, and EWCT
3.5	Select and train functional DIT [ACT]	Select and train DIT	Coordinated by PIT and EWCT in consultation with the QC (or EIT); done by appropriate persons (may be outside consultants)
3.6	DIT works on improving own process [ACT]	DIT focuses on internal process improvement efforts	DIT, PIT, and EWCT
3.7	Select and train local area TTs [ACT]	Select and train TTs	Coordinated by the PIT, in cooperation with the EWCT, DIT; training done by appropriate persons
3.8	Identify emergent opportunities [STUDY]	Identify opportunities for quality improvement efforts based on process and problem analysis	TTs, DITs, PITs, and EWCTs
3.9	Integrate quality and ethical work culture into planning [ACT]	Integrate quality and organizational ethics improvement principles and techniques into organization planning	Led by the QC (or EIT), in cooperation with the other teams that have been formed

Table 7.1 (continued) Total Quality Integrated Implementation Plan

No.	Why	How	When	Indicators
3.4	To ensure collective ownership and commitment to the mission, vision, guiding principles, and overarching goals	Discussion of assessment report and development of material related to the mission, vision, principles, and goals. "Challenge process" to enable all employees to provide input and shape the future context.	Months 1 and 2 Months 2–6 (as needed to reach all employees)	QC (or EIT), PIT, and EWCT minutes; draft statement of vision, mission, guiding principles, and goals
3.5	To increase understanding of and commitment to quality improvement efforts among key persons in the major functional areas	Select, appoint, and train DIT	Months 3 and 4	PIT and EWCT minutes; training designed and delivered to DIT
3.6	To provide team members with the opportunity to analyze and improve internal processes	Process and problem analysis	Months 5 and 6	PIT, EWCT, and DIT minutes
3.7	To have local area TTs address issues related to major core process	Select persons directly involved in the processes to be addressed and train TTs	Months 6 and 7	Minutes of QC (or EIT), PIT, EWCT, and DIT
3.8	To assist the QC (or EIT) in identifying opportunities for quality improvement efforts	Analysis of all materials produced by the assessment and process management activities	Months 6 and 7	Reports to DITs, PITs, EWCTs, and QC (or EIT)
3.9	To institutionalize quality and ethical work culture improvement principles and techniques into ongoing planning of activities of the organization	Train all team members in quality and organizational ethics improvement principles and techniques, development of policies and procedures	Month 6 and continuously throughout the effort	Training designed and delivered to all team members; written policies and procedures

Table 7.1 (continued) Total Quality Integrated Implementation Plan

No.	Action	What	Who
4.0 PROCESS IMPLEMENTATION			
4.1	Identify initial process improve- ment projects [PLAN]	Identification of the core processes	QC (or EIT), PIT, and EWCT
4.2	Select and train DIT and TTs [DO]	Select and train DITs and TTs	QC (or EIT), PIT, and EWCT
4.3	Solve process improvement problems [DO]	Identify and solve process improvement problems with PIT, DIT, and EWCT	Cross-functional process improvement with PIT, DIT, and EWCT
4.4	Prioritize organ- izational process improvement issues [STUDY]	Identify issues and priorities of the organization	PITs, DITs, TTs, and EWCT
4.5	Gain organiza- tional endorse- ment of process improvement efforts [ACT]	Process management improve- ment efforts recommended and approved	PITs, DITs, TTs, EWCT, QC (or EIT)
5.0 PROJECT IMPLEMENTATION			
5.1	Identify and plan initial project management projects [PLAN]	Identify and initiate projects based on the list of core processes of the organization (step 4.1)	DITs and TTs in coop- eration with PIT, EWCT, and QC (or EIT)

Table 7.1 (continued) Total Quality Integrated Implementation Plan

No.	Why	How	When	Indicators
4.0 PROCESS IMPLEMENTATION				
4.1	To assure that all key processes are working in harmony to maxim-ize organizational effectiveness	Systematic effort by the QC (or EIT), PIT, or EWCT to identify core processes of the organization	Months 3 and 4	List of core processes of the organization
4.2	To enhance the under-standing of and commit-ment to quality and ethics improvement principles and techniques	Selected reading materials on quality improvement prin-ciples and techniques, workshops on improvement prin-ciples and techniques	Months 4 and 5	Training design-ed and delivered to DITs and TTs
4.3	To ensure that the major processes of the organi-zation are effective, efficient, and meet customer needs and expectations	Systematic efforts using PIT, DIT, and EWCT	Months 5 and 6	Process improve-ment problems identified and addressed by PIT, DIT, and EWCT
4.4	To have an accepted set of issues that need to be addressed by the organization	PITs, DITs, TTs, EWCT	Months 6 and 7	Reports on activ-ities and results of PITs, DITs, TTs, and EWCT
4.5	To ensure selection of appropriate processes, authorization, commit-ment, and support	DITs and TTs recom-mend priorities and target processes; they are reviewed and approved by PITs, EWCT, and QC (or EIT)	Months 7 and 8	Approved reports on process improvement priorities and target processes
5.0 PROJECT IMPLEMENTATION				
5.1	To select projects based on core processes and ensure that initial problems have a high chance of successful solution	Each DIT and TT iden-tifies the problem processes they would like to initially address and develops the over-all plan and strategy for the selected projects	Months 8 and 9	Approved list of initial projects. Fully developed plan for each selected project; DIT and TT minutes

Table 7.1 (continued) Total Quality Integrated Implementation Plan

No.	Action	What	Who
5.2	Organize the project manage-ment activities [DO]	Coordinate the organizational framework of each project; conduct training on shared responsibilities (cross-training)	DITs and TTs
5.3	Implement and control the project manage-ment activities [STUDY]	Begin each project based on the developed plan and organiza-tional framework. Utilize the control strategies developed in the plan.	DITs and TTs
5.4	Complete the projects and disseminate results [ACT]	Complete each project within the designated objective, specified time, and budget. Disseminate results to other parts of the organization.	DITs and TTs
6.0 INDIVIDUAL PERFORMANCE IMPLEMENTATION			
6.1	Plan personal performance assessment and development [PLAN]	Provide assessment and training for personal performance improvement	Each person in the organization on a voluntary basis, and preferably in teams to facilitate co-development
6.2	Align personal performance with organizational priorities [DO]	Provide education in developing personal vision, mission, objectives, and plans	Each person in the organization on a voluntary basis, and preferably in teams to facilitate co-development

Table 7.1 (continued) Total Quality Integrated Implementation Plan

No.	Why	How	When	Indicators
5.2	To organize all the necessary steps, required resources, and areas of shared responsibilities for each project	Each team collaboratively organizes its project, with the help of a lead person as the facilitator; conduct workshops on cross-training	Months 8 and 9	Fully developed and understood organizational framework for each project
5.3	To initiate the selected team-centered quality improvement projects and to assure the progress of each project	"Just do it"; get started with the projects, applying PDSA and appropriate quality tools and techniques, and use appropriate quality evaluation and feedback tools	Months 9 and 10	Visible indication of projects beginning, scheduled progress reports from DITs and TTs
5.4	To demonstrate the success of team-centered project management. To use the project results in other areas of the organization.	Successful implementation of steps 4.5, 5.1–5.4, and 6.4	Months 10 and 11	Scheduled progress and end-of-project reports from DITs and TTs

6.0 INDIVIDUAL PERFORMANCE IMPLEMENTATION

No.	Why	How	When	Indicators
6.1	To develop the organization's most important resource, its people, for the benefit of the people and the company	Provide courses and seminars on total quality skills, personal improvement, and team building	Begin in month 4 (see step 4.2) and continue throughout the effort	Positive evaluation of the courses/seminars; measurable impact on personal effectiveness
6.2	To demonstrate the organization's commitment to personal empowerment and self-direction; to align team development with personal development	Provide courses and seminars in developing personal and team vision, mission, and objectives/plans	Begin in month 4 (see step 4.2) and continue throughout the effort	Positive evaluation of the courses/seminars; measurable impact on personal effectiveness

Table 7.1 (continued) Total Quality Integrated Implementation Plan

No.	Action	What	Who
6.3	Personalize customer–supplier orientation [STUDY]	Sensitivity to meeting, even anticipating, needs of customers/constituents; establish long-term relations with suppliers	Each person in the organization within the framework of the teams and in cooperation with the PIT, EWCT, and QC (or EIT)
6.4	Develop personal skills matrix. Extend through-out the organization. [ACT]	Development of personal skills matrix and database	Each person in the organization within the framework of DIT and TT

7.0 EVALUATION AND CONTROL IMPLEMENTATION

No.	Action	What	Who
7.1	Conduct process and project evaluation [PLAN]	Evaluation criteria and procedures built into *all* quality improvement efforts; quality improvement efforts reviewed and evaluated	DITs and TTs responsible for improvement effort, with reports reviewed by PIT, EWCT, and QC (or EIT)
7.2	Provide training, remediation, and enhancement opportunities [DO]	Develop and deliver additional training for persons identified in steps 4.1 and 4.2 or on topics identified through the bench-marking process (step 7.3)	DIT and EWCT, in cooperation with the DITs and TTs

Table 7.1 (continued) Total Quality Integrated Implementation Plan

No.	Why	How	When	Indicators
6.3	To actualize the two basic purposes of the project: implement the basic mission of the organization and totally serve the customers/constituents	Provide courses and seminars on customer service; team-based projects addressing customer service process (steps 4.1–4.5 and 5.1–5.4)	Begin in month 6 (see step 4.4) and continue throughout the effort	Successful completion of and measurable impacts on customer service and supplier orientation projects
6.4	To provide a personal skills matrix for each person, identifying present and future skills; facilitate the cross-training of each team and its members	Establish a personal skills matrix database for each person; coordinate with a team-centered database	Begin in month 6 (see step 3.7) and continue throughout the effort	Personal skills matrix database of each person established, coordinated with a team-centered database

7.0 EVALUATION AND CONTROL IMPLEMENTATION

No.	Why	How	When	Indicators
7.1	To learn whether the improvements occurred in terms of effectiveness, efficiency, and meeting the needs of the customers; to maintain orientation to continuous improvement	Application of total quality tools such as control charts and other more formal evaluation techniques	Begin with initiation of the project (steps 4.1–4.5 and 5.1–5.4) and continue throughout the effort	Evaluation criteria and procedures identified for each project; periodic project reports
7.2	To maintain the relevance of the established education and training program; to enhance the knowledge, skills, and attitudes of everyone	Formal training programs, newsletters with an educational focus, written material (job aids, manuals, performance guidelines)	Begin with initiation of the effort and continue throughout	Additional training completed and evaluated; written materials published

Table 7.1 (continued) Total Quality Integrated Implementation Plan

No.	Action	What	Who
7.3	Benchmark best practices [STUDY]	Develop and deliver additional training for persons identified in steps 4.1 and 4.2 or on topics identified through the benchmarking process (step 7.3)	DIT and EWCT, in cooperation with the DITs and TTs
7.4	Measure overall quality and ethical work culture programs [ACT]	Conduct monitoring and evaluation activities to determine impact of the quality and ethical work culture improvement efforts	QC (or EIT), PIT, and EWCT in cooperation with DITs and TTs

Key to abbreviations: DIT = department improvement team, EIT = executive improvement team, EWCT = ethical work culture team, PIT = process improvement team, QC = quality council, TT = task team.

The implementation action plan provided in Table 7.1 integrates concepts and suggests ways to make them operational for firms that want to apply total quality principles to total quality OD/HR activities. This integrated conceptual model provides guidelines for changing the organization's strategy and structure to conform to total quality principles. It is important to recognize that many organizations are moving in this direction.

QUALITY FUNCTION DEPLOYMENT: AN INTEGRATED IMPLEMENTATION TOOL

Quality function deployment (QFD) was introduced in Chapter 3 as an element of *hoshin* planning. It begins where mission leaves off and extends down through every level of the organization. Although we will discuss some of Florida Power & Light's shortcomings later, the company provides a model of implementation for both *hoshin* planning and QFD. First, we will consider the basics of QFD. Then we will discuss how FPL implemented its quality improvement strategy using QFD.

Table 7.1 (continued) Total Quality Integrated Implementation Plan

No.	Why	How	When	Indicators
7.3	To maintain the relevance of the established education and training program; to enhance the knowledge, skills, and attitudes of everyone	Formal training programs, newsletters with an educational focus, written material (job aids, manuals, performance guidelines)	Begin with initiation of the effort and continue throughout	Additional training completed and evaluated; written materials published
7.4	To obtain data on the impact of the quality and ethics improvement efforts; to ensure a fact-driven organizational environment	Use of quality audit and ethical work culture audit to evaluate and control; identification of successes and failures; corrective measures taken when warranted	Begin with initiation of the effort and continue throughout	Completed quality audits and ethical work culture audits, with identification of goal fulfillment and shortfalls; corrective recommendations

QFD is one of the primary technical tools for business process planning within an organization.[4] It is a planning methodology used to ensure that customers' requirements are met throughout the product design process and in the design and operation of production systems. A set of matrices is used to relate the voice of the customer to technical features and production planning and control requirements. Because of its structure, the first phase of QFD is often referred to as the House of Quality (Figure 7.1), not to be confused with the House of Total Quality in Chapter 1. The latter is the conceptual framework for the entire book; the former is one phase of a business process improvement tool.

Building the House of Quality requires six basic steps:[5]

1. Identify customer and consumer attributes.
2. Identify technical features.
3. Relate the customer attributes to the technical features.
4. Conduct an evaluation of competing products.
5. Evaluate technical features and develop targets.
6. Determine which technical feature to deploy in the production process.

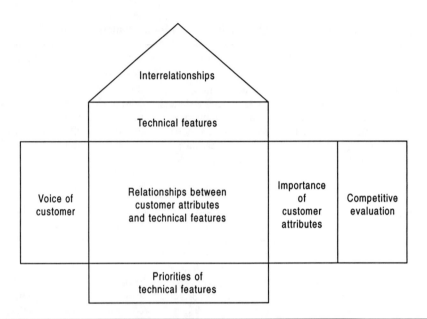

Figure 7.1 The House of Quality (Source: Reprinted by permission from Dean, James W. Jr. and Evans, James R. (1994). *Total Quality: Management, Organization and Strategy*, p. 70. Copyright ©1994 by West Publishing Company. All rights reserved.)

The first step is correctly identifying customer and consumer attributes. This requires ongoing market research to stay in touch with changing demand.

The second step is listing the technical features that are necessary to meet customer requirements. These technical features are design attributes expressed in the technical language of the designer and engineer. They form the basis for subsequent design, manufacturing, and service process activities. They must be measurable, because the output will be controlled and compared to objective targets.

The roof of the House of Quality shows the interrelationships between any pair of technical features. Various symbols are used to denote these relationships. A typical scheme is to use the symbol ⊙ to denote a very strong relationship, o for a strong relationship, and Δ to denote a weak relationship. These notations help determine the effects of changing one product feature and enable planners to assess the trade-offs between features. This process enables designers to focus on features collectively rather than individually.

Third, a relationship matrix between the customer attributes and the technical features is developed. Customer attributes are written down the left column, and technical features are listed across the top. In the matrix itself, the same symbols (as those used in the roof of the house) are utilized to indicate the degree of relationship. The purpose of the relationship matrix is to show whether the final technical features adequately address the customer attributes. This assessment may be based on expert experience, customer responses, or controlled experiments.

Technical features can relate to customer attributes in a variety of ways. The lack of a strong relationship between a customer attribute and any of the technical features suggests that either the attributes are not being addressed and the final product will have difficulty meeting customer needs or more market research on customer attributes is necessary. Similarly, if a technical featured does not affect any customer attribute, it may be unnecessary, redundant, or the designers may have missed an important customer attribute.

The fourth step is adding market evaluation and key selling points. This step includes rating the importance of each customer attribute and evaluating existing products with respect to each of the attributes. Customer importance ratings represent the areas of greatest interest and highest expectations to the customer. Competitive evaluation helps highlight the absolute strengths and weaknesses of competing products/services. This step enables designers to see opportunities for improvement. It also links QFD to a company's strategic position and allows priorities to be set in the design process. For example, focusing on a high-priority attribute that receives a low evaluation on all competitors' products can help a company gain a competitive advantage. Such attributes become key selling points and help establish promotion strategies.

Fifth, the evaluation of the technical features of competitive products and the development targets is produced. This is usually accomplished through in-house testing and translated into measurable terms. These evaluations are compared with the competitive evaluation of customer attributes to detect any inconsistencies. If a competing product best satisfies a customer attribute, but the evaluation of the related technical feature indicates otherwise, then either the measures used are faulty or the product has an image difference (either positive toward the competitor or negative toward the product) that affects customer perceptions. In either case, the findings can guide future company action. Targets for each technical feature are determined on the basis of customer importance ratings and existing product strengths and weaknesses.

The sixth and final step in building the House of Quality is selecting technical features to be deployed in the remainder of the process. This means identifying the characteristics that have a strong relationship to customer needs, have poor competitive performance, or are strong selling points. These characteristics, in turn, need to be deployed—or translated into the language of each function—in the design and production process, so that proper actions and controls are taken to address the voice of the customer.

The House of Quality provides marketing with an important tool to understand customer needs and gives top management strategic direction. However, it is only the first of four stages in the QFD process. The other houses of quality are:

- The *technical features deployment matrix*, which translates technical features of the final product into design requirements for critical components
- The *process plan and quality control charts*, which translate component features into critical process and product parameters and control points for each
- The *operating instructions*, which identify operations to be performed by plant employees to assure that important process and product parameters are achieved

Most of the QFD activities represented by the first two houses of quality are performed by people in the product development and engineering functions. At the next stage, the planning activities begin to involve supervisors and production line operators. This represents the transition from planning to implementation. If a product component parameter is critical and is created or affected during the process, it becomes a control point. The linkage of critical indicators provides the basis for measurement, monitoring, and improvement of the business process system to achieve customer satisfaction. The last house relates the control points to specific requirements for system quality assurance. This includes specifying control methods, sample sizes, and related technical operations, to achieve the necessary level of quality.

It has been estimated that the majority of QFD applications in the United States concentrate on the first, and to some extent the second, house of quality. Lawrence Sullivan, who brought QFD to the West, suggests that the third and fourth houses offer far more significant benefits, especially in the United States.[6] Japanese employees are more naturally cross-functional and tend to promote group effort and consensus thinking. U.S. employees are more vertically oriented and tend to suboptimize for individual and/or departmental achievements. Beginning to emphasize effective cross-functional processes as supported by QFD will enable U.S. firms to be more competitive with foreign rivals. The third and fourth houses of quality utilize the knowledge of about 80% of a company's employees; if they are not used, this potential is wasted.

Application of Quality Function Deployment at Florida Power & Light

An excellent U.S. example of the application of QFD is Florida Power & Light (FPL), the first non-Japanese company ever to win the Deming Prize.[7] FPL is the fourth largest and fastest growing electric utility in the United States. Currently the primary investor-owned subsidiary of FPL Group, Inc., a diversified holding company organized in 1984, the utility was established in 1925 to supply reliable electric light and power to parts of southeastern Florida.

The present-day service area, which consists of five major divisions (northeastern, eastern, southeastern, southern, and western), encompasses the east coast of Florida and virtually the whole lower half of the state (27,650 square miles), providing power to 6 million residents (3 million customer accounts). With its general office in Miami, the company operates 13 power plants (total capacity 16,000 megawatts), two of which are nuclear (St. Lucie and Turkey Point). It also runs 45 customer service offices, 72 service centers, and pays nearly 15,000 employees from an operating budget of $4.75 billion.

The company's rapid growth between the 1940s and 1970s led to an unwieldy expansion of management ranks and a lack of ability to rapidly respond to the needs of a changing customer base. Although FPL had a limited team-based quality program, there was no internal comprehensive process system that could achieve its expanded vision of becoming the best-managed electric utility in the United States. After examining domestic and global management process models, FPL decided to adapt the Japanese total quality process system used by the Kansai Electric Power Company in Osaka, Japan. Dr. Tetsiuchi Asaka, an eminent TQM process educator in Japan who was affiliated with the Union of Japanese Scientists and Engineers (JUSE), served as the lead counselor to FPL from Kansai Electric.

The basic QFD model was adopted to more precisely detect the voice of diverse customers. This led to the focus on eight general customer attributes: reduce customer dissatisfaction, increase customer satisfaction, reduce service unavailability, reduce transmission-line forced outages, increase nuclear availability, reduce fossil-forced outages, improve nuclear safety, and improve employee safety. Technical features related to these customer attributes were identified, and measurement indicators to scientifically determine critical changes were set up. Competing utilities were benchmarked for process and outcome results. Detail process records were kept, increased numbers of employee suggestions were encouraged, successive PDSA cycles were used to focus on process improvements, and extensive training in quality techniques was provided.

FPL's coordinated efforts resulted in stunning results:

1. Overall customer complaints dropped from 0.9 per 1000 in 1984 to 0.23 in 1989. FPL went from one of the worst utilities in Florida to one of the best in the state of Florida in terms of number of customer complaints.
2. The percentage of times when improvement is needed in the caring and concern for the customer dropped from 13% to 3.5% by the end of 1988. Monitored positive interactions registered customer delight and noted

the reduction of times when customer contact was not as pleasant and courteous as possible.
3. Service unavailability dropped from an average of 75 minutes per year per customer in 1983 to 47 minutes in 1989.
4. The number of transmission-line forced outages dropped from an average of 730 in 1983 to 604 in 1989.
5. The number of unplanned days nuclear plants are off-line dropped from 310 in 1983 to 267 in 1989.
6. The percentage of time the fossil-fueled plants are not available to make electricity dropped from 5.95% in 1983 to 3.62% in 1989. In 1990, this indicator went below 3%, the best record for a utility company in the United States.
7. With regard to nuclear safety, the occurrence of nuclear plant shutdowns dropped from 0.85 shutdowns per 1000 critical hours in 1983 to 0.20 shutdowns per 1000 critical hours in 1989.
8. With regard to employee safety, lost-time injuries per 100 employees dropped from 1.17 per 100 employees in 1983 to 0.40 lost-time injuries per 100 employees in 1989.

The aggregate, "bottom-line" impact of these efficiency efforts was to reduce the cost of electricity to FPL customers. From the mid-1970s to 1985, FPL was never able to keep the price of electricity below the rate of the Consumer Price Index. From 1985 to 1989, however, when the total quality processes were operational, the price of electricity in actual dollars was down 10%. In constant dollars, the price was down 30%. Furthermore, for the years 1985 through 1989, FPL earned the full amount allowed by the Florida Public Service Commission and still provided refunds to customers.

These findings are not unique to process improvements at FPL. For the period 1965 to 1985, the Deming Prize winners had increases in sales and profits of 14%. By comparison, other Japanese companies during the same period averaged 12%. For the same period, U.S. companies averaged only 8%.[8]

Interestingly, Voehl reported that James Broadhead, who succeeded Marshall MacDonald as chairman of the board at FPL Group in 1989, briefly considered calling off the Deming Prize audit that was being completed by the JUSE audit team.[9] While senior leadership has dramatically changed at FPL since that date and the extensive, detailed processes required for the Deming Prize have been severely reduced, the commitment to a total quality orientation persists today.[10]

An important lesson was learned at FPL: if a firm wants to achieve a quality prize, be sure that winning the prize is organizationally perceived as worth the sustained effort, that the award criteria are suited to organizational human resource capacities, and that the quality challenge will not overstrain resources, prompting a backlash.

The Deming Prize emphasizes the JUSE penchant for detailed statistical process documentation. As in Japan, organizations and individuals in them are expected to provide extensive, ongoing statistical documentation for all incremental improvements to operational systems. This emphasis of the prize, however, may not be as well suited to *sustainable commitment* in U.S organizations as one that accords more weight to individual interaction with systems. In the United States, the Baldrige Award emphasizes that interaction between individuals and systems, with much less focus on statistical documentation for incremental improvements and more on the need for visible, involved leadership.[11] In Europe, the ISO 9000 standards and the European Quality Award emphasize detailed policies and standards, with a broad environmental concern, not typical of either the Japanese or the U.S. award criteria.

While FPL's success demonstrates that QFD can work elsewhere, perhaps adopting regionally appropriate award criteria might facilitate sustained organizational commitment and more recognition/celebration rituals along the way would maintain the morale and momentum for change.

BARRIERS TO TOTAL QUALITY IMPLEMENTATION

Organization behavior is a relatively mature field, and quality management is beginning to "come of age," so that some lessons learned about the barriers to implementation and the reasons for failures may be of benefit to theoreticians and practitioners in the field of total quality OD. There are several perspectives from which barriers may be viewed: (1) theoretical accounts of implementation barriers, (2) cases of implementation failures, or (3) conclusions based on implementation problems through the eyes of experts such as Baldrige Award examiners. We will give an overview of all three perspectives in this section.

Theoretical Accounts of Implementation Barriers

The *issues and actions* related to *actual implementation* receive little attention when compared to planning or even evaluation of policies and programs, despite the fact that implementation failure has long been identified as a source of policy or program failure. We would much rather plan and talk about TQM than do the hard work of *implementing* it! Three reasons why policy and program innovations appear to languish include:

1. **Programmatic overexpectation**—Unrealistic expectations for success
2. **Conceptual failure**—The theories about causation and the relationships underlying the policies and programs are inaccurate or incomplete

3. **Implementation failure**—The failure to carry out the policy or program as designed

There is very little one can do to avoid failures due to programmatic expectations except to: (1) warn potential customers to be careful (if it sounds too good to believe, it probably is) or (2) warn advocates to avoid excess (do not promise what you can't deliver).

Regarding the second and third causes of failure, stories abound of how quality improvement efforts have been tried and have failed. A review of these stories indicates that many (perhaps most) of the reported failures are due to programmatic overexpectations and/or implementation failure. They are full of similar phrases (e.g., "we thought the situation would be turned around in six months" or "the president told us we were now 'empowered' to make decisions" or, "the president didn't even attend the training sessions for the quality improvement program").

A recent article by Reger et al. throws a different perspective on why total quality efforts often fail. It addresses the question of how members of the organization "see" and understand it (cognitive "maps" or "organizational identity") and how these organizational members might be persuaded to make the commitment to consciously change from "the way things are" to "the way things should be." At the risk of oversimplifying a well-constructed and somewhat complex theory, we will quote from the authors' abstract and briefly explain the model that they presented. They stated:[12]

> ...The theory suggests that employees resist total quality because their beliefs about the organization's identity constrain understanding and create cognitive opposition to radical change. We propose a dynamic model in which successful implementation of fundamental organizational transformation is partly dependent on management's ability to reframe the change over time. Implementation may best be accomplished through a series of middle-range changes that are large enough to overcome cognitive inertia and relieve an organization stress, but not so large that members believe the proposed change is unobtainable or undesirable.

Their model is shown in Figure 7.2. In it, they show the "identity gap" scale (narrow to wide) on the horizontal axis, the "acceptance of change" scale (implying low to high probability of change acceptance) on the vertical axis, and the three zones of "high inertia," "change acceptance zone," and "high stress." The "identity gap" is defined as[13] "the perceived gap between 'who we are' and 'who we want to be' [that] creates pressure for change within the minds of organizational members—managers and employees alike." Obviously, based on the model, the chances for failure in implementation are more than 50%, since it is only within the change acceptance zone

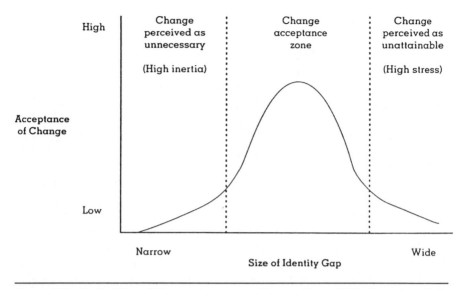

Figure 7.2 Probability of Change Acceptance (Source: Reger, R.K., Gustofson, L.T., Demaire, S.M., and Mullane, J.V. (1994). *Academy of Management Review.* Vol. 19, No. 3, p. 576.)

that there is a significantly high probability of acceptance of the changes necessary for development of a total quality culture.

Reported Cases of Implementation Failure

Although "true believers" in total quality *hate* to talk about failures, because of the "can do" success ethic of the movement, it is often instructive to do so. The Japanese have an easier time dealing with quality problems and failures than we in the West do. Their culture and their quality slogans reflect this. To the Japanese, "a defect is a treasure." By this they mean that much can be learned from examining the root causes and possible cures for failure.

A flurry of articles in various media about the lack of success of total quality efforts in the United States was brought on by a $2 million study of 584 companies in the United States, Canada, Germany, and Japan, performed by Ernst and Young for the American Quality Foundation in 1992.[14] The study painted a rather gloomy picture of the lack of successful implementation and use of such quality practices as employee involvement in improvement efforts, using customer complaints to aid in the design of new products and services, and tying quality performance measures to pay for senior managers. Perhaps the most widely read and caustic critique of the movement was found in a *Newsweek* article entitled "The Cost of Quality." The authors stated: "Until recently, TQM was seen as the doctrine that would rescue American business from flabby management techniques and shoddy products. Now many executives and their consultants have moved on to other methods, and while several firms remain true to TQM, it has stumbled badly over its early inflated expectations."[15]

Fortunately, several later articles were publishing stating that reports of TQM's demise were slightly or grossly exaggerated. A *Fortune* magazine article noted:[16] "But make no mistake: thoughtfully applied and modified, total quality's principles still represent a sound way to run a company."

An early example of an OD article on implementation failures, with a focus on diffusion of innovations, was written by Walton.[17] He described an OD project at Shell, U.K., the British arm of Shell Oil Company. The top managers decided to do a company-wide, comprehensive work redesign effort which was planned to last from five to ten years. Teams spent over two years in planning—developing a phased approach, organizing and performing a process designed to obtain maximum management commitment and buy-in across the organization of 6000 people, and planning to implement the results at selected pilot sites. Despite many conferences, management discussions, staff preparation and rule changes by management–labor committees, and final implementation efforts at three selected sites, the diffusion effort bogged down and was eventually abandoned. Walton concluded that despite early efforts and successes based on his observations across several companies, there were numerous factors that could cause innovations not to be diffused throughout organizations such as Shell, U.K., including:

- Internal inconsistencies in the original design
- Loss of support from levels above the experimental unit
- Premature turnover of leaders, operators, or consultants directly associated with a project
- Stress and crises that lead to more authoritarian management
- Tension in the innovative unit's relations with other parties—peer units, staff groups, superiors, labor unions
- Letdown in participants' involvement after initial success, with its attendant publicity
- Lack of diffusion to other parts of the organization, which isolates the original experiment and its leaders

This list appears to be very similar to many that have appeared in literature on the causes of failure in implementation of quality circles and subsequent critiques of TQM efforts. One of the most widely publicized of the TQM successes that turned out negatively was the FPL story, as mentioned earlier. FPL was widely heralded as the first company outside of Japan to win the Deming Prize. However, even as the prize was being awarded, a change of CEO was beginning to bring about drastic changes.

Jeremy Main, a former editor of *Fortune* magazine, gave a detailed account of the rise and fall of TQM at FPL.[18] The company formally adopted its quality improvement program in 1985 and changed from a management-by-objectives approach to a *hoshin* planning approach (adapted from Kansai Electric's process) at the top level of management. The roots of the change extended back to Marshall MacDonald, chairman and CEO of FPL Group (the holding company), who had set up pilot quality circle teams in 1981 which had attained some significant improvements in quality. In about 1984, John Hudiburg, CEO of FPL (the operating company), began using consultants from JUSE to help set up a detailed, Japanese-style quality improvement process. He and the top management from the holding company stated their intention to seek the Deming Prize in 1989. After spectacular improvements in such performance measures as power outages due to lightning strikes, consumer complaints, and injuries to employees, FPL applied for, and won, the Deming Prize. It became the first company outside of Japan to do so. It also became the first company to win the prize and immediately begin to dismantle the organization structure that had been instrumental in making it happen. Voehl[19] reported that when he called Dr. Deming to tell him the news that FPL had won the Deming Prize, Deming was singularly unimpressed. His response was "So?" When pressed, he finally elaborated by saying:

> What is really important is to decide what is next. The prize by itself is meaningless and can be destructive if not carefully dealt with. Chasing prizes is like chasing too many rabbits. You can never catch them all and you'll get worn out in the process. So challenge them with—what's next.

It was quickly apparent that James L. Broadhead, the CEO who was hired in 1989 to head FPL Group, did not have a philosophy on quality that was compatible with that of MacDonald, his predecessor, or Hudiburg, his subordinate. In fact, Hudiburg quickly determined this and planned to retire immediately after he accepted the Deming Prize in Japan. After a series of interviews with various managers and employees in mid-1990, Broadhead determined that he needed to: (1) deemphasize the use of indicators, charts, graphs, reports, and meetings in which they were reviewed; (2) abandon the requirement that certain tools and techniques be used by everyone for problem solving; (3) dismantle the bureaucracy that had been created to oversee the corporate quality improvement efforts; (4) balance the training program to reduce its focus on quality; and (5) streamline and simplify the quality process in general.

Main suggested several things that went wrong and may have led to the dismantling of the quality organization at FPL.[20] He also suggested that the process was not completely "scrapped," despite the bad publicity that surrounded the turnabout. What went wrong included:

- Hudiburg did not keep the FPL operating company and group boards informed of the progress of the quality improvement efforts.
- Because Hudiburg did not explain the important role of TQM as the "engine" that was behind the improvements in performance at FPL, MacDonald and others lost sight of this, while assuming that the improvements were just due to "better management."* Thus, quality philosophy was not a key consideration when the board chose Broadhead as CEO.
- The effort to win the Deming Prize may have overburdened the employees with numerous tedious reports, measures, and bureaucracy that created "burnout."
- The effort to win the Deming Prize may also have made managers less attentive to other business goals, thus creating problems in other parts of the business.
- There is evidence that quality has indeed become a way of life in many parts of the organization. Main quotes a team leader who had led a successful quality improvement project in downtime reduction due to pump failures at a fossil fuels plant: "No one here could kill quality improvement. Now that we know how to solve problems that have been bothering us for years, why would we stop just because some manager doesn't support it?"

Implementation Problems Through the Eyes of Baldrige Award Examiners

The most systematic framework for understanding and implementing TQM in the western world is the Malcolm Baldrige National Quality Award criteria, discussed earlier. Significant experience has been gained by examiners who have had the opportunity to compare good and excellent companies and the way they successfully implement TQM. Some interesting insights have been developed by George S. Easton, a Baldrige examiner.[21] Based on his experiences evaluating the Baldrige applications of 22 companies and participating in site visits at three firms, he identified four "cross-cutting themes" as areas that need improvement by companies that want to develop outstanding quality processes:

- A lack of understanding of "process"
- A lack of effective management-by-fact

* It should be noted that the FPL Group had possibly lost its strategic focus several years earlier by diversifying into insurance and other businesses that were unrelated to the power business. Thus, there were indications that there were problems in other divisions that Broadhead would have the ability to "fix."

- Failure to set clear priorities
- Primary focus on the work force (leaving out the roles of management and technical staff)

Because managers tend to misunderstand processes, processes are often poorly defined, unstable, and lack uniformity. Planning is based on goals and objectives, incentives, and feedback after the fact, rather than a more process-oriented focus that would emphasize strategies, methods for implementation and improvement of the plan, and "building in" quality before attempting to execute the process. Easton gives an example of how this problem affects improvement teams. Although most teams are trained in the basics of the Plan-Do-Study-Act process, along with basic quality tools, the team process is not fully developed. Consequently, teams are not trained in how to function as a team, use the tools effectively, document their results, and deploy their findings in other areas. They tend to use informal approaches (such as brainstorming), fail to gather and use data, fail to use available quality tools, and are ineffective in root cause analysis.

Management-by-fact suffers because there are few direct operating performance or customer measures available that can be used for problem analysis. Instead, managers tend to use downstream financial measures that rarely can be applied to operational planning and decision making.

The failure to set clear priorities can be attributed to the tendency of top managers to set too many top priorities and failure to clearly and consistently communicate their importance to middle-level and line employees. Thus, employees are either confused or left on their own to pick and choose as to which is the most important priority.

In many companies, the primary focus in TQM implementation efforts is on the work force (leaving out the roles of management and technical staff). Thus, managers tend to focus on proper worker attitude and motivating the work force. This causes them to neglect the fact that only managers and technicians can bring about significant changes in the business systems.

Despite the fact that there is much room for improvement, Easton's overall conclusion about the current state of TQM in the United States is positive:[22]

> An increasing number of companies are actively focused on quality as a key approach to improving competitiveness....U.S. companies that are committed to quality have a large number of areas of true strength. In many cases, they also demonstrate some exceptional management innovation. Further, their efforts are yielding clear results in terms of customer satisfaction, operational improvement and employee involvement.

IMPLEMENTING PLANNED CHANGE THROUGH ORGANIZATION DEVELOPMENT AT MIDVALLEY ELECTRIC[23]

Midvalley Electric Company (MVE) is an investor-owned regional utility that operates in the midwestern United States (the state of MW). It encompasses a service region of approximately 2200 square miles and serves a population of more than 1.1 million people, roughly centered in the city of Gotham.

Pressures for Radical Change

In about 1985, with the appointment of Mr. James Watts as CEO and president, a conscious effort to change the "corporate culture" at MVE was begun. Watts was determined to inculcate certain "desired behaviors" into employees (see Exhibit 7.1)—perhaps an early form of "human reengineering." He wanted to make a radical change in the way that MVE did business. With the agreement of the board of directors, a culture change was to be undertaken in order to "grow as an independent company, empower employees to reach their fullest potential, and better meet changing customer expectations."

Corporate Environment

In the late 1970s, the utility industry went through wrenching changes in the business environment, described by John J. Hudiburg, former CEO of FPL, as follows:

> Two oil shocks, high inflation, falling prices, and rising bond interest rates all contributed to an increasingly hostile financial environment. Meanwhile, increasing government regulation of nuclear power, as a result of the Three Mile Island accident in 1979, and increasing environmental regulation added to the pressure that FPL was facing. The price of electricity was rising faster than the Consumer Price Index, and our customers were becoming less and less satisfied with the level of service that they were receiving. This left both us and our customers in a sad state.[24]

In addition to the common problems that all companies in the industry had, MVE had another major "image" problem to overcome at this time as well. In 1984, after over five years of attempting to complete its first nuclear generating facility, the Magnum Station in Podunk, MW, the company and its co-owners announced plans to convert the project to a conventional coal-

---

PARTICIPATIVE MANAGEMENT

Participative Management is a way of doing business that pools the efforts of knowledgeable and affected employees in workplace decision making and problem solving. It promotes higher quality business decisions by allowing employees who have the necessary knowledge and information, regardless of their level, to make decisions whenever possible and appropriate. Participative Management produces positive changes in:

CULTURE: *The new culture, or atmosphere, gives employees flexibility and independence as they take responsibility for, and are held accountable for, meeting overall objectives.*

COMMITMENT: *Employees support and are willing to implement their own departments' goals, plans, and decisions as well as those of the Company.*

OWNERSHIP: *Employees feel that they are part of, and have ownership in, their work and their Company.*

COMMUNICATION: *Employees can communicate freely upward, downward, and among departments.*

COOPERATION: *Individual employees work together as a team within their own departments and with employees of other departments.*

OPENNESS, TRUST, AND RESPECT: *Employees feel comfortable in openly expressing their opinions.*

INVOLVEMENT: *Employees feel that their degree of participation is appropriate for each situation.*

Not to be confused with "democratic management," Participative Management supports Company management's right and duty to manage and to continue making key business decisions.

(Internal MVE document)

Exhibit 7.1 MVE Definitional Statement on Participative Management

---

fired generating unit. The decision was prompted by mounting community opposition, quality problems in the welding work done on a major portion of the plant's piping, and the likelihood that it would take many more years of redesign and rebuilding to get a permit from the Nuclear Regulatory Commission to operate the plant. This decision was made despite the fact that over $1.4 billion had been "sunk" in the construction effort and another $1.3 billion would be required to bring the plant on line. The share price of MVE stock plunged from around $40 to $19 when the decision was announced. Public confidence in the company was at a historic low.

Vision, Philosophy, and Goals

Watts began his change process internally with a program entitled "We're Moving," based on the tenets of Tom Peters' book, *In Search of Excellence*. There was a lot of "management by walking around" (MBWA), but many managers did not "buy in" to the program. As it was obvious that very little was happening, Watts began a more intensive effort, called the "We're Changing" approach, which was focused on customers.

The overall vision for the company was set out in a corporate document in 1988.[25] It stated that it was MVE's vision to "be the best energy company in the midwest." To realize the vision, the corporate philosophy had to change, goals had to be set, and employees had to be trained and empowered to change the structure and business processes in the firm.

The philosophy of MVE had been a top-down, bureaucratic production-oriented approach since the beginning of the company in the 1880s. In fact, every CEO from 1944 to 1985 came out of the electric production department with an engineering background. At a week-long retreat of the executive planning committee in 1988, where the vision was adopted, some radical objectives were set to change the philosophy and culture to:

- Understand and respond to customer needs
- Have motivated, qualified, productive, customer-oriented employees
- Create a complete customer service system comprised of the necessary systems, organizations, and processes
- Be a high-quality investment
- Have respect for and be respected by our regulators and foster community service objectives

Their goals included:

- Improve overall customer perceptions of the company
- Improve overall customer satisfaction
- Establish and meet customer service standards
- Raise employee morale
- Increase gas and electric sales
- Maintain gas and electric prices
- Limit budget variances
- Improve productivity
- Complete Podunk Station conversion

The retreat resulted in the preparation of a number of carefully worded statements by management, including one on "participatory management" (Exhibit 7.1), designed to provide a clear signal to employees that the focus and culture of the organization were about to undergo massive change.

Spreading the Vision and Empowering Employees

The vision, objectives, and goals were made known to the employees, and natural work teams were formed to look at four areas for process change and improvement. The four teams were focused on:

- Customer needs
- Systems
- Organization
- Communications

The teams were multilevel and cross-functional and consisted of salaried and hourly (bargaining unit) employees. The four teams came up with 25 recommendations that were essentially "action items" for implementation of the reengineering process. A representative sample included:

- Follow up service contacts to solicit customer service feedback
- Move salaried employees across departmental lines to enhance career development and broaden their knowledge base and improve communications throughout the company
- Perform interdepartmental and intradepartmental team-building and training exercises
- Extend office hours at the main office, and extend telephone contact hours
- Combine into one department the contacts for large gas and electric customers, area development, and marketing

In addition to a steering committee that was set up to guide the natural action teams, a transition coordinator was named to guide the transition process. Charters were written for natural action teams to work in two areas: corporate culture and customer service. The corporate culture teams included ones for productivity reporting, employee recognition, management/culture, area concept, management effectiveness, facility image, facilities management, telecommunications, and career development and job enhancement review. The customer service teams included commitment to customer (internal expansion of employee commitment), Don't Hang Up (optimum use of customer service telephone system), TRAC&FIELD (consolidated field functions for customer contact and marketing), Time on Your Hands (expansion of business hours for customer convenience), Ready Kilowatt...Now (search for ways to minimize service times), and Pay 30 (process improvement for accounts payable).

Results of the Change Process

To support the culture change transition process, a cadre of external consultants was established. A senior consultant (also external) coordinated their efforts and reported to an executive sponsor at the vice president level and to the CEO.

Scores of recommendations were made by the natural action/"We're Changing" teams. These recommendations were presented to company officers, and action was taken on their disposition. One of the many recommendations that was approved was to form an internal change management function composed of internal OD professionals. The work of the external consultants, coordinated by a highly qualified senior consultant, had demonstrated its value added.

In December 1990, an internal OD function was established at MVE. A national search yielded its senior consultant and supporting OD practitioners.

Implementation Actions

MVE took a number of actions to implement its planned change process. Despite some initial skepticism, massive training of employees was undertaken to improve their capabilities to be involved in planning, goal setting, decision making, creativity/innovation, and team building.

The new customer focus also received a great deal of attention. Customer service training was given to a large number of front-line customer service employees. Focus groups were being used to gain internal customer insights throughout the company. These groups were used to tap into employee opinions and gain perspective on current problems and potential solutions.

Other steps were taken to align the mission, goals, and objectives with tangible results. Employee surveys were done about every three years to determine if measurable change could be detected in employee attitudes, supervisory behavior, and culture change. The Encore! Encore! program was developed, with employee input, to recognize employees for exceptional job performance, ideas, and team spirit. Recognition ranged from the Qual-o-gram (employee-to-employee thank-you's) to the James R. Watts Award (several employees selected by the CEO were presented with $5000 for outstanding service, after receiving earlier "New Highs" awards for exceptional work). Early in the culture change process, it was determined that the performance appraisal review system was a major barrier to the ongoing change effort. The system, which had assumed a "bell curve" by placing employees into five performance categories ranging from provisional to exceptional, was discarded and a new one developed, with cross-sectional departmental input.

Harsh Realities: Downsizing and Merger

Successful change, participative management results, and an announced intention to merge with a regional utility in a neighboring state, Public

Service of Near West (PSNW), brought about the need for corporate downsizing at the end of 1992. Cuts that were made in 1993 and 1994 were felt most heavily at the middle management level. A combination of an early retirement plan and forced separations, where they were considered necessary, was used by MVE. A generous severance package, career placement, and counseling services were provided by the company to help ease the pain.

In November 1994, a newspaper article[26] on the completion of the merger of the two firms into a parent firm, called OHMS (Onward and Higher Midvalley Service), provided interesting insights into the possible corporate culture issues and accompanying pain that were involved. MVE was still trying to overcome its past cultural legacy of being a traditional, bureaucratic, "by the book" utility. PSNW, in contrast, was seen as a more innovative, flatter organization. An example of how the companies differ in symbolic appearances occurred when MVE employees visited PSNW's corporate headquarters outside Athens. "We have casual day on Friday here," said one MVE employee who didn't want his name used. "They have it every day."

On the much more difficult question of people's jobs, executives of the firm say that cuts will be "surgical." Independent observers suggested that this could mean that from 900 to 2200 of the existing 8755 jobs in the combined company could be eliminated. Given that the CEOs of both firms (Watts, CEO of MVE, is retiring in 1995, and William E. Voltz, CEO of PSNW, will take over as CEO of OHMS) voiced commitment to participation, corporate change, and a flat organization structure, there seems to be hope that previous work done on changing the "old MVE" to a participative corporate culture may yet bear fruit. However, an ominous sign of deterioration is the fact that the OD department that led the change process for about two years has been absorbed into the human resources department. Some OD people have already resigned.

Summary

OHMS has made significant progress since 1988, when it initiated its transformation to "be the best energy company in the midwest." In setting its sights at the highest level possible, the former company, MVE, took a number of calculated risks in initiating a massive culture change. One of the most difficult parts of a merger is the requirement to integrate diverse cultures. As seen in the process of attempting to change the culture at FPL in order to win the Deming Prize, culture change is difficult even if no merger is involved, and "holding the gains" is even harder. It seems as if the "stuff" of which organizations are made has a built-in memory that makes it want to go back to the old "status quo" if it is permitted to do so. Nevertheless, there are lessons to be learned, even from less than perfect attempts at change.

Total Quality Organization Development Lessons for the Entire Organization

Employees at MVE were made to feel that they had the freedom to make decisions and try new things/take risks. Employees perceived they had real support, which took away their fear of failure. Thus, managers were credited with giving power to workers, and workers took that power with a sense of boldness to responsibly create change.

The dedication of group members, their personal commitment to a common goal, and their ability to adapt to constant changes were seen as crucial. They were able to involve the total group; there were no "fence sitters." The groups created and lived by their own ground rules, listening to each other, respecting everyone's opinion (no titles), and communicating openly and honestly with no fear of repercussions.

Teams were effective at researching and analyzing problems, seeking feedback, planning, and following through. But effective problem solving was not enough; effective teamwork was also a key. Teams learned to address problems and come to agreements through patience and did not take disagreements personally. They also learned the importance of recognizing and celebrating organizational results and individual contributions.

Total Quality Organization Development Lessons for Front-Line Employees

In drawing lessons from their experiences, teams have some important advice to offer. The advice itself is not new; it may serve only as a common-sense reminder to those who know the power of employee involvement and support it on a regular basis.

The source of the following advice was a collection of front-line employees who rose to a new challenge together and, through no small effort, achieved breakthrough results in a changing environment, which gives their advice special weight. The recommendations of front-line employees at a utility that is very similar to OHMS (MichCon, Michigan Consolidated Gas Company, headquartered in Detroit)[27] are presented in their own words as a gift to front-line employees everywhere who want to succeed at quality at the "grass roots" level:

- Think about what you *can* do, not what you cannot.
- Be objective.
- Be willing to give feedback. Be straightforward and honest.
- Establish ground rules as a team and live by them.
- Be a good coach!
- Ensure that the overall philosophy is shared and participants support vision and values.

- Get commitment!
- Recognize that people may select not to participate.
- Keep others informed (co-workers, other departments, team members, management, etc.).
- Allow people to live with the consequences of their behavior.
- Respect others' decisions. Don't force it.
- Make it easy to participate.
- Make achievements visible (i.e., goal boards).
- Thank people, appreciate people. Remind them that their contributions are invaluable.
- Treat our co-workers (internal customers) as external customers.
- Share positive experiences! Take time to enjoy what you did.
- Start small and build.
- Be willing to listen to others and adjust your thinking.
- Avoid having different levels have different power. There are no BIG "I's and little "you's" (everyone is equal).
- Share the "big picture" with employees (company goals).
- Set a good example for others.
- Provide personal recognition that doesn't happen every day.
- Just do it—don't wait for someone else to do it.
- Constant communication is essential (e.g., talk about what's going on in section meetings, solve problems).
- Stop blaming others. Let people know why decisions are made.
- Foster pride in the work and in others. Support others in developing positive self-esteem.
- Reach out and include others...*invite* others to participate.
- Recognize that we are all in this together (management and employees).
- Talk about the fear and see how actions can actually work.
- Avoid making excuses. Admit mistakes and work them through.

Total Quality Organization Development Lessons for Senior Management

Another set of lessons emerged for senior management, given the role they had played throughout the early years of the effort:

1. The need for leaders to "walk the talk" is paramount. In the midst of such continuous and substantive change, leadership behaviors become intensely magnified.
2. Officer time commitment is extensive and should not be underestimated.
3. Some 20% of the employee population will be ready and willing to step out and make change. Senior leaders need to utilize and support that 20% right from the start.

4. The path of change is not smooth; therefore, consistency and persistence are essential to ensure long-term success of a quality transformation of this magnitude.

As the OHMS experience documents, the challenges of creating a premier organization characterized by quality service and total quality OD/human resource management (HRM) are not inconsequential. Business news stories provide dramatic reminders almost daily that nobody can take livelihoods for granted anymore and traditional ground rules no longer apply. New answers must be created by effectively developing and tapping *all* available resources, most importantly, people. OHMS's investment in applying total quality principles in managing organizational change has reaped significant returns, but consumers of their services are constantly asking, "What have you done for me lately?"

Having provided a conceptually integrated total quality implementation action plan and an empirical case study of OHMS as a domestic success story, it is time to turn to information about the global implementation of total quality practices as a vital part of the organizational change process.

INTERNATIONAL QUALITY FACTORS IN IMPLEMENTATION

At least four factors relate to quality implementation in the increasingly important global arena: culture and values, product/service standards and measurement, empowerment and motivation of employees, and organizing for quality. Culture and values affect the acceptance of the philosophy and goals of quality, as well as ethical standards, which are considered "norms" for operating within a company. Product/service standards and measurements are frequently imposed by government or industry standard-setting organizations to maintain minimum requirements for the purpose of standardization or consumer safety. Employee empowerment (which has been covered in detail in earlier chapters) is often related to norms of both the culture within the organization and the culture of the country or geographic region. Organizing for quality has to do with "organizational motivation" to excel through development of structures, hierarchies, and systems for quality management, control, and improvement.

Culture and Values

Most Americans are generally aware of the fact that the Japanese view quality differently from they do. Genichi Taguchi takes the view that quality is focused on aiming for zero variance from a specified tolerance. Therefore, any deviation from "perfection" represents a loss to society in the form of waste. In addition, once the product is in the hands of the consumer, any deviation from the ability to perform its intended use is also defined as a loss to society which has theoretically measurable costs. Taguchi defined quality as: "[avoidance of] loss a product causes to society after being shipped, other than any losses caused by its intrinsic functions."[28] Thus, in Japanese terms, quality of design and quality of conformance are defined by the capability to minimize the loss to society caused by failure to meet the targeted specifications or fitness for intended use characteristics of the product or service.

Americans are traditionally less demanding in relation to both quality of design and quality of conformance; they tend to take a situational view of quality. Garvin observed that quality has at least eight dimensions that must be recognized:[29]

- **Performance**—A product's primary operating characteristics
- **Features**—The "bells and whistles" of a product
- **Reliability**—The probability of a product's surviving over a specified period of time under stated conditions of use
- **Conformance**—The degree to which physical and performance characteristics match preestablished standards
- **Durability**—The amount of use one gets from a product before it physically deteriorates or until replacement is preferable
- **Serviceability**—The speed, courtesy, and competence of repair
- **Aesthetics**—How a product looks, feels, sounds, tastes, or smells
- **Perceived quality**—Subjective assessment resulting from image, advertising, or brand names

The traditional view of Americans toward quality is that there are tradeoffs, which often involve product characteristics, but almost invariably relate to costs. The traditional view still held by many managers is that in order to obtain higher quality, more and more time, money, and effort must be invested in preventing poor quality. Beyond a certain point, "diminishing returns" set in, making further improvements in quality more costly than the warranty costs of repair or replacement of products for those customer who receive defective items. Once again, the contrast between the American and Japanese view of quality is instructive. Robert E. Cole,[30] a leading expert on Japanese management, explained how the Japanese have managed to work around the "trade-off" model that has limited the Americans' concept of quality. He points out that the Japanese have been able to shift the trade-off point "down and to the right" by using six "achievements" that are not well-recognized during studies of quality implementation by Japanese firms: (1) [Japanese] management realized that the costs of poor quality were far larger than had been recognized. (2) It recognized that focusing on quality improvement as a firm-wide effort improved a wide range of firm-wide performance measures. (3) Management established a system that moves toward quality improvement and toward low-cost solutions simultaneously. (4) It focused on preventing error at the source, thereby dramatically reducing appraisal costs. (5) It shifted the focus of quality improvement from product attributes to operational procedures. (6) It evolved a dynamic model in which customer demands for products rise (along with their willingness to pay for these improvements).

Cultural Archetypes®

AT&T has done some interesting work on American views of quality versus those in other societies.[31] Building on the work of Dr. G. Clotaire Rapaille, a cultural anthropologist and psychoanalyst who now assumes the title of archetypologist™, AT&T performed *cultural studies* to determine the quality attitudes that were unique to people who are representative of the American culture.

Rapaille has developed a theory which says that people who grow up in a particular culture share common *imprint* structures due to similar experiences and languages. These typically occur in early childhood, from ages one to six, when children are acquiring language knowledge, which is strongly grounded in emotional episodes. He calls the common, unconscious imprint structure a cultural archetype™.

The study was performed by Rapaille and a team of AT&T quality staff personnel on a sample of AT&T and non-AT&T individuals who were chosen to represent a wide range of Americans from various age, race, religious, sex, economic, cultural, and geographic categories. To discover hidden attitudes and associations with quality, Rapaille took participants in the study through a series of word association, guided relaxation, and exploration of childhood experience exercises that probed how early *imprinting* of the concept of quality had taken place for these typical Americans. After studying a number of carefully selected sample groups, a cultural archetype™ was identified.

Although a detailed explanation of the findings from the AT&T study cannot be given here, the American Quality Archetype model in Figure 7.3 shows the results in graphical form. The typical "quality story" of an individual or group usually starts in the lower left-hand quadrant of the graph, where we have feelings of embarrassment and negative experience as a result of not producing what others expect and want. Gradually, a transformation takes place, often with the assistance of older or more experienced people (coaches or mentors), so that the individual or group ultimately triumphs over difficulty. Thus, they move from the lower left quadrant to the upper right, as shown by the dotted line on the model.

The things to be learned from this model and archetype studies in various cultures include:

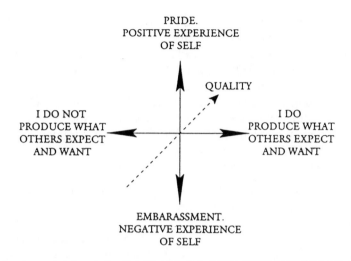

PRIDE.
POSITIVE EXPERIENCE
OF SELF

QUALITY

I DO NOT
PRODUCE WHAT
OTHERS EXPECT
AND WANT

I DO
PRODUCE WHAT
OTHERS EXPECT
AND WANT

EMBARASSMENT.
NEGATIVE EXPERIENCE
OF SELF

Figure 7.3 The American Quality Archetype Model (Source: Zuckerman, Marilyn R. and Hatala, Lewis J. (1992). *Incredibly American: Releasing the Heart of Quality.* Milwaukee: ASQC Quality Press, p. 52.)

- Quality is ultimately an emotional subject with many individual aspects.
- Quality is experienced in unique ways by those in different countries and cultures.
- To achieve quality using the American archetype, it is necessary to go through pain and failure to reach success.

Product/Service Standards and Measurement[32]

In Chapter 5, we developed the concept of measurement as a key requirement for "speaking with facts." Quality standards and measurement are often taken as either: (a) the essence of total quality or (b) are ignored as being irrelevant once total quality has been embraced as a philosophy. To answer the first fallacy, it must be realized that quality measurement is a necessary but not a sufficient condition for implementing a total quality system. One can have an excellent measurement process but still not have a total quality system, or even high-quality products or services. The second fallacy is that measurement will "take care of itself" if we have a total quality philosophy. This is not a viable position, because continuous improvement is not possible without an understanding of where one is starting from.

Any measurement system has three components: (1) a standard or objective, (2) a means of measuring and comparing the actual achievement versus the standard, and (3) a method for feedback of results to those who must make corrections or improvements. Unfortunately, there are often psychological barriers built into the system. Frequently, those who measure are inspectors—auditors for the IRS, quality control inspectors on the production line, or police officers with their radar guns. A more "user-friendly" approach, in step with the TQM philosophy, is to promote self-measurement, self-correction, and self-improvement.

The process of implementing an integrated total quality OD system will only be successful if managers and employees at every level understand the "why" of the measurement process. To do this, measurement must be actively performed at three levels: the mission level, the process output level, and the process variable level.

- **Mission measures** are the business results of the sum of all processes at a macro *system* level. Mission measures indicate fundamental accomplishment of business objectives by processes. If a process team has a charter with objectives clearly stated, then the mission measures will quantitatively indicate the team's degree of success in meeting or exceeding those objectives that are linked to corporate values. Mission measures, in the form of quantified objectives, will include indicators of quality, speed, cost, customer satisfaction, employee satisfaction, revenue, and profitability.
- **Process output measures** are indicators of the success or worth of the process outputs. They are used to track the products or services of an operation and to drive mission measures. Examples might include number of reports generated, number of projects completed on time, amount of scrap and rework from a production process, etc.
- **Process variable measures** are the measures that indicate the performance of the process itself, before outputs are produced. They are used to maintain and improve quality by tracking the process. Examples might include calls answered before the third ring, time to produce a program design, effort needed to correct errors, etc.

The development, appropriate use, and continuous improvement of measurement and measurement systems are *vital* to the implementation of a sound total quality OD philosophy. Total quality OD practitioners must understand, assist in development, and support the measurement systems in an organization because employee performance, morale, and commitment often directly depend on the measurement system and how it is applied. In the following section, we will look at how quality practices are being carried out in three countries. Many of the quality approaches and their associated measures that are used are applied in vastly different ways in the United States and Canada (North America) versus Japan and Germany.

International Quality Practices

In 1989, the American Quality Foundation and Ernst and Young conducted a massive international study of quality practices on three continents.[33] This study analyzed 580 organizations in Japan, the United States, Canada, and Germany. It focused on more than 900 separate management practices from the organizations; 84% of the firms responded to the last comprehensive questionnaire, which provided a measure of the use of quality management practices in general, as well as the quality developments in different parts of the world.

The firms selected for the study came from four industries: automotive, banking, computer, and health care. The firms were selected from these industries regardless of their commitment to the principles of the quality revolution. The study indicates the degree of implementation of total quality in these industries in each country.

From the more than 900 quality practices, ten core practices were identified as distinguishing firms that implemented total quality from those that had not.[34] The ten practices are categorized as those related to strategic planning, customer expectations, core technology, evaluating performance, and teams and participation.[35] These practices address many of the key elements of the House of Total Quality. They point toward the use of customer information to guide strategic decisions and develop new products, process improvement efforts using simplification and cycle time analysis to guide internal quality efforts, and the interaction of employees in teams or other participatory involvement.

1. Strategic Planning—*Customer satisfaction (CS) is used as a primary criterion in the strategic planning process.* Using CS information in the strategic planning process shows the depth of the quality commitment in the organization. With the pervasive use of CS data, all parts of the organization will adjust to, sustain, and/or improve the level of the customer's satisfaction.

- *Japan*—About 42% of the firms currently use quality information in the strategic planning process. About 80% of the Japanese firms intend to use quality information in the next three years.
- *North America*—Canadian firms lead the world in considering CS information primary in strategic planning. About 80% of the Canadian firms forecast using CS as a primary indicator over the next three years. About 70% of U.S. firms thought they would use CS as a primary criterion in the future. About 17% of U.S. firms relegate CS to secondary importance.
- *Germany*—Only about 22% presently consider CS to be of primary importance in the strategic planning process. About 27% of the firms put CS in a secondary role, while 51% consider it major.

- *Summary*—CS is not as important a measure in Germany as it is in the other countries. Japan leads, with about 95% of the firms considering CS a major or primary measure in the planning process. The United States and Canada still have a significant percentage of firms that do not use CS in their planning process. All organizations are increasing their use of CS information as a primary criterion. Germany still lags significantly behind in its use of CS information.

2. Strategic Planning—*Importance of competitor comparisons in the strategic planning process.* Competitor comparisons (CC), benchmarking exercises, and reverse engineering products are some of the ways organizations obtain competitor information. Comparing the organization against information from competitors illustrates strengths and weaknesses of the present organization. Maturity in this area indicates an organization that is confident about the competitive quality of its product or service.

- *Japan*—More than 90% of the Japanese firms use CC in the strategic planning process.
- *North America*—Canadian firms use CC less than U.S. firms do (67% to 82%) in a primary or major way. About 31% of the Canadian firms feel that such comparisons are secondary in importance.
- *Germany*—Less than 5% of the German firms use CC as a component in strategic planning. About 56% of the firms consider it of major importance, while 39% relegate it to secondary in importance.
- *Summary*—The Japanese place greater importance on CC than do other countries. The Germans give it less importance, with a large percentage giving it secondary importance (39%). About 31% of the Canadian firms also consider CC to be of secondary importance.

3. Customer Expectations and New Product Development—*Departments develop new products or services based on customer expectations.* If an organization is going to sustain quality leadership, the design unit has to be very effective. Success in this criterion depends on a commitment to the customer, a well-developed information system, and the depth of the product or service design system.

- *Japan*—About 90% of the firms usually or always use customer expectations to develop new products.
- *North America*—In both countries, less than 70% of the firms usually or always use customer expectations in product development. About 30% of the firms do not use customer expectations at all.
- *Germany*—About 83% of the German firms always or usually use customer expectations for new product development.
- *Summary*—German and Japanese firms lead the North American firms in usually or always using customer expectations in developing new prod-

ucts. About 30% of the North American firms use customer expectations occasionally or less, compared to about 20% of German and 10% of Japanese firms.

4. Customer Expectations and Technology—*Importance of technology in meeting customer expectations.* The use of technology can enable an organization to meet customer expectations. There are numerous ways technology enhances problem solving, decision making, and service capabilities of the front-line worker. Technology enables superior service or manufacturing because it empowers people to rapidly respond to customer inquiries.

- *Japan*—About 98% of the Japanese firms consider technology to be of prime or major importance in meeting customer expectations. The intensity of the use of technology to meet customer expectations will increase in the next three years.
- *North America*—About 80% of the firms in North America place primary or major emphasis on technology in meeting customer expectations. A surprising 20% relegate technology to secondary importance. Over the next three years, both countries will increase their intensity dramatically.
- *Germany*—About 93% of the German firms place primary or major emphasis on the use of technology. Only 7% relegate technology to secondary importance. Over the next three years, German firms intend to use technology more intensely as a primary strategy.
- *Summary*—Both Japan and Germany place significantly more importance on the use of technology than do the North American firms. About 23% of the U.S. firms relegate technology to secondary or no value. More Japanese firms use technology as a primary support in their quality efforts.

5. Core Technology—*The use of process simplification to improve business processes.* Process simplification (PS) is the focus on continually understanding smaller subprocesses of key business processes, as indicated in Chapter 4. The overall philosophy is the basic approach of both the functional and the quality network structures. Continual improvement is based on the logic of PS.

- *Japan*—About 82% usually or always use PS.
- *North America*—Significantly more Canadian firms than U.S. firms use PS (72% to 47%). About 54% of the American firms use PS occasionally or less, indicating a lack of emphasis on improving operations.
- *Germany*—Only 34% of the German firms usually or always use PS. About 66% use it occasionally or less.
- *Summary*—Using PS as a measure of the maturity of the quality commitment in the operations area puts the Japanese and Canadians in the lead. The Americans and Germans place less value on the process. In the

American case, there is a tendency to rely on innovation to bring the company's quality up. German firms tend to emphasize heavy engineering in the first place and fixing it at the end. The Japanese work at improving the process constantly.

6. Cycle Time Technology—*The use of process cycle time (PCT) analysis to improve business processes.* In the changing external world, a firm's rapid cycle time gives it a competitive advantage. When customer expectations are turned into requirements, then into specifications, and finally into a product/service in a rapid sequence, this cycle time technology is perceived as superior and deserving of customer allegiance.

- *Japan*—About 84% of the Japanese firms usually or always use cycle time to improve business processes.
- *North America*—About 84% of Canadian firms usually or always use cycle time. About 60% of the U.S. firms use cycle time.
- *Germany*—Less than 47% of the German firms usually or always use PCT. About 53% use cycle time occasionally or less.
- *Summary*—Japanese and Canadian firms use cycle time significantly more than firms in other countries. Over half the German firms use PCT only occasionally or seldom. About 40% of the U.S. firms use PCT occasionally or less.

7. Evaluating Executive Performance—*Executive compensation depends on a performance–compensation–quality criterion.* Executive compensation has traditionally been based on increasing profits. Bonuses, stock options, and profit pools are some of the traditional approaches, particularly in North America. Relating incentives to quality is an important change in for-profit enterprises.

- *Japan*—About 20% of Japanese executives' salaries are dependent on the firm's quality performance. This soon will increase to about 30%.
- *North America*—The number of firms applying incentives to quality criteria has doubled in the last couple of years. This trend is expected to double again in the next three years. Canada will go to about 40% and the United States to about 50% of executives with quality incentives. This is greater than in any of the other countries.
- *Germany*—The Germans just began to look at quality items for their incentives, currently increasing to about 10%. Other companies are planning to convert to quality incentives, which will raise Germany's total to about 30% in three years.
- *Summary*—Germany lags behind the other countries in providing quality incentives for top management. The Japanese adaptation to quality incentives is moderate. They are not adopting quality incentives as readily as the North Americans. It is clear, however, that providing quality incentives is increasing in world executive suites.

8. Evaluating Business Performance—*Quality information used to evaluate business performance.* The commitment to use quality information has to be supported by the appropriate information system. How frequently quality information makes it to the desk of the decision makers is a measure of the commitment of a firm to quality.

- *Japan*—About 90% of the Japanese firms use quality information at least quarterly to evaluate performance.
- *North America*—About 70% of the U.S. firms use quality information at least quarterly. An interesting statistic is that about 18% of the firms use it less than annually or not at all. Canadian firms showed some of the same tendencies as U.S. firms.
- *Germany*—About 70% of the German firms use quality information at least quarterly. About 25% use quality information yearly for evaluation.
- *Summary*—About 15% of North American firms do not use quality information to evaluate business performance. This is an indication of how far the quality revolution has to go in North America in terms of using data collection in decision making. About the same number of German and North American firms use quality information quarterly or better. Japan's organizations are most likely to use quality information to evaluate performance during the year.

9. Teams and Participation—*Percentage of employees in quality-related teams (QRTs).* The team network is a key component of the quality effort, as indicated in Chapters 4 and 5. Teams are formed to deal with unit problem solving (functional teams) or with cross-functional processes (process management teams). This question determines the percentage of firms that have one of three levels of employees involved in a team.

- *Japan*—About 36% of Japanese firms have more than 25% of their employees in QRTs. They intend to increase this percentage only slightly to about 39% in the next three years.
- *North America*—U.S. firms have about 49% of their employees in QRTs, about 10% more than the Canadians. The Canadians and Americans expect to increase their QRTs significantly, to 77 and 70%, respectively.
- *Germany*—Only 20% of the German firms have more than 25% of their employees in QRTs. The intent is to double this to about 42% in the next three years.
- *Summary*—The U.S. and Canadian firms use QRTs more than other countries do and intend to increase the intensity of their use of QRTs. The Germans use QRTs less than the others, and the Japanese only have moderate usage. The heavy union/government socialism in Germany has an impact on this criterion.

10. Teams and Meetings—*Percentage of employees participating in meetings about quality (QM)*. Meetings are another component of the quality leadership firm. Meetings to problem solve, communicate, coordinate, and control quality-related efforts are an important form of employee involvement. Such firms depend on a high-intensity communication structure to sustain their success. A willing commitment to QMs is a major indicator of a maturity of the new organization.

- *Japan*—About 65% of the firms have over 25% of their employees participate in QMs.
- *North America*—About 40% of the North American firms use QMs, where over 25% of employees participate.
- *Germany*—About 32% of the firms have more than 25% of their employees participating in QMs.
- *Summary*—About 39% of Japan's firms have more than 75% of their employees involved in regular QMs. About 68% of German firms have 25% or less of their employees in QMs.

The above ten international total quality practices impact total quality OD/HRM policies and indicate the range of relative global quality implementation. It is clear that Japanese organizations use total quality practices more intensively than do firms in other major global trading regions. North American firms exhibit the widest range of implementation variation, with heavy reliance on executive incentive programs rather than internal system improvements to stimulate total quality initiatives. German firms have implemented the fewest total quality practices, in part because their fastidious concentration on internal operational detail detracts from their concern for either the competition or customers.[36] Nevertheless, the extent of total quality implementation indicates that it is a pervasive world phenomenon that has or will impact the global competitiveness and total quality OD/HRM policies of any firm.

Organizational Motivation of International Firms

Among the many motivations to implement total quality systems and practices are two major ones: winning a significant quality prize/award and meeting international quality certification standards. Table 7.2 provides a comparison profile of both the quality prizes/wards (Deming Prize in Japan, Baldrige Award in the United States, and the European Quality Award) and the leading quality certification standard (ISO 9000 certification). Firms that win a quality prize/award and meet global quality process certification are, with rare exceptions, leaders in their respective industries. The best total quality firms do not approach winning awards and certification as ends in and of themselves, but as valuable and sometimes necessary vehicles for institutionalizing continuous improvement and competitive advantage.

Table 7.2 Comparison of International Quality Prize/Awards and Certification Standards

	Deming Prize	Baldrige Award	European Quality Award	ISO 9000 Certification
Year created	1951	1987	1992	1987
Basic form	Long-term prize	Annual contest for award	Long-term award	Certification
Primary geographic applicability	Japan	U.S.	Europe	World
Winners	Few	Few	Very few	Many
Emphasis	Statistical control, problem solving, continual incremental improvement	Customer leadership, support organization, measurement, benchmarking	Organizational enablers and results; leadership processes and results	Equal minimal global quality standards; documentation of system control, operating processes, and support activities
Cost	High	Medium–high	Medium–high	Low–medium

The respective emphases of the Deming Prize, which focuses on statistical control, problem solving, and continual incremental improvement, and the Baldrige and European Quality awards, which focus on organizational-level systems and leadership development, are partly due to cultural differences and partly due to historical changes in the quality movement. The technical approach of the Deming Prize in Japan is due to the prize being structured and administered by academic scientists and engineers (Deming and JUSE). The less technical organizational management approach of the Baldrige and European Quality awards is due to their formulation and determination by groups of businesspeople concerned about quality from the managerial leadership perspective. The early historical advances in technical quality control procedures catapulted many Japanese firms into world-class status in manufacturing in the 1970s and accelerated the comeback of select U.S. firms in the 1980s. However, the organizational management approach to the quality movement has incorporated the broader strategic implications of change management, the impact of information technology, the leadership influence on human resource performance, and the service/nonprofit sectors, in addition to the manufacturing sector, in its widespread use in the 1990s in the United States and Europe. The total quality leadership and HRM criteria in all the prizes/awards are useful tactical guides for continuous improvement of performance by people within all types of organizations.

ISO 9000 is a set of certification standards designed to promote international trade by creating a level playing field for producers worldwide to compete equally.[37] The intent is to certify individual firms, making it easy for an organization to purchase goods and services from around the world and be assured of their minimal uniform quality. While the ISO 9000 series of standards was developed in Europe, it is gaining global applicability.[38] The certification series consists of five standards: ISO 9000 provides concepts and definitions; ISO 9001, 9002, and 9003 cover specific aspects of a quality assurance program; and ISO 9004 focuses on creating and sustaining a quality management system, including specific human resource training and development issues, leadership issues, and performance recognition issues.

By meeting ISO 9004 standards regarding managing human resources according to total quality principles and policies and by remaining competitive for major quality prizes/awards, organizations gain world-class performance from their total quality OD/HRM efforts. It is this external global challenge, as much as the internal, intrinsic merit of managing organizational change by total quality principles, that is propelling firms to examine the Total Quality Integrated Implementation Plan in Table 7.1, emulate the success of OHMS, and begin applying total quality approaches to managing organizational change at all levels in every country in the world.

CONTINGENCIES OF IMPLEMENTATION

An OD approach to implementation requires that changes be planned organization-wide, orchestrated from the top, people oriented, and sensitive to the need to develop a supporting value structure. Based on our House of Total Quality, we must carefully plan, manage, and implement total quality from the strategy level, to the process, team project, and individual task levels. Only in this way will the management, social, technical, and educational systems be enhanced.

Managers and academicians are beginning to reexamine the assumption that TQM principles and practices are universal and can be applied to all organizations. There are, no doubt, limitations to what can be achieved via the implementation of total quality practices. Sitkin et al.[39] propose that a sharp distinction should be made between the concepts of what they call total quality control (TQC) and total quality learning (TQL) approaches. Their basic argument is that TQC practices that are applied to the quality precepts of customer satisfaction, continuous improvement, and treating the organization as a system result in a traditional closed-system "cybernetic" control system. A closed-loop control system has a standard, a way of measuring actual performance versus the standard, feedback on variances between actual versus the standard, and a way to modify the system. The TQL approach, in contrast, applies practices to the precepts in such a way as to indicate an open-system view that is experimentally oriented rather than control oriented. The authors argue that the "control" aspects of TQC are appropriate to stable, routine environments where repetitive operations (such as high-volume manufacturing or service delivery) take place. The environment in which innovative, highly uncertain operations (such as production of newly designed semiconductors or research and engineering departments) take place would require a TQL focus that was experimentally oriented and tolerant of mistakes in order to successfully "invent" new products and approaches. If their theory is confirmed, it would suggest that TQM would need to be modified in order to "fit" various environmental and contextual factors such as stage of the life cycle of the product, industry in which the company operates, level of education and training of the work force, etc. Implementation issues may need to be directly addressed in other categories of organizations and in the business environment in general. In addition to differentiating between closed-system versus open-system organizations, distinctions could be made between manufacturing, service, and government organizations. Regardless of the method of categorization, implementation contingencies can be seen as focusing on managerial "blind spots" and cultural biases. The key issues include environmental conditions, lack of systems orientation, lack of customer focus, learning disabilities, and cultural barriers to change.

Future Directions in Total Quality Organization Development Implementation

The direction in which total quality is evolving promises to have profound implications for how total quality OD practitioners go about their tasks of facilitating planned organizational change. The above key issues will be changing and evolving well into the 21st century. Various "gurus" and theoreticians have reflected on the direction and on what is "beyond" total quality.

Environmental conditions have been seen by many as the key obstacle to overcome if total quality is to be successful. As pointed out by Hyde,[40] in the context of total quality in government organizations, there are three environmental barriers to the adoption of total quality: (1) labor–management relations, (2) management policies and philosophies, and (3) downsizing realities. All three of these are also present, to some degree, in private, profit-making organizations. Unless they are addressed by individual organizations and local, regional, and national interest groups, it is unlikely that total quality will ever become as pervasive as it is in Japan.

Lack of systems orientation is identified by Ackoff[41] as the *key issue* of total quality that has led to widespread reports of its failure in surveys. By focusing on systems, organizations and their managers are often able to overcome the barriers and address the issues that are stated above. Ackoff suggests that the keys to understanding systems were often far removed from the traditional concepts of total quality. He makes the following major points:

- Quality should be defined as meeting or exceeding the expectations of all the *stakeholders*.
- Involving *all* stakeholders in design is key.
- Focusing on removing defects is insufficient.
- It is the interactions, not the parts of the system, that need improving.
- The 1990s manager has three functions: shaping the environment, developing employees, and managing interactions.
- There is too little theory in total quality.

To Ackoff, "customer focus" must include the customer, the consumer of the product, and the *stakeholders* (those who have an interest in the product, including employees). He says that you cannot just survey those who are buying a product, since often they are not the ultimate consumer. For example, Procter and Gamble would be foolish to survey executives at Wal-Mart on their need for disposable diapers. They would also be (and were for a while) foolish to ignore the needs of Wal-Mart to keep inventories low and delivery times short.

Stakeholders are rarely involved in the actual design of the product or process, which makes it impossible to know how they will react when the product is "rolled out." Similarly, Ackoff points out the requirement for designing a quality program that will provide quality results from employees (key stakeholders), saying: "Therefore, the focus of the total movement should be on producing work that's fun, a higher quality of work life. Then the quality of products and services will take care of itself."

Ackoff observed that you will never be able to compete with another company by using the incremental approach to improvement. There are two reasons for this: (1) there is no guarantee that eliminating what you do not want will yield something better and (2) even if you focus on getting what you want, you generally have to aim for discontinuous (breakthrough) improvements, instead of just removing the defects.

"It's the interactions, not the system's parts that need improving." This is illustrated by Ackoff in his example of putting together a superior automobile. If you take 100 of the best automotive engineers and put them in a room with all 142 varieties of automobiles sold in the United States, they could probably determine which engine, transmission, or brakes were the best in class. However, if they were asked to take out those components from each automobile and reassemble them into a world-class car, they could not do it. The interaction of those parts is *critical* to their proper functioning as a system.

The 1990s manager has three functions: (1) "...to create an environment in which our subordinates can do as well as they know how," (2) "...to enable our employees to do better tomorrow than the best they can do today," and (3) "...to manage the interactions of those for and to whom they are responsible; the interactions of their units with other units of the organization; and the interactions of their organizations with other organizations in their environments." Thus, to avoid *learning disabilities* in organizations, "Managers must become educators because education is the means to development. Quality can be improved more by education than it can by supervision."

Finally, Ackoff charges that: "There's too little theory in TQM." The lack of theory creates cultural barriers to change. Managers prefer to use knowledge and intuition, rather than theory, when implementing total quality. Unfortunately, when they do not understand the system, they frequently go about making changes that only make things worse. Control (a major value in total quality) can be increased by increasing vertical and horizontal integration, replacing cooperation with conflict, developing the ability to respond rapidly to changes, and applying incentives. Many of these are known to managers, but are not well applied. For example, prior to total quality, vertical integration was overapplied, while horizontal integration was often ignored. This resulted in "chimneys" with thick functional "walls" between departments. Ackoff gives the example of a company that had tens of thousands of repair trucks on the road every day, each carrying thousands of parts. A manager asked Ackoff how he could reduce the millions of dollars worth of costly inventory that was being carried, since only a few dozen parts were used on the typical day. After talking to repair people, Ackoff discovered that the problem was in the system. Each repair person was compensated according to the number of calls completed. If a part was missing from the truck, he lost compensation by going back to the warehouse to get the part. Thus, there was no *incentive* to deal with this aspect of quality in daily work.

Taking the systems perspective to its ultimate conclusion, Ackoff states:

> Summarizing, total quality management requires a revision of management and restructuring of the organizations involved. Incremental change of an organization, and particularly of its parts taken separately, will not do it.
>
> TQ requires a revolution, not reform. The challenge is to make it and to make it bloodless.

Ackoff, one of the founding fathers of operations research, sounds strangely like a total quality OD practitioner. Perhaps the answer to "What's beyond TQM?" is total systems integration with a focus on quality.

REVIEW QUESTIONS

7.1 Describe the six distinct theoretical models for implementing total quality.

7.2 Relying upon Table 7.1, describe goal setting implementation.

7.3 Relying upon Table 7.1, describe strategy implementation.

7.4 Relying upon Table 7.1, describe project implementation.

7.5 What are the major components of the QFD House of Quality?

7.6 What role does ISO 9000 play in motivating international firms to improve their quality?

7.7 Summarize the major findings of international quality practices.

DISCUSSION QUESTIONS

7.1 Talk to a manager or executive of a company that has recently implemented TQM and determine what process and steps were used. How has/will the company avoided/overcome some of the barriers to implementation?

7.2 How might the Total Quality Integrated Implementation Plan for managing an OD change process have to be modified to be useful to managers/owners of small firms (say 50 to 75 employees)?

7.3 Discuss how the cultural archetypes™ model applies to some well-known companies.

7.4 Do a study of the ISO 9000 certification process. Determine how feasible it would be to obtain certification in the firm you work for or have access to.

ENDNOTES

1. Crosby, Philip B. (1992). *Completeness: Quality for the 21st Century*. New York: Dutton, p. xi.
2. Lewis, Ralph G. and Smith, Douglas H. (1994). *Total Quality in Higher Education*. Delray Beach, FL: St. Lucie Press, pp. 234–236
3. Copyright ©Strategy Associates, Inc. and adapted by the authors.
4. Brossert, James L. (1991). *Quality Function Deployment: A Practitioner's Approach*. Milwaukee: ASQC Quality Press; Sullivan, L.P. (1988). "Policy Management Through Quality Function Deployment." *Quality Progress*. Vol. 10, No. 6, pp. 20–25; Akao, Yogi, Ed. (1990). *Quality Function Deployment*. Cambridge, MA: Productivity Press.
5. This section relies on material from Dean, James W. Jr. and Evans, James R. (1994). *Total Quality: Management, Organization and Strategy*. Minneapolis: West Publishing, pp. 70–74.
6. Sullivan, L.P. (1990). "Quality Function Deployment: The Latent Potential of Phases III and IV." In Shores, Richard A. *A TQM Approach to Achieving Manufacturing Excellence*. Milwaukee: ASQC Quality Press, pp. 47–59.
7. Hudiburg, John (1991). *Winning with Quality: The FPL Story*. White Plains, NY: Quality Resources, pp. 5–87.
8. Ibid., p. 88
9. Voehl, Frank, Ed. (1995). *Deming: The Way We Knew Him*. Delray Beach, FL: St. Lucie Press, p. 131.
10. Shiba, S., Graham, A., and Walden, D. (1993). *A New American TQM: Four Practical Revolutions in Management*. Portland, OR: Productivity Press, p. 524.
11. Petrick, J., Scherer, R., Wilson, J.C., and Westfall, F. (1994). "Benchmarking and Improving Core Competencies." *Journal for Quality and Participation*. Vol. 17, No. 4, pp. 76–78.
12. Reger, Rhonda K., Gustofson, Loren T., Demaire, Samuel M., and Mullane, John V. (1994). "Reframing the Organization: Why Implementing Total Quality Is Easier Said than Done." *Academy of Management Review*. Vol. 19, No. 3, p. 565.
13. Ibid., p. 576.
14. Fuchsberg, Gilbert (1992). "Quality Programs Show Shoddy Results." *The Wall Street Journal*. May 14, p. B1.
15. Mathews, Jay with Katel, Peter (1992). "The Cost of Quality." *Newsweek*. September 7, p. 48.
16. Jacob, Rahul (1993). "TQM: More than a Dying Fad?" *Fortune*. October 18, p. 66.
17. Walton, Richard E. (1975). "The Diffusion of New Work Structures: Explaining Why Success Didn't Take." *Organizational Dynamics*. As found in Nadler, David A., Tushman, Michael L., and Hatvany, Nina G. (1982) *Managing Organizations: Readings and Cases*. Boston: Little Brown, pp. 404–405.

18. Main, Jeremy (1994). *Quality Wars: The Triumphs and Defeats of American Business*. New York: Free Press, pp. 203–206.

19. Voehl (endnote 9), p. 133.

20. Main (endnote 18), pp. 208–210.

21. Easton, George S. (1993). "The 1993 State of U.S. Total Quality Management: A Baldrige Examiner's Perspective." *California Management Review*. Spring, pp. 32–48.

22. Ibid., p. 48.

23. The name of the company has been disguised, but the events that took place are true, according to accounts of employees and published reports. Much of the information on corporate change at OHMS is excerpted from term projects performed between 1988 and 1993 by students in the MBA classes of one of the authors. Appreciation is expressed to Richard J. Baute, Michael L. Connley, David G. Jones, Jeff Kern, John R. Kreinest, Kathleen H. Smith, and Constance Toler for their insightful contributions. Special thanks goes to Ms. Liz Demotte, former internal OD consultant with the company.

24. Hudiburg (endnote 7), p. 13.

25. *The Best in the Midwest—The Corporate Plan*. Midvalley Electric Co. (disguised name of report and company name an actual company), 1988.

26. Ward, Leah Beth and Boyer, Mike (1994). "Energizing Utilities." *Mill Valley News* (disguised name). November 27, pp. G1–3.

27. Petrick, Joseph A. and Furr, Diana S. (1995). *Total Quality in Managing Human Resources*, Delray Beach, FL: St. Lucie Press, pp. 333–334.

28. Taguchi, Genichi (1986). *Introduction to Quality Engineering*. Tokyo: Asian Productivity Organization, p. 1.

29. Garvin, David A. (1984) "What Does Product Quality Really Mean?" *Sloan Management Review*. Vol. 26, No. 1, pp. 25–43.

30. Cole, Robert E. (1992) "The Quality Revolution." *Production and Operations Management Journal*. Vol. 1, No. 1, pp. 118–120.

31. Zuckerman, Marilyn R. and Hatala, Lewis J. (1992). *Incredibly American: Releasing the Heart of Quality*. Milwaukee: ASQC Quality Press.

32. Portions of this section were adapted from materials supplied by Frank W. Voehl, Strategy Associates, Inc.

33. Ernst and Young (1991). *International Quality Study*. Cleveland: Ernst and Young.

34. Ernst and Young (1991). *Top-Line Findings*. Cleveland: Ernst and Young.

35. Vroman, H. William and Luchsinger, V.P. (1994). *Managing Organizational Quality*. Burr Ridge, IL: Irwin, pp. 287–296. This section of the chapter relies heavily on this work.

36. Tillier, Alan (1993). *Doing Business in Today's Western Europe*. Lincolnwood, IL: NTC Books, pp. 207–208.

37. Voehl, Frank, Jackson, Peter, and Ashton, David (1994). *ISO 9000: An Implementation Guide for Small to Mid-Sized Businesses*. Delray Beach, FL: St. Lucie Press, pp. 12–34; Kalinsky, I.S. (1993). "The Total Quality System: Going Beyond ISO 9000." *Quality Progress*. Vol. 3, No. 5, pp. 50–54; Jackson, S.L. (1992). "What You Should Know About ISO 9000." *Training*. Vol. 15, No. 4, pp. 48–50.

38. Timbers, M.J. (1992). "ISO 9000 and Europe's Attempts to Mandate Quality." *Journal of European Business*. Vol. 4, No. 4, pp. 22–24.

39. Sitkin, Sim B., Sutcliffe, Kathleen M., and Schroeder Roger G. (1994). "Distinguishing Control from Learning in Total Quality Management: A Contingency Perspective." *Academy of Management Review*. Vol. 19, No. 3, pp. 537–564.
40. Hyde, A.C. (1993). "Barriers in Implementing Quality Management." *The Public Manager–The New Bureaucrat*. Spring, pp. 35–37.
41. Ackoff, Russell L. (1993). "Beyond Total Quality Management." *The Journal for Quality and Participation*. March, pp. 66–78

ABSTRACTS

ABSTRACT 7.1
CORPORATE CULTURE AS AN IMPEDIMENT TO EMPLOYEE INVOLVEMENT

Chelte, Anthony F., Hess, Peter, Fanelli, Russell, and Ferris, William
Work and Occupations, Vol. 16, No. 2, May 1989, pp. 153–164

This article focuses on the failure of TQM to take hold in a manufacturing firm with a top-level reluctance to give up traditional management practices. The Grayworks Company, a northeastern firm with production and distribution operations at five sites, is a subsidiary of a multinational Fortune 500 corporation. It has 1500 employees and a $100-million-a-year income. Production-level employees are unionized, and management is on stable terms with the union. In the early 1980s, the company made adjustments to increase productivity to meet increased demand for company products. This increase in production led to a decrease in quality, which had previously been among the highest in the industry. Management decided to take steps to get quality back in line through increased employee involvement.

Beginning in 1983, the vice president of operations brought in the authors, who were outside consultants, to develop a training program for first-line supervisors. The supervisors, plant managers, and the CEO expressed optimism and support for the concept of employee involvement. However, the supervisors expressed concern about the true feelings of upper management. Several new programs had been previously launched and then dropped due to lack of management enthusiasm. Despite the assurances of the CEO that upper management was committed to change, in its heart the company, and the CEO, was still a top-down organization. The company culture—its characteristic set of values, principles, and expectations—was still autocratic and had been so for over 100 years. The authors, by their own admission, made a mistake in not paying more attention to supervisor misgivings about management's commitment.

By sitting in on supervisor meetings and asking for and taking supervisor input on capital budget priorities, the CEO convinced the supervisors, and the authors, of his commitment to change. However, six months later, after the supervisors had completed their training, the company had backpedaled from employee involvement to traditional top-down techniques. Two issues marked the retreat. The first was the vice president's initiation of accountability reports for each supervisor. These reports, accumulated and posted weekly, measured each supervisor's productivity. The CEO thought this information would motivate supervisors with weak performance by revealing problems. As the supervisors pointed out, the reports measured productivity and ignored quality, which was, according to management's recent statements, the company's first priority. The supervisors now had a conflict between making decisions to increase productivity versus making decisions to increase quality or, in other words, giving management what it said it wanted versus giving it what it *really* wanted. The authors agreed with the supervisors and advised the CEO to abolish, or at least change, the accountability reports. (To do so, they said, would further show management's commitment to employee involvement.) But the CEO took a hard line, claiming that the supervisors wanted to avoid their responsibilities and that some did not have the initiative and ability to work out their production problems.

The second issue marking the retreat from total quality was the doubled capital expenditures budget for badly needed maintenance and repairs to equipment and facilities at the plants. Previously, management's inability to enact simple maintenance procedures at the plants (supervisors cited repeatedly ignored requests to fix a leaking roof at one plant) was noted as evidence of management's lack of concern for employee involvement. Now, with the money in place to make repairs, the schedule called for 75% of the equipment or repairs to be delivered or completed within 120 days of the new fiscal year. At the end of that time, a progress report showed that, due to various problems, many maintenance projects had yet to be initiated.

The authors questioned the ability of the vice president of operations to make decisions, noting his habit of passing the buck to the CEO. Charged with the impossible task of increasing both productivity *and* quality, the vice president felt uncomfortable confronting the CEO, who, despite his claims to the contrary, was not amenable to suggestions in opposition to his views. In a difficult meeting with the vice president and CEO, the authors confronted both men with the communication problem. The CEO saw the vice president's inability to fight for his own point of view as a sign of incompetence and called for his resignation. The new vice president of operations was the former head of marketing and sales, who had the ability to push for production. He claimed he had the ability to take a hard line with the CEO when necessary, but in practice the authors saw no evidence of this.

In this case, the corporate culture placed an emphasis on profit rather than integrating other values relating to communication, decision making, feedback, discipline, and delegation. The secret of job survival at Grayworks was not to get caught making a mistake. In recent years, with higher product demands, meeting production numbers was the easiest way to avoid mistakes. Feedback at Grayworks has negative aspects. Communication is often a tool for punishing mistakes rather than reinforcing positive behavior. Supervisors in this environment would be reluctant to take on a team, since they (the supervisors) would be increasing their exposure to punishment for mistakes made by someone else. Finally, it is routine to pass even simple decisions up the command ladder, to avoid bad decisions or even decisions in conflict with management's views.

While even the most hesitant plant supervisors at Grayworks made some steps toward quality improvements, the CEO's unwillingness to give up the company's 100-year tradition of top-down management (which, until recently, had been profitable) killed the effort. The company, say the authors, may not decide to change until the old-style management threatens the company's existence. They warn that unless a company's culture is transformed, and unless a company understands the influence of its corporate culture on employee behavior, efforts to implement effective change are likely to be frustrated.

ABSTRACT 7.2
UNDERSTANDING AND APPLYING QFD IN HEAVY INDUSTRY

Maduri, Omnamasivaya
The Journal for Quality and Participation, Vol. 15, No. 1, January/February 1992, pp. 64–68

This article develops the basic theory of quality function deployment and applies it to the design of a piece of heavy earth-moving equipment. The author states that:

> We can all agree that understanding the customer's needs and turning requirements into actions is a necessity in today's business environment. Quality Function Deployment (QFD) is a technique that translates the "voice of the customer" into design parameters that can be deployed horizontally through the product planning, engineering, manufacturing, assembly, and service departments.

QUALITY FUNCTION DEPLOYMENT PLANNING, TEAMWORK, AND MANAGEMENT

QFD can be viewed as a planning and communication tool as well as a way to build the "voice of the customer" into the product. According to Maduri, it is a disciplined process for managing:

- Determination of consumer needs and demands
- Estimation of what competitors are doing or planning to do
- Integration of information
- Prioritization of required actions
- Identification and resolution of engineering bottlenecks

The QFD process is usually managed by a team which consists of marketing, R&D, product design, manufacturing, quality assurance, and other representatives of functions that have a stake in the design of the product. QFD is designed to anticipate and correct impediments to quality at various stages in the design, development, and production of the product. If done correctly, it should result in making the product right the first time, every time. Care must be taken to ensure that the corporate communication circle does not distort or alter the requirements set by the customer.

Every level of management has a role to play in the QFD process. In the early stages, product development work must be managed. Later comes the quality improvement stage, as the product goes through changes. After changes are standardized, but before the next product improvement project, quality maintenance through daily work must be emphasized as a routine requirement.

CASE STUDY OF QUALITY FUNCTION DEPLOYMENT IMPLEMENTATION AT BHARAT EARTH MOVERS LTD.

The author applied QFD to the R&D of a 30- to 40-ton world-class rear dumper earth-moving machine at Bharat Earth Movers, Ltd. in India. Its QFD system was based on four key documents:

1. The product planning matrix, which translates the voice of the customer into counterpart control characteristics; that is, it provides a way of turning general customer requirements drawn from market evaluations, comparisons with competitors, and marketing plans into specified final product control characteristics.
2. A product deployment matrix translates the output of the planning matrix into critical components or areas. Thus, it moves one step further back in the design and assembly process.
3. Component deployment charts identify the design and process parameters, as well as control or check points for each of those parameters.
4. Operating instructions are based on the critical process parameters; these instructions identify operations to be performed by plant personnel to assure that important parameters are achieved.

The overall QFD system based on these documents traces a continuous flow of information from the customer requirements to the plant operating instructions. It thus provides a clear operational definition, a common purpose, priorities, and a focus of attention.

The Planning Matrix—The purpose of the planning matrix is to translate customer requirements into important final product control characteristics that are to be deployed through the product design, development, processing, and production control system. The planning matrix (shown in Figure 7.A1) is built step by step as follows:

1. The product requirements in customer terms are stated and laid out vertically.
2. The primary requirements, which are very basic customer wants, are normally expanded into the secondary and tertiary requirements to obtain a more definitive list. This information comes from a variety of sources (marketing research data, sales department wants, international magazines, special customer opinion surveys, etc.). This step is the most critical part of the process and usually the most difficult, because it requires obtaining and expressing what the customer really wants and not what we think that he or she expects.
3. The product control characteristics, which are believed to be the assurances that meet customer-stated product requirements, are laid out hori-

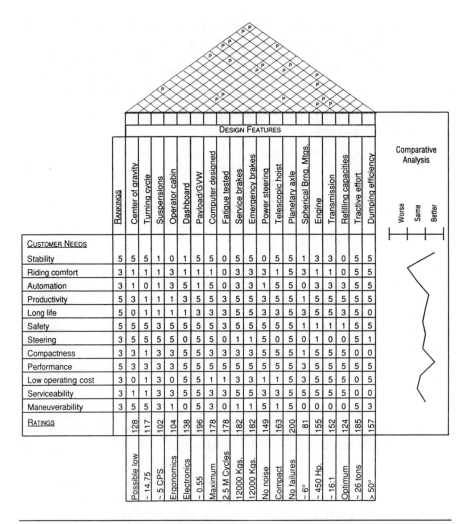

Figure 7.A1 QFD Planning Matrix (House of Quality)

CUSTOMER NEEDS	RANKINGS	Center of gravity	Turning cycle	Suspensions	Operator cabin	Dashboard	Payload/GVW	Computer designed	Fatigue tested	Service brakes	Emergency brakes	Power steering	Telescopic hoist	Planetary axle	Spherical Brng. Mtgs.	Engine	Transmission	Refilling capacities	Tractive effort	Dumping efficiency
Stability	5	5	5	1	0	1	5	5	0	5	5	0	5	5	1	3	3	0	5	5
Riding comfort	3	1	1	1	3	1	1	1	0	3	3	3	1	5	3	1	1	0	5	5
Automation	3	1	0	1	3	5	1	5	0	3	3	1	5	5	0	3	3	3	5	5
Productivity	5	3	1	1	1	3	5	5	3	5	5	3	5	5	1	5	5	5	5	5
Long life	5	0	1	1	1	1	3	3	3	5	3	3	5	3	5	5	3	5	3	0
Safety	5	5	5	3	5	5	5	5	3	5	5	5	5	5	1	1	1	1	5	5
Steering	3	5	5	5	5	0	5	5	0	1	1	5	0	5	0	1	0	0	5	1
Compactness	3	3	1	3	3	5	5	3	3	3	3	5	5	5	1	5	5	5	0	0
Performance	5	3	3	3	3	5	5	5	5	5	5	5	5	5	3	5	5	5	5	5
Low operating cost	3	0	1	3	0	5	5	1	1	3	3	1	1	5	3	5	5	5	0	5
Serviceability	3	1	1	3	3	5	5	3	3	5	5	3	3	5	5	5	5	5	0	0
Maneuverability	3	5	5	3	1	0	5	3	0	1	1	5	1	5	0	0	0	0	5	3
RATINGS		128	117	102	104	138	196	178	178	182	182	149	163	200	81	155	152	124	185	157
		Possible low	~14.75	~5 CPS	Ergonomics	Electronics	~0.55	Maximum	2.5 M Cycles	12000 Kgs.	12000 Kgs.	No noise	Compact	No failures	~6°	~450 Hp.	~16:1	Optimum	~26 tons	≥50°

zontally. These are the product requirements that relate directly to the customer requirements and must be selectively deployed throughout the design, manufacturing, assembly, and service process to manifest themselves in final product performance and customer acceptance. These characteristics must be capable of being expressed in measurable terms since characteristic outputs are to be controlled and compared to objective targets. The question to be asked is: "Do we have the right ones in terms of customer requirements?"

4. After labeling the vertical and horizontal axes of the planning matrix, the relationships between the customer requirements and the final product con-

trol characteristics are established. Since there are varying degrees of correlation between customer requirements and product characteristics, a type of rating is assigned to identify the significance of the relationships. In this case, 5, 3, and 1 were used to show strong, average, and weak relationships, with 0 indicating no relationship.

5. The rankings and ratings are then assigned to each of the customer requirements and the design features. The rankings are the weights given to each of the customer requirements as 5, 3, and 1. Next, the ratings are obtained as a product of the relationships and the rankings. Also, a comparative analysis is drawn as a line diagram to each of the competitive products in the same range.

The Product Deployment Matrix—Once the planning matrix is completed, the product deployment matrix (Figure 7.A2) is made for each of the product control characteristics from the overall vehicle down to the subsystem and component level.

In this phase, the customer requirements and final product control characteristics are listed in greater detail. The finished component characteristics affecting the final product characteristics are identified, and a deployment matrix is developed to show whether, and to what extent, the relationships between component and product characteristics are critical.

Component Deployment Matrix—If the component is very critical, then it is further deployed and monitored. The component deployment matrix (shown in Figure 7.A3) expands the list of components or the exact parameters required to

Product Deployment Matrix

Computer Designed:	Application:	Layouts	Dimensional checks	Drafting	Strength evaluation	Kinematic analysis	System dynamics	Methods planning	Manufacturing	Aesthetics	Stability
Power train		x	x	x	x	x					x
Chassis		x	x	x	x				x	x	x
Steering system		x	x	x		x			x		x
System pipings		x	x	x					x	x	
Dumping efficiency		x	x	x			x		x		x
Sub–systems		x	x	x	x			x			x
Components		x	x	x					x	x	

Figure 7.A2 Product Deployment Matrix

Component Deployment Chart (hydraulic tank)		
PARAMETER	VALUE	REASONS/REMARKS
Operating pressure	0.6 KSC	System limits
Factor of safety	10	Design criteria
Material strength	410 KSC	Design and cost
Plate thickness	6 mm	Design and cost
Tank volume	326 litres	Design
Gauge volume	225 litres	Maintenance
Length/width	1.3:1	Aesthetics
Length/height	1.1:1	Aesthetics
Length	775 mm	Design
Width	596 mm	Design
Height	705 mm	Design
Gauge height	487 mm	Maintenance

Figure 7.A3   Component Deployment Matrix

design the complete component. These parameters should relate directly or indirectly to the customer-set requirements. Parameters such as time, temperature, and dimensions are also monitored to assure component requirements.

Operating Instruction Sheet—The operating instruction sheet is the final key document. It basically defines operator requirements, the process plan chart check points, and the quality control plan chart check points.

CONCLUSION

The author concluded that QFD is a challenging approach that requires more work in the early planning stages and makes it more difficult to change direction once the project is underway. However, the advantages of a team approach that fosters better understanding of requirements and what is needed to meet those requirements outweigh the potential problems. Maduri concludes that more companies will use QFD to reduce prototype development cycle time, improve overall quality, and lower cost. He says that "the applications of QFD are limited only by the degree of the individual's imagination."

CASE STUDY

JOY INDUSTRIES*

Joy Industries' plastics products division (PPD) primarily manufactures and markets commercial and residential plastic components for a variety of end-use applications including toys, kitchen and home storage containers, and casings for control equipment. Its U.S. distribution system includes service to large national retail outlets such as Home Depot and Wal-Mart for home products and a network of 73 independent distributors for commercial products. Seven manufacturing plants are dispersed throughout the United States, with a network of eight regional sales offices in major metropolitan areas. Of the 5120 employees, 88% are in manufacturing. A corporate staff located in Landisville, Pennsylvania, supports PPD in the legal, research, quality management, and engineering areas. Three of the seven plants are unionized. Relationships with the unions are excellent, with a relatively low number of grievances and a high degree of cooperation in improving the business through employee involvement. PPD is a market leader and has used its ten-year-old quality management process to continually improve its market position, quality service, and costs. It has followed the Malcolm Baldrige National Quality Award criteria for three years to further refine its approaches and achieve improved company performance.

The quality improvement process (QIP) is based as much on culture, behavior, and values as on quality of products and services. Extensive changes have been implemented, redefining the internal customer/supplier among all employees and their relationships to markets and customers. Of the 14 QIP actions, 9 are focused on human resource issues.

The 23 quality improvement teams (QITs) use the 14 QIP actions to localize divisional strategies, which makes employees themselves—in all locations—the owners of change. Through the success of the QIP and human resource strategies, the PPD has significantly redefined an industry once steeped in tradition.

PPD's human resource strategy (Table 7.C1) is based on the corporate quality goal:

> To achieve total customer satisfaction by involving our employees in the improvement of our business processes at a rate that sustains global leadership.

* This case was developed by the National Institute of Standards and Technology (NIST) and is used to train Baldrige Award Examiners. It is in the public domain and may be freely reproduced.

Table 7.C1 Plastic Products Division Human Resource Strategy

Strategic Components	Plans and Approaches
Employee Involvement/Empowerment • Team Based • Individual	• Ongoing multifunctional teams • Ad hoc improvement teams • High performance organization • Process/function sharing • Opportunities for improvement
People Development	• Performance review • Learning • Career concept
Recognition/Reward	• Corporate awards • QIT recognition programs • Incentive rewards
Well-Being and Satisfaction	• Communications • Employee feedback • Benefits • Compensation • Community interaction • Quality of life

The leadership in this culture change has given the company a significant competitive advantage. In large part, leadership is the reason Joy Industries has been recognized for the second time by Robert Levering and Milton Moskowitz in *The 100 Best Companies to Work for in America* (only 55 companies were chosen for both the 1984 and 1993 editions). Levering and Moskowitz cited several human resource issues: pay and benefits, career concept, security, fairness, camaraderie, pride in work, and company openness.

According to a company spokesperson, the reason for the company's success is:

> Because of the maturity of our Quality Improvement Process, our approaches are fundamentally integrated into every aspect of our business. Pursuit of the ideals behind the concept of a high-performance organization is never-ending. Therefore, these approaches exist at various stages, are constantly refined and advanced, and have their own subset of tactics.

Specific short-term tactics are planned and implemented by each QIT to create a monolithic approach, but each QIT is empowered to interpret and manage what is best for its organization. This authority is especially important because of the different types of products made at each plant (88% of the employees work in manufacturing).

For instance, at some plants (Seattle, Tulsa, and Akron), the manufacturing strategy creates a continuous-flow, integrated line for commodity products. Such lines require fewer people with higher process and team skills. The QIT takes the elements of the human resource strategy and the 14 QIP actions that best enable it to achieve its goals.

In plants that make higher end specialty products (Tampa and Pittsburgh), the manufacturing strategy requires flexible manufacturing lines. At those plants, the QITs and human resource strategies focus on employees' capabilities in quick changeovers and a high degree of teamwork.

Longer term plans involving all plants include flatter organizations, pay-for-knowledge systems, gainsharing, employee involvement, safety, and a size limit of 500 employees per plant for optimum flexibility.

HUMAN RESOURCE IMPROVEMENT

Human resource plans and practices are improved through external and internal benchmarking, studying Baldrige winners, use of employee and process improvement teams, feedback, and corporate human resource experts in industrial relations and employment practices and services. The division's general management team (GMT) reviews all human resource goals to assure alignment with PPD's stretch goals and business plans. The plant managers, regional sales managers, and their QITs implement activities toward the goals locally. A variety of performance indicators are used to measure improvement, as outlined in Table 7.C2. Information about employees is collected on three levels:

1. **QIT locations (plants, regional sales offices)**—QITs collect data on a variety of approaches including employee interviews, team participation and results, gainsharing, safety, recognition, training and education, absenteeism, and grievances. These data are routinely shared with crews, QITs, and departments.
2. **Divisional (PPD)**—The division's GMT routinely reviews results in person and by conference calls with plant managers. The general managers of manufacturing and sales and marketing each cross-reference their human resource data with goal achievements. Gainsharing and employee interviews accurately measure the effectiveness of employee involvement in improvement activities and serve as a basis for evaluation and refinement.

    Global plant managers' meetings always include reports on key human resource initiatives. Once a year, QIT chairpersons attend the PPD quality council meeting to evaluate performance and plan the future initiatives. These are held at rotating sites so that facility tours can be conducted. The group vice president visits every PIT yearly to review progress and future plans.
3. **Corporate (Joy Industries)**—Using its corporate human resource information systems (CHRIS), the company collects and maintains information about all employees in a permanent database. The data are used for numerous evaluations, including education and training, awards for excellence and other

Table 7.C2 Plastics Products Division Performance Measurement Metrics

Strategies/goals	Key performance indicators	QIT initiatives (sample)
Increase involvement of employees in improvement efforts	• Number of corrective action teams • Number of process improvement teams • Number of opportunities for improvement • Number of gainsharing plants • Number of natural work teams	• Measure current level of involvement; develop plan for continued improvement • Improve education/training for improvement teams • Provide on-site facilitators to support teams • Improve recognition effectiveness • Improve communication of team activities
Improve safety	• Zero lost-time accidents • Reduce OSHA recordables 60% by 1996	• Provide S.T.O.P. safety training • Benchmark National Safety Council industries • Increase effectiveness of safety audits
Flatter organizations	• Reduce layers to four • Number of natural work teams	• Benchmark Akron, OH, plant
Improve recruitment	• Number of job offers • Acceptance rate • Rejection rate	• Improve process of selecting candidates • Assess division's requirements • Provide more accurate data to potential candidates about jobs
Improve recognition and reward systems to drive process improvement	• Number of recognition systems • Percent of employees recognized • Number of gainsharing plants • Number of pay-for-knowledge systems	• Encourage participation in improvement activities • Provide timely recognition • Develop day-to-day informal and formal approaches • Measure, assess, and improve, based on employee feedback • Implement and monitor gainsharing
Improve employee satisfaction and feedback	• Number of employee interviews • Number of comments, favorable and unfavorable	• Develop follow-up plans • Provide timely communication
Focus learning	• Extent of education/training • Stretch goal and gainsharing achievement	• Just-in-time training • Improve needs assessment

recognition, benefits preferences, performance reviews, and job histories. The CHRIS information is used by the GMT and corporate support departments.

At all levels, managers use the employee interview process established in 1960. Employee interviews are confidential, one-on-one efforts to determine satisfaction for all categories of employees. Nearly 9000 comments were made in 1992 interviews. Only one other company in the United States is known to use employee interviews the way Joy Industries does—not to "put out fires," but on a regular basis to prevent them.

Each location QIT analyzes the data and identifies not only overall employee satisfaction factors, but specific issues that directly impact absenteeism, turnover, grievances, and safety issues, as well as site-related concerns, and then develops plans for improvement.

In addition to employee interviews, Joy Industries uses employee satisfaction surveys. In May 1992, the company R&D center conducted a written employee survey; employees indicated an exceptionally high 82% satisfaction level. Sales organizations conducted surveys, and employees had a satisfaction rating of 71.4%. QITs worked closely to follow up this information. The appropriate general managers review the aggregate data and address division issues not handled locally.

Employee exit interviews are conducted in all cases at the site involved. Issues not within the scope of a QIT are passed on to the general managers of manufacturing or of sales and marketing for action and to corporate recruiting for analysis and preventive action.

QUESTIONS FOR DISCUSSION

1 What are some of the factors that have made Joy Industries successful in its implementation of TQM?
2 What role might total quality OD practitioners play in bringing about such a corporate transformation?

INDEX